Semantic–Enabled Advancements on the Web:

Applications Across Industries

Amit P. Sheth
Wright State University, USA

Information Science
REFERENCE

Managing Director:	Lindsay Johnston
Senior Editorial Director:	Heather Probst
Book Production Manager:	Sean Woznicki
Development Manager:	Joel Gamon
Development Editor:	Hannah Abelbeck
Acquisitions Editor:	Erika Gallagher
Typesetter:	Lisandro Gonzalez
Cover Design:	Nick Newcomer, Lisandro Gonzalez

Published in the United States of America by
Information Science Reference (an imprint of IGI Global)
701 E. Chocolate Avenue
Hershey PA 17033
Tel: 717-533-8845
Fax: 717-533-8661
E-mail: cust@igi-global.com
Web site: http://www.igi-global.com

Library of Congress Cataloging-in-Publication Data

Semantic-enabled advancements on the Web: applications across industries /
Amit P. Sheth, editor.
    p. cm.
  Includes bibliographical references and index.
  Summary: "This book reviews current and future trends in Semantic Web research with the aim of making existing and potential applications more accessible to a broader community of academics, practitioners, and industry professionals"--Provided by publisher.
  ISBN 978-1-4666-0185-7 (hardcover) -- ISBN 978-1-4666-0186-4 (ebook) -- ISBN 978-1-4666-0187-1 (print & perpetual access) 1. Semantic Web--Research. 2. Application software--Development. 3. Knowledge management. I. Sheth, A. (Amit), 1959-
  TK5105.88815.S4237 2012
  025.04'27--dc23
                                                    2011051815

British Cataloguing in Publication Data
A Cataloguing in Publication record for this book is available from the British Library.

All work contributed to this book is new, previously-unpublished material. The views expressed in this book are those of the authors, but not necessarily of the publisher.

Table of Contents

Section 3
Semantic Applications

Detailed Table of Contents

Section 1
Ontology Development and Ontology-Based Services

Efficient and user friendly ontologies are crucial for the effective use of chemical structural data on compounds. This paper describes an automated technique to create a structural ontology for compounds like ligands, co-factors and inhibitors of protein and DNA molecules using a technique developed from Perl scripts, which use a relational database for input and output, called Chem-BLAST (Chemical Block Layered Alignment of Substructure Technique). This technique recursively identifies substructures using rules that operate on the atomic connectivity of compounds. Substructures obtained from the compounds are compared to generate a data model expressed as triples. A chemical ontology of the substructures is made up of numerous interconnected 'hubs-and-spokes' is generated in the form of a data tree. This data-tree is used in a Web interface to allow users to zoom into compounds of interest by stepping through the hubs from the top to the bottom of the data-tree. The technique has been applied for (a) 2-D and 3-D structural data for AIDS[1]; (b) ~60,000 structures from the PDB. Recently, this technique has been applied to approximately 3,000,000 compounds from PubChem. Plausible ways to use this data model for the Semantic Web are also discussed.

#### Chapter 2

To speed up the ontology development process, ontology developers are reusing all available ontological and non-ontological resources, such as classification schemes, thesauri, lexicons, and so forth, that have already reached some consensus. Non-ontological resources are highly heterogeneous in their data model and storage system (or implementation). The reuse of these non-ontological resources involves their re-engineering into ontologies. This paper presents a method for re-engineering non-ontological resources into ontologies. The method is based on so-called re-engineering patterns, which define a procedure that transforms the non-ontological resource components into ontology representational primitives using WordNet for making explicit the relations among the non-ontological resource terms. The paper also provides the description of NOR_2O, a software library that implements the transformations suggested by the patterns. Finally, it depicts an evaluation of the method, patterns, and software library proposed.

Annett Mitschick, Technische Universität Dresden, Germany

Stefan Pietschmann, Technische Universität Dresden, Germany

Klaus Meißner, Technische Universität Dresden, Germany

Context awareness is a key issue for applications within heterogeneous and networked environments. In terms of efficiency and reusability, such applications need to be separated from the problems of context gathering and modeling, but should instead profit from and contribute to *cross-application context information*. For this purpose, an ontology-based, cross-application context modeling and management service is required to provide appropriate support for the variety of conceivable application scenarios. Although there have been numerous approaches dealing with application-independent context management, none of them sufficiently supports the vision of cross-application context handling. Therefore, this paper presents CROCO, an ontology-based context management service that allows for cross-application context gathering, modeling, and provision. The authors successfully verified and tested the application independency and practicability of this novel concept within three different projects with disparate application scenarios.

Section 2
Annotation, Mappings and Tools

Bernhard Schandl, University of Vienna, Austria

Bernhard Haslhofer, University of Vienna, Austria

With the increasing storage capacity of personal computing devices, the problems of information overload and information fragmentation are apparent on users' desktops. For the Web, semantic technologies solve this problem by adding a machine-interpretable information layer on top of existing resources. It has been shown that the application of these technologies to desktop environments is helpful for end users. However, certain characteristics of the Semantic Web architecture that are commonly accepted in the Web context are not desirable for desktops. To overcome these limitations, the authors propose the sile model, which combines characteristics of the Semantic Web and file systems. This model is a conceptual foundation for the Semantic Desktop and serves as underlying infrastructure on which applications and further services can be built. The authors present one service, a virtual file system based on siles, which allows users to semantically annotate files and directories and keeps full compatibility to traditional hierarchical file systems. The authors also discuss how Semantic Web vocabularies can be applied for meaningful annotation of files and present a prototypical implementation of the model and analyze the performance of typical access operations, both on the file system and metadata level.

Brian Davis, Digital Enterprise Research Institute, National University of Ireland, Ireland

Pradeep Dantuluri, Digital Enterprise Research Institute, National University of Ireland, Ireland

Siegfried Handschuh, Digital Enterprise Research Institute, National University of Ireland, Ireland

Hamish Cunningham, University of Sheffield, UK

Richly interlinked metadata constitute the foundation of the Semantic Web. Manual semantic annotation is a labor intensive task requiring training in formal ontological descriptions for the otherwise non-expert user. Although automatic annotation tools attempt to ease this knowledge acquisition barrier, their development often requires access to specialists in Natural Language Processing (NLP). This challenges researchers to develop user-friendly annotation environments. Controlled Natural Languages (CNLs) offer an incentive to the novice user to annotate, while simultaneously authoring his/her respective documents in a user-friendly manner. CNLs have been successfully applied to ontology authoring, but little research has focused on their application to semantic annotation. This paper describes two novel approaches to semantic annotation, which permit non-expert users to simultaneously author and annotate meeting minutes using CNL. Finally, this work provides empirical evidence that for certain scenarios applying CNLs for semantic annotation can be more user friendly than a standard manual semantic annotation tool.

    Mariano Rico, Universidad Autónoma de Madrid, Spain
    Óscar Corcho, Universidad Politécnica de Madrid, Spain
    José Antonio Macías, Universidad Autónoma de Madrid, Spain
    David Camacho, Universidad Autónoma de Madrid, Spain

Current web application development requires highly qualified staff, dealing with an extensive number of architectures and technologies. When these applications incorporate semantic data, the list of skill requirements becomes even larger, leading to a high adoption barrier for the development of semantically enabled Web applications. This paper describes VPOET, a tool focused mainly on two types of users: web designers and web application developers. By using this tool, web designers do not need specific skills in semantic web technologies to create web templates to handle semantic data. Web application developers incorporate those templates into their web applications, by means of a simple mechanism based in HTTP messages. End-users can use these templates through a Google Gadget. As web designers play a key role in the system, an experimental evaluation has been conducted, showing that VPOET provides good usability features for a representative group of web designers in a wide range of competencies in client-side technologies, ranging from amateur HTML developers to professional web designers.

    Matthias Klusch, German Research Center for Artificial Intelligence (DFKI), Germany
    Patrick Kapahnke, German Research Center for Artificial Intelligence (DFKI), Germany
    Ingo Zinnikus, German Research Center for Artificial Intelligence (DFKI), Germany

In this paper, the authors present an adaptive, hybrid semantic matchmaker for SAWSDL services, called SAWSDL-MX2. It determines three types of semantic matching of an advertised service with a requested one, which are described in standard SAWSDL: logic-based, text-similarity-based and XML-tree edit-based structural similarity. Before selection, SAWSDL-MX2 learns the optimal aggregation of these different matching degrees off-line over a random subset of a given SAWSDL service retrieval test collection by exploiting a binary support vector machine-based classifier with ranking. The authors present a comparative evaluation of the retrieval performance of SAWSDL-MX2.

Section 3
Semantic Applications

Chapter 8

Rachanee Ungrangsi, Shinawatra University, Thailand

Chutiporn Anutariya, Shinawatra University, Thailand

Vilas Wuwongse, Asian Institute of Technology, Thailand

While Flickr, a widely-known photo sharing system, allows users to describe their own photos with tags (aka. folksonomy tags) for indexing purposes, its tag-based photo retrieval function is severely hampered by the inherent nature of folksonomy tags. This paper presents SemFlickr, an application which enhances the search in Flickr with its semantic query suggestion feature. SemFlickr employs SQORE, an ontology retrieval system, to retrieve relevant ontologies from the Semantic Web and then derives query term suggestions from those ontologies. To ensure that the highly related photos will appear at the top of the results, SemFlickr takes the ontological relations among the given query terms to assign tag scores and then generates its ranked results. Experimental outcomes are encouraging and reveal a number of useful insights for developing applications that integrate the Semantic Web and Web 2.0 together.

Chapter 9

Alex Kohn, Roche Diagnostics GmbH, Germany

François Bry, University of Munich, Germany

Alexander Manta, Roche Diagnostics GmbH, Germany

Studies agree that searchers are often not satisfied with the performance of current enterprise search engines. As a consequence, more scientists worldwide are actively investigating new avenues for searching to improve retrieval performance. This paper contributes to YASA (Your Adaptive Search Agent), a fully implemented and thoroughly evaluated ontology-based information retrieval system for the enterprise. A salient particularity of YASA is that large parts of the ontology are automatically filled with facts by recycling and transforming existing data. YASA offers context-based personalization, faceted navigation, as well as semantic search capabilities. YASA has been deployed and evaluated in the pharmaceutical research department of Roche, Penzberg, and results show that already semantically simple ontologies suffice to considerably improve search performance.

Chapter 10

Heiko Paulheim, SAP Research CEC Darmstadt, Germany

Florian Probst, SAP Research CEC Darmstadt, Germany

Ontologies have been increasingly used in software systems in the past years. However, in many of those systems, the ontologies are hidden "under the hood". While a lot of useful applications of ontologies on the database and business logic layer have been proposed, the employment of ontologies in user interfaces has been gaining comparatively little attention so far. For providing a deeper understanding of that field as well as assisting developers of ontology-enhanced user interfaces, the authors give an overview of such applications and introduce a schema for characterizing the requirements of ontology-enhanced user interfaces. With this article, a state of the art survey of approaches is presented along with promising research directions.

Interactive TV has started to penetrate broadcasting markets, providing a new user experience through novel services to subscribers and new revenue opportunities for companies. Personalization and intelligent behavior, such as proactive content delivery are considered key features for the services of the future TV. However, most of the work in this area is limited to personalization of electronic program guides and advanced program recommendation. In this article, the authors adopt a more horizontal approach and describe the application of concepts, practices and modern Web trends to the TV domain in the context of the POLYSEMA platform. A key characteristic of this approach is the formal modeling of multimedia and user semantics that enables novel TV services. Specifically, Semantic Web methodologies are employed (e.g., ontologies and rules) while compatibility with the MPEG-7 standard is also pursued. The paper describes the overall architecture of the platform, provides implementation details and investigates business issues.

#### Chapter 12

A typical music clip consists of one or more segments with different moods and such mood information could be a crucial clue for determining the similarity between music clips. One representative mood has been selected for music clip for retrieval, recommendation or classification purposes, which often gives unsatisfactory result. In this paper, the authors propose a new music retrieval and recommendation scheme based on the mood sequence of music clips. The authors first divide each music clip into segments through beat structure analysis, then, apply the k-medoids clustering algorithm for grouping all the segments into clusters with similar features. By assigning a unique mood symbol for each cluster, one can transform each music clip into a musical mood sequence. For music retrieval, the authors use the Smith-Waterman (SW) algorithm to measure the similarity between mood sequences. However, for music recommendation, user preferences are retrieved from a recent music playlist or user interaction through the interface, which generates a music recommendation list based on the mood sequence similarity. The authors demonstrate that the proposed scheme achieves excellent performance in terms of retrieval accuracy and user satisfaction in music recommendation.

Preface

A decade has passed since the term Semantic Web was first used in Tim Berners-Lee's book "Weaving the Web." It has also been a decade since this book's editor founded Taalee, initially a Semantic Search company, fully knowing the power of modeling relationship as a first class model (as in RDF) and faceted search. The work presented at the 2000 keynote given at the first international event of Semantic Web (http://slidesha.re/sw-ib), in a patent filed in 2000 and awarded in 2001 (http://bit.ly/sw-p) and in an article (http://bit.ly/sw-ic) that describes the Semantic Web technology based application development platform as well as a variety of semantic search, browsing, personalization, interactive marketing (advertisement), and analysis applications for a variety of content within enterprises and on the Web. By the time you read this, it would also be a decade since the highly cited Scientific American article on Semantic Web by Tim Berners-Lee, James Hendler and Ora Lassila.

Some of the technologies, which involve minimal human training and experience to use, get adapted at a faster rate. One example is that of tablets. Another example is social networks. Both of these came about after Semantic Web was conceived of, and after RDF, the key underlying standard for Semantic Web data, was developed, and they were widely accepted within five years. However, technologies that require development of broader infrastructure, are complicated or have multiple components, require an ecosystem of trained programmers, best practices, and mature products and services, take at least a decade. I remember that it was 15 years after the first relational database management system came out that large corporations were seriously considering migrating their IMS and CODASYL based databases. In that context, Semantic Web's adoption is quite reasonable.

At the core of it, Semantic Web technology involves three components. The first is development of domain/conceptual models or ontologies. These capture agreements regarding a domain of discourse--ranging from shared vocabulary to extensive factual knowledge. This component has seen extensive progress in a number of domains, with the domain of life sciences as perhaps the most prominent one. There are now over 300 ontologies in the repository maintained by the Nation Center of Biomedical Ontologies (bioportal.org). There are also existing or emerging ontologies that are domain-independent or general purpose, including time, natural language, and provenance. Some, especially in the search community and those dealing with broad variety of content, argue that while ontologies can help with Enterprise content, they cannot scale to the Web. Others disagreed and believed it possible to develop simple models or identify relevant domain ontologies that are appropriate to interpreting and understanding content. You can find an example of the debate at http://bit.ly/s-search. The validation of the latter position came in the form of recent collaboration between the three Web search companies to create schema.org which provides schemas, or conceptual models, for several common domains.

The second component of Semantic Web approach is to semantically annotate any content. This essentially means adding semantic metadata where the semantics is conveyed through associating what is in the content with what is in described in the domain/conceptual model or ontology. For general web content that is described using HTML, better support for microdata and RDFa with HTML5 is making it easier to add or describe metadata. Followed by early progress in annotating documents found in enterprises and on the Web, there is now extensive growth in annotating social media data (such as Facebook's Open Graph protocol) and e-commerce data (i.e., BestBuy's use of the GoodRelations ontology). While my start up Taalee did semantic annotation of audio and video content over a decade ago, there was little progress until recently; an example can be found in discussions at a recent VW3C Video on the Web workshop (http://www.w3.org/2007/08/video/). As the Web 3.0 takes shape, the growth in the "Internet of the Thing" or "Web of the Thing", including sensors data made accessible over the Web, is significantly outpacing that of textual content. Correspondingly we see the rise of Semantic Social Web, Semantic Sensor Web and other ecosystems emerging around new forms of largely non-textual data, each with its own form of techniques for annotating data, storing those annotations and accessing them. In 2010, W3C's Semantic Sensor Networking has made significant progress in designing both a core ontology for Sensor, as well as in developing best practices for annotating sensor data.

Much of the initial Semantic Web data started with the annotations. However, parallel to the growth of conceptual models and ontologies, and their use for annotations, during last five year, we have seen even stronger growth of Semantic Web data in the form of Linked Open Data (LOD). This has involved representing unstructured data in the form of more structured data while capturing semantics-- such as representing Wikipedia as DBpedia. LOD has also started to become important knowledge as an anchor for semantics. Given that various sources of LOD are independent, although overlapping or related, there is an extensive need for semantic interoperability and integration needs. These are now being investigated in terms of robust sub-areas of ontology alignment.

In terms of the third component, analysis and reasoning, we have started to find ways to deal with large graphs - to find patterns, paths and subgraphs. There is a slow but steady progress in understanding and exploiting the power of relationships. An area that received concrete attention is that of the challenges in getting "same_as" right. Same_as has recieved the most attention in the context of LOD. This fundamentally gets to the issue of disambiguation and context- as things might be the same in one context, but not all.

This volume contains chapters organized in three sections. The first section is related to ontology development and applications primarily focused on using ontology for specific Semantic Web capabilities. The second section focuses on building semantic annotations and the tools that provide middleware and services that utilize ontologies and annotations. The third section includes chapters on semantic applications, starting with the use of semantics and Semantic Web technologies for improving retrieval, search, et cetera.

SECTION 1: ONTOLOGY DEVELOPMENT AND ONTOLOGY-BASED SERVICES

Section 1 begins with Chapter 1: Building Chemical Ontology for Semantic Web Using Substructures Created by Chem-BLAST, by Talapady N. Bhat. Having led the development of a few tens of ontologies, many of which are used in real-world applications, the author's empirical observation is that ontologies developed to conceptualize and describe the natural world (e.g, life sciences) are usually lot more complicated and intricate compared to ontologies to describe the domains, system and processes humans have created (e.g., sports, travel, entertainment). This chapter belongs to the first category, and primarily deals with biochemistry. It discusses an automated technique to create a structural ontology for compounds like ligands, co-factors and inhibitors of protein and DNA molecules using a technique developed from Perl scripts, which use a relational database for input and output, called Chem-BLAST (Chemical Block Layered Alignment of Substructure Technique). This technique recursively identifies substructures using rules that operate on the atomic connectivity of compounds. Substructures obtained from the compounds are compared to generate a data model expressed as triples. A chemical ontology of the substructures is made up of numerous interconnected 'hubs-and-spokes' is generated in the form of a data tree. This data-tree is used in a Web interface to allow users to zoom into compounds of interest by stepping through the hubs from the top to the bottom of the data-tree.

Chapter 2, A Pattern-Based Method for Re-Engineering Non-Ontological Resources into Ontologies, was written by by Boris Carmen Villazón-Terrazas, Mari Suárez-Figueroa, and Asunción Gómez-Pérez. Manually building ontologies that would involve humans to find and add each of the facts or component of its knowledgebase is not scalable. So a key to scalability is to find existing sources which are already based on ontological commitment, or consensus of the community of experts and users regarding the validity and interpretation of the facts that constitute the knowledgebase. If such sources are well structured, transforming or mapping them into the structure needed for ontological representation is easier, compared to the cases when unstructured sources. An even harder case to source ontological knowledge is presented by non-ontological resources (NORs), defined as "knowledge resources whose semantics have yet to be formalized by an ontology". These NORs can be in a variety of heterogeneous forms, including textual corpora, classification schemes, thesauri, lexicon, and folksonomy. This chapter first characterizes NORs based on the type of inner organization of the resource, design data model used to represent the knowledge encoded by the resources, and resource implementation. The chapter then presents a comparative framework for re-engineering NORs. The core of the chapter presents a method that is based on so-called re-engineering patterns along with a software library that implements the transformations suggested by the patterns. The chapter also presents an evaluation framework.

Chapter 3, An Ontology-Based, Cross-Application Context Modeling and Management Service, was written by Annett Mitschick, Stefan Pietschmann, and Klaus Meißner. Context-awareness is important for both information providers (software agents, sensors, applications) and information consumers, including applications that use information in a specific context. While there is a body of work in context awareness and context-aware applications, this work takes the next step in building cross-application context management that provides context support for diverse applications, application plug-ins, software agents and sensors acting in the roles of producers and consumers. They use ontology-based approach to support what they term "domain profiles" to build their cross-application context management services, and demonstrate the use in three applications: personal multimedia document management, adaptive co-browsing and context-aware user interface mashups.

SECTION 2: ANNOTATION, MAPPINGS AND TOOLS

Section 2 begins with Chapter 4, Files are Siles: Extending File Systems with Semantic Annotations, by Bernhard Schandl and Bernhard Haslhofer. Nowadays, extensive applications of Semantic Web technologies have added to the challenges in Web and enterprise environments. One of the next frontiers, which has already been started to be explored, is desktops, with an initial body of research in semantic desktops. Examples include incomplete information, broken links, or disruption of content and annotations. This chapter investigates a model authors call siles, which combine features of Semantic Web with files systems. The intent of this work is to show that siles model can provide a better infrastructure to build semantic desktops of the future. The chapter presents one component of this infrastructure, a virtual file system, which allows users to semantically annotate files and directories with RDF descriptors while keeping full compatibility to traditional hierarchical file systems. The chapter also provides the context of this work with respect to hierarchical file systems and metadata-centric file systems, and presents a prototype implementation and evaluates performance of typical access operations at file system and semantic metadata levels.

Chapter 5, Towards Controlled Natural Language for Semantic Annotation, was written by Brian Davis, Pradeep Dantuluri, and Hamish Cunningham. Semantic annotation is a core component of most Semantic Web approaches- it is how one uses controlled vocabulary or more formal representation as an ontology to associate meaning and common interpretations to words and objects on the Web. There are several approaches to achieve semantics annotations, including (a) manual annotation, semi-automatic annotation, and fully automatic annotations. Simple manual annotations found in unrestricted tagging is often of limited value due to little consistency and uncontrolled quality. Manual annotations, with respect to a formal ontology, can be time consuming as well as a complex job, especially if it involves the annotator to gain expertise in using a formal ontology. For a well-defined domain, which can have high quality ontology or ontologies when applied on certain high quality textual content, automatic annotations can give good and scalable results. A number of semi-automated approaches use natural language processing and/or machine learning techniques with ontologies described in a Semantic Web language (typically OWL). Such solutions require significant initial investment in building ontologies as well as sophitrication required for developing the technical solution. This chapter focuses on empowering content creators with an approach that involves a lower learning curve and little initial investment. It advocates and demonstrates use of Controlled Natural Languages (CNLs) that are subsets of natural language whose grammar and dictionaries have been restricted in order to reduce or eliminate both ambiguity and complexity. The approach is demonstrated for meeting notes.

Chapter 6, A Tool Suite to Enable Web Designers, Web Application Developers and End-users to Handle Semantic Data, was written by Mariano Rico, Óscar Corcho, José Antonio Macías, and David Camacho. Web application development is no longer an easy task. A developer is faced with a large collection of technologies with significant increases in the complexity and novelty on the client side. While Semantic Web developers have often failed to pick up necessary skills to develop sophisticated but end user friendly interfaces, coercing traditional Web application developers to add Semantic Web technologies to their mix of skill is too burdensome for them. This work discusses a semantic template based strategy to provide Web designers ability to incorporate semantic data into their applications without getting too involved in Semantic Web technologies. This strategy seeks to provide collaborative features to create templates, allowing forms to enter user's data that will be converted to semantic data and support semantic data transformation, all in a simpler albeit somewhat constrained ways compared to contemporary strategies. Evaluations include investigating how well it supports web designers in a wide range of competencies in client-side technologies, ranging from amateur HTML developers to professional Web designers.

Chapter 7, Adaptive Hybrid Semantic Selection of SAWSDL Services with SAWSDL-MX2, was written by Matthias Klusch, Patrick Kapahnke, and Ingo Zinnikus. Web services are a primary way for making applications and tools available over the Web using standardized descriptions. Semantic annotations of services make services easier to find, match, map, and integrate. In 2007, W3C adopted SAWSDL as a recommendation for describing Semantic Web Services. This chapter presents what is termed "hybrid semantic matchmaker" for services described in SAWSDL. It incorporates three types of semantic matching, including logic-based, text-similarity-based and XML-tree edit-based structural similarity, and combines them using an adaptive matching approach by using a training set to help decide semantic relevance to rank component matching in the aggregated matching process.

SECTION 3: SEMANTIC APPLICATIONS

Section 3 begins with chapter 8, Enhancing Folksonomy-Based Content Retrieval with Semantic Web Technology, by Rachanee Ungrangsi, Chutiporn Anutariya, and Vilas Wuwongse. This work is at the intersection of Web 2.0 and Semantic Web for image content. Quality of so called folkonomy tagging in current systems such as Flickr is usually poor due to lack of common terminology, use of single word tagging, lack of synonym support, and lack of adequate context. This work discusses the SemFlickr system that supports semantic querying which involves a system that first retrieves relevant ontologies from among existing ontologies and finding term suggestions for use as tags from those ontologies. It takes the ontological relations among the given query terms to assign tag scores and then generates its ranked results. SemFlickr's ability to boost image retrieval using semantics is demonstrated with respect to Flickr.

Chapter 9 is titled Semantic Search on Unstructured Data: Explicit Knowledge through Data Recycling, and it was written by Alex Kohn, François Bry, and Alexander Manta. Search is the most important Web application, and using semantics to improve search is something researchers have been investigating since the very early days of Semantic Web. Early examples include a semantic search engine called MediaAnywhere from Taalee, perhaps the earliest US Semantic Web company (details can be found in a patent awarded in 2001 titled "System and method for creating a Semantic Web and its applications in browsing, searching, profiling, personalization, and advertising), and a paper on Semantic Search in 2003 World Wide Web Conference. This chapter presents a semantic search system called YASA that uses ontology to improve information retrieval within an enterprise. The novel feature of YASA is that a large part of the ontology's fact base is automatically built by recycling and transforming existing data. YASA is a fully implemented system that is evaluated in a pharmaceutical company with very positive results. The systems features include context-based personalization, faceted navigation, and of course, semantic search.

The tenth chapter, Ontology-Enhanced User Interfaces: A Survey, was composed by Heiko Paulheim and Florian Probst. Ontologies have been used as part of engineering numerous software systems. However, only a few of these systems are user interfaces. This chapter discusses a variety of the ways in which user interface developers can enhance their systems using ontologies. Examples include adapting user interfaces to a user's needs and providing input assistance. It then outlines the corresponding requirements for the ontologies and their use in the context of enhancing user interface functions. This characterization serves two purposes: it allows for a better understanding of ontology-enhanced user interfaces, and it supports developers who want to use ontologies for a certain purposes in a user interface by pinpointing the relevant requirements. The survey ends with identifying new interesting research directions.

Chapter 11, Integrating Interactive TV Services and the Web through Semantics, was written by Vassileios Tsetsos, Antonis Papadimitriou, Christos Anagnostopoulos, and Stathes Hadjiefthymiades. The concept of interactive TV (iTV) has been around for a while, and Electronic Program Guides and program recommendation services can provide some useful capabilities. However, semantics and Semantic Web technologies have the promise to repurpose TV content more easily, support more advanced features, and even make access easier for end users. This chapter shows use of custom-made ontologies and rules, along with relevant standards in TV and Semantic Web areas, to support formal modeling of multimedia and user semantics, to create an iTV system that includes personalization and proactive content delivery to end users.

Chapter 12, Music Retrieval and Recommendation Scheme Based on Varying Mood Sequences, was written by Sanghoon Jun, Seungmin Rho, and Eenjun Hwang. This chapter deals with semantics in a broader sense, unlike other chapters; in this value, it does not use Semantic Web technologies. Music recommendation systems already utilize high-level musical features such as harmonics, beat, loudness, tonality, et cetera This chapter utilizes low-level features as base knowledge for music classification and recommendation, and develops an alternative strategy that involves measuring the similarity of music by using musical mood variation. Its recommendation system is based on applied artificial neural network algorithm to component ratio vectors of each music sequence and user preference rated playlist. It succeeds in achieving an average 70% classification accuracy.

Section 1
Ontology Development and Ontology–Based Services

Chapter 1
Building Chemical Ontology for Semantic Web Using Substructures Created by Chem-BLAST

Talapady N. Bhat
National Institute of Standards and Technology, USA

ABSTRACT

Efficient and user friendly ontologies are crucial for the effective use of chemical structural data on compounds. This paper describes an automated technique to create a structural ontology for compounds like ligands, co-factors and inhibitors of protein and DNA molecules using a technique developed from Perl scripts, which use a relational database for input and output, called Chem-BLAST (Chemical Block Layered Alignment of Substructure Technique). This technique recursively identifies substructures using rules that operate on the atomic connectivity of compounds. Substructures obtained from the compounds are compared to generate a data model expressed as triples. A chemical ontology of the substructures is made up of numerous interconnected 'hubs-and-spokes' is generated in the form of a data tree. This data-tree is used in a Web interface to allow users to zoom into compounds of interest by stepping through the hubs from the top to the bottom of the data-tree. The technique has been applied for (a) 2-D and 3-D structural data for AIDS[1]; (b) ~60,000 structures from the PDB [2,3]. Recently, this technique has been applied to approximately 3,000,000 compounds from PubChem[4,5,6]. Plausible ways to use this data model for the Semantic Web are also discussed.

1. INTRODUCTION

Established methods, e.g. PSI-BLAST (Altschul et al., 1997) that use amino-acid sequences to compare and organize structural data are widely used to build structural ontology for protein and DNA molecules. These proteins and DNA molecules are often found to contain small molecules such as toxins, drugs, and co-factors. These small molecules fall under a broad category called ligands (*compounds*) in the Protein Data Bank. *Compounds* are one of the most abundant entities created by nature and they are key components of

DOI: 10.4018/978-1-4666-0185-7.ch001

information space for several technological areas such as drug-discovery (Blundell et al., 2006; Drews, 2000), chemical, agricultural and biofuel research. These *compounds* come as add-ons to macromolecular structures either during their creation or later on at various steps ranging from sample preparation to crystallization. Building an ontology for *compounds* is a major challenge for developers of structural databases such as the Protein Data Bank (Berman et al., 2000; Berman, Westbrook, Feng, et al., 2000) and the HIV structural database (Prasanna, Vondrasek, Wlodawer, & Bhat, 2005).

Here we present a new rule-based automated technique to develop ontology for *compounds*. We also describe its application to structures chosen from three major databases (1) AIDS structural database[7], (2) Protein Data Bank[8], (3) PubChem[9]. Web tools[10] to query and intersect structural data from these databases using this ontology will also be presented. The terms of the ontology are defined using rules operating on the atomic connectivity of *compounds*. Atomic arrangements are invariants for a given compound and therefore the ontology described here may be considered as "formal" (Gruber, 1993) and thus it is subject to machine reasoning. The terms that form the ontology are of the type Object, Classifier and Value and thus they can be used to generate RDF triples (Lassila & Swick, 1999). An ontology developed by this method for about 3 million compounds obtained from PubChem is available for download[11].

2. BACKGROUND

Structural informatics deals with both large molecules such as proteins and small molecules (*compounds*) such as drugs and co-factors. *Compounds* are usually not peptides and therefore they may not be broken into standard amino-acid like fragments and classified using the rules applicable to protein sequences. Without automated and rule-based methods to classify them, the huge volume and large structural variations in

compounds pose difficulties for Web tools that try to present and compare *compounds* using their fragments in a predictable and orderly fashion. For instance, during the course of the last twenty years, researchers working on developing AIDS drugs have synthesized thousands of *compounds* that bind to HIV protease (Wlodawer & Erickson, 1993) and these *compounds* share many fragments among them. Identifying these shared fragments (also knows as scaffolds) is a challenge for a Webpage that distributes biological and structural data. Here we describe an automated rule-based method to present and compare *compounds* using their structural ontology built on their fragments.

Figure 1 shows the cavity formed by the HIV protease and an AIDS drug, amprenavir, held inside it. This figure is made from the three-dimensional x-ray structure of the protease (PDBID =1YT9) obtained from the Protein Data Bank. The protease cavity is shown as depressions and the grey colored surface shows the vicinity of carbon atoms of a drug molecule in its bound state. The oxygen atom of the drug molecule binds around the red regions of the cavity. Scaffolds of drug molecules that bind to this cavity tend to be structurally very similar since they all have to provide similar interactions to the protein surface around them. The focus of this paper is the automated development of a structural ontology for such drugs using their scaffolds.

2.2 Basic Concepts of the Rules Used to Define Ontological Terms

Compounds that bind to the active site of a particular protein, such as the HIV protease, can be quite different from one another. However, they possess certain common structural components called – scaffolds. Scaffolds are a part of *compounds* (Figure 2) and they are made up of a set of atoms arranged in a certain fashion. These scaffolds bind to specific pockets (HIV protease is considered to have six pockets denoted as P1, P2, P3, P1', P2' and P3') of the active site (Figure 1) of a protein

Figure 1. Cavity formed by the HIV protease and an AIDS drug, amprenavir, held inside it

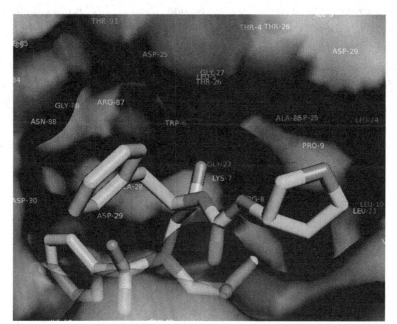

Figure 2. Several drug-like chemical compounds that bind to the active site of HIV protease – an AIDS drug target. This paper describes an automated method to build ontology for such compounds by using their scaffolds (Figure 3). PDB Ids are also shown.

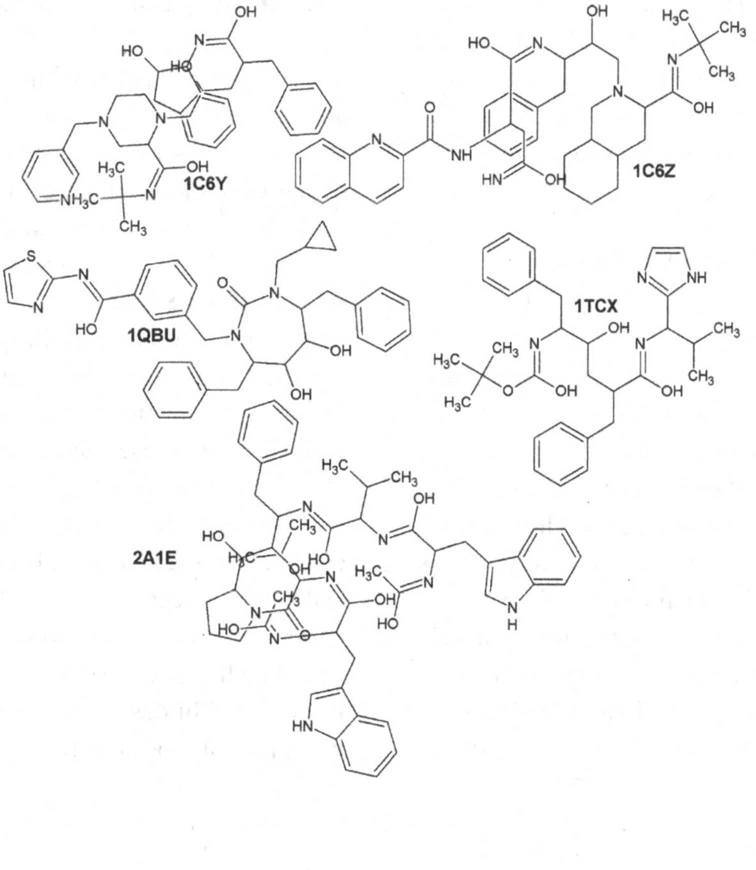

Figure 3. Some of the scaffolds used to build triples from the compounds such as those shown in Figure 2. Three types of names are used to denote scaffolds; one, short IUPAC names such as Valine, Indene, and the second are InChI (Table 1). InChI are generated by open source software that encodes the information on the atomic connectivity of the atoms of the scaffolds into strings. The third names are unique identifiers used by our database to identify each scaffold and its image. These are about 10 character long strings and they get assigned by an automated step as new scaffolds are discovered.

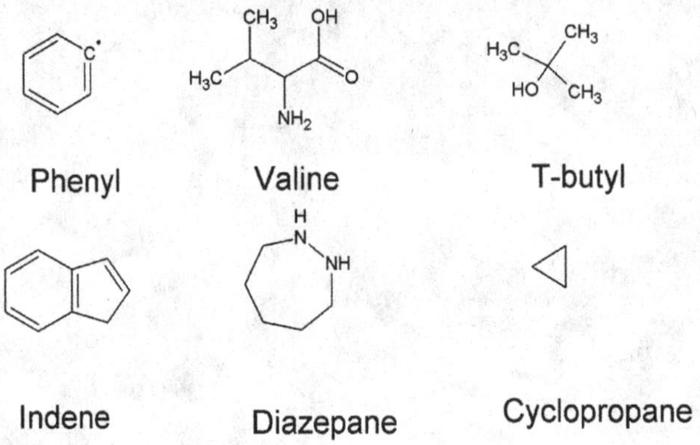

and therefore, in general, one or more scaffolds are conserved among *compounds* that bind to the same protein. The method that we describe here builds an ontology on *compounds* using their scaffolds (Figure 3) and based on programmable rules that are used to define scaffolds (ontological terms) in terms of their atomic bonds. Ontological terms that are commons to multiple *compounds* are used to classify and compare *compounds* and to establish RDF.

2.3 Automated Generation of Scaffolds

In our method, the scaffolds (Figure 4) are generated by automated procedures working on rules that operate on their atomic connectivity. For instance, a six member ring is coded as a collection of six atoms connected to each other such that starting from any one of these atoms one gets back to the same atom after stepping through six atomic bonds. If any one of those atoms is nitrogen, then it is noted as a nitrogen-containing six member ring. Two rings that share a bond is denoted as a double fused ring. Similar rules are used to define

and generate scaffolds of other ring and non-ring scaffolds. These scaffolds are used as elements of RDF triples as described in section 2.4.

2.4 Linking Scaffolds to Form Triples

Triples (Object, Property, Value) of RDF (Table 1) are generated by linking scaffolds that have shared structural features. For instance, consider some of the *compounds* (Figure 2) that bind to HIV protease. They have several common structural scaffolds (Figure 3). A six member-ring is one such scaffold. Some of these six member rings have a nitrogen atom in them. Some of the six member rings are fused to another six or five member ring. Some *compounds* have a seven member ring. These shared features of scaffolds are used to form their triples as shown in Figure 4. In this table, the middle column lists the Property, and the left and the right columns list Object and Value respectively. IUPAC names of some of these Objects are also shown in Figure 3 and a complete list of IUPAC names can be generated from the InChI described in section 4.1. Though it is plausible to build RDF for scaffolds using

Figure 4. Examples of triples generated by the method described here. Structural elements though identified by text strings in our database are shown also as images for clarity.

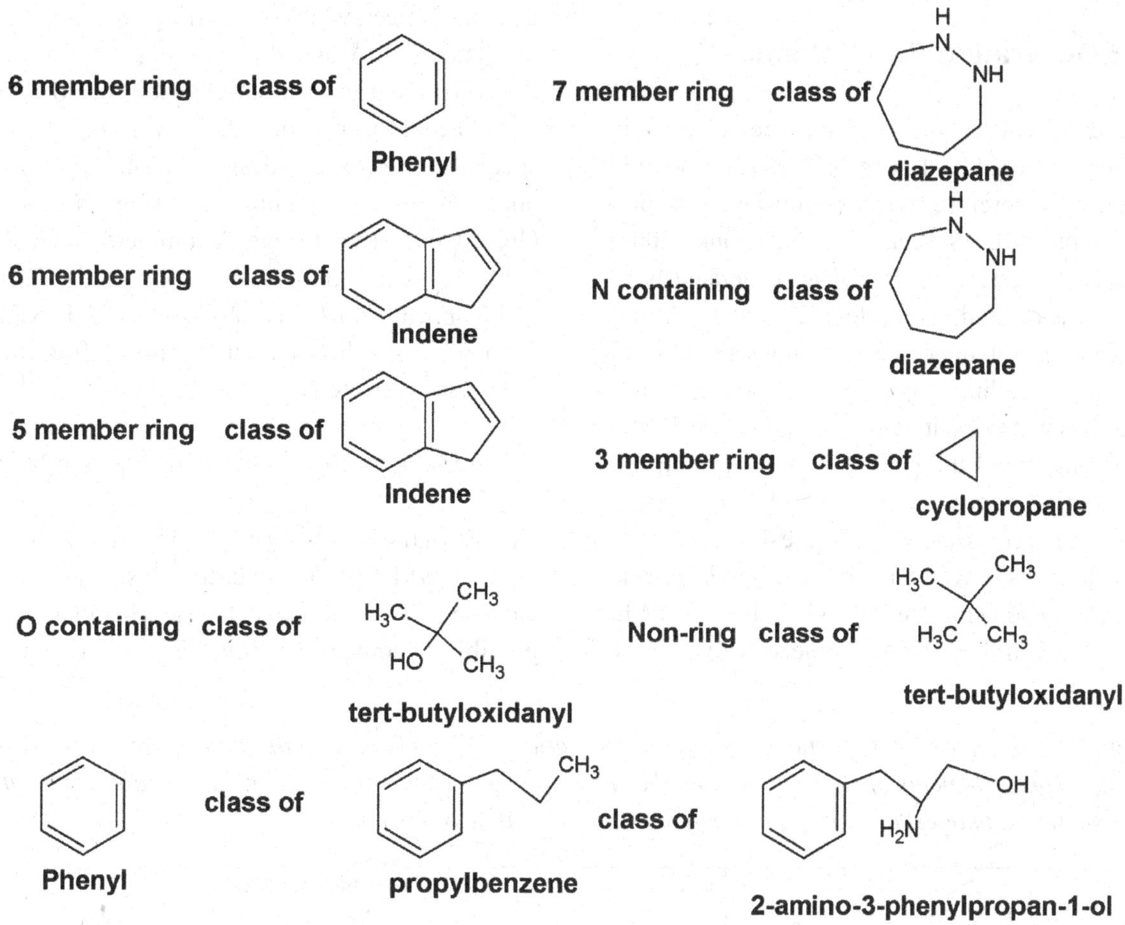

Table 1. Elements of RDFS using text-based names and rule-based names -InChI. InChI is used to assign a unique identifier for each element and to ensure that all identical elements get the same identifier regardless when they are added to the ontology. InChI is also used to re-generate the chemical structure of the elements of RDFS for re-validation purposes.

Phenyl InChI=1/C6H5/c1-2-4-6-5-3-1/h1-5H	level1	Six member ring
Benzyl InChI=1/C7H7/c1-7-5-3-2-4-6-7/h2-6H,1H2	level2	phenyl InChI=1/C6H5/c1-2-4-6-5-3-1/h1-5H
1-phenylethyl InChI=1/C8H9/c1-2-8-6-4-3-5-7-8/h2-7H,1H3	leveln-m	Benzyl InChI=1/C7H7/c1-7-5-3-2-4-6-7/h2-6H,1H2
Phe InChI=1/C9H11NO2/c10-8(9(11)12)6-7-4-2-1-3-5-7/h1-5,8H,6,10H2,(H,11,12)	leveln	1-phenylethyl InChI=1/C8H9/c1-2-8-6-4-3-5-7-8/h2-7H,1H3

IUPAC names, for clarity in recognizing the RDF elements we chose to use images instead.

2.5 Generating RDF Schema

Structural data are too complex to be expressed in a single layer of RDF such as 'Class of' shown in Figure 4. Therefore, a richer multi-layered representation of RDF Schema (Brickley & Guha, 2000) is used. Several layers of RDF are generated using properties called level1, level2,.. leveln. Atoms of an Object in the nth level includes all atoms of its corresponding Object in the (n-1)th level plus the ones in its vicinity. Conceptually, these RDFS gradually build the picture of a more complete *compound* starting from certain basic scaffolds such as the rings shown in Figure 4. Examples of the elements of RDFS are given using images in Figure 5 and using the IUPAC names and InChI in Table 1. In Figure 5 the Objects shown in the left column are a subclass of the ones shown in the corresponding right column. The rules used to generate Objects which contain rings are discussed in section 2.3. Atoms that are not part of a ring are considered to form an Object either if they are adjacent to a ring or if they form scaffolds of special interest to drug-design or molecular modeling. Phosphate and t-butyl are two examples of Objects that are not rings. A complete molecule is always considered as an Object of the RDF and it appears in the last (nth) level of RDF. RDF for a subset of the compounds chosen from the PubChem Website is downloadable[12].

2.5.1 Generating OWL from the Triples

Our use of the RDFS did not involve OWL per se. We convert RDFS into data-tree-based ontology and use it in a relational database. However, it is possible to convert the RDFS into OWL and to

Figure 5. RDFS for a hypothetical compound. The actual implementation of this concept may vary with usage. These elements of RDF all put together form a RDF schema or ontology. In this table elements are shown as images for clarity in specifying as to what they represent.

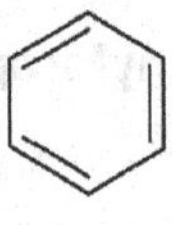 benzene	Level1	Six member ring
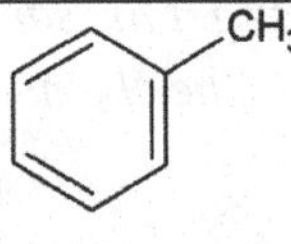 methylbenzene	Level2	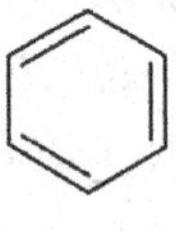 benzene
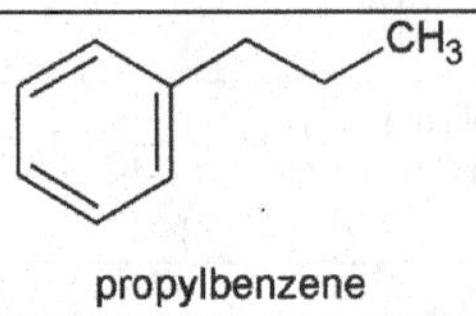 propylbenzene	Level3	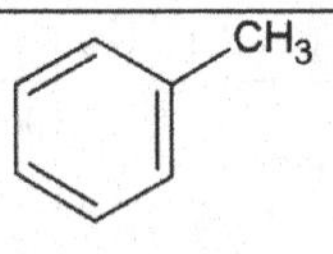 methylbenzene
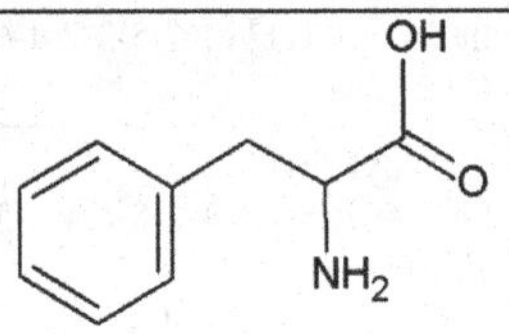 phenylalanine	Level4	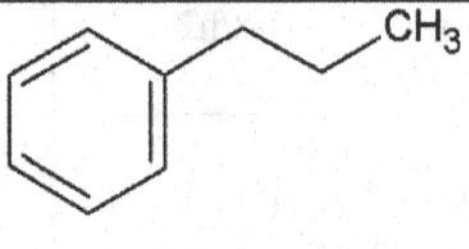 propylbenzene

support SPARQL type queries on them. An example of the OWL for a limited set of structures may be downloaded[13].

2.6 Generation of Ontology

The above described data model with triples provides a source of precisely defined and closely knitted terms that can be used and exchanged across Web applications as ontology. This technique of generating a data model is called Chem-BLAST (Bhat, 2009a, 2009b; Bhat & Barkley, 2007, 2008; Prasanna, Vondrasek, Wlodawer, & Bhat, 2005; Prasanna, Vondrasek, Wlodawer, Rodriguez, & Bhat, 2006) – Chemical Block Layered Alignment of Substructure Technique. The code that does this is written in Perl. This code, first extracts all rings from a *compound.* Following that, it examines each ring to look for other rings, if any, around them. Following the identification of all individual and adjacent rings, it extracts non-ring atoms that are adjacent to them, a few atoms at a time. The substructures (rings and non-rings) extracted in these steps are also called scaffolds or fragments. It organizes the scaffolds into groups based on their types such as six or seven member rings. Additionally, it also places scaffolds into an alternative group if any of the atoms they contain, such as Fe, are of ontological interest. Each unique group is considered a 'hub' and a means of association of a hub to another hub through a data model is called 'spoke'. These 'hubs' and 'spokes' collectively form the Objects and Value for building triples and structural ontologies. Keywords such as level1, level2 define the hierarchy (Figure 6) of these Objects. A full *compound* and the type of the ring extracted from it in the first step are the two terminal hubs of the ontology. Additionally, a terminal hub of ontology may be followed or preceded by biological information such as the binding constant of the *compound* or the abstract of the paper that describes the compound.

2.6.1 Application of the Method and a Schematic View of the Results

The proposed method was applied to all the *compounds* available in the Protein Data Bank (PDB)[14,15] and also to a subset of the *compounds* in the PubChem Website. A schematic view of the results is shown in Figure 7. This figure shows two layers, an outer layer consisting of Objects e.g., '6 member ring' and an inner layer consisting of Value, e.g., a structure of a benzene ring. Each Object is associated through RDFS to one or more *compounds* in the PDB or in PubChem as the case may be. Figure 7 shows databases as cyclodecane.

2.6.2 An Integrated Ontology of All Compounds: Hub-and-Spoke Model of the Elements

An integrated ontology that relates different layers (Figure 7) of information on *compounds* is generated first by collecting distinct InChI of elements of all layers and then by re-naming them so that identical elements have the same name everywhere. The result of this operation is a hub-and-spoke model for the elements of all *compounds* where hubs and spokes are uniquely labeled and classified. In this model similar or identical *compounds* share one or more hubs formed by their scaffolds. Number of hubs shared between two *compounds* depends on the structural similarity between them.

3. BUILDING A USER-INTERFACE

Although triple store with capabilities to query in SPARQL is a preferred method to query RDF, our interface works differently. Our Web interface deals with RDF elements of structural scaffolds that can be more elegantly presented in a Web as hyperlinked molecular images rather than as concatenated text-strings of their IUPAC names

Figure 6. A schematic view of a structural ontology of a hypothetical compound. The left most layer, called level1, has hubs for the general classification of a scaffold. Next layer, called level2 has hubs for type of the rings it has. The following layer, called level3, has hubs made up of rings and few atoms around them. Actual number of hubs that stack up between the top and bottom layers may vary depending on the size and the chemical structure of a compound.

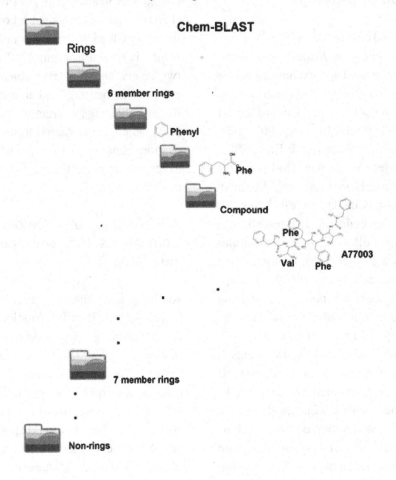

or InChI. Web interface lays out the images in layers of hyperlinked image-tiles for inspection and subsequent selection. Each layer of the image-tile holds images of elements of a particular layer of ontology denoted by the RDF. On selection of a particular image, the Web interface performs a query on the element denoted by that image and displays the result set as new images (Figure 6) for further selection.

The gradual increase in the precision of the image-tiles to define a *compound* in successive layers provides a convenient mechanism to present the images in a predictable order over the Web. The image-tile displayed initially by the Web tool have the scaffolds that point to a collection of both closely and distantly similar *compounds* and the image-tiles displayed subsequently have the scaffolds that point to a collection of *compounds* that are more closely related.

Figure 7. A schematic view of some of the results obtained by the method on compounds in the PDB (top) and in a subset of the ones from PubChem (bottom). The method organizes information on each compound into several layers of low to high granularity and connects these layers using RDFS. Elements in these layers and their relationships are used by Chem-BLAST to query and intersect data from these resources.

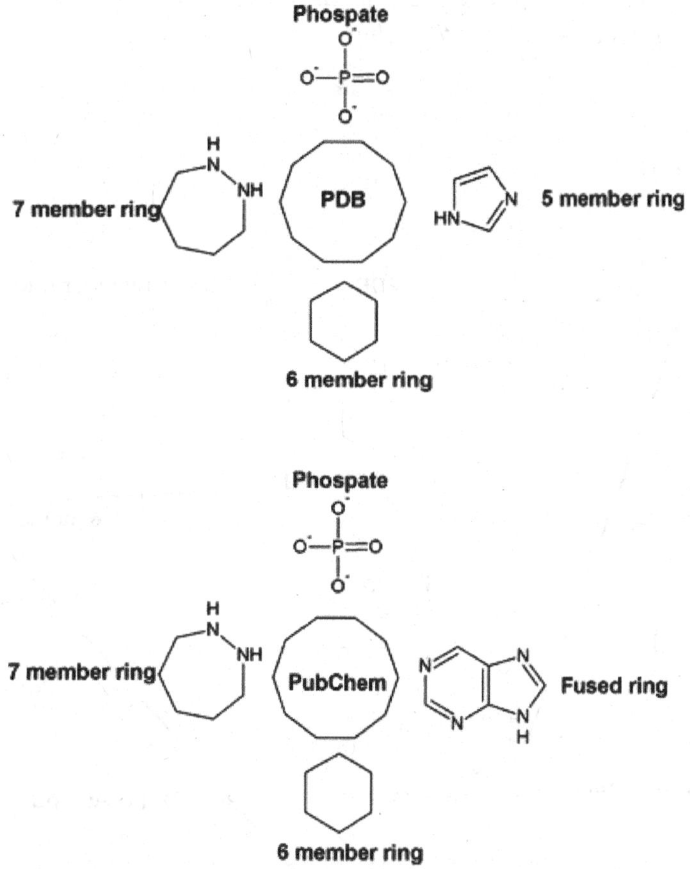

4. ON THE INTEGRATION/ INTERSECTION OF DATABASES USING TRIPLES

We have used *compounds* both from the PDB and PubChem to build a data model using triples and Website to query them. Its schematic view is shown in Figure 8. This Website[16] uses triples to index and integrate/intersect related structures from the PDB and PubChem. Using this Website a user can search similar or identical compounds from the PDB and/or PubChem using the hyperlinks. The

hyperlink on a complete *compound* generates list of all entries of that compound in the database.

4.1 Unique IDs for the RDF Elements

Each element is assigned a unique identifier using the open source software[17]. This identifier is called InChI (International Chemical Identifier). InChI (Murray-Rust, Rzepa, Tyrrell, & Zhang, 2004; Prasanna, Vondrasek, Wlodawer, & Bhat, 2005) is a text string generated from the atomic connectivity of the atoms of the element. The InChI of structurally identical elements will be identical

Figure 8. A schematic view of a user interface to query either the PDB or the PubChem Websites using the RDF elements (shown as images) that are established by the Chem-BLAST. In this interface a user clicks on a molecular image to query for structures either in the PDB or in the PubChem Website. These RDF can be maintained independent of the data resources such the PDB and the PubChem Websites. Therefore, they provide a convenient mechanism to query and intersect federated structural resources without creating a local copy of those resources. This mechanism may help to bring the vision of Semantic Web for structural resources a step closer to reality.

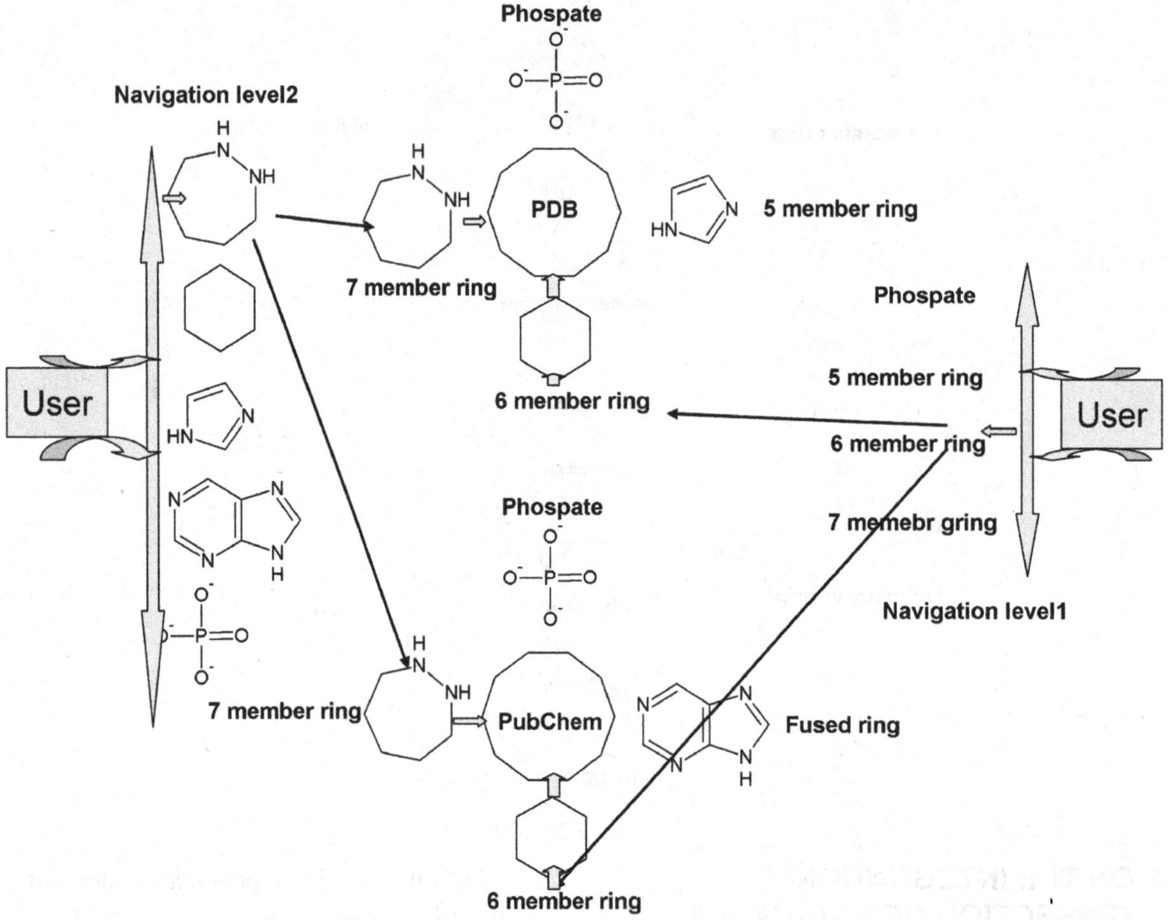

and therefore, all identical elements receive the same identifier regardless of which *compound* they belong to or when they were added to the ontology. InChI encodes the entire atomic connectivity of the element that it identifies, and thus, it may have several hundred characters. Therefore, although InChI provides a convenient method to establish unique identifiers for the elements, it is not suitable as a name of a file that holds the atomic connectivity or image of a scaffold that it

identifies. For this reason, a short (usually, less that 10 character long) identifier is also assigned to each element using a look-up table. The current version of InChI is unable to properly handle metal co-ordination and therefore, a separate identifier may be also needed for accurate representations of *compounds* with metals.

Figure 9. A part of the Web interface of the AIDS database. It displays the text-based information as folders (left panel) and substructure as image-tiles (right panel). Each Image is hyperlinked to provide query on that scaffold.

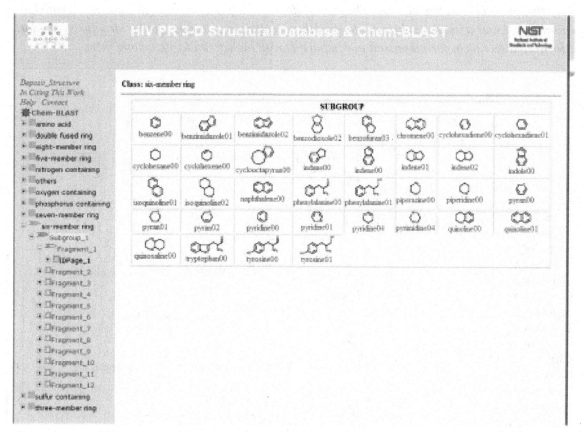

5. RESULTS AND DISCUSSION

Chem-BLAST was initially developed to build ontology for *compounds* of interest to AIDS[18]. As the paper was being written, we extended the work to about 3 million compounds chosen from the PDB and from PubChem. Since the results of the work on the PDB and PubChem have been already discussed in previous sections of this paper, in this section we intend to focus mostly on the *compounds* of interest to AIDS. These *compounds* are traditionally classified on the basis of the mechanism by which they prevent the replication of the AIDS virus. Some of these classes are HIV Protease, HIV Integrate, HIV Reverse Transcriptase, and CCR 5. A few thousand compounds from these classes were used in our work. Figure 9 shows the Web interface that was developed to query *compounds* belonging to one of these classes. In that figure, the left panel displays information from the top layer of the ontology and this layer holds text-only type information such as amino-acids, and double-fused rings. In the right panel, information on scaffolds from the middle layers is displayed as images.

Each data item displayed by the Webpage is a hub for one or more *compounds*. Each hub is hyperlinked to perform query to produce results from its adjacent hubs. The default direction of propagation of a query using a hyperlink is towards its lower level in the ontological tree. Some of the hyperlinks work differently and they propagate

Figure 10. A snapshot from the Webpage of HIVSDB that provides hyperlinks to query both in the forward (top to bottom of the ontology tree) and the reverse direction. A user may use a hyperlink in the forward direction to query on spokes to go to its lower layers. Similarly, the reverse arrows provide queries on spokes that connect to its higher layer. The reverse direction hyperlinks result in compounds with lower similarity as it uses a smaller subset of atoms of the structure to query for similar structures. Similarly, the forward direction hyperlinks result in compounds with higher similarity among them.

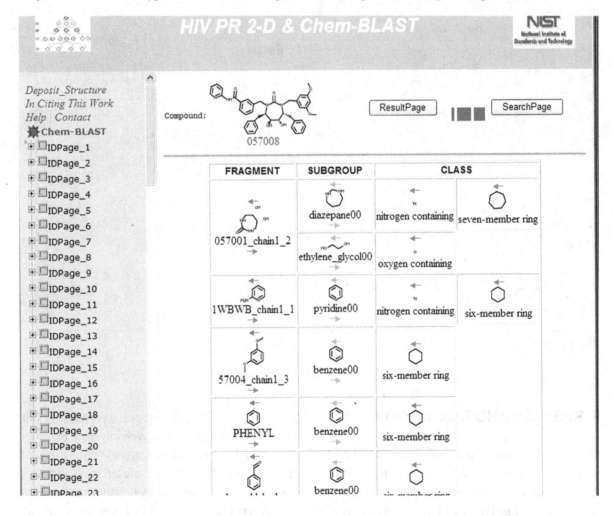

query in the reverse (lower to higher) direction and they are shown explicitly using arrows (Figure 10).

Though we store the ontology in a relational database, it can be stored [19] in OWL or RDF using adjacent hubs of the ontological tree as elements and their relationships as predicates.

Chemical *compounds* are an important part of information technology and there have been several major efforts and publications[20,21,22](Batchelor,

2008) on developing their ontology. The primary focus of many of those efforts has been to develop ontology using a complete *compound*. Though, the work described here has a component of developing ontology for complete *compounds*, its primary focus is to develop ontology for *compounds* using their sub-components (scaffolds) by an automated and rule-based method. The proposed ontology on scaffolds may be integrated with other ontology using either a *compound* or its scaffolds such as the metals and phosphates as the point of intersection between them. A full discussion on published efforts to develop chemical ontology on full *compounds* per se is beyond the scope of this paper.

One of the fundamental properties of a class of *compounds* that bind to a particular target protein, for example the HIV Protease is the reuse of certain scaffolds. This property of a class of *compounds* arises from the fact that all those *compounds* fill the same pocket of the protein (Figure 1). For this reason, we believe that the ontology on scaffolds built by the technique, Chem-BLAST that we describe here has direct applications in chemi-informatics and drug design.

The scaffolds that we used to build the ontology are generated in several levels. Scaffolds at the first level are smaller than the one in its higher level. Scaffolds at the higher levels have atoms from the immediate lower level plus the atoms around them. For instance, (see Figure 5) one of the scaffolds at the first level is a six member ring. The next level of its ontological tree is a six member ring with an additional carbon atom. The ontological tree of scaffolds is presented over a Web as clickable folders (see Figure 9) (Prasanna et al., 2006)[23]. At the first level, they allow a user to select hubs of general descriptions such as six member rings and at the next levels they allow a user to gradually wean through hubs with more precise definitions of a *compound*.

5.1 Naming of Scaffolds and the Generation of RDF

Atomic bonds between atoms of a scaffold provide a unique mechanism to develop a rule-based method, InChI (McNaught, 2003), for naming them. For instance, the InChI (International Chemical Identifier) for indane molecule (Figure 3) is InChI=1S/C9H10/c1-2-5-9-7-3-6-8(9)4-1/h1-2,4-5H,3,6-7H2. The first part (between the first two "/ ") of an InChI is the chemical formula of the *compound* and the rest is a coded form of its atomic connectivity. It is possible to re-generate the structure of a *compound* (in this case indane) from its InChI using the InChI software[24]. For this reason, InChI provides a novel, rule-based method for naming *compounds* and their scaffolds. However, the InChI does not allow humans to instantly infer the structure of a scaffold. For this reason we developed Chem-BLAST which uses molecular images to scaffolds. Chem-BLAST identifies each scaffold as a file of its image. InChI is not convenient to be used as file names. Therefore, we assign a shorter text-based identifier to identify its molecular image and bond connectivity file. Using this identifier, we generate an RDF (Resource description framework[25]) (Wang, Gorlitsky, & Almeida, 2005) as *compound – has – scaffold A; scaffold A – has – scaffold A1; scaffold A – has – scaffold A2*. Elements of an RDF are joined head-to-tail to generate ontology as *compound -> scaffold A -> scaffold A1; compound ->scaffold A ->scaffold A2*.

5.2 Integration of Ontologies

InChI (InChIKey or an alternate shorter identifier described in 4.1) encodes the atomic connectivity of the entire *compound* and thus it may be used to create an invariant URI for a *compound*. However, an integration of information using InChI particularly of a scaffold though can be technically done its ontological relevance to a focus area is less guaranteed. Relevance of a scaffold to a particular focus area such as drug-discovery or patenting depends on the rules used to define it. Moreover, even within a particular focus area for example drug discovery, relevance may be affected depending upon whether it is drug discovery for AIDS or cancer or a target protein. For this reason, a scaffold and its InChI may be treated instead as semi-invariant and used in an ontological URI (OURI) ((Bhat & Barkley, 2007, 2008). OURI may foster 'dialects' with less than perfect overlaps in their meaning in different focus areas and they get their designed meaning only in the context they are designed for.

Compound identifiers used by different databases are often not the same and therefore, the intersection of ontology on *compounds* held by them using their identifiers is a major problem. For instance, the PDB uses what is called a three-letter-code and PubChem uses what is called CID to identify *compounds*. The method proposed here attempts to alleviate this problem by proposing a rule-based system (Bhat, 2009a, 2009b) for generating, and naming elements to build ontology on *compounds* and their scaffolds. Description of a *compound* and scaffolds in the Web is another problem. Chemical structures are too complex to be recognized by their commercial or IUPAC names. For this reason in our Webpage ontological terms, namely scaffolds and *compounds*, are stored and displayed as images. However, from their identifiers descriptive IUPAC names could have been generated for ontological terms and a descriptive RDF could have been also built (Figure 3). Such an RDF would have been of the type *Indane – has – Six member ring* and *Indane – has – four member ring. Compound 006688 – has – Indane.* Additional examples of this type of RDF have been posted[26] in a downloadable OWL document[27]. In our application, we generate the ontology as triples and store them in a relational database. However, these triples could have been stored in a triple store and queried using SPARQL as well. After we started to write this paper, we extended our work to few million compounds chosen from the PubChem Webpage. A part of its result is downloadable[28]. This result is also available to the community as a standard reference data distributed by NIST.

ACKNOWLEDGMENT

Work on HIVSDB was done in part in collaboration with Anh-Dao Nguyen of NIST, G. Noble and L. Cooney of Cygnus Corporation, M. Nasr of NIAID, A. Wlodawer of NCI and K. Das and E. Arnold of University of Rutgers. Certain trade and company products are identified in this paper to specify adequately the computer products needed to develop this data system. In no case does such identification imply endorsement by the National Institute of Standards and Technology (NIST), or does it imply that the products are necessarily the best available for the purpose.

REFERENCES

Altschul, S. F., Madden, T. L., Schaffer, A. A., Zhang, J., Zhang, Z., & Miller, W. (1997). Gapped BLAST and PSI-BLAST: a new generation of protein database search programs. *Nucleic Acids Research, 25*(17), 3389–3402. doi:10.1093/nar/25.17.3389

Batchelor, C. (2008). Formal ontology in information systems. In *Frontiers in Artificial Intelligence and Applications* (Vol. 183, pp. 195-207).

Berman, H. M., Bhat, T. N., Bourne, P. E., Feng, Z., Gilliland, G., & Weissig, H. (2000). The PDB and the Challenge of Structural Genomics. *Nature Structural Biology, 11*, 957–959. doi:10.1038/80734

Berman, H. M., Westbrook, J., Feng, Z., Gilliland, G., Bhat, T. N., & Weissig, H. (2000). The Protein Data Bank. *Nucleic Acids Research, 28*, 235–242. doi:10.1093/nar/28.1.235

Bhat, T. N. (2009a). Chemical Taxonomies and Ontologies for Semantic Web. *Semantic Universe.* Retrieved from http://www.semanticuniverse.com/articles-chemical-taxonomies-and-ontologies-semantic-web.html

Bhat, T. N. (2009b). *On the creation of structural FaceBook using rule-based methods to build and exchange ontology for drug design.* Retrieved from http://sunsite.informatik.rwth-aachen.de/Publications/CEUR-WS/Vol-549

Bhat, T. N., & Barkley, J. (2007). Semantic Web for the Life Sciences - Hype, Why, How and Use Case for AIDS Inhibitors. In *Proceedings of the IEEE Congress on Services* (pp. 87-91).

Bhat, T. N., & Barkley, J. (2008). Development of a Use case for Chemical Resource Description Framework for Acquired Immune Deficiency Syndrome Drug Discovery. *The Open Bioinformatics Journal, 2*, 20–27. doi:10.2174/1875036200802010020

Blundell, T. L., Sibanda, B. L., Montalvao, R. W., Brewerton, S., Chelliah, V., & Worth, C. L. (2006). Structural biology and bioinformatics in drug design: opportunities and challenges for target identification and lead discovery. *Philosophical Transactions of the Royal Society B. Biological Sciences, 361*(1467), 413–423. doi:10.1098/rstb.2005.1800

Brickley, D., & Guha, R. V. (2000). *Resource Description Frame Work (RDF) Schema Specification 1.0, W3C Candidate Recommendation.* Retrieved from http://www.w3.org/TR/rdf-schema

Drews, J. (2000). Drug discovery: a historical perspective. *Science, 287*, 1960–1964. doi:10.1126/science.287.5460.1960

Gruber, T. R. (1993). A Translation Approach to Portable Ontology Specification. *Knowledge Acquisition, 5*, 199–220. doi:10.1006/knac.1993.1008

Lassila, O., & Swick, R. (1999). *Resource Description Framework (RDF) Model and Syntax Specification, W3C Recommendation.* Retrieved from http://www.w3.org/TR/REC-rdf-syntax

McNaught, A. (2003). *What's in a Name.* The Alchemist.

Murray-Rust, P., Rzepa, H. S., Tyrrell, S. M., & Zhang, Y. (2004). Representation and use of chemistry in the global electronic age. *Organic & Biomolecular Chemistry, 2*(22), 3192–3203. doi:10.1039/b410732b

Prasanna, M., Vondrasek, J., Wlodawer, A., & Bhat, T. N. (2005). Application of InChI to curate, index and query 3-D structures. *Proteins, Structure, Function, and Bioinformatics, 60*, 1–4. doi:10.1002/prot.20469

Prasanna, M. D., Vondrasek, J., Wlodawer, A., Rodriguez, H., & Bhat, T. N. (2006). Chemical compound navigator: a web-based chem-BLAST, chemical taxonomy-based search engine for browsing compounds. *Proteins, 63*(4), 907–917. doi:10.1002/prot.20914

Wang, X., Gorlitsky, R., & Almeida, J. S. (2005). From XML to RDF: how semantic web technologies will change the design of 'omic' standards. *Nature Biotechnology, 23*(9), 1099–1103. doi:10.1038/nbt1139

Wlodawer, A., & Erickson, J. W. (1993). Structure-based inhibitors of HIV-1 protease. *Annual Review of Biochemistry, 62*, 543–585. doi:10.1146/annurev.bi.62.070193.002551

ENDNOTES

1. http://bioinfo.nist.gov/SemanticWeb_pr2d/chemblast.do
2. http://www.rcsb.org/pdb/explore/external-References.do?structureId=3GGT
3. http://xpdb.nist.gov/chemblast/pdb.html
4. http://xpdb.nist.gov/chemblast/chemlevel1.pl?T1=IMD
5. http://xpdb.nist.gov/pubchem_chem_blast/rdf/pubchem.rdf
6. http://xpdb.nist.gov/hiv2_d/download.html
7. http://bioinfo.nist.gov/SemanticWeb_pr2d/chemblast.do

8 http://www.pdb.org/pdb/home/home.do

9 http://pubchem.ncbi.nlm.nih.gov/summary/summary.cgi?cid=00001199

10 http://xpdb.nist.gov/chemblast/pdb.pl?pdbid=3GGT

11 http://xpdb.nist.gov/pubchem_chem_blast/rdf/pubchem.rdf

12 http://xpdb.nist.gov/pubchem_chem_blast/rdf/pubchem.rdf

13 http://xpdb.nist.gov/hiv2_d/download.html (The Properties used here are subject to change).

14 http://www.pdb.org/pdb/home/home.do

15 http://pubchem.ncbi.nlm.nih.gov/

16 http://xpdb.nist.gov/chemblast/pdb.pl?pdbid=3GGT

17 http://www.iupac.org/inchi/

18 http://bioinfo.nist.gov/SemanticWeb_pr2d/chemblast.do

19 http://esw.w3.org/topic/HCLS/Chemical-TaxonomiesUseCase

20 http://www.semanticuniverse.com/

21 http://pubs.acs.org/doi/abs/10.1021/ci060139e

22 http://www.ebi.ac.uk/chebi/

23 http://bioinfo.nist.gov/SemanticWeb_pr2d/chemblast.do

24 http://www.iupac.org/inchi/

25 http://www.w3.org/RDF/

26 http://esw.w3.org/topic/HCLS/Chemical-TaxonomiesUseCase

27 http://xpdb.nist.gov/hiv2_d/download.ht

28 http://xpdb.nist.gov/chemblast/chemlevel1.pl?T1=1T3R_ll_2

This work was previously published in International Journal of Semantic Web and Information Systems, Volume 6, Issue 3, edited by Amit P. Sheth, pp. 22-37, copyright 2010 by IGI Publishing (an imprint of IGI Global).

Chapter 2
A Pattern-Based Method for Re-Engineering Non-Ontological Resources into Ontologies

Boris Villazón-Terrazas
Universidad Politécnica de Madrid, Spain

Mari Carmen Suárez-Figueroa
Universidad Politécnica de Madrid, Spain

Asunción Gómez-Pérez
Universidad Politécnica de Madrid, Spain

ABSTRACT

To speed up the ontology development process, ontology developers are reusing all available ontological and non-ontological resources, such as classification schemes, thesauri, lexicons, and so forth, that have already reached some consensus. Non-ontological resources are highly heterogeneous in their data model and storage system (or implementation). The reuse of these non-ontological resources involves their re-engineering into ontologies. This paper presents a method for re-engineering non-ontological resources into ontologies. The method is based on so-called re-engineering patterns, which define a procedure that transforms the non-ontological resource components into ontology representational primitives using WordNet for making explicit the relations among the non-ontological resource terms. The paper also provides the description of NOR$_2$O, a software library that implements the transformations suggested by the patterns. Finally, it depicts an evaluation of the method, patterns, and software library proposed.

INTRODUCTION

Research on Ontology Engineering methodologies has provided methods and techniques for developing ontologies from scratch. Well-recognized methodological approaches such as METHON-TOLOGY (Gómez-Pérez, Fernández-López & Corcho, 2003), On-To-Knowledge (Staab, Schnurr, Studer & Sure, 2001), and DILIGENT (Pinto, Tempich & Staab, 2004) give guidelines that help researchers to develop ontologies. However, researchers face an important limitation: no guidelines are provided for building ontologies

DOI: 10.4018/978-1-4666-0185-7.ch002

by re-engineering existing knowledge resources widely used by a particular community.

During the last decade, specific methods, techniques and tools were proposed for building ontologies from existing knowledge resources. First, ontology learning methods and tools have been proposed to extract relevant concepts and relations from structured, semi-structured, and non-structured resources (Gómez-Pérez & Manzano-Macho, 2004; Maedche & Staab, 2001) in order to form a single ontology. One important constraint to these methods and tools is that they propose *ad-hoc* solutions to transforming such resources, mainly texts, into ontologies. Hepp et al. (Hepp, 2006; Hepp & Brujin, 2007; Hepp, 2007) stated that employing methods and techniques when ontologizing non-ontological resources to the level of ontologies is key for the success of semantic technology for two main reasons: (1) if the use of semantic technologies for real-world data integration challenges is required, it is possible to refer to the original conceptual elements, and (2) for many domains, the existing category systems, XML schemas, and normative entity identifiers are the most efficient resources for engineering ontologies.

The ontologization of non-ontological resources has led to the design of several specific methods, techniques and tools (Hepp & Brujin, 2007; Hyvönen, Viljanen, Tuominen & Seppälä, 2008; Gangemi, Guarino, Masolo & Oltramari, 2003; García & Celma, 2005). These are mainly specific to a particular resource type, or to a particular resource implementation. Thus, everytime ontology engineers face a new resource type or implementation, they develop *ad-hoc* solutions for transforming such resource into a single ontology.

In parallel, and within the context of the NeOn project[1], a novel scenario-based methodology for building ontology networks[2] has been proposed: the NeOn Methodology (Suárez-Figueroa, 2010; Gómez-Pérez & Suárez-Figueroa, 2009). One of these novel scenarios is *Building Ontology Networks by Reusing and Re-engineering Non-*

Ontological Resources. As opposed to custom-building silos of single ontologies from scratch, this new scenario emphasizes the re-engineering of knowledge resources for building ontologies that are connected with other ontologies in the ontology network.

The motivation of this paper lies in this scenario of the NeOn Methodology and the use of re-engineering patterns to transform the non-ontological resources components into ontology representational primitives. Along this paper we will try to demonstrate that the use of re-engineering patterns for transforming non-ontological resources into ontologies has several advantages: (1) they embody expertise about how to guide a re-engineering process, (2) they improve the efficiency of the re-engineering process, and (3) they make the transformation process easier for ontology engineers.

In this paper we present first our proposed categorization of non-ontological resources. Then, we provide a framework for comparing methods for re-engineering non-ontological resources into ontologies, and the conclusions drawn on the comparative study. After that, we analyze the role of patterns in software engineering and ontology engineering with particular emphasis on re-engineering patterns. Then, we present our pattern-based method for re-engineering non-ontological resources into ontologies. Then, we explain NOR$_2$O, a software library that performs the transformation automatically. Next, we present an evaluation of the method, patterns and software library. Finally we draw the conclusions and provide future lines of work.

NON-ONTOLOGICAL RESOURCES

Non-Ontological Resources (NORs) are knowledge resources whose semantics have not yet been formalized by an ontology (García-Silva, Gómez-Pérez, Suárez-Figueroa & Villazón-Terrazas, 2008). There is a great number of NORs that embody knowledge about some particular domains and that represent some degree of consensus. These resources are present in the form of textual corpora, classification scheme, thesauri, lexicons, etc. NORs have usually implicit semantics that allows interpreting the knowledge they contain. Regardless of whether the semantics is explicit or not, the main problem is that the semantics of NORs is not always formalized, and this lack of formalization prevents them from being used as ontologies. Using non-ontological resources that already have reached a consensus for building ontologies can have several benefits, e.g. interoperability in terms of the vocabulary used, browsing/searching information, decrease the knowledge acquisition bottleneck, and increase the reuse.

An analysis of the literature has revealed that there are different ways of categorizing NORs. Thus Maedche et al. (Maedche & Staab, 2001) classify NORs into unstructured (free text), semi-structured (folksonomies) and structured

(databases) resources; whereas Gangemi et al. (Gangemi, Pisanelli & Steve, 1998) distinguish catalogues of normalized terms, glossed catalogues, and taxonomies; finally, Hodge (Hodge, 2000) proposes characteristics such as structure, complexity, relationships among terms, and historical functions for classifying them. However, an accepted and agreed on typology of NORs does not exist yet.

In this paper we propose a categorization of NORs, according to the three features presented in Figure 1: (1) type of NOR, which refers to the type of inner organization of the information; (2) data model[3], that is, the design data model used to represent the knowledge encoded by the resource; and (3) resource implementation.

According to the *type of NOR* we classify them into

- **Glossary:** A glossary is an alphabetical list of terms or words found in or relating to a

Figure 1. NORs categorization

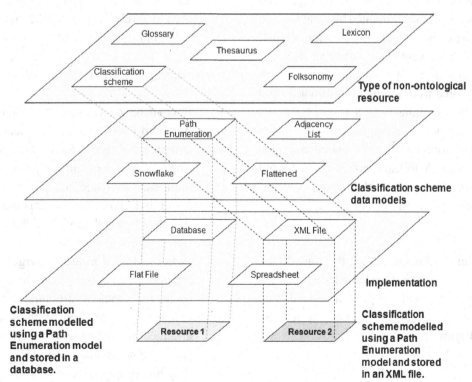

specific topic or text. It may or may not include explanations, and its vocabulary may be monolingual, bilingual or multilingual (Wright & Budin, 1997). One example is the FAO Fisheries Glossary[4].

- **Classification scheme:** A classification scheme refers to the descriptive information required to arrange or divide objects into groups according to the characteristics that they have in common (ISO/IEC, 2004). A clear example is the Fishery International Standard Statistical Classification of Aquatic Animals and Plants (ISSCAAP)[5].

- **Thesaurus:** A thesaurus is a controlled vocabulary of terms in a particular domain with hierarchical, associative, and equivalence relations between terms. Thesauri are mainly used for indexing and retrieving articles in large databases (ISO, 1986). A good example is the AGROVOC[6] thesaurus.

- **Lexicon:** In a restricted sense, a computational lexicon is considered as a list of words or lexemes hierarchically organized and normally accompanied by meaning and linguistic behaviour information (Hirst, 2004). A relevant example is WordNet[7].

- **Folksonomy:** A folksonomy is the result of personal free tagging of information and objects (anything with a URL) for one's own retrieval. The tagging is done in a social environment (usually shared and open to others). A folksonomy is created from the act of tagging by the person consuming the information[8]. An example is *del. icio.us*[9].

According to the *data model*, there are different ways of representing the knowledge encoded by the resource. Next we present several *data models for classification schemes*, which are shown in Figure 2.

- **Path Enumeration** (Brandon, 2005): A path enumeration model (see Figure 2b) is a recursive structure for hierarchy representations defined as a model that stores for each node the path (as a string) from the root to the node. This string is the concatenation of the nodes code in the path from the root to the node.

- **Adjacency List** (Brandon, 2005): An adjacency list model is a recursive structure for hierarchy representations comprising a list of nodes with a column linking to their parent nodes. Figure 2c shows this model.

- **Snowflake** (Malinowski & Zimányi, 2006): A snowflake model is a normalized structure for hierarchy representations. For each hierarchy level a table is created. In this model each hierarchy node has a linked column to its parent node. Figure 2d shows this model.

- **Flattened** (Malinowski & Zimányi, 2006): A flattened model is a denormalized structure for hierarchy representations. The hierarchy is represented with a table in which each hierarchy level is stored on a different column. Figure 2e illustrates this model.

Next, we present two *data models for thesauri*:

- **Record-based model** (Soergel, 1995): A record-based model is a denormalized structure that uses a record for every term. The record keeps information about the term, such as synonyms, and broader, narrower and related terms. This model looks like the flattened model of the classification scheme.

- **Relation-based model** (Soergel, 1995): A relation-based model leads to a more elegant and efficient structure. Information is stored in individual pieces that can be arranged in different ways. Relationship types are not defined as fields in a record, they are simply data values in a relation-

Figure 2. Classification scheme example

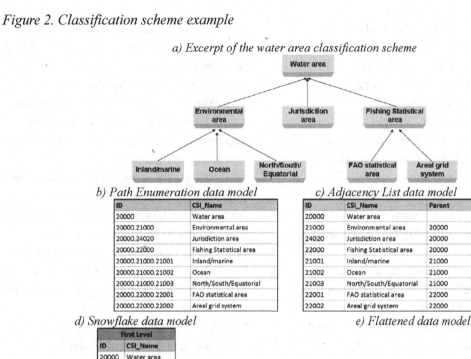

a) Excerpt of the water area classification scheme

b) Path Enumeration data model

ID	CSI_Name
20000	Water area
20000.21000	Environmental area
20000.24020	Jurisdiction area
20000.22000	Fishing Statistical area
20000.21000.21001	Inland/marine
20000.21000.21002	Ocean
20000.21000.21003	North/South/Equatorial
20000.22000.22001	FAO statistical area
20000.22000.22002	Areal grid system

c) Adjacency List data model

ID	CSI_Name	Parent
20000	Water area	
21000	Environmental area	20000
24020	Jurisdiction area	20000
22000	Fishing Statistical area	20000
21001	Inland/marine	21000
21002	Ocean	21000
21003	North/South/Equatorial	21000
22001	FAO statistical area	22000
22002	Areal grid system	22000

d) Snowflake data model

First Level

ID	CSI_Name
20000	Water area

Second Level

ID	First Level ID	CSI_Name
21000	20000	Environmental area
24020	20000	Jurisdiction area
22000	20000	Fishing Statistical area

Third Level

ID	Second Level ID	CSI_Name
21001	21000	Inland/marine
21002	21000	Ocean
21003	21000	North/South/Equatorial
22001	22000	FAO statistical area
22002	22000	Areal grid system

e) Flattened data model

First Level		Second Level		Third Level	
ID	CSI_Name	ID	CSI_Name	ID	CSI_Name
20000	Water area	21000	Environmental area	21001	Inland/marine
20000	Water area	21000	Environmental area	21002	Ocean
20000	Water area	21000	Environmental area	21003	North/South/Equatorial
20000	Water area	22000	Fishing Statistical area	22001	FAO statistical area
20000	Water area	22000	Fishing Statistical area	22002	Areal grid system
20000	Water area	24020	Jurisdiction area		

f) XML implementation for the adjacency list data model

```
<WaterAreaClassificationScheme>
  <CSI>
    <ID>20000</ID><Name> Water area</Name>
  </CSI>
  <CSI>
    <ID>21000</ID><Name>Environmental area</Name>
    <Parent>20000</Parent>
  </CSI>
  <CSI>
    <ID>21001</ID><Name>Inland/marine</Name>
    <Parent>21000</Parent>
  </CSI> ....
</WaterAreaClassificationScheme>
```

g) Spreadsheet implementation for the path enumeration data model

	A	B
1	ID	CSI_Name
2	20000	Water area
3	20000.21000	Environmental area
4	20000.24020	Jurisdiction area
5	20000.22000	Fishing Statistical area
6	20000.21000.21001	Inland/marine
7	20000.21000.21002	Ocean
8	20000.21000.21003	North/South/Equatorial
9	20000.22000.22001	FAO statistical area
10	20000.22000.22002	Areal grid system
11		

ship record, thus new relationship types can be introduced with ease. There are three entities: (1) a term entity, which contains the overall set of terms; (2) a term-term relationship entity, in which each record contains two different term codes and the relationship between them; and (3) a relationship source entity, which contains the overall resource relationships.

After analysing several *data models for lexicons*, we have identified the same data models already identified for thesauri:

- **Record-based model** (Soergel, 1995): This model can also be used for lexicons, because it is possible to use a record for every lexical resource and for the information about that lexical resource.
- **Relation-based model** (Soergel, 1995): It can also be used for lexicons, because it is possible to store the information about any lexicon in individual pieces.

According to the *implementation* we classify NORs into databases, spreadsheets, XML files and flat files.

To sum up, Figure 1 shows how a given type of NOR can be modelled following one or more data models, each of which could be implemented in different ways at the implementation layer. As an example, Figure 1 shows a classification scheme modeled following a path enumeration model. In this case, the classification scheme is implemented in a database and in an XML file.

To exemplify the non-ontological categorization here presented with a real life classification scheme, we use an excerpt from the FAO water area classification shown in Figure 2a. This classification schema is modelled following a path enumeration model (Figure 2b), an adjacency list model (Figure 2c), a snowflake model (Figure 2d), and a flattened model (Figure 2e). Figure 2f presents an XML implementation of the path enumeration model and Figure 2g presents a spreadsheet implementation of the path enumeration model of the same classification scheme.

It is worth mentioning that this first categorization of NORs is neither exhaustive nor complete. Currently, we are enriching it by adding examples taken from RosettaNet[10] and Electronic Data Interchange, EDI[11].

Moreover, we can map available non-ontological resources to our categorization. In the following we present a brief list of them.

- The United Nations Standard Products and Services Code, UNSPSC[12], is a classification scheme, modelled with the path enumeration data model, and it is stored in a relational database.
- WordNet[13], a lexical database for English, is a lexicon, modelled with the relation-based data model, and it is stored in several implementations, a particular implementation is a relational database.
- UMLS[14], a very large, multi-purpose, and multilingual thesaurus that contains information about biomedical and health related concepts, is modelled with the record-based model and it is stored in a flat file.
- MeSh[15], the Medical Subject Headings, is a classification scheme, modelled with the path enumeration data model.
- The Art and Architecture Thesaurus[16], is modelled with the record-based data model and it is implemented in XML.
- The ISCO-08 International Standard Classification of Occupations[17] is a classification scheme modelled with the path enumeration data model, and implemented in a database and spreadsheet.
- The European Training Thesaurus, ETT[18], is modelled with the record-based data model and it is implemented in XML.
- The Classification of Fields of Education and Training, FOET[19], is a classification scheme modelled with path enumeration data model, and implemented in XML and spreadsheet.
- The Aquatic Sciences and Fisheries Abstracts thesaurus, ASFA[20], is modelled with the record-based data model and it is implemented in XML.
- The AGROVOC thesaurus[21] is modelled with the relation-based data model and implemented in a database.
- The Fisheries Global Information System, FIGIS[22] is modelled with the adjacency list data model and implemented in a database.
- The Classification of Italian Education Titles published by the National Institute

of Statistics, ISTAT[23], is a classification scheme modelled with the flattened data model and implemented in a spreadsheet.

A COMPARATIVE FRAMEWORK FOR RE-ENGINEERING NORS INTO ONTOLOGIES

In this section we provide an overview of a comparative study of the most outstanding methods for re-engineering NORs into ontologies. First, we describe briefly the representative methods. Then, we have established a common framework with which to compare the main characteristics of the different methods. Finally, we evaluate the methods against the proposed framework.

Methods for Transforming NORs into Ontologies

This section overviews existing methods for transforming NORs into ontologies. The methods are centred on the NOR type (classification schemes, lexica, and thesauri) and on the NOR implementation (databases, XML, flat files, and spreadsheets).

Methods Centred on the NOR Type

- **GenTax** is a method presented by Hepp et al. (Hepp & Brujin, 2007) for semi-automatically deriving consistent RDF(S) and OWL ontologies from hierarchical classifications, thesauri and informal taxonomies. These authors have implemented SKOS2GenTax to support their method. Human intervention in the transformation is limited to checking some conceptual properties and to identifying frequent anomalies. The idea underlying this method is to derive two ontology classes: one generic concept and one broader taxonomic concept from each category. The method produces one single ontology in OWL-DLP or RDF(S). The ontology components generated are classes and relations.

- **Hakkarainen et al.** (Hakkarainen, Hella, Strasunskas & Tuxen, 2006) present a study of the semantic relationship between the ISO 15926-2[24] and OWL-DL. The ISO 15926-2 is built on EXPRESS[25]; and stored in a flat file to specify its data model. This method consists of (a) two transformation protocols, which are based on transformation rules; and (b) two inverse transformation protocols for examining the possible loss of semantics. Transformation protocols include a formal specification of the conversions and their functions are to manage a single ontology, expressed in OWL-DL. The ontology components generated are classes, attributes, and relations.

- **van Assem et al.** (Assem, Gangemi & Schreiber, 2006) propose a method for a standard conversion of WordNet into the RDF/OWL representation language. This method is based on version 2.0 of Princenton's WordNet Prolog distribution. The process for designing the conversion consists in (1) analyzing the existing conversions, which helps to understand the different ways in which WordNet is used on the Semantic Web; (2) formulating the requirements; (3) analyzing the source files and documentation; (4) designing the RDF/OWL schema; (5) designing a program for converting Prolog data to RDF/OWL; (6) drafting a Working Group Note explaining the requirements and design choices; and (7) reviewing the draft note and schema/data fields. The method produces one single ontology in RDF(S)/OWL Full. The ontology components generated are classes, attributes, relations, and instances.

- **Gangemi et al.** (Gangemi, Navigli & Velardi, 2003; Gangemi, Guarino, Masolo & Oltramari, 2003) present a method that explains how WordNet information can be bootstrapped, mapped, refined and modularized. Their method employs WordNet 1.6, stored in relational databases. The method automatically extracts association relations from WordNet, and interprets those associations in terms of a set of conceptual relations, formally defined in the DOLCE[26] ontology. It manages a single ontology implemented in DAML+OIL. The ontology components generated are classes, attributes, and relations.

- **Hahn et al.** present (Hahn, 2003; Hahn & Schulz, 2003) a method that extracts conceptual knowledge from UMLS[27], and semi-automatically converts this conceptual knowledge into a formal description logics model in LOOM[28]. It produces a single ontology. The ontology components generated are classes and relations.
- **van Assem et al.** present (Assem, Menken, Schreiber & Wielemaker, 2004) a method for converting thesauri from their native format to RDF(S)/OWL Full. This method deals with resources implemented in (1) a proprietary text format, (2) a relational database, and (3) an XML representation. It produces one single ontology in RDF(S)/OWL Full. The ontology components generated are classes, attributes, and relations.
- **van Assem et al.** present (Assem, Malaisé, Miles & Schreiber, 2006) a method for converting thesauri to the SKOS[29] RDF/OWL schema. This SKOS schema is a proposal for a standard that is being developed by the W3Cs Semantic Web Best Practices Working Group. The method produces one single ontology expressed in SKOS RDF. The ontology components generated are classes, attributes, and relations.
- **Wielinga et al.** present (Wielinga, Schreiber, Wielemaker & Sandberg, 2001) a method for transforming the Art and Architecture Thesaurus (AAT) into an RDF(S) ontology. The AAT is available in XML files. The method produces one ontology. The ontology components generated are classes, attributes, and relations.
- **Hyvönen et al.** present (Hyvönen et al., 2008) a method for transforming thesauri into ontologies. This method has been applied to the YSA thesaurus[30] where DOLCE was employed for the transformation. The resultant ontology, based on the YSA thesaurus, is the General Finnish Ontology YSO[31]. The ontology components generated are classes, attributes, and relations, which are expressed in RDF(S).
- **Soergel et al.** (Soergel et al., 2004), and **Lauser et al.** (Lauser & Sini, 2006) present a method for the re-engineering of traditional thesaurus, AGROVOC, into a full-fledged ontology. The AGROVOC thesaurus is stored in a database. The authors plan to build an inventory of patterns, namely, content ontology design patterns which are specific for the agricultural domain. The method produces one ontology in OWL-DL, and the ontology components generated are classes, attributes, and relations.

Methods Centered on the NOR Implementation

- **Stojanovic et al.** present (Stojanovic, Stojanovic & Volz, 2002) an integrated and semi-automatic approach to generating shared and understandable metadata of data-intensive Web applications. This method is based on mapping a relational schema into F-Logic ontology by means of a reverse engineering process. The method deals with any NORs stored in a database and transforms the database content into instances of an existing ontology (in the form of RDF files) by applying the generic mapping rules specified by the authors.

- **Barrasa et al.** present (Barrasa, 2007; Barrasa, Corcho & Gómez-Pérez, 2004) an integrated framework for the formal specification, evaluation and exploitation of the semantic correspondences between legacy ontologies and legacy relational data sources. The framework consists of two main components: R_2O, which is a declarative language for the description of complex mapping expressions between ontology elements and relational elements, and ODEMapster processor, which generates RDF instances from relational instances based on the mapping description expressed in an R_2O document.

- **García et al.** (García & Celma, 2005) introduce a method to create an ontology from the XML schema and populate it with instances generated from the XML data. This method has been applied to the MPEG-7[32] XML Schemas and has generated a single MPEG-7 ontology[33] in OWL Full. The ontology components generated are classes, attributes, relations, and instances.

- **An et al.** present (An & Mylopoulos, 2005) a method to translate an XML web document into an instance of an OWL-DL ontology. In that work the authors take advantage of the semi-automatic mapping discovery tool (An, Borgida & Mylopoulos, 2005) for discovering the relationship between XML schema and the ontology. The method produces a single ontology in OWL-DL. The ontology components generated are classes, attributes, relations, and instances.

- **Cruz et al.** present (Cruz, Xiao & Hsu, 2004) a method to transform XML schema into RDF(S) ontology while preserving the XML document structure, i.e., modelling the knowledge implicit in XML schema with RDF(S). In order to support the method, a specific tool has been developed. This method produces a single ontology.

The ontology components generated are classes, attributes, and relations.

- **Foxvog et al.** present (Foxvog & Bussler, 2006) a method to transform Electronic Data Interchange (EDI)[34] messages into ontologies. The method produces several ontologies. The ontology components generated are classes, attributes, relations, and instances, expressed in OWL Full, CycL, and WSML.

Evaluation Framework

In this section we establish a framework for comparing the methods for re-engineering NORs. Next, we present the characteristics identified, which are grouped according to the NOR, the transformation process, and the resultant ontology.

NOR Characteristics

- **Types of NOR:** (1) classification schemes, (2) folksonomies, (3) glossaries, (4) lexica, and (5) thesauri.

- **Implementation of a NOR:** (1) databases, (2) XML files, (3) flat files, or (4) spreadsheets.

- A NOR belongs to a specific and concrete domain or it can fit in any domain.

- The NOR *data model* information is known. The data model depicts the logical entity types, the data attributes describing those entities, and the relationships between entities (Carkenord, 2002).

Characteristics of the Transformation Process

- The transformation approach can be: (1) an *ABox transformation* (Caracciolo, Heguiabehere, Presutti & Gangemi, 2009), which converts the resource schema into an ontology schema and the resource content into ontology instances; (2) an *TBox transformation* (Caracciolo et al., 2009), which transforms the resource content into an ontology schema; or (3) *Population*, for transforming the resource content into instances of an existing ontology.

- The transformation process can be (1) *automatic*, (2) *semi-automatic*, or (3) *manual*.
- The transformation process considers the *implicit, formal semantics of the NOR relationships* (*subClassOf, partOf*, etc.).
- The transformation process uses *additional resources* to carry out the conversion.
- The research work provides some *methodological guidelines* to support the transformation process.
- The list of the *techniques employed* serves to guide the transformation process, e.g., mapping rules, re-engineering patterns.
- If a specific *tool* is provided, then this should give technological support to the transformation process.

Characteristics of the Resultant Ontology

- The *ontology components* generated are classes, attributes, relations, or instances.
- The *ontology implementation language*: for instance OWL or RDF(S).
- The research work generates a *single ontology* or *several ontologies*. We do not distinguish whether the ontologies generated are interconnected or not.

Results

After having analyzed the state of the art of the methods available for re-engineering NORs, we present the results of applying the evaluation framework.

Table 1 summarizes the methods presented according to the characteristics of the NOR.

- According to the type of non-ontological resource, we can state that most of the methods are focused on thesauri, some on classification schemes, lexicons and folksonomies, and then there is a small group which does not contemplate the type of resource. Only one method is focused in thesauri and classification schemes. In general the methods consider only a particular type of resource.
- According to the implementation of the non-ontological resource, we can state that most of the methods are focused on databases, some on XML, and flat files, and some are independent of resource implementation. In addition, one method is focused on resources implemented in Prolog whereas another includes resources implemented in proprietary format, relational database, and XML.
- In relation to the data model, we can observe the half of the methods does not contemplate the data model of the resource for the transformation, whereas half does it.

To sum up, we can conclude that most of the methods presented are based on *ad-hoc* transformations for the resource type, and the resource implementation. Only a few take advantage of the resource data model, an important artifact for the re-engineering process (García-Silva et al., 2008). There is no any integrated framework, method or corresponding tool, that considers the resources types, data models and implementations identified in an unified way. In conclusion, we can state that there is a clear need for some sort of re-engineering methods that simultaneously

- Cope with the overall set of non-ontological resources, i.e. classification schemes, thesauri, and lexica.
- Consider the internal data model of the resource.

Table 1. NOR characteristics of the methods

Research work	Type of resource	Resource implemented in	Specific/Any	Data model is used
Hepp et al.	Classification scheme, thesaurus	Database	Any	No
Hakkarainen et al.	Classification scheme	Flat file	ISO15926-2	Yes
Abbasi et al.	Folksonomy	Not mentioned	Any	No
Maala et al.	Folksonomy	Not mentioned	Flickr	No
van Assem et al.	Lexicon	Prolog	Any	Yes
Gangemi et al.	Lexicon	Database	Any	Yes
Hahn et al.	Thesaurus	ASCII files	UMLS	Yes
van Assem et al.	Thesaurus	Proprietary text format, relational database, XML	Any	No
van Assem et al.	Thesaurus	Not mentioned	IPSV, GTAA, MeSH	No
Wielinga et al.	Thesaurus	XML	AAT	Yes
Hyvö nen et al.	Thesaurus	Not mentioned	YSA	Yes
Soergel et al.	Thesaurus	Database	AGROVOC	Yes
Stojanovic et al.	Not mentioned	Database	Any	Yes
Barrasa et al.	Not mentioned	Database	Any	Yes
Garc´ıa et al.	Not mentioned	XML	Any	No
An et al.	Not mentioned	XML	Any	No
Cruz et al.	Not mentioned	XML	Any	No
Foxvog et al.	Not mentioned	Flat file	EDI X12	No

- Cope with non-ontological resources implemented in databases, XML files, flat files, or spreadsheets.
- According to the explicitation of the hidden semantics in the relations of the resource components, we can state that the methods that perform a TBox transformation make explicit the semantics in the relations of the resource components. Most of those methods identify *subClassOf* relations, others identify *ad-hoc* relations, and some identify *partOf* relations. However, only a few methods make explicit the three types of relations.
- With regard to the transformation approach (Table 2), the majority of the methods perform a TBox transformation, many others perform an ABox transformation and some perform a population. However, no method includes the possibility to perform the three transformation approaches.
- Regarding to the degree of automation, almost all the methods perform a semi-automatic transformation of the resource, followed by three automatic methods, and then by a manual method.
- With respect to how the methods make explicit the hidden semantics in the relations of the resource terms, we can say that three methods rely on the domain expert for making explicit the semantics, and two rely on an external resource, e.g., DOLCE ontology. Moreover, there are two methods that rely on external resources but not for making explicit the hidden semantics, but for finding out a proper ontology for populating it.

- According to the provision of the methodological guidelines, almost all the methods provide methodological guidelines for the transformation. However these guidelines are not finely detailed; for instance, they do not provide information about who is in charge of performing a particular activity/task, nor when that activity/task has to be carried out.
- With regard to the techniques employed, most of the methods do not mention them at all. Only a few methods specify techniques as transformation rules, lexico-syntactic patterns, mapping rules and natural language techniques.
- According to the tool support, most of the methods rely on ad-hoc tools for the transformation. And only a few methods integrate a public available tool, such as KAON-REVERSE, ODEMapster, XSD2OWL, and XML2RDF.

In summary, after having analyzed the features related to the transformation process, we can conclude that (1) methods are mostly focused on the TBox transformation approach; (2) only a few methods make explicit the hidden semantics in the relations of the NOR terms, and most of them rely on domain expert for doing it; (3) almost all the methods provide methodological guidelines for the transformation, but they are not finely detailed; (4) only a few methods specify the techniques employed for the transformation; and (5) there is no method that considers the possibility to perform the three transformation approaches. In a nutshell, we can state that there is a clear need for some sort of re-engineering methods that

- Include the three transformation approaches (TBox, ABox and Population).
- Make explicit the hidden semantics in the relations of the NOR terms, by means of external resources in a semi-automatic way, for saving the transformation time.

- Provide fully detailed guidelines for the transformation, including information on who is in charge of performing a particular activity/task and when this activity/task has to be carried out.
- Integrate in a single framework the method and its corresponding tool support for the transformation.
- Employ techniques that improve the efficiency of the re-engineering process.

Table 3 summarizes the methods presented regarding the characteristics of the resultant ontology.

- In relation to the ontology components, we can observe that this feature is closely related to the transformation approach performed by the methods. Methods that perform TBox transformation generate classes, relations, and optionally attributes. Methods that perform ABox transformation generate classes, attributes, relations and instances. Methods that perform population generate instances.
- As for the ontology implementation language, despite of the variety of existing languages, the ontology languages mostly used are OWL for the ontology and RDF for the instances.
- As for whether the method generates one or several ontologies, almost all the methods generate a single ontology.

After having analyzed the characteristics related to the resultant ontology, we can conclude that there is a lack of re-engineering methods that support several ontologies, and the generation of ontologies that includes classes, attributes, relations and instances.

In this paper, we solve the needs above mentioned introduce a method that

Table 2. Transformation process of the methods

Research work	Transformation Approach	Automatic/ Semi-automatic/ Manual	Semantics of NOR relations	Additional Resources	Methodological Guidelines	Technique	Tool support
Hepp et al.	TBox	Semi-automatic	subClassOf ad-hoc relation	No	Yes	Not mentioned	SKOS2Gen-Tax
Hakkarainen et al.	ABox	Semi-automatic	subClassOf ad-hoc relation	No	Yes	Transformation rules	Not mentioned
Abbasi et al.	Population	Automatic	Not mentioned	Swoogle Google	Yes	Lexico Syntactic Patterns	T-ORG
Maala et al.	Population	Automatic	Not mentioned	WordNet	Yes	Not mentioned	Not mentioned
van Assem et al.	ABox	Semi-automatic	Not mentioned	No	Yes	Not mentioned	Swi-Prolog
Gangemi et al.	TBox	Semi-automatic	Not mentioned	DOLCE	Yes	NLP Techniques	Not mentioned
Hahn et al.	TBox	Semi-automatic	subClassOf partOf ad-hoc relation	No	Yes	Ontology Design Patterns	Ad-hoc tool
van Assem et al.	TBox	Semi-automatic	subClassOf ad-hoc relation	No	Yes	Not mentioned	Ad-hoc tool
van Assem et al.	TBox	Automatic	Not mentioned	No	Yes	Not mentioned	Swi-Prolog
Wielinga et al.	TBox	Semi-automatic	Not mentioned	No	Yes	Not mentioned	Ad-hoc tool
Hyvö nen et al.	TBox	Semi-automatic	Not mentioned	DOLCE	Yes	Not mentioned	Ad-hoc tool
Soergel et al.	TBox	Manual	subClassOf ad-hoc relation	No	Yes	Not mentioned	Not mentioned
Stojanovic et al.	Population	Semi-automatic	ad-hoc relation	No	Yes	Mapping rules	KAON-RE-VERSE
Barrasa et al.	Population	Semi-automatic	subClassOf ad-hoc relation	No	Yes	Mapping rules	ODEMapster
Garc'ia et al.	ABox	Semi-automatic	ad-hoc relation	No	Yes	Mapping rules	XSD2OWL XML2RDF
An et al.	ABox	Semi-automatic	ad-hoc relation	No	No	Not mentioned	Discovery tool
Cruz et al.	ABox	Semi-automatic	Not mentioned	No	Yes	Mapping rules	Ad-hoc tool
Foxvog et al.	ABox	Semi-automatic	Not mentioned	No	Yes	Not mentioned	Ad-hoc tool

Table 3. Ontology characteristics of the methods

Research Work	Components	Implementation language	Single/Several
Hepp et al.	classes, relations	RDF(S) / OWL-DLP	Single
Hakkarainen et al.	classes, attributes, relations	OWL-DL	Single
Abbasi et al.	instances	Not mentioned	Several
Maala et al.	instances	RDF	Single
van Assem et al.	classes, attributes, relations, instances	RDF(S) / OWL Full	Single
Gangemi et al.	classes, attributes, relations, instances	DAML+OIL	Single
Hahn et al.	classes, relations	LOOM / ALC	Single
van Assem et al.	classes, attributes, relations	RDF(S) / OWL Full	Single
van Assem et al.	classes, attributes, relations	SKOS RDF	Single
Wielinga et al.	classes, attributes, relations	RDF(S)	Single
Hyvö nen et al.	classes, attributes, relations	RDF(S)	Single
Soergel et al.	classes, attributes, relations	OWL-DL	Single
Stojanovic et al.	instances	F-Logic / RDF	Single
Barrasa et al.	instances	RDF	Single
Garc´ıa et al.	classes, attributes, relations, instances	OWL Full/ RDF	Single
An et al.	classes, attributes, relations, instances	OWL-DL	Single
Cruz et al.	classes, attributes, relations	RDF(S)	Single
Foxvog et al.	classes, attributes, relations, instances	CycL / OWL Full / WSML	Several

- Includes the three transformation approaches (TBox, ABox and Population).
- Makes explicit the hidden semantics in the relations of the NOR terms, by means of external resources in an semi-automatic way, for saving the transformation time.
- Provides fully detailed guidelines for the transformation, including information on who is in charge of performing a particular activity/task and when this activity/task has to be carried out.
- Employs techniques that improve the efficiency of the re-engineering process.

PATTERNS FOR RE-ENGINEERING

In this section we introduce briefly the role that patterns play in software and ontology engineering, with a particular focus on re-engineering patterns.

Patterns were introduced by Christopher Alexander (Alexander, 1979) to encode knowledge and experience in designing buildings. He defines a pattern as the core of a solution to a problem in context. The solution can be applied in different situations and has to be adapted to fit the needs of the specific situation (Alexander, 1979).

In the (Object Oriented) software community, patterns are used to describe software design structures that can be used over and over again in different systems. Patterns provide a general solution that has to be applied in a particular context, where design considerations are used to decide whether the pattern is useful and how it could be best implemented (Edwards, Puckett & Jolly, 2006).

A kind of software patterns are the re-engineering software patterns (Pooley & Stevens, 1998). These describe how to change a legacy system into a new, refactored system that fits current conditions and requirements. Their main goal is

Figure 3. Ontology Design Pattern Categorization (Presutti et al., 2008)

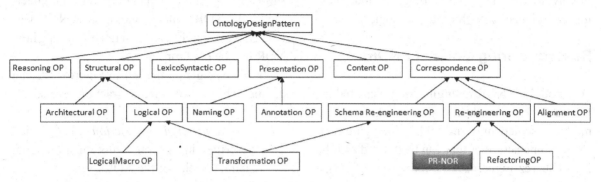

to offer a solution for re-engineering problems. They are also on a specific level of abstraction and describe a process of re-engineering without proposing a complete methodology; sometimes these re-engineering patterns can suggest which type of tool should be used.

The idea of applying patterns for modelling ontologies was proposed by (Clark, Thompson & Porter, 2000). Since then, several relevant works on patterns have appeared, such as: Semantic Web Best Practices and Deployment Working Group[35], the Ontology Design Patterns Public Catalog[36], the Ontology Design Patterns (ODP) Portal[37] and the Linked Data Patterns[38], which is a catalogue of Linked Data (Bizer, 2009) patterns. According to (Presutti et al., 2008) Ontology Design Patterns are modelling solutions to solving a recurrent ontology design problem. They distinguish different types of Ontology Design Patterns by grouping them into six families (see first level in Figure 3). Each family addresses different kind of problems and can be represented with different levels of formality. For a detailed description of each family of patterns, please refer to (Presutti et al., 2008).

As shown in Figure 3, *Correspondence OPs* are templates for representing alignments between models. They include Schema Re-engineering OPs, Re-engineering OPs and Alignment OPs. *Re-engineering OPs* are transformation rules applied to create a new ontology starting from elements of a source model, and *Refactoring OPs*.

In this paper we focus on *Patterns for Re-engineering NORs (PR-NOR)*. These patterns define a procedure that transforms the NOR components into ontology representational primitives. PR-NORs are considered as Re-engineering Patterns (Presutti et al., 2008), because they share the same goal, i.e., to generate a new ontology from elements of a source model. The rest of the patterns are out of the scope of this paper.

In this paper we propose the use of re-engineering patterns for transforming NORs into ontologies. The re-engineering patterns proposed take advantage of the use of logical patterns for creating the ontology code. So, most of the code generated follows the best practices already identified by the community. Up to present, none of the methods presented in the evaluation framework section use re-engineering patterns as a technique for the transformation.

PATTERN-BASED RE-ENGINEERING METHOD

In this section we present the method we have devised for re-engineering non-ontological resources into ontologies. The method is based on a model for re-engineering non-ontological resources. In it, we first provide a description of this re-engineering model for NORs, then we introduce the notion of patterns for re-engineering NORs.

Finally, we depict the methodological guidelines for re-engineering NORs into ontologies.

Re-Engineering Model for NORs

Our model for NOR re-engineering, depicted in Figure 4, is based on the software re-engineering[39] model presented in (Byrne, 1992). The figure also shows some activities that can be defined as follows (Suárez-Figueroa & Gómez-Pérez, 2008):

- NOR reverse engineering is defined as the activity of analyzing a non-ontological resource to identify its underlying components and to create a representation of the resource at higher levels of abstraction.
- NOR transformation is defined as the activity of generating an ontological model at different levels of abstraction from the NOR.
- Ontology forward engineering refers to the activity of outputting a new implementation of the ontology on the basis of the new conceptual model.

Since we consider NORs as a kind of software resources, we use the software abstraction levels shown in Figure 4 to depict the reverse engineering of the NOR. Understanding how NOR was created is extremely useful for understanding how NOR can be re-engineered.

In the triangle on the left in Figure 4 we can distinguish four software abstraction levels:

- *The conceptual abstraction level*, which describes in general terms the functional characteristics of the NORs.
- *The requirements level*, which is the specification of the problem being solved.
- *The design level*, which is the specification of the solution.
- *The implementation level*, which refers to the coding, testing and delivering of the operational resource.

As the level of abstraction decreases, a resource description becomes more detailed and the amount of information increases. Moreover, the higher the abstraction level, the less information about a resource.

Since the goal, of the *forward engineering process,* is to transform the resources into ontologies, we use the ontology levels of abstraction (Gómez-Pérez, Fernández-López & Corcho, 2003) to depict

Figure 4. Re-engineering model for NORs

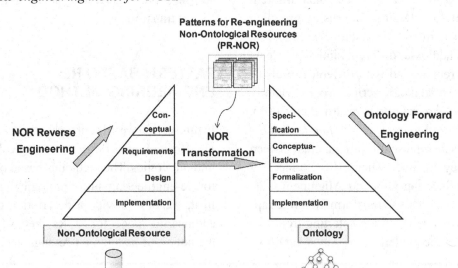

the ontology forward engineering. In the triangle on the right in Figure 4 we can distinguish the four ontology abstraction levels that define each activity in ontology engineering:

- *The specification level*, which describes the collection of requirements that the ontology should fulfil.
- *The conceptualization level*, which organizes the information from the acquisition process into meaningful conceptual models.
- *The formalization level*, which represents the transformation of the conceptual model into a formal or semi-computable model according to a knowledge representation paradigm.
- *The implementation level*, which refers to the generation of computable models according to the syntax of a formal representation language.

Finally, the model in Figure 4 suggests the path from the existing NOR to the target ontology. This transformation is guided by a set of Patterns for Re-engineering NORs (PR-NOR), and goes from the NOR requirements/design level to the conceptualization level of the ontology.

Requirements for the Transformation

In this section we describe the identified requirements for the transformation, we list the requirements according to the three transformation approaches identified in the Evaluation Framework section.

- *TBox transformation* (Caracciolo et al., 2009), that transforms the resource content into an ontology schema. This transformation approach tries to enforce a formal semantics to the re-engineered resources, even at the cost of changing their structure.

The requirements for this transformation are:

- ○ Full conversion, the resultant ontology has all the information that is present in the original resource. In other words, all queries that are possible on the original source should be also possible on the ontology generated.
- ○ Conversion on the semantic level, which implies the schema translation to interpret the semantics of the data. In other words, the conversion should not stay agnostic to possible interpretations, e.g., relations among the NOR entities.

- *ABox transformation* (Caracciolo et al., 2009), that transforms the resource schema into an ontology schema, and the resource content into ontology instances. This transformation approach leaves the informal semantics of the re-engineered resources mostly untouched. The requirements for this transformation are:

- ○ Full conversion, the same requirement of the TBox transformation. Again, this implies that all queries that are possible on the original source should be also possible on the ontological version.
- ○ Structure preserving translation, the opposite of the second requirement of the TBox transformation. The translation should as much as possible reflect the original structure of the resource, in other words, the conversion should stay agnostic to possible interpretations.

- *Population* that transforms the resource content into instances of an existing ontology. The requirements of the transformation are:

- ○ Full conversion, the same requirement of the TBox and ABox transformation.

○ The ontology instances generated should reflect the target ontology structure as closely as possible. In this case, the class structure of the ontology already exists and is extended with instance data. In other words, the ontology instances must conform the existing ontology schema.

Patterns for Re-Engineering NORs

In this section we present the patterns that perform the transformations of NORs into ontologies. Patterns for re-engineering NORs (PR-NOR) define a procedure that transforms the NOR components into ontology representational primitives (García-Silva et al., 2008).

According to the NOR categorization presented in a previous section, the data model can be different even for the same type of NOR. For every data model we can define a process with a well-defined sequence of activities with which to extract the NORs components and then to map these components to a conceptual model of an ontology. Each of these processes can be expressed as a pattern for re-engineering NORs.

The re-engineering patterns take advantage of the use of Ontology Design Patterns[40] for creating the ontology code. Therefore, most of the code generated follows the best practices already identified by the community.

Template for the PR-NOR

In this section we present the template proposed, which describes the patterns for re-engineering NORs (PR-NOR). In order to present the patterns for re-engineering NORs we have modified the tabular template used in (García-Silva et al., 2008). The template and the meaning of each field are shown in Table 4.

Although we have identified five types of NORs, here we just list patterns for re-engineering three: classification schemes, thesauri, and

lexica (see Table 5). It is worth pointing out that we refer to ontology schema as the TBox, and to ontology as the TBox and the ABox. These patterns are included in the ODP Portal. Regarding the time complexity of the algorithm included in the patterns, we can say that the time complexity of the TBox transformation algorithm is polynomial $O(n^2)$, and of the ABox transformation algorithm is linear $O(n)$.

Due to space reasons, Table 6 presents only an excerpt of the PR-NOR-CLTX-01 pattern which is instantiated to the classification scheme presented in Figure 2.

Semantics of the Relations between the NOR terms

The TBox transformation approach converts the resource content into an ontology schema. The TBox transformation tries to enforce a formal semantics to the resource, by making explicit the semantics hidden in the relations of the NOR terms. To this end, each NOR term is mapped to a class, and then, the semantics of the relations among those entities must be discovered and then made explicit. Thus, patterns that follow the TBox transformation approach must discover first the semantics of the relations among the NOR terms. To perform this task, we rely on WordNet, which organizes the lexical information into meanings (senses) and synsets. What makes WordNet remarkable is the existence of various relations explicitly declared between the word forms (e.g. lexical relations, such as synonymy and antonymy) and the synsets (meaning to meaning or semantic relations e.g. hyponymy/hypernymy relation, meronymy relation). In this paper, we want to prove that we can rely on an external resource for making explicit the relations. For this purpose, we rely first on WordNet, but for a future work we may rely on other information resources, such as DBpedia[41].

Table 4. PR-NOR Template

Slot	Value
General Information	
Name	Name of the pattern.
Identifier	An acronym composed of component type + abbreviated name of the component + number
Component Type	Pattern for Re-engineering Non-Ontological Resource (PR-NOR).
Use Case	
General	Description in natural language of the re-engineering problem addressed by the pattern for re-engineering NORs.
Example	Description in natural language of an example of the re-engineering problem.
Pattern for Re-engineering Non-Ontological Resource	
INPUT: Resource to be Re-engineered	
General	Description in natural language of the NOR.
Example	Description in natural language of an example of the NOR.
Graphical Representation	
General	Graphical representation of the NOR.
Example	Graphical representation of the example of NOR.
OUTPUT: Designed Ontology	
General	Description in natural language of the ontology created after applying the pattern for re-engineering the NOR.
Graphical Representation	
General	Graphical representation, using the UML profile (Brockmans & Haase, 2006), of the ontology created for the NOR being re-engineered.
Example	Example showing a graphical representation, using the UML profile (Brockmans & Haase, 2006), of the ontology created for the NOR being re-engineered.
PROCESS: How to Re-engineer	
General	Algorithm for the re-engineering process.
Example	Application of the algorithm to the NOR example.
Time Complexity	The time complexity of the algorithm.
Additional Notes	Additional notes of the algorithm.
Formal Transformation	
General	Formal description of the transformation by using the formal definitions of the resources.
Relationships (Optional)	
General	Description of any relation to other PR-NOR patterns or other ontology design patterns.

Algorithm 1 describes how to make explicit the semantics of the relations in the NOR terms. The shortname of the algorithm is *getRelation*.

The most important parts of algorithm are explained:

- (Line 1) Take two related terms from the NOR.
- (Line 2) For the *userDefinedRelation* one recommendation is to use the *subClassOf* relation by default. However, we recommend considering the type of non-ontolog-

Table 5. Set of patterns for re-engineering NORs

Identifier	Type of NOR	NOR Data Model	Target
PR-NOR-CLTX-01	C. Scheme	Path Enumeration	O. Schema
PR-NOR-CLTX-02	C. Scheme	Adjacency List	O. Schema
PR-NOR-CLTX-03	C. Scheme	Snowflake	O. Schema
PR-NOR-CLTX-04	C. Scheme	Flattened	O. Schema
PR-NOR-CLAX-10	C. Scheme	Path Enumeration	Ontology
PR-NOR-CLAX-11	C. Scheme	Adjacency List	Ontology
PR-NOR-CLAX-12	C. Scheme	Snowflake	Ontology
PR-NOR-CLAX-13	C. Scheme	Flattened	Ontology
PR-NOR-TSTX-01	Thesaurus	Record-based	O. Schema
PR-NOR-TSTX-02	Thesaurus	Relation-based	O. Schema
PR-NOR-TSAX-10	Thesaurus	Record-based	Ontology
PR-NOR-TSAX-11	Thesaurus	Relation-based	Ontology
PR-NOR-LXTX-01	Lexicon	Record-based	O. Schema
PR-NOR-LXTX-02	Lexicon	Relation-based	O. Schema
PR-NOR-LXAX-10	Lexicon	Record-based	Ontology
PR-NOR-LXAX-11	Lexicon	Relation-based	Ontology

Table 6. Excerpt of the PR-NOR-CLTX-01 pattern

PR-NOR-CLTX-01.
PROCESS: How to Re-engineer
General
1: noParentTerms ← classification scheme terms without parent 2: if noParentTerms.length > 1 then 3: entityName ← name of the entity that contains the classification scheme terms 4: rootClass ← createClass(entityName) 5: for ri ∈ noParentTerms do 6: Ri ← createClass(ri) 7: relation ← ExternalResource.getRelation(rootClass,Ri) 8: relate(relation,rootClass,Ri) 9: end for 10: end if 11: repeat 12: for cei ∈ noParentTerms do 13: if not alreadyCreatedClassFor(cei) then 14: Ci ← createClass(cei) 15: end if 16: children ← childrenOf(cei) 17: for cej ∈ children do 18: if not alreadyCreatedClassFor(cej) then 19: Cj ← createClass(cej) 20: end if 21: relation ← ExternalResource.getRelation(cei,cej) 22: relate(relation,cei,cej) 23: end for 24: add(allChildren,children) 25: end for 26: noParentTerms ← allChildren 27: removeAllTerms(allchildren) 28: until isEmpty(noParentTerms)
Example

continued on following page

Table 6. Continued

PR-NOR-CLTX-01.
1: noParentTerms ← [Legislators, senior officials and man- agers;Professionals] 2: // noParentTerms.length=2 > 1 3: entityName ← Occupation 4: rootClass ← createClass(entityName) 6: R1 ← createClass(Legislators, senior officials and managers) 7: relation1 ← ExternalResource.getRelation(rootClass,R1) 8: relate(relation1,rootClass,R1) 6: R2 ← createClass(Professionals) 7: relation2 ← ExternalResource.getRelation(rootClass,R2) 8: relate(relation2,rootClass,R2) 13: // Legislators, senior officials and managers class, R1, already created 16: children ← childrenOf(Legislators, senior officials and managers) 16: children ← [Legislators and senior officials;Corporate managers] // using the path enumeration model 19: C1 ← createClass(Legislators and senior officials) 21: rel1 ← ExternalResource.getRelation(R1,C1) 22: relate(rel1,R1,C1) 19: C2 ← createClass(Corporate managers) 21: rel2 ← ExternalResource.getRelation(R1,C2) 22: relate(rel2,R1,C2) 24: allChildren ← [Legislators and senior officials;Corporate managers] 13: // Professionals, R2, already created 16: children ← ∅ ← childrenOf(Professionals) 26: noParentTerms ← [Legislators and senior officials;Corporate managers] 27: removeAllTerms(allChildren) 13: // Legislators and senior officials, C1, already created 16: children ← ∅ ← childrenOf(Legislators and senior officials) 13: // Corporate managers, C2, already created 16: children ← ∅ ← childrenOf(Corporate managers) 24: allChildren ← ∅ 26: noParentTerms ← allChildren ← ∅

ical resource and the source relation. For instance, if the input terms come from a classification scheme from the classification scheme item relation, we recommend using the *subClassOf* relation by default. If the input terms come from a thesaurus (1) of the BT/NT relation, we recommend to use the *subClassOf* relation by default, and (2) of the RT relation, we recommend using the *relatedTerm* relation by default.

- (Lines 3-6) Check whether it is possible to get the *subClassOf* relation by identifying attributive adjetives[42] within the two terms.
- (Line 7) If it is not possible to get the *subClassOf* relation.
    ◦ (Line 8) Search in WordNet for a relation between those two terms.

- (Line 9-10) the hyponym in the relation is interpreted as *subClassOf*.
- (Line 11-12) the hypernym in the relation is interpreted as *superClass*.
- (Line 13-14) the member meronym in the relation is interpreted as *Part*.
- (Line 15-16) the member holonym in the relation is interpreted as *Whole*.

- (Line 18) if WordNet gives an empty result, relate the two terms by means of the default relation, which was set by the user (Line 1).

Algorithm 1. Discovering the semantics of the relations

```
1:   Take two related terms from the NOR, ti and t j
2:   de f aultRelation ← userDe f inedRelation
3:   if contains(ti,t j) then
4:     relation ← ti.subClassO f.t j
5:   else if contains(t j,ti) then
6:     relation ← t j.subClassO f.ti
7:   else
8:     wordnetRelation ← W ordNet(ti, t j)
9:     if wordnetRelation == hy ponym then
10:        relation ← ti.subClassO f.t j
11:     else if wordnetRelation == hy pernym then
12:        relation ← t j.subClassO f.ti
13:     else if wordnetRelation == meronym then
14:        relation ← ti. partO f.t j
15:     else if wordnetRelation == holonym then
16:        relation ← t j. partO f.ti
17:     else
18:        relation ← de f aultRelation
19:     end if
20:   end if
21:   return relation
```

It is worth mentioning that for asserting the *partOf* relation the algorithm takes advantage of the use of the *PartOf content pattern*[43], to guarantee that the OWL code generated follows common practices in Ontological Engineering.

Regarding the time complexity of the algorithm, it is constant, i.e. $O(1) + K$. Where K represents the time complexity of accessing WordNet method.

Method for Re-engineering NORs into Ontologies

The aim of the Method for Re-engineering Non-Ontological Resources is to transform a non-ontological resource into an ontology. Therefore, the output of the process is an ontology. The pattern-based method consists of three activities, which are depicted in Figure 5.

Activity 1. NOR Reverse Engineering. The goal is to analyze a NOR, to identify its underlying components, and to create representations of the resource at the different levels of abstraction, i.e. design, requirements and conceptual (see Figure 4). This activity is carried out by domain experts, software developers and ontology practitioners.

- **Task 1.1 Data gathering.** The goal is to search and compile all the available data and documentation about the NOR, including purpose, components, data model and implementation details.
- **Task 1.2 Conceptual abstraction.** The goal is to identify the schema of the NOR, including the conceptual components and their relationships. If the conceptual schema is not available in the documentation,

Figure 5. Re-engineering process for NORs

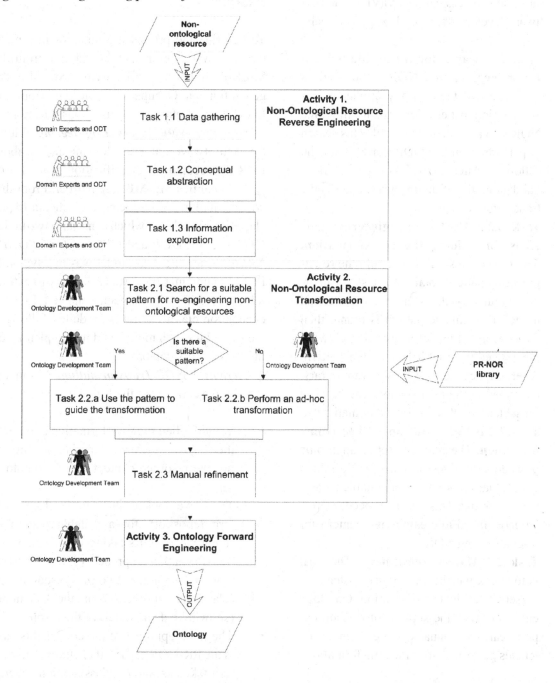

the schema should be reconstructed manually or with a data modelling tool.

- **Task 1.3 Information exploration.** The goal is to find out how the conceptual schema of the NOR and its content are represented in the data model. If the NOR data model is not available in the documenta-

tion, the data model should be reconstructed manually or with a data modelling tool.

Activity 2. NOR Transformation. The goal here is to generate a conceptual model from the NOR, using for that purpose the Patterns for Re-engineering NORs (PR-NOR), which guide the transformation process. This activity is carried out by software developers and ontology practitioners.

- **Task 2.1 Search for a suitable pattern for re-engineering NOR.** The goal is to find out if there is any applicable re-engineering pattern for transforming the NOR into a conceptual model. This search is performed in the ODP Portal, with the following criteria: (1) NOR type, (2) internal data model of the resource, and (3) the transformation approach.
- **Task 2.2.a Use of re-engineering patterns for guiding the transformation.** The goal of this task is to apply the re-engineering pattern obtained in task 2.1 in order to transform the NOR into a conceptual model. If a suitable pattern is found, then the conceptual model is created following the procedure established in the pattern. Alternatively, the NOR₂O software library, described in the next section, can be used for generating the ontology automatically.
- **Task 2.2.b Carry out an ad-hoc transformation.** The goal is to set up an *ad-hoc* procedure to transform the NOR into a conceptual model, when a suitable pattern was not found. This *ad-hoc* procedure may be generalized to create a new pattern for re-engineering NORs.
- **Task 2.3 Manual refinement.** The goal is to check whether some inconsistency is present after the transformation. Ontology engineers with the support of domain experts can fix manually some of inconsistencies generated after the transformation.

Activity 3. Ontology Forward Engineering. The goal here is to generate the ontology. We use the ontology levels of abstraction to depict this activity because they are directly related to the ontology development process. This activity is carry out by software developers and ontology practitioners.

Example

To describe the proposed guidelines in a more practical way, we present an example from the SEEMP Project[44], specifically we exemplify the generation an Occupation Ontology from the EURES proprietary occupation classification[45].

Activity 1. NOR Reverse Engineering. Within this activity we gathered documentation about EURES occupation classification from European Dynamics SEEMP user partner. From this documentation we extracted the schema of the classification scheme which consists of two tables *CVO_OCCGROUP* and *CVO_OCCUGROUP_ NAME*. Since the data model was not available in the documentation, it was necessary to extract it for the resource implementation itself. EURES occupation classification is modelled following the snowflake data model, and it is implemented in a MS Access database.

Activity 2. NOR Transformation. Within this activity we carried out the following tasks:

- We identified the transformation approach, the TBox transformation, i.e. transforming the resource content into an ontology schema.
- Then, we looked into in our local pattern repository for a suitable pattern to re-engineer NORs taking into account the transformation approach (TBox transformation), the non-ontological resource type (classification scheme), and the data model (snowflake data model) of the resource.
- The most appropriate pattern for this case is the PR-NOR-CLTX-03 pattern. This pattern takes as input a classification scheme modelled with a snowflake data model and produces an ontology schema.
- Because of the number of occupations of the EURES classification, more than five hundred occupations, it was not practical to create the ontology manually. Therefore, we used the NOR₂O software library, de-

Figure 6. Modules of the NOR2O software library

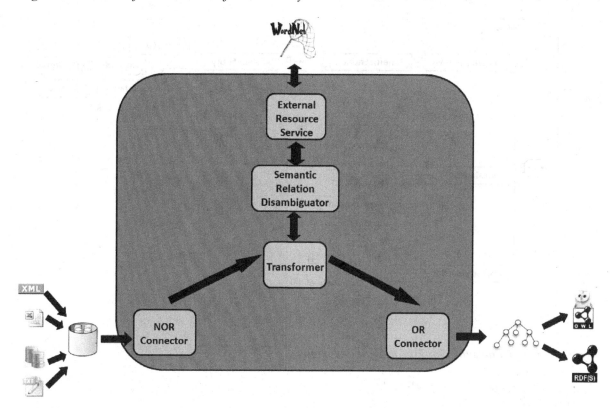

scribed in the next section, for generating the ontology automatically.

NOR₂O SOFTWARE LIBRARY

In this section we present NOR_2O^{46} (Villazón-Terrazas, Gómez-Pérez & Calbimonte, 2010), a Java library that implements the transformation process suggested by the Patterns for Re-engineering Non-Ontological Resources (PR-NOR) described in the previous section. This library performs the ETL process[47] for transforming the non-ontological resource components into ontology primitives. A high-level conceptual architecture diagram of the modules involved is shown in Figure 6.

Figure 6 depicts the modules of the NOR_2O software library: NOR Connector, Transformer, Semantic Relation Disambiguator, External Resource Service, and OR Connector. These modules are described in detail in the following section.

For illustrating the modules, the transformation of the ASFA thesaurus[48] into an ontology schema[49] has been taken as example.

NOR Connector

The NOR Connector loads classification schemes, thesauri, and lexicons modelled with their corresponding data models, and implemented in databases, XML, flat files and spreadsheets.

This module utilizes an XML configuration file for describing the NOR. Figure 7 shows the graphical representation of the NOR connector XSD file, including the following main sections:

- The *Schema* section. It describes the schema entities of the resource and the relationships among the entities.

Figure 7. Graphical representation of the NOR connector XSD file

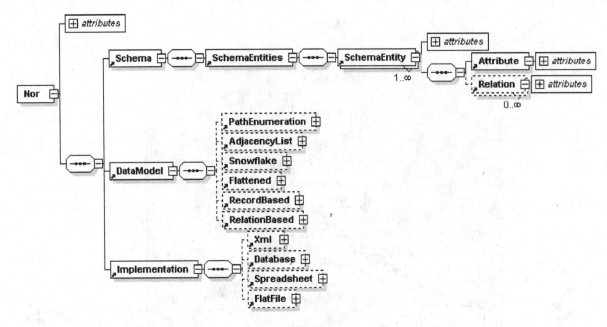

Figure 8. NOR Connector configuration file example

```
<Nor type="Thesaurus" name="ASFA">
  <Schema>
    <SchemaEntities>
      <SchemaEntity name="Term">
        <Attribute name="Identifier" valueFrom="DESCRIPTOR" type="string"/>
        <Relation name="NT" using="RecordBased" valueId="NT" destination="Term"/>
        <Relation name="BT" using="RecordBased" valueId="BT" destination="Term"/>
        <Relation name="RT" using="RecordBased" valueId="RT" destination="Term"/>
        <Relation name="UF" using="RecordBased" valueId="UF" destination="NonPreferredTerm"/>
      </SchemaEntity>
      <SchemaEntity name="NonPreferredTerm">
        <Attribute name="Identifier" valueFrom="NON-DESCRIPTOR" type="string"/>
      </SchemaEntity>
    </SchemaEntities>
  </Schema>
  <DataModel>
    <RecordBased>
      <Entity>CONCEPT</Entity>
    </RecordBased>
  </DataModel>
  <Implementation>
    <Xml xmlFile="asfa.xml" xsdFile="asfa.xsd"/>
  </Implementation>
</Nor>
```

Figure 9. Graphical representation of the PRNOR XSD file

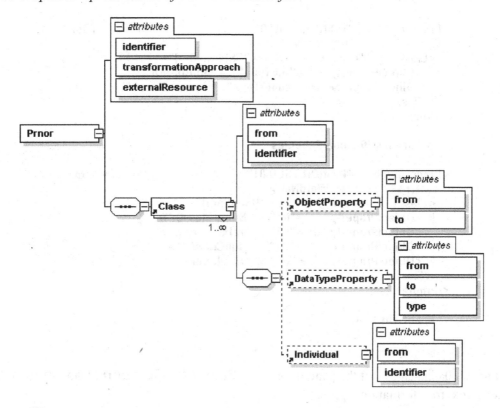

- The *DataModel* section. It includes the descriptions of the resource's internal data model.
- The *Implementation* section. It defines the information needed to physically access the resource.

An example of the XML configuration file is presented in Figure 8. The figure shows that the file describes a thesaurus. The thesaurus has two schema entities, *Term* and *NonPreferredTerm*, and is modelled following the record-based data model; it is implemented in XML.

Transformer

This module performs the transformation suggested by the patterns, by implementing the sequence of activities included in such patterns. The module transforms the NOR elements, loaded by the NOR Connector module, into internal model representation elements. And it interacts with the Semantic Relation Disambiguator module for obtaining the suggested semantic relations of the NOR elements.

The Transformer also utilizes an XML configuration file, called prnor.xml, for describing the transformation between the NOR elements and the ontology elements. This XML configuration file has only one section, *PRNOR*, which includes the description of the transformation from the NOR schema components (e.g. schema entities, attributes and relations) into the ontology elements (e.g. classes, object properties, data properties and individuals). Additionally, it indicates the transformation approach, e.g. TBox, ABox or Population.

Figure 9 shows the graphical representation of the PRNOR XSD file. Two examples of the XML configuration file are shown in Figure 10.

Figure 10. PRNOR configuration file examples

```
<Prnor identifier="PR-NOR-CLTX-01" transformationApproach="TBox"
  externalResource="WordNet">
  <Class from="CSItem" identifier="[CSIdentifier]">
    <ObjectProperty from="subType" to="subClassOf"/>
    <ObjectProperty from="superType" to="superClassOf"/>
  </Class>
</Prnor>
```

a) For Classification Schemes

```
<Prnor identifier="PR-NOR-TSLO-01" transformationApproach="TBox"
  externalResource="WordNet">
  <Class from="Term" identifier="[Identifier]">
    <ObjectProperty from="NT" to="superClassOf"/>
    <ObjectProperty from="RT" to="relatedTerm"/>
    <ObjectProperty from="BT" to="subClassOf"/>
    <ObjectProperty from="UF" to="rdfs:label"/>
  </Class>
</Prnor>
```

b) For Thesauri

The Figure 10a indicates that the pattern follows the TBox transformation approach and transforms the elements of the *CSItem* schema component into ontology classes. Also by default, it transforms the *subType* schema relation into a *subClassOf* relation and the *superType* schema relation into a *superClassOf* relation, unless the Semantic Relation Disambiguator module suggests another relation. Figure 10b indicates that the pattern follows the TBox transformation approach and it transforms the elements of the *Term* schema component into ontology classes. Also by default, it transforms the *NT* schema relation into a *superClassOf* relation, the *RT* schema relation into a *relatedTerm* relation, and the *BT* schema relation into a *subClassOf* relation, unless the Semantic Relation Disambiguator module suggests another relation. Finally, the *UF* schema relation is transformed into a *rdfs:label*, and the module uses WordNet as external resource for disambiguating

Semantic Relation Disambiguator

This module works only with the TBox transformation approach, which converts the resource content into an ontology schema. To this end, each NOR term is mapped to a class, and then, the semantics of the relations among those entities is made explicit. The algorithm presented in previous section describes how to make explicit the semantics of the relations in the NOR terms.

Figure 11. Graphical representation of the OR XSD file

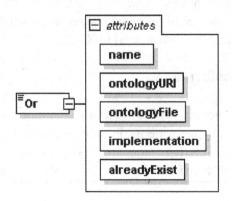

Figure 12. OR Connector configuration file example

```
<Or name="asfa ontology"
    ontologyURI="http://droz.dia.fi.upm.es/ontologies/asfa.owl"
    ontologyFile="asfa.owl" implementation="OWL" alreadyExist="no">
</Or>
```

External Resource Service

This is in charge of interacting with external resources for obtaining the semantic relations between two NOR terms. At this moment the module interacts with WordNet. We are implementing the access to DBpedia[50].

OR Connector

The Ontological Resource (OR) Connector generates the ontology in OWL-DL. To this end, this module relies on the OWL API[51]. It also utilizes an XML configuration file for describing the ontology to be generated. Figure 11 shows the graphical representation of the OR connector XSD file. The XML configuration file has only one section, *OR*, which includes the descriptions of the name, URI, file and implementation language of the ontology. Additionally, this section indicates if the ontology already exists, in the case we want to populate an existing ontology.

An example of the XML configuration file is shown in Figure 12. The figure indicates that the ontology generated will be stored in the *asfa.owl* file, its name will be *asfa ontology* and it will be implemented in OWL.

Finally, to conclude the description of the software library, it is worth mentioning that the implementation of this library follows a modular approach; therefore, it is possible to extend it in order to include other types of NORs, data models, and implementations in a simple way, as well as to exploit other external resources for relation disambiguation.

EXPERIMENTAL EVALUATION

In this section we describe two experiments we conducted with the objective of evaluating the methodological and technological aspects of our NOR Re-engineering approach. First, we assess the understandability and usability of the methodological guidelines. Second, we evaluate the quality of the set of patterns proposed in this paper. We focus on the TBox transformation because it is the most challenging transformation, however we intend to experiment the rest of transformation approaches in the future.

Methodological Evaluation

In this section we present the setting of the experiment we have carried out on the methodological guidelines proponed in this paper. This example refers to the manual transformation of an excerpt from a thesaurus, by using the guidelines and the proposed set of patterns. The purpose here is to assess the understandability and usability both the methodological guidelines and the set of patterns for carrying out the NOR Re-engineering when WordNet is used for disambiguating the relations between terms. Moreover, we present a comparison of the three most representative methods, introduced previously, with our pattern-based method.

Settings

The evaluation was carried out with participants whose background included databases, software engineering, AI, and had some experience in ontology engineering.

- The "Ontologies and Semantic Web" course within the "Athens Programme" taught at the Facultad de Informática (UPM). Fourteen international students attended the course.
- The "Ontologies and Semantic Web" course within the "Information Technology" Master, taught at the Facultad de Informática (UPM). Twenty Spanish students attended the Master course.

We carried out the evaluations in two separate experiments that were performed at different points in time, leaving an interval of one or two weeks between them. During this time, we did not modify the patterns and disambiguation algorithm.

We selected the ETT thesaurus. The excerpt from this thesaurus contains twenty terms[52]. The participants had to build manually the conceptual model from the resource, by analyzing the methodological guidelines and the set of patterns. They had 30 minutes for generating the conceptual model.

Execution

The experiment was executed in four phases:

1. The students were provided with the proposed guidelines.

2. The students were organized in groups of two.

3. The groups of students analyzed the methodological guidelines and the set of patterns in order to carry out the NOR re-engineering process. They generated manually the conceptual model.

4. The students filled in a questionnaire.

Next, we show the tasks performed within phase 3 to generate the conceptual model from the excerpt of the resource.

NOR Reverse Engineering. Within this activity the groups gathered documentation about the thesaurus from the ETT web site. From this documentation they extracted the schema of the thesaurus. Since the data model was not available in the documentation, they extracted it for the resource implementation itself.

NOR Transformation. Within this activity the groups looked into the ODP portal for a suitable PR-NOR, taking into account the following criteria: (1) the resource type, the thesaurus; (2) the resource data model, the record-based model; and (3) the transformation approach selected, the TBox transformation. The most appropriate pattern was the PR-NOR-TSTX-01. Finally, students followed the procedure suggested by the pattern, for creating manually the conceptual model. Each thesaurus term was mapped to a class. For the disambiguation of the semantics of the BT, NT

Table 7. Answers to the questionnaire proposed

Questions	Answers
Q1.	Ninety seven percent of the participants indicated that guidelines were well explained.
Q2.	Eighty eight percent of the students considered that more detail was not necessary in the guidelines; however twelve percent explained that they would welcome the improvement of the explanations of: i) how to search for a suitable pattern (task 2.1 in the guidelines), and ii) how to perform the ontology formalization (activity 3 in the guidelines).
Q3.	One hundred percent of the participants believed that the techniques and patterns to execute each activity of the guidelines were sufficient.
Q4.	Eighty five percent of the participants proposed to include more examples of how to use the proposed guidelines and what results were expected.
Q5.	One hundred percent of the participants believed that the guidelines were useful, but also necessary.

relations among thesaurus terms, the participants checked whether they could get the *subClassOf* relation by identifying attribute adjectives. If this was not the case, they searched the WordNet web site. When the query results were empty, they related the terms by means of the default relations (see Figure 10).

Ontology Forward Engineering. Since the goal was to create a conceptual model, the students did not perform this activity.

Collecting Results

Students were asked to answer the following questionnaire.

Q1. Are the guidelines proposed well explained?
Q2. Do the guidelines need to be more detailed? If so, please elaborate on your comments.

Q3. Do you think that more techniques and patterns should be provided?
Q4. How can we improve the guidelines proposed? And in which tasks?
Q5. Did you find these guidelines useful?

Findings and Observations

Table 7 presents the 34 answers to the questionnaire. As a general conclusion we can say that the students did not seem to find any problems with the use and understanding of each of the activities and tasks identified in the methodological guidelines.

Based on the comments obtained in this experiment, we can say that the main strength is that the methodological guidelines were useful and understandable.

Table 8. Comparative analysis of the three representative methods and the pattern-based method

Features	Heep et al.	Hyvo¨nen et al.	Soerger et al.	Pattern-Based Method
Non-Ontological Resource				
Type	classification scheme, thesaurus	thesaurus	thesaurus	classification scheme, thesaurus, lexicon
Data model is used	No	No	Yes	Yes
Implementation	database	Not mentioned	database	database, XML, spreadsheet, flat file
Transformation				
Transformation approach	TBox	TBox	TBox	TBox, ABox, Population
Semantics of the NOR relations	*subClassOf*, ad-hoc relation	*subClassOf*, *partOf*	*subClassOf*, ad-hoc relation	*subClassOf*, *partOf*
Additional resources	No	DOLCE	Domain expert	WordNet
Technique	Not mentioned	Not mentioned	Not mentioned	Re-engineering patterns
Tool support	SKOS2GenTax	ad-hoc tool	Not mentioned	NOR$_2$O
Ontology				
Components	classes, relations	classes, attributes, relations	classes, attributes, relations	classes, attributes, relations, instances
Language	RDF(S)/OWL-DLP	RDF(S)	OWL-DL	OWL-DL/RDF
Single / Several	single	single	single	single

Table 9. Resources utilized in the experiment

Name	Type	Data Model	Implemen- tation	N. of terms	N.of terms covered
ASFA	thesaurus	record- based	XML	9882	188
ETT	thesaurus	record- based	XML	2522	337
ACM	classification scheme	adjacency list	XML	1606	223
FOET	classification scheme	path enumeration	spreadsheet	127	112
BioLexicon	lexicon	relation- based	database	53876	150

Comparison with the Methods of the State of the Art

In this section we review the main contributions of our pattern-based method, against the existing methods introduced in the comparative framework for re-engineering NORs into ontologies. Table 8 presents the three most representative methods: Hepp et al. (Hepp & Brujin, 2007), Hyvönen et al. (Hyvönen et al., 2008), and Soergel et al. (Soergel et al., 2004), compared against our pattern-based method by using the evaluation framework defined previously.

Technological Evaluation: Quality of the Patterns and NOR₂O

The main purpose of this study is to evaluate the quality of the re-engineering patterns being used for transforming the NOR into an ontology by a disambiguation algorithm that lies on WordNet, the algorithm is implemented in the NOR_2O software library. The ontology generated is compared against a reference ontology (or gold standard) that was built manually by external ontology experts not involved in the experiment.

Settings

For this experiment, two ontology engineering experts built five ontologies, in OWL, from existing NORs (two classification schemes, two thesauri and one lexicon) of different domains.

One expert built two ontologies and the other built three ontologies. Then, the experts exchanged their ontologies in order to evaluate them. Later, the experts refined the ontologies by following the comments provided in the review. At the end of this process we obtained five "gold standard" ontologies[53]. It is worth mentioning that the ontologies cover an excerpt of the resources. Table 9 shows the resources utilized in this experiment:

Execution

The experiment was executed in the three phases:

1. Each NOR has been transformed automatically using the following patterns
    ◦ ASFA, using the PR-NOR-TSTX-01 pattern.
    ◦ ETT, using the PR-NOR-TSTX-01 pattern.
    ◦ ACM, using the PR-NOR-CLTX-02 pattern.
    ◦ FOET, using the PR-NOR-CLTX-01 pattern.
    ◦ BioLexicon, using the PR-NOR-LXTX-02 pattern.
2. For disambiguating the relations between entities of a particular resource we have executed the disambiguation algorithm using WordNet.
3. In order to assess the quality of the ontologies generated, we compared, the "gold standard" ontologies with the five ontologies gener-

Table 10. Similarity values of each of the ontologies generated with the "Gold Standard" ontology

Similarity values between ontologies generated with the gold standard		
	Cider	StrucSubsDistAlignment
ASFA	0.754	0.631
ETT	0.713	0.745
ACM	0.620	0.870
FOET	0.621	0.753
BioLexicon	0.515	0.793

ated automatically by means of similarity measures based on (1) the Cider System (Gracia, 2009), which considers the structure of the ontologies, i.e. classes, object properties and datatype properties; and (2) the *StrucSubsDistAlignment* measure taken from the Ontology Alignment Evaluation Initiative[54], which contemplates the structure of the ontologies.

Collecting Results

We built a table for comparing each one of the "Gold Standard" ontologies to the ontologies generated, by means of the similarity measures.

Finding and Observations

Table 10 presents the similarity values of each of the ontologies generated. We can say that the ontologies generated have an acceptable similarity degree to the gold standard ones.

Based on the results obtained, we can say that the main strength of the NOR_2O software library is that generates ontologies with an acceptable level of quality, meaning by quality how similar are the ontologies to the gold standard.

CONCLUSION

In this paper we have introduced a categorization of NORs according to three different features: type of NOR, data model, and implementation. Additionally, we have presented a framework that compares the existing methods for re-engineering NORs and we provided conclusions for the comparative study. The main contributions of this paper are (1) the model for re-engineering NORs into ontologies; (2) the patterns for re-engineering NORs; (3) the NOR_2O software library that implements the transformations suggested by the patterns; and (4) the method for re-engineering NORs into ontologies. Finally, we have depicted an evaluation of the method, patterns and software library.

We have shown that the approach presented: (1) copes with the following set of NORs, i.e., classification schemes, thesauri, and lexica, in an uniform way; (2) deals with NORs implemented in databases, XML files, flat files or spreadsheets; (3) takes into account the internal data model of the resources; and (4) contemplates the semantics of the NOR relations. Moreover, we have demonstrated that the use of patterns (1) embodies expertise about how to guide a re-engineering process, (2) improves the efficiency of the re-engineering process, and (3) makes the transformation process easier for both ontology engineers and domain experts.

Regarding the evaluation of the methods, patterns and software library, the main conclusions are: (1) NOR_2O software library generates ontologies with an acceptable level of quality; (2) the majority of participants find that the methodological guidelines are useful and understandable; and (3) NOR_2O software library really makes ontology development easier and faster. Therefore, the user saves time and effort in the development of ontologies. The results of the experiments provide an indication of the real value and practical usability of the method, patterns, and software library proposed in this paper. Moreover, we have compared our pattern-based method against the three most representative methods of the state of the art.

Although in this paper we address open research problems in the context of re-engineering non-ontological resources, there are still further works that can be done in the near future, and they are (1) the improvement of the disambiguation algorithm by including DBpedia as an additional external resource; (2) the creation of richer and more complex ontologies, by including more knowledge in the patterns, for example the disjoint knowledge; (3) the integration of several NORs into one ontological model; and (4) the enrichment of the patterns by including a section that explains how to generate instances following the Linking Open Data[55] recommendations.

ACKNOWLEDGMENT

This work has been partially supported by the European Commission projects NeOn (FP6-027595) and SEEMP (FP6-027347), as well as by an R+D grant from the UPM. We would like to kindly thanks María Poveda, Esther Nuñez, and Rosario Plaza.

REFERENCES

Alexander, C. (1979). *The Timeless Way of Building*. New York: Oxford University Press.

An, Y., Borgida, A., & Mylopoulos, J. (2005). Constructing Complex Semantic Mappings between XML Data and Ontologies. In *Proceedings of the International Semantic Web Conference* (pp. 6-20).

An, Y., & Mylopoulos, J. (2005). Translating XML Web Data into Ontologies. In *Proceedings of the OTM Workshops* (pp. 967-976).

Barrasa, J. (2007). *Modelo para la Definición Automática de Correspondencias Semánticas entre Ontologías y Modelos Relacionales*. Madrid, Spain: Facultad de Informática, Universidad Politécnica de Madrid.

Barrasa, J., Corcho, O., & Gómez-Pérez, A. (2004). R_2O, an Extensible and Semantically Based Database-to-Ontology Mapping Language. In *Proceedings of the Second Workshop on Semantic Web and Databases (SWDB2004)*.

Bizer, C. (2009). The Emerging Web of Linked Data. *IEEE Intelligent Systems*, *24*(5), 87–92. doi:10.1109/MIS.2009.102

Brandon, D. (2005). Recursive Database Structures. *Journal of Computing Sciences in Colleges*.

Byrne, E. J. (1992). A Conceptual Foundation for Software Re-engineering. In *Proceedings of the International Conference on Software Maintenance and Reengineering* (pp. 226-235). Washington, DC: IEEE Computer Society.

Caracciolo, C., Heguiabehere, J., Presutti, V., & Gangemi, A. (2009). *Initial Network of Fisheries Ontologies*. NeOn project.

Carkenord, B. (2002). *Why Build a Logical Data Model*. Retrieved from http://etnaweb04.embarcadero.com/resources/tech_papers/datamodel.pdf

Clark, P., Thompson, J., & Porter, B. W. (2000). Knowledge Patterns. In *Proceedings of KR2000* (pp. 591–600). Principles of Knowledge Representation and Reasoning.

Cruz, I. F., Xiao, H., & Hsu, F. (2004). An Ontology-Based Framework for XML Semantic Integration. In *IDEAS '04: Proceedings of the International Database Engineering and Applications Symposium* (pp. 217-226). Washington, DC: IEEE Computer Society.

Edwards, H., Puckettm, R., & Jolly, A. (2006). Analyzing Communication Patterns in Software Engineering Projects. In *Software Engineering Research and Practice* (pp. 310-315).

Foxvog, D., & Bussler, C. (2006). Ontologizing EDI Semantics. In *Proceedings of the ER Workshops* (pp. 301-311).

Gangemi, A., Guarino, N., Masolo, C., & Oltramari, A. (2003). Sweetening WordNet with DOLCE. *AI Magazine, 24*(3), 13–24.

Gangemi, A., Navigli, R., & Velardi, P. (2003). The OntoWordNet Project: Extension and Axiomatization of Conceptual Relations in WordNet. In *Proceedings of the CoopIS/DOA/ODBASE Conference*.

Gangemi, A., Pisanelli, D., & Steve, G. (1998). Experiences with Medical Terminologies. In *Ontology in Information Systems* (pp. 163–178). Ontology Integration.

García, R., & Celma, O. (2005). Semantic Integration and Retrieval of Multimedia Metadata. In *Proceedings of the ISWC 2005 Workshop on Knowledge Markup and Semantic Annotation (Semannot'2005)*.

García-Silva, A., Gómez-Pérez, A., Suárez-Figueroa, M. C., & Villazón-Terrazas, B. (2008). A Pattern Based Approach for Re-engineering Non-Ontological Resources into Ontologies. In *ASWC '08: Proceedings of the 3rd Asian Semantic Web Conference* (pp. 167-181). Berlin: Springer-Verlag.

Gómez-Pérez, A., Fernández-López, M., & Corcho, O. (2003). *Ontological Engineering*. Berlin: Springer-Verlag.

Gómez-Pérez, A., & Manzano-Macho, D. (2004). An overview of methods and tools for ontology learning from text. *The Knowledge Engineering Review, 19*(3), 187–212. doi:10.1017/S0269888905000251

Gómez-Pérez, A., & Suárez-Figueroa, M. C. (2009). Scenarios for Building Ontology Networks within the NeOn Methodology. In *Proceedings of the Fifth International Conference on Knowledge Capture (K-CAP 2009)*.

Gracia, J. (2009). *Integration and Disambiguation Techniques for Semantic Heterogeneity Reduction on the Web*. Zaragoza, Spain: University of Zaragoza.

Haase, P., Rudolph, S., Wang, Y., & Brockmans, S. (2006). *Networked Ontology ModelNetworked Ontology Model*. NeOn project.

Hahn, U., & Schulz, S. (2003). Towards a broad-coverage biomedical ontology based on description logics. *Pacific Symposium on Biocomputing, 8*, 577-588).

Hahn, V. (2003). Turning informal thesauri into formal ontologies: a feasibility study on biomedical knowledge re-use. *Comparative and Functional Genomics, 4*(1), 94–97. doi:10.1002/cfg.247

Hakkarainen, S., Hella, L., Strasunskas, D., & Tuxen, S. (2006). A Semantic Transformation Approach for ISO 15926. In *Proceedings of the OIS 2006 First International Workshop on Ontologizing Industrial Standards*.

Hepp, M. (2006). Products and Services Ontologies: A Methodology for Deriving OWL Ontologies from Industrial Categorization Standards. *International Journal on Semantic Web and Information Systems, 2*(1), 72–99.

Hepp, M. (2007). Possible Ontologies: How Reality Constrains the Development of Relevant Ontologies. *IEEE Internet Computing, 11*(1), 90–96. doi:10.1109/MIC.2007.20

Hepp, M., & de Brujin, J. (2007). GenTax: A generic Methodology for Deriving OWL and RDF-S Ontologies from Hierarchical Classifications, Thesauri, and Inconsistent Taxonomies. In *Proceedings of the 4th European Semantic Web Conference (ESWC2007)*. Berlin: Springer-Verlag.

Hirst, G. (2004). Ontology and the Lexicon. In *Handbook on Ontologies in Information Systems* (pp. 209–230). Berlin: Springer.

Hodge, G. (2000). Systems of Knowledge Organization for Digital Libraries: Beyond Traditional Authority Files.

Hyvönen, E., Viljanen, K., Tuominen, J., & Seppälä, K. (2008). Building a National Semantic Web Ontology and Ontology Service Infrastructure - The FinnONTO Approach. In *Proceedings of the European Semantic Web Conference, ESWC* (pp. 95-109).

ISO. (1986). *Documentation - Guidelines for the establishment and development of monolingual thesaurus (Rep. ISO 2788)*. Geneva, Switzerland: ISO.

ISO/IEC. (2004). *Information technology - Metadata registries - Part 1: Framework (Rep. ISO/IEC FDIS 11179-1)*. Geneva, Switzerland: ISO.

Kimball, R., & Caserta, J. (2004). The Data Warehouse ETL Toolkit: Practical Techniques for Extracting, Cleaning. In *The Data Warehouse ETL Toolkit*. New York: John Wiley & Sons.

Lauser, B., & Sini, M. (2006). From AGROVOC to the agricultural ontology service/concept server: an OWL model for creating ontologies in the agricultural domain in the agricultural domain. In *DCMI '06: Proceedings of the 2006 International Conference on Dublin Core and Metadata Applications* (pp. 76-88). Dublin, Ireland: Dublin Core Metadata Initiative.

Maedche, A., & Staab, S. (2001). Ontology Learning for the Semantic Web. *IEEE Intelligent Systems*.

Malinowski, E., & Zimányi, E. (2006). Hierarchies in a multidimensional model: From conceptual modeling to logical representation. *Data & Knowledge Engineering, 59*(2). doi:10.1016/j.datak.2005.08.003

Pinto, H. S., Tempich, C., & Staab, S. (2004). DILIGENT: Towards a fine-grained methodology for DIstributed, Loosely-controlled and evolvInG Engineering of oNTologies. In *Proceedings of the 16th European Conference on Artificial Intelligence (ECAI 2004)* (pp. 393-397).

Pooley, R., & Stevens, P. (1998). *Software Reengineering Patterns*. Retrieved from http://www.reengineering.ed.ac.uk/csgrep.pdf

Presutti, V., Gangemi, A., David, S., de Cea, G. A., Suárez-Figueroa, M. C., & Montiel-Ponsoda, E. (2008). *NeOn Deliverable D2.5.1: A Library of Ontology Design Patterns: reusable solutions for collaborative design of networked ontologies*. Retrieved from http://www.neon-project.org

Soergel, D. (1995). *Data models for an integrated thesaurus database*. Retrieved from http://www.dsoergel.com/cv/B54.pdf

Soergel, D., Lauser, B., Liang, A., Fisseha, F., Keizer, J., & Katz, S. (2004). *Reengineering Thesauri for New Applications: The AGROVOC Example*. Rome, Italy: FAO.

Staab, S., Schnurr, H., Studer, R., & Sure, Y. (2001). Knowledge Processes and Ontologies. *IEEE Intelligent Systems, 16*(1), 26–34. doi:10.1109/5254.912382

Stojanovic, L., Stojanovic, N., & Volz, R. (2002). A Reverse Engineering Approach for Migrating Data-intensive Web Sites to the Semantic Web. In *Proceedings of the Conference on Intelligent Information Processing*.

Suárez-Figueroa, M. C. (2010). *NeOn Methodology for Building Ontology Networks: Specification, Scheduling and Reuse.* Madrid, Spain: Facultad de Informática, Universidad Politécnica de Madrid.

Suárez-Figueroa, M. C., & Gómez-Pérez, A. (2008). First Attempt towards a Standard Glossary of Ontology Engineering Terminology. In *Proceedings of the 8th International Conference on Terminology and Knowledge Engineering (TKE2008),* Copenhagen, Denmark.

Van Assem, M., Gangemi, A., & Schreiber, G. (2006). Conversion of WordNet to a standard RDF/OWL representation. In *Proceedings of the Fifth International Conference on Language Resources and Evaluation (LREC'06),* Genova, Italy.

Van Assem, M., Malaisé, V., Miles, A., & Schreiber, G. (2006). A Method to Convert Thesauri to SKOS. In *The Semantic Web* (pp. 95–109). Research and Applications.

Van Assem, M., Menken, M., Schreiber, G., & Wielemaker, J. (2004). A Method for Converting Thesauri to RDF/OWL. In *Proceedings of the Third International Semantic Web Conference (ISWC).* Berlin: Springer.

Villazón-Terrazas, B., Gómez-Pérez, A., & Calbimonte, J. P. (2010). NOR₂O: a Library for Transforming Non-Ontological Resources to Ontologies. In *Proceedings of the Seventh Extended Semantic Web Conference (ESWC 2010).*

Wielinga, B., Schreiber, A. T., Wielemaker, J., & Sandberg, J. (2001). From thesaurus to ontology. In *K-CAP '01: Proceedings of the 1st international conference on Knowledge capture* (pp. 194-201). New York: ACM Press.

Wright, S., & Budin, G. (1997). *Handbook of terminology management, Basic aspects of terminology management.* Amsterdam, The Netherlands: John Benjamins Publishing Company.

ENDNOTES

[1] http://www.neon-project.org

[2] An ontology network is a collection of ontologies together through a variety of different relationships such as mapping, modularization, version, and dependency relationships (Haase, Rudolph, Wang & Brockmans, 2006).

[3] A data model (Carkenord, 2002) is an abstract model that describes how data is represented and accessed. There are three basic styles of a data model: (1) the conceptual data model, which presents the primary entities and relationships of concern to a specific domain; (2) the logical data model, which depicts the logical entity types, the data attributes describing those entities, and the relationships between entities; and (3) the physical data model, which is related to a specific implementation of the resource. In this paper we will use the term data model when referring to the logical data model.

[4] http://www.fao.org/fi/glossary/default.asp

[5] http://www.fao.org/figis/servlet/RefServlet

[6] http://www.fao.org/agrovoc/

[7] http://wordnet.princeton.edu/

[8] http://www.vanderwal.net/folksonomy.html

[9] http://del.icio.us/

[10] http://www.rosettanet.org/

[11] http://www.edibasics.co.uk/

[12] http://www.unspsc.org/

[13] http://wordnet.princeton.edu/

[14] http://www.nlm.nih.gov/pubs/factsheets/umlsmeta.html

[15] http://www.nlm.nih.gov/mesh/

[16] http://www.getty.edu/research/tools/vocabularies/aat/index.html

[17] http://www.ilo.org/public/english/bureau/stat/isco/index.htm

[18] http://libserver.cedefop.europa.eu/ett/en/

[19] http://ec.europa.eu/eurostat/ramon/nomenclatures/index.cfm?TargetUrl=DSP_GEN_

DESC_VIEW_NOHDR&StrNom=EDU_TRAINI&StrLanguageCode=EN

[20] http://www.fao.org/fishery/asfa/8/en

[21] http://aims.fao.org/website/AGROVOC-Thesaurus/sub

[22] http://www.fao.org/figis/servlet/RefServlet

[23] http://en.istat.it/

[24] http://www.iso.org/iso/iso_catalogue/catalogue_tc/catalogue_detail.htm?csnumber=29557

[25] The EXPRESS file is a computer-interpretable of ISO 15926-2 http://www.iso.org/iso/iso_catalogue/catalogue_tc/catalogue_detail.htm?csnumber=38047

[26] http://www.loa-cnr.it/DOLCE.html

[27] http://www.nlm.nih.gov/research/umls/

[28] http://www.isi.edu/isd/LOOM/

[29] http://www.w3.org/2004/02/skos/

[30] http://vesa.lib.helsinki.fi/

[31] http://www.yso.fi/onto/yso

[32] http://mpeg.chiariglione.org/

[33] http://rhizomik.net/html/ontologies/mpeg7ontos/

[34] http://www.ifla.org/VI/5/reports/rep4/42.htm\#chap2

[35] http://www.w3.org/2001/sw/BestPractices/OEP/

[36] http://www.gong.manchester.ac.uk/odp/html/index.html

[37] http://ontologydesignpatterns.org

[38] http://patterns.dataincubator.org/book/

[39] According to (Byrne, 1992) software re-engineering is the examination and alteration of a software system to reconstitute it in a new form and the subsequent implementation of the new form.

[40] Ontology Design Patterns are included in the ODP portal http://ontologydesignpatterns. org. The ODP portal is a Semantic Web portal dedicated to ontology design best practices for the Semantic Web, specially focused on ontology design patterns (OPs).

[41] http://www.dbpedia.org/

[42] Attributive adjectives are part of the noun phrase headed by the noun they modify; for example, happy is an attributive adjective in "happy people". In English, attributive adjectives usually precede their nouns in simple phrases, but often follow their nouns when the adjective is modified or qualified by a phrase acting as an adverb.

[43] http://ontologydesignpatterns.org/wiki/Submissions:PartOf

[44] http://www.seemp.org

[45] http://www.eurodyn.com/

[46] http://mccarthy.dia.fi.upm.es/nor2o/

[47] The extraction, transformation, and loading (ETL) of legacy data sources, is a process that involves: (1) extracting data from the outside resources, (2) transforming it to fit operational needs, and (3) loading into the end target resources (Kimball, Ralph & Caserta, 2004).

[48] http://www4.fao.org/asfa/asfa.htm

[49] http://droz.dia.fi.upm.es/ontologies/asfa.owl

[50] http://dbpedia.org/

[51] http://owlapi.sourceforge.net/

[52] http://droz.dia.fi.upm.es/master/rd/homework/resources/ett.xml

[53] Ontologies available at http://droz.dia.fi.upm.es/ontologies

[54] http://oaei.ontologymatching.org/

[55] http://esw.w3.org/topic/SweoIG/TaskForces/CommunityProjects/LinkingOpenData

This work was previously published in International Journal of Semantic Web and Information Systems, Volume 6, Issue 4, edited by Amit P. Sheth, pp. 27-63, copyright 2010 by IGI Publishing (an imprint of IGI Global).

Chapter 3
An Ontology–Based, Cross–Application Context Modeling and Management Service

Annett Mitschick
Technische Universität Dresden, Germany

Stefan Pietschmann
Technische Universität Dresden, Germany

Klaus Meißner
Technische Universität Dresden, Germany

ABSTRACT

Context awareness is a key issue for applications within heterogeneous and networked environments. In terms of efficiency and reusability, such applications need to be separated from the problems of context gathering and modeling, but should instead profit from and contribute to cross-application context information. For this purpose, an ontology-based, cross-application context modeling and management service is required to provide appropriate support for the variety of conceivable application scenarios. Although there have been numerous approaches dealing with application-independent context management, none of them sufficiently supports the vision of cross-application context handling. Therefore, this paper presents CroCo, an ontology-based context management service that allows for cross-application context gathering, modeling, and provision. The authors successfully verified and tested the application independency and practicability of this novel concept within three different projects with disparate application scenarios.

INTRODUCTION

Context awareness and context-aware applications have been the focus of extensive research work in recent years. Accordingly, a number of solutions for context gathering and modeling have been

suggested (Baldauf et al., 2007; Chen & Kotz, 2000) or already found their ways into practice, especially within the field of *Location-based Services*, e. g., *Mobi.Ubiq*[1] services or *Urban Mediator*[2]. A context managing solution has to take account of appropriate support for *context providers* (e. g., software agents, applications,

DOI: 10.4018/978-1-4666-0185-7.ch003

or sensors, which supply context data) and *context consumers* (e. g., applications, which utilize context data for specific purposes).

Cross-application context management must allow diverse applications, application plug-ins, software agents, and sensors to act as context providers or consumers. Therefore, a corresponding context management service needs to offer a generic and flexible mechanism for dynamic registration of such agents. Registered context consumers should be able to fetch (i. e., query) relevant data from the service at any time (*pull*), or be notified if relevant data managed by the service has changed (*push*). Furthermore, context consistency needs to be ensured, e. g., with the help of appropriate consistency rules based on a confidence and reputation system for context providers, as well as a context history. Moreover, dynamic cross-application context management necessitates special care to be taken of security and privacy issues. Further challenges include the ambiguity and redundancy of context entities used in different domain models.

The majority of the proposed approaches exclusively fulfill the requirements of the according research projects and application scenarios, i. e., they support only specific context providers and context consumers or use a specialized domain model. Gathering, modeling, and supply of context information *across application boundaries* has still not been designed, implemented, and tested for and within heterogeneous scenarios. Thus, the vision of cross-application context awareness based on semantic technologies has not been fulfilled, yet. This vision could be fulfilled with the help of an application-independent, stand-alone context management component, which provides adequate interfaces for context providers and consumers to enter and access consistent, up-to-date context information for their particular application scenarios. In this article we therefore present *a Cross-application Context management Service*, called (CRoCo). It allows for cross-application context handling, with the help of a new concept

of so called *Domain Profiles*. As a stand-alone context service, CRoCo separates the modeling and management functionality from the context-aware applications themselves.

In the first section we discuss relevant work related to ontology-based cross-application context modeling. Afterwards, the design of CRoCo is presented, followed by a discussion of the implementation details and usage scenarios to illustrate the practicability of our approach. Three "orthogonal" application scenarios are described: *personal multimedia document management*, *adaptive co-browsing applications* and *context-aware user interface mashups*. The last section summarizes this article and suggests future research directions.

Related Work

A lot of research has been carried out regarding context modeling and management (Strang & Linnhoff-Popien, 2004; Baldauf et al., 2007), especially in the fields of Adaptive Hypermedia (Hinz et al., 2007) and, more recently, Ubiquitous Computing (Bardram, 2005). In this research process the means for context representation have changed from basic key-value models to logic- and ontology-based models, which provide much better support for aspects like partial validation, disambiguity and applicability. We do not discuss these advantages in detail here, as this has already been extensively done, e. g., in (Strang & Linnhoff-Popien, 2004). In the following we shortly present related concepts for ontology-based context management.

Context infrastructures are usually similar in the components they consist of, which resemble the basic tasks of the system (e. g., management, inferencing and storage). However, they differ in important additional features, such as a *Context History* and *Security* support, as well as regarding their architectural style.

CoBrA (*Context Broker Architecture*) (Chen et al., 2003) and DAIDALOS (Roussaki et al.,

2006) are two powerful approaches that – similar to our concept – comply to the *Blackboard* model using a central component for storage, management and provision of context data (Baldauf et al., 2007). Both are designed to support smart spaces, though, and are therefore not suited for our application scenarios. Furthermore, they either do not consider privacy aspects (DAIDALOS) or provide a context history (CoBrA), which is crucial for sophisticated context reasoning.

In (Floréen et al., 2005) a context framework for *MobiLife* is presented that is similar to our concept in using a provider-consumer metaphor and facilitating easy access via a service interface. However, its distribution among a network implies that there is no central context history and additional effort regarding security needed. Another promising distributed context management concept proposed in (Power et al., 2004) differs from common approaches by not using a specific ontology. Instead, during registration, *Context Services* (providers) exchange their domain models and corresponding mapping rules. When context data is requested, these rules are used to match the request with the correct provider and map its data automatically to the requested model. In contrast to our approach, to benefit from cross-application context authors here need to define mapping rules and are therein limited to previously known concepts.

SOCAM (*Service-Oriented Context-Aware Middleware*) (Gu et al., 2005), based on a hybrid architectural style with distributed components and central server, seems to be the closest to our approach, as it allows for cross-application context management and exchange by subclassing a domain-independent ontology. Opposed to our concept, this does not include time-related concepts for describing context dynamics and hence does not provide a context history.

Within the IST-Project *Amigo*[3] Bonino da Silva Santos et al. (2007) developed a context middleware consisting of a *Context Management Service* (CMS) and an *Awareness and Notification Service* (ANS). The strength of their approach is the messaging service which enables applications to register for context events with the help of a simple script language. However, there is no central context store, context history and reasoning service, similar to the approach described in (Euzenat et al., 2008).

The *Middleware for Adaptive Coordination* (MAC), presented in (Zhou et al., 2007), provides a three-tier architecture for the development of context-aware self-managing systems. Although, the middleware offers a general framework for the interaction of different applications, domain ontologies are specified and integrated at design time and cannot be dynamically edited at run time.

The *CoCa Platform* (Collaborative Context-aware service Platform), described in (Ejigu et al., 2008), was designed as a data independent environment for proactive context-aware computing services in pervasive environments. It is based on a hybrid context model, to separate *context data management* and *knowledge management*. Nevertheless, the handling of cross-application context and dynamic integration of domain ontologies is not part of this approach.

Rocha et al. (2008) introduces a *Middleware for Ubiquitous Context-Awareness* which provides cross-domain access to context information in heterogeneous, dynamic environments. A domain is managed by a so called *Context Management Node*, which is a "generic building block" within the middleware. This approach of isolated domains is very interesting, but does not deal explicitly with the idea of cross-domain or cross-application context querying.

Our study of the related work revealed that currently no approach supports all aspects needed for cross-application context usage sufficiently. Therefore, we developed a new solution for ontology-based, cross-application context management, which is described in the next section.

CRoCo: An Ontology-Based, Cross-Application Context Service

In this section we present our concept of an ontology-based, cross-application context modeling and provision service, called CRoCo. First of all, we describe the general architecture of our ontology-based, cross-application context service, followed by a presentation of its functionality and the used upper ontology called CRoCoON (Cross-application Context Ontology).

Architecture

We have designed our ontology-based, *Cross-application Context management Service* (CRoCo) as a generic system allowing arbitrary *Context Providers* to submit, and *Context Consumers* to request context data via specific service interfaces.

Clients may act as providers *and* consumers at the same time. With the help of consistency and inference rules, higher-level information that may not be provided by any sensor is derived by CRoCo (inferring contextual information from basic sensor data) and serves as a general context supplier for the external context-aware applications (see next section). Imagine we want to adapt web content directly to the users' age, so that inappropriate content is filtered out. As the age of consent differs from country to country, we need to bind the adaptation to the semantic concept of *adulthood*, which can be dynamically reasoned from other contextual information of a user, such as his/her age and location, by our service, i. e., separate from the adaptive application.

Figure 1 shows the overall architecture of CRoCo. As already mentioned, it follows the *Blackboard* model, which promotes a data-centric

Figure 1. Conceptual architecture of CRoCo

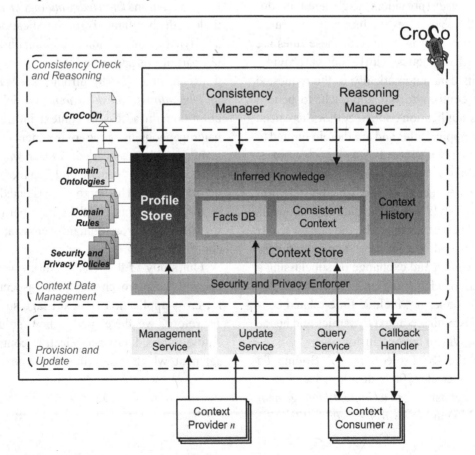

approach in which external processes can post context information on a blackboard, or subscribe for change notifications. Thus, it is rather easy to add new Context Providers and Consumers and ensure context integrity.

CroCo has three responsibilities: *(Context) Data Management, Consistency Checking and Reasoning, and Context Data Update and Provision.*

Data Management comprises four parts: the *Profile Store*, which manages so called *Domain Profiles*, the *Context History*, which contains the history of updates to the context model, the *Consistent Context*, representing the currently valid, consistent contextual data, and finally the *Inferred Knowledge* – a layer which encapsulates all information derived, i. e., reasoned from current context information. More precisely, while the Consistent Context contains the explicit data passed by context providers, the Inferred Knowledge comprises implicit data inferred from the Consistent Context based on rules and facts. Consumers always request data from the *Context Store*, which manages Consistent Context and Inferred Knowledge, so their division is transparent to external components. The Context History is completely hidden and only used internally for statistical analysis or by reasoners that include the time variance of context data into their inferencing process. It may as well be extended to predict future context changes. The Profile Store facilitates processing of context information within cross-application scenarios. Therefore, it is responsible for the management of (and access to) Domain Profiles that contain domain-specific models, security policies, facts and inferencing rules, as well as supplementary metadata.

Consistency checking is controlled by the *Consistency Manager* based on rules and facts of the according application domain. It is triggered every time new data is added to the context model. An arbitrary number of *Consistency Enforcers*, each responsible for ensuring consistency of a certain aspect (e. g., data type or cardinality),

can register at the Consistency Manager to be included in the consistency checking and conflict detection process.

Reasoning is carried out by the *Reasoning Manager*. Similar to the Consistency Manager, arbitrary *Reasoners* can register there to be invoked as soon as relevant contextual data changes. Context reasoning is based on facts stored in a *Facts Database* and its result is, of course, subject to subsequent consistency checks. The Facts Database is subdivided into separate corpora according to existing domain profiles, handled and managed by the Profile Store as described above. Since inferred data must not overwrite existing data – it would interfere with the confidence mechanism – it is stored separately in the Inferred Knowledge base. This allows for the dynamic integration of additional reasoners at run time without negative impact on the Consistent Context.

To support Context Data Update and Provision, CroCo provides two services: the *Update Service* and *Query Service*. The former is responsible for updates and changes to the context model, while the latter provides both a synchronous and asynchronous way to retrieve context information from CroCo. Context Consumers, i. e., systems that are interested in context changes, can register for specific context data, so that they are notified by a *Callback Handler* once it changes. Alternatively, consumers can request data synchronously. These two different approaches facilitate the use of CroCo in different application scenarios. In any case, the *Privacy Enforcer* ensures that consumers have the necessary authorization to provide and access data by utilizing security policies from the corresponding domain profiles or CroCo itself.

Finally, to allow for the entry and modification of Domain Profiles CroCo provides a dedicated *Management Service* for *Profile Publishers*. Those are specialized Context Providers who define their own application domain with the help of their own domain ontologies, rules and facts.

Figure 2. Example workflow of CroCo

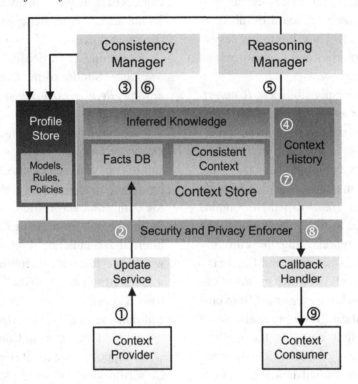

Functionality

Figure 2 presents the main components of CroCo. With the help of an example workflow we discuss its functionality in more detail, i. e., how its components work together at run time during context updates and requests.

At first, a Context Provider, e. g., a sensor, sends new data in the form of regular RDF triples to the Context Update Service ①. Additional information, such as a time stamp, provider id, and confidence value, are transferred as well, which we discuss later on.

First, the Security Enforcer checks, whether the provided data complies to general and profile-specific security policies ②, i. e., whether the provider is registered and has the necessary rights. If it has, the context information is forwarded to the Context Store, which internally manages the consistent and inferred context. It uses CroCoOn (cf. next section) or a domain-specific profile

derived from it to model persons (users), groups, hard- and software on client devices, time, geographic information, preferences, and much more. To ensure that the submitted context information is consistent with the internal model, it is validated by the Consistency Manager ③, which internally triggers all registered Consistency Enforcers. A consistency report is returned to the Context Store, which is added to the Context History together with the submitted data ④. If the data is validated as consistent, the reasoning process, which is controlled by the Reasoning Manager and carried out by several registered Reasoners, is started ⑤. The inferred knowledge is then again checked for consistency ⑥ and stored in the Context History ⑦ as well as in the Inferred Knowledge base. Finally, the Callback Handler is informed that the context model has changed. If there are Context Consumers, which had previously registered as change listeners, they are notified of these changes ⑧ once authorization for access to this data has been granted by the Privacy Enforcer ⑨. Context Consumers can alternatively request data from the Context Update Service directly, i. e., synchronously.

Several mechanisms facilitate sound and useful consistency checks and reasoning in CroCo: For one, each Context Provider is assigned an internal *confidence value* (cf. Schmidt, 2006) representing its accuracy and reliability, which is also reflected in the Context History. This value is initialized with the confidence value sent by the Context Provider, which rates the reliability and accuracy of the sensed context data. The determination of this value is left to the Context Provider. The internal representation of a Context Provider's confidence value is based on the sent confidence value and its reputation (see below). Based on this value it is possible to include the quality of context updates into consistency checks. Furthermore, the Context History stores information about the *variability* of contextual data. As an example, the birth date of a user is static, while his/her location may be highly dynamic. This implies that context information can get outdated over time and may need to be updated with new, even low-confidence data. A last additional parameter used in CroCo is the *reputation* of context providers, which depends on their data quality. If a provider constantly sends inconsistent data, its reputation decreases, ultimately resulting in scaling down the confidence values for context data sent by this provider. So, consistency checks and conflict detection are influenced by the age and variability of context data, as well as the reputation and confidence values of its providers.

The CroCoOn Context Model

In contrast to most prevalent, static XML-based approaches, we use an ontology-based model similar to those described by Chen et al. (2003) and Kernchen et al. (2006). This allows for the integration of external ontologies describing relevant contextual aspects (preferences, device characteristics, location, time, etc.) as well as domain-specific knowledge and reasoning. Traditional approaches either directly store sensed contextual data, or they incorporate a static mapping from sensor data to context parameters. In contrast to this, an ontological basis provides machine-processable semantic metadata, domain-inherent integrity constraints and inferencing rules to derive higher-level contextual knowledge from basic sensor data. Thus, it becomes possible to model implicit knowledge and to establish a semantic context (meaning) on top of the purely technical context (parameters).

We have developed a generic, ontology-based context model, called CroCoOn (Cross-application Context Ontology)[4], for the use within CroCo. As can be seen in Figure 3, it consists of several sub-ontologies that model different aspects of context, e. g., time, place, the user and the device. Therefore, we reused concepts from several well-known ontologies, such as SOUPA (Chen et al., 2004), PROTON[5] and the W3C Time Ontology[6].

Based on this Upper Ontology it is possible – and intended by all means – to extend the model and integrate domain-specific knowledge to facilitate the usage of CroCo in diverse application scenarios. We call these extensions Domain Profiles as already mentioned above. In addition to CroCoOn, they describe a certain *type* of activity (application scenario) in more detail, e. g., a co-browsing session, a video conference, etc. Thus, they represent the common conceptualization of context providers and consumers for a particular application scenario. Some examples are given in the next section.

Implementation and Usage of CroCo

In the following we present the implementation of the designed context management component CroCo and go into detail on three application scenarios that heavily depend on cross-application context use and were used with our CroCo to prove its practicability and validity.

Figure 3. Import relations within CRoCoON

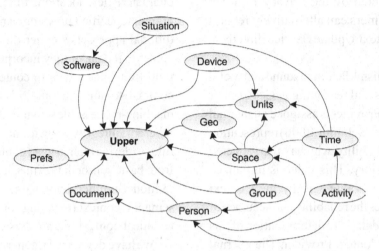

Based on the concept explained in the last section, we have implemented CRoCo in Java. It heavily relies on the Jena Semantic Web Framework[7] for RDF and OWL processing tasks. Consistent and inferred context data is modeled and processed in RDF and stored in a MySQL database. The reasoner to date is based on the GenericRuleReasoner provided by Jena's inference support. It processes Jena rules which can be stored in separate files and can thus be updated and adjusted very easily. Thus, consistency checking and reasoning mechanisms in CRoCo are based on the Jena inference engine which processes declared domain rules in Jena Rules Syntax. The Context History has been implemented as logger that allows for easy future extension. Also, basic privacy mechanisms, i. e., consumer-based access control is provided by the Privacy Enforcer using declarative privacy rules. The service interfaces were built based on Apache Axis2. The Update Service and Query Service both support SPARQL requests (Prud'hommeaux & Seaborne, 2008) – the former to allow consumers to register for relevant data, the latter to query the current context model. The Management Service provides methods to access and manage (CRUD) registered Domain Profiles.

In the following we give three examples of application domains, i. e., scenarios that heavily depend on contextual knowledge and may benefit as well from the use of a joint context management facility. Namely, these are *personal multimedia document management*, *context-aware co-browsing* and the *composition of context-aware user interface mashups*. The context management service explained above was used within these scenarios to prove its independence and cross-application usability. Therefore, it has been deployed in the projects K-IMM (*Knowledge through Intelligent Media Management*) (Mitschick et al., 2008), VCS (*Virtual Consulting Services*) (Pietschmann et al., 2007; Niederhausen et al., 2009), and CRUISe (*Composition of Rich User Interface Services*) (Pietschmann et al., 2009), using their application-specific Domain Profiles. However, as all three scenarios are realized as research prototypes, a real-world evaluation has not yet been accomplished.

Personal Multimedia Document Management

Managing a considerable quantity of documents involves administration efforts and certain strategies for ordering and arrangement to keep track of content and structure of the collection – esp. over a long period. With the help of Semantic Web technologies, which ensure machine-processability and interchangeability, it is possible to apply semantic knowledge models and paths to organize and describe heterogeneous multimedia items. In this application area context plays a very important role and can be applied within annotation and retrieval scenarios. Retrieval tasks can be supported with the help of context-dependent adaptation and personalization techniques. Furthermore, to generate rich semantic annotation and description of multimedia content the context of its creation, modification, usage, sharing, etc. (i. e., the whole *life cycle* of a document) is highly valuable. Thus, a system for personal multimedia document management is primarily a context consumer and profits from cross-application context modeling. Relevant context concerning a document's life cycle comes from desktop applications, like e-mail clients (transmission of a document via e-mail),

authoring or editing tools (e. g., photo correction software), or browser information (e. g., file upload for online photo printing). The variety of context providers necessitates a flexible solution capable of cross-application context gathering and modeling.

As a practical application scenario, we utilized CRoCo within the K-IMM project[8] to access context information about a document's usage. As a prototypical personal multimedia document management system, the K-IMM service platform autonomously manages documents stored on the local file system of the user. An overview of the system is depicted in Figure 4.

The architecture, which is presented in more detail in (Mitschick et al., 2008), is composed of three layers: (I) a media-specific layer for the import and indexing of multimedia assets (of different type), performed by background tasks,

Figure 4. K-IMM Architecture (overview)

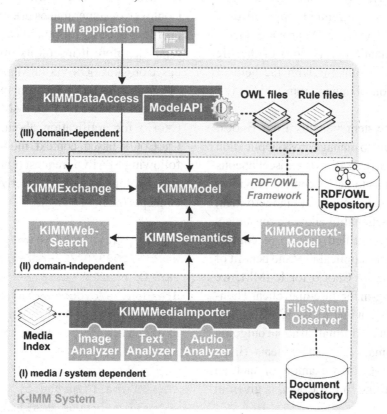

Figure 5. Usage of context information within the K-IMM document life cycle modeling process

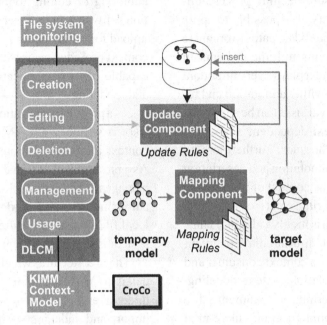

(II) a domain-independent layer for the semantic data modeling and consolidation, and (III) a domain-dependent layer as an interface for personal document management applications. Within the second layer K-IMM provides facilities to model semantic descriptions of the life cycle of personal documents with the help of context information obtained from CRoCo (cf. Figure 5).

The K-IMM System benefits from CRoCo because of its ability to manage cross-application context information (i. e., allowing miscellaneous desktop applications to act as context providers for information about document usage activities) and its callback functionality, allowing consumers to be immediately notified in case of context changes. To show the applicability and benefit of context acquisition by CRoCo for K-IMM, we implemented a plug-in for the e-mail client Thunderbird[9] as context provider for CRoCo. It gathers and sends contextual information about outgoing and incoming e-mail with attachments (i. e., documents) to CRoCo. An example of such an description, according to CRoCoOn, is given in Box 1.

As a unique identifier of the attached document the description provides the SHA1 hash code of the whole file. The K-IMM System, acting as Context Consumer makes use of its own domain profile to specify information about e-mail transfers. Therefore it inserts its own sub-ontology, based on CRoCoOn, via the Management Service. Assuming that the image from the example above has been indexed by K-IMM, it registers at CRoCo for notification about changes of the CRoCoOn based context model regarding the following SPARQL request (cmail is the derived sub-ontology based on the activity:MailTransfer concepts of CRoCoOn[10]):

```
PREFIX rdf: <http://www.
w3.org/1999/02/22-rdf-syntax-ns#>
PREFIX cmail: <http://mmt.inf.tu-
dresden.de/crocoon/context-mail.owl#>
PREFIX upper: <http://mmt.inf.tu-
dresden.de/crocoon/context-upper.
owl#>

SELECT ?mail ?property ?value WHERE {
   ?mail rdf:type cmail:Email.
```

Box 1.

```
<rdf:RDF
  xmlns:rdf="http://www.w3.org/1999/02/22-rdf-syntax-ns#"
  xmlns:document="http://mmt.inf.tu-dresden.de/crocoon/context-document.owl#"
  xmlns:activity="http://mmt.inf.tu-dresden.de/crocoon/context-activity.owl#"
  xmlns:upper="http://mmt.inf.tu-dresden.de/crocoon/context-upper.owl#"...
  xml:base="http://mmt.inf.tu-dresden.de/crocoon/consistent-context">
<activity:MailTransfer rdf:ID="Transfer_238">
  <activity:transfers>
    <document:EMail rdf:ID="Mail_45">
      <document:hasAttachment rdf:resource="#Image_18"/>
      <!-- information about subject, addressee, sender,... -->
    </document:EMail>
  </activity:transfers>
... <!-- information about time, tool,... -->
</activity:MailTransfer>
<document:DigitalImage rdf:ID="Image_18">
  <upper:uniqueID>d07149922d9f84c097f7ccf6ed5c7b658c4229d0
  </upper:uniqueID>
  <document:fileName>landschaft.jpg</document:fileName>
</document:DigitalImage>
...
</rdf:RDF>
```

```
  ?mail cmail:hasAttachment ?doc.
  ?doc upper:uniqueID "d07149922d9f-
84c097f7ccf6ed5c7b658c4229d0".
  ?mail ?property ?value.
}
```

Being notified and provided with information about the event, K-IMM processes the result using the document's transmission information to extend the existing semantic information about the document, stored within the K-IMM System.

Adaptive Co-Browsing Applications

Co-browsing is a collaborative extension of traditional web browsing. It allows for synchronous view and interaction with web pages between multiple users and includes means for collabora-

tion and mutual awareness. Therefore, it can be used for various application scenarios such as online discussions, remote presentations, and collaborative, i. e., guided shopping. The recent development of the Web towards a software platform has further pushed the need for such tools, e. g., for professional, web-based consulting and support, but it also poses some serious problems. Time- and location-independent access to the Web implicates that applications are used in extremely different contexts, so that the "one-size-fits-all"-approach of traditional web applications does no longer meet today's requirements. Even more, co-browsing can not simply follow the WYSIWIS ("What You See Is What I See") paradigm (Greenberg & Roseman, 1996), because it fails in typical, highly heterogeneous scenarios with different browsers, screen sizes and application-specific roles involved. Therefore, a co-browsing system needs to provide a common ground for all participants by adapting the shared view to the context of single participants as well as the whole group.

While traditional Adaptive Hypermedia approaches include their own context modeling algorithms, this is no longer appropriate taking into account a rising amount and complexity of context data. An adaptive web system needs access to diverse contextual information it can not necessarily sensor itself. Examples include the users' location (provided by a GPS sensor), their contacts (provided by a web-based CRM software) and topics they are interested in or currently work on (provided by their email client installation). In this regard, availabiliy and interoperability – esp. of context data from different applications – becomes a key requirement for a reasonable, context-aware web experience. Hence, an independent, cross-application context management system is needed.

To support co-browsing scenarios with CROCO, we developed the domain profile *CoCAB* (*Context-Aware Co-Browsing*) and a corresponding model containing co-browsing-specific concepts, some of which are shown in Figure 6 and extend CRO-COON. As an example, it allows us to model a user's

"SystemProfile" representing his/her hard- and software, e. g., his/her browser ("WebBrowserInstallation"), and that he/she is co-browsing within a "CoCAB-Session". These sessions represent the group context of all its members and may contain information on their lowest common denominator (e. g., regarding end device capabilities) as well as higher-level information that directly results from the combination of all users' parameters (e. g., that "all participants of a session are project members"), either by properties or relationships to such concepts.

In the VCS[11] project we developed a co-browsing platform which uses CROCO as a context modeling and storage service. The architecture of the VCS platform is presented in detail by Niederhausen et al. (2010). Therein, server-side components of VCS act as context providers and consumers of CROCO, which handles user-specific context data and infers additional context data like the "lowest common denominator" explained above. Furthermore, it allows for using context data from external providers in VCS, such as a CRM client providing information on the project membership of certain users as in the example above. The *Adaptation Engine* – a DOM-based adaptation pipeline in VCS – represents a context consumer that requests contextual information

Figure 6. Part of the concepts and relations modeled for the co-browsing scenario

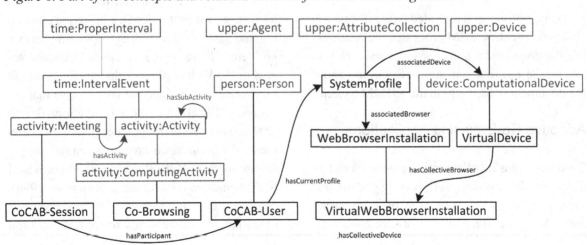

from CroCo for inclusion into the adaptation process. Thus, the views of co-browsing participants are adapted based on the contextual data modeled with CroCo so that they have a common ground. If, for example, all members of a co-browsing session are members of the same project and this is modeled as a shared (group) property, it can result in the inclusion of confidential project information into the shared content.

As can be seen, VCS benefits from using CroCo for a number of reasons. The complex and costly tasks of context management, reasoning, and consolidation are separated from the VCS system, whose functionality focuses on the efficient and error-prone co-browsing support. In contrast to an interal solution, CroCo can provide a larger number of context information provided by heterogeneous, distributed providers, and more sophisticated reasoning mechanisms at low cost.

Context-Aware User Interface Mashups

In recent years, the so-called *programmable web* has become a vibrant platform for a large number of applications. An enabling factor and basic foundation for these applications are *services* in the form of SOAP, REST, open Web APIs, or feeds. They provide data and application logic in a reusable and distributed fashion. As a result, new types of applications, especially *mashups* have gained momentum. They combine distributed resources, i. e., data and application logic from multiple services, in a new way to generate an added value.

While service-orientation has certainly simplified development on the lower layers, programming the user interface remains a complex and complicated task due to heterogeneous technologies to choose from, and the need to support heterogeneous user, usage and device contexts, as pointed out above. There exist several mashup authoring tools and platforms already. However, none has addressed flexibility and context-awareness of mashup user interfaces, yet. To introduce adap-

tive behavior, however, a corresponding platform needs access to high-quality context data. Ideally, it should be accessed and integrated following the same, service-oriented paradigm.

Within the CRUISe[12] project we extend the idea of service-orientation to the presentation layer of web applications. Therein, a mashup UI is composed from services providing reusable, configurable UI components. A primary goal of CRUISe is the dynamic, context-aware selection, configuration and exchange of these UI services to enable adaptation of the mashup UI at initialization and run time. Figure 7 gives an overview of the CRUISe infrastructure, which is presented in more detail in (Pietschmann et al., 2009). As can be seen, generated UI mashups utilize a specific *Runtime* which controls their presentation logic as well as the binding of back end services. The overall user interface is composed from generic UI components provided by so-called *User Interface Services* (UIS). At application initialization, the Runtime invokes the *Integration Service* to select, configure and integrate such components into a homogeneous, composite UI.

In CRUISe, CroCo is used at distinct deployment and runtime stages by different components. Both the Runtime and the Integration Service use CroCo as an external context management and storage solution as explained in the following.

The integration request issued by the Runtime usually contains characteristics and constraints for the UI component to be integrated. The *Integration Service* is responsible for finding UIS in a *UIS Registry* that provide components which match the given requirements. In the case of multiple eligible UIS, they are ranked by their accuracy of fit, the best one being invoked and the resulting, configured UI component returned to the Runtime. This selection and ranking process relies on context data provided by CroCo, so the Integration Service acts a Context Consumer. As an example, some UIS may require a certain plug in to be installed on the client, or some may be

Figure 7. Usage of CROCO in the CRUISe project

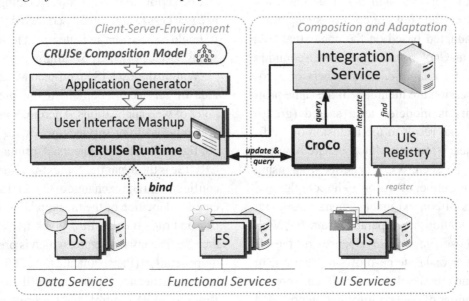

specific for mobile devices – information that is modeled and stored within CROCO.

All the information on the user and his/her device need to be monitored beforehand. This is done by the *Runtime*, which contains sensors, e. g., for device characteristics, that constantly publish information to CROCO. In this regard we could reuse some of the client-side sensors developed within the VCS project mentioned above. Nevertheless, certain information can only be provided by external monitors, such as a built-in GPS monitor on a device.

The *Runtime* also acts as a consumer of context data. Within a UI mashup there exist several components which are wired based on the composition model already mentioned. Besides UI, logic and service components, *Context Components* are part of the mashup. They either sensor contextual data directly, or they request it from CROCO. One could, for example, request a user's current location from CROCO (published there by a GPS sensor) and send it as input for a Google Map. Furthermore, we are currently working on runtime adaptation mechanisms, e. g., layout, UI component configuration and exchange, based on certain rules. Therefore, we plan to use CROCO's

callback mechanism to be notified of relevant context changes.

As with previous approaches, CRUISe benefits from outsourcing the costly task of context management, validation and consolidation to an external service. Application composition and integration are ensured by the system – independently from aspects of context modeling. Context data can be included into the service selection and configuration process by consequently integrating CROCO in a service-oriented manner. The reason for this can be seen in the distributed character of the CRUISe infrastructure. As different components provide or access contextual data, it is favorable to externalize context management to a dedicated service. Moreover, this allows unforeseen providers, e. g., sensors from other context frameworks, to be used with CRUISe without any changes to the overall architecture.

CONCLUSION

In this article we have presented design and implementation of an ontology-based, cross-application and domain-independent context management service called CʀᴏCᴏ. It handles arbitrary context data which is supplied by context providers and requested by context consumers via service interfaces. In contrast to existing solutions, CʀᴏCᴏ allows for the cross-application exchange of context data with the help of so called *Domain Profiles* and further separates the modeling and management process from context-aware applications themselves. We did validate the practicability of our approach by using it successfully within three "orthogonal" application scenarios, namely personal multimedia document management, adaptive co-browsing and the context-aware composition of user interface mashups.

In the future we will concentrate on the development of additional profiles for different domains. Moreover, we are interested in improving the context history, e. g., by realizing a more sophisticated logger or by integrating mechanisms to predict future context changes as proposed by Mayrhofer (2004). Another challenging task is the extension of security and privacy mechanisms in CʀᴏCᴏ to provide a more fine-grained access control to contextual data.

ACKNOWLEDGMENT

The CRUISe project is funded by the German Federal Ministry of Education and Research (BMBF) under promotional reference number 01IS08034-C. The VCS project was funded with means of the European Regional Development Fund 2000-2006 and by the Free State of Saxony.

REFERENCES

Baldauf, M., Dustar, S., & Rosenberg, F. (2007). A Survey on Context-Aware Systems. *Intl. Journal of Ad Hoc and Ubiquitous Computing, 2*(4), 263–277. doi:10.1504/IJAHUC.2007.014070

Bardram, J. E. (2005). The Java Context Awareness Framework (JCAF). In *Proceedings of the 3rd intl. conf. on pervasive computing.*

Bonino da Silva Santos, L. O., Wijnen, R. P.-v., & Vink, P. (2007, November). A Service-Oriented Middleware for Context-Aware Applications. In *Proceedings of the 5th international workshop on middleware for pervasive and ad-hoc computing (mpac 2007),* Newport Beach, CA (pp. 37-42). New York: ACM. Retrieved from http://eprints. eemcs.utwente.nl/11446/.

Chen, G., & Kotz, D. (2000, November). *A Survey of Context-Aware Mobile Computing Research* (Tech. Rep. No. TR2000-381). Hanover, NH: Dartmouth College, Dept. of Computer Science.

Chen, H., Finin, T., & Joshi, A. (2003). An Ontology for Context-Aware Pervasive Computing Environments. In *Proceedigns of the Workshop on ontologies and distributed systems (ijcai-2003).*

Chen, H., Perich, F., Finin, T., & Joshi, A. (2004). SOUPA: Standard Ontology for Ubiquitous and Pervasive Applications. In *Proceedings of the Intl. conf. on mobile and ubiquitous systems: Networking and services.*

da Rocha, R. C. A., Endler, M., & de Siqueira, T. S. (2008). Middleware for ubiquitous context-awareness. In *Proceedings of the 6th international workshop on middleware for pervasive and ad-hoc computing (Mpac '08)* (pp. 43-48). New York: ACM.

Ejigu, D., Scuturici, M., & Brunie, L. (2008). Hybrid Approach to Collaborative Context-Aware Service Platform for Pervasive Computing. *JCP, 3*(1), 40–50. doi:10.4304/jcp.3.1.40-50

Euzenat, J., Pierson, J., & Ramparany, F. (2008). Dynamic context management for pervasive applications. *The Knowledge Engineering Review, 23*(1), 21–49. doi:10.1017/S0269888907001269

Floréen, P., Przybilski, M., Nurmi, P., Koolwaaij, J., Tarlano, A., & Wagner, M. (2005). Towards a Context Management Framework for MobiLife. In *Proceedings of the ist summit*.

Greenberg, S., & Roseman, M. (1996). GroupWeb: A WWW Browser as Real Time Groupware. In *Proceedings of the Conference companion on human factors in computing systems (Chi96)* (pp. 271-272). New York: ACM.

Gu, T., Pung, H. K., & Zhang, D. Q. (2005). A Service-Oriented Middleware for Building Context-Aware Services. *Journal of Network and Computer Applications*, *28*(1), 1–18. doi:10.1016/j.jnca.2004.06.002

Hinz, M., Pietschmann, S., & Fiala, Z. (2007). A Framework for Context Modeling in Adaptive Web Applications. *IADIS Intl. Journal of WWW/Internet, 5*.

Kernchen, R., Bonnefoy, D., Battestini, A., Mrohs, B., Wagner, M., & Klemettinen, M. (2006, June). Context-Awareness in MobiLife. In *Proceedings of the 15th ist mobile summit,* Mykonos, Greece.

Mayrhofer, R. (2004). *An Architecture for Context Prediction*. Unpublished doctoral dissertation, Johannes Kepler University of Linz, Austria.

Mitschick, A., Nagel, R., & Meißner, K. (2008). Semantic Metadata Instantiation and Consolidation within an Ontology-based Multimedia Document Management System. In *Proceedings of the Int. Workshop on Semantic Metadata Management and Applications (ESWC 2008),* Tenerife, Spain.

Niederhausen, M., Pietschmann, S., Ruch, T., & Meißner, K. (2009). *Web-Based Support By Thin-Client Co-Browsing*. Berlin: Springer.

Niederhausen, M., Pietschmann, S., Ruch, T., & Meißner, K. (2010, April). Emergent Web Intelligence: Advanced Semantic Technologies. In Badr, Y., Chbeir, R., Abraham, A., & Hassanien, A. E. (Eds.), *Web-Based Support By Thin-Client Co-Browsing* (*Vol. XVI*). Berlin: Springer.

Pietschmann, S., Niederhausen, M., Ruch, T., Wilkowski, R., & Richter, J. (2007). Instant Collaborative Web-Browsing with VCS. In *Proceedings of the "virtuelle organisationen und neue medien" (geneme 2007)*.

Pietschmann, S., Voigt, M., Rümpel, A., & Meißner, K. (2009, June). CRUISe: Composition of Rich User Interface Services. In M. Gaedke, M. Grossniklaus, & O. Díaz (Eds.), *Proceedings of the 9th intl. conf. on web engineering (icwe 2009),* San Sebastian, Spain (pp. 473-476). Berlin: Springer Verlag.

Power, R., O'Sullivan, D., Conlan, O., Lewis, D., & Wade, V. (2004). Utilizing Context in Adaptive Information Services for Pervasive Computing Environments. In *Proceedings of the pervasive web services and contex aware computing workshop (ah'2004)*.

Prud'hommeaux, E., & Seaborne, A. (2008). *SPARQL Query Language for RDF* (W3C Recommendation). Retrieved from http://www.w3.org/TR/rdf-sparql-query/

Roussaki, I., Strimpakou, M., Pils, C., Kalatzis, N., & Anagnostou, M. (2006). Hybrid Context Modeling: A Location-Based Scheme Using Ontologies. In *Proceedings of the 4th annual iee intl. conf. on pervasive computing and communications workshop*.

Schmidt, A. (2006). The Challenges of Imperfection and Time-Dependence. In *Proceedings of odbase 2006, on the move federated conferences (otm)*. Ontology-Based User Context Management.

Strang, T., & Linnhoff-Popien, C. (2004). A Context Modeling Survey. In *Proceedings of the Workshop on advanced context modeling, reasoning and management - 6th intl. conf. on ubiquitous computing*.

Zhou, Y., Pan, J., Ma, X., Luo, B., Tao, X., & Lu, J. (2007). Applying ontology in architecture-based self-management applications. In Cho, Y., Wainwright, R. L., Haddad, H., Shin, S. Y., & Koo, Y. W. (Eds.), *Sac* (pp. 97–103). New York: ACM.

ENDNOTES

[1]   http://www.mobiubiq.org/

[2]   http://mlab.taik.fi/urbanmediator/

[3]   http://www.hitech-projects.com/euprojects/amigo/

[4]   The according OWL files can be found at http://mmt.inf.tu-dresden.de/crocoon

[5]   http://proton.semanticweb.org/

[6]   http://www.w3.org/TR/owl-time/

[7]   http://jena.sourceforge.net

[8]   http://mmt.inf.tu-dresden.de/K-IMM/

[9]   http://www.mozilla.com/products/thunderbird

[10]   the according domain ontology can also be found at http://mmt.inf.tu-dresden.de/crocoon

[11]   http://mmt.inf.tu-dresden.de/VCS/

[12]   http://mmt.inf.tu-dresden.de/cruise/

This work was previously published in International Journal of Semantic Web and Information Systems, Volume 6, Issue 1, edited by Amit P. Sheth, pp. 39-54, copyright 2010 by IGI Publishing (an imprint of IGI Global).

Section 2
Annotation, Mappings and Tools

Chapter 4
Files are Siles:
Extending File Systems with Semantic Annotations

Bernhard Schandl
University of Vienna, Austria

Bernhard Haslhofer
University of Vienna, Austria

ABSTRACT

With the increasing storage capacity of personal computing devices, the problems of information overload and information fragmentation are apparent on users' desktops. For the Web, semantic technologies solve this problem by adding a machine-interpretable information layer on top of existing resources. It has been shown that the application of these technologies to desktop environments is helpful for end users. However, certain characteristics of the Semantic Web architecture that are commonly accepted in the Web context are not desirable for desktops. To overcome these limitations, the authors propose the sile model, which combines characteristics of the Semantic Web and file systems. This model is a conceptual foundation for the Semantic Desktop and serves as underlying infrastructure on which applications and further services can be built. The authors present one service, a virtual file system based on siles, which allows users to semantically annotate files and directories and keeps full compatibility to traditional hierarchical file systems. The authors also discuss how Semantic Web vocabularies can be applied for meaningful annotation of files and present a prototypical implementation of the model and analyze the performance of typical access operations, both on the file system and metadata level.

INTRODUCTION

Large amounts of information are stored on personal desktops. We use our personal computing devices—both mobile and stationary—to communicate, to write documents, to organize multimedia content, to search for and retrieve information, and much more. With the increasing computing and storage power of such devices, we face the problem of *information overload*: the amount of data we generate and consume is permanently increasing, and because of the availability of cheap storage space, each and every bit of information

DOI: 10.4018/978-1-4666-0185-7.ch004

is stored. Another problem is even more prevalent on the desktop than on the Web: *information fragmentation*. Data of different kinds are stored in heterogeneous silos, and—contrary to the Web, where hyperlinks can be defined between documents and across site boundaries—there exist only limited means to define and retrieve relationships between different desktop resources. In the best case such relationships can be represented using additional infrastructure (e.g., relational databases or specific applications), but these are usually not tightly integrated with file systems.

The Semantic Web aims to deal with the problems mentioned before by adding a layer on top of the existing Web infrastructure, wherein descriptions about web resources are expressed using the Resource Description Framework (RDF) using commonly accepted vocabularies or ontologies. This allows machines to interpret the published data and thus helps end users to find information more efficiently. A large number of data sets[1] and vocabularies[2] have already been published and form a solid data corpus that can be indexed by (semantic) search engines and serves as foundation for applications.

Recent research in the field of the Semantic Desktop (Blunschi et al., 2007; Groza et al., 2007; Karger, 2007) has shown that a number of features provided by Semantic Web technologies are also suitable for the problem of information management on the desktop; especially, the provision of unified identifiers, the ability to represent data in an application-independent generic format, the flexibility to describe resources using formalized vocabularies, and the possibility to reason over these descriptions. It has also been shown (Sauermann & Heim, 2008; Franz et al., 2009) that the inclusion of semantic technologies on the desktop can significantly improve the user's perceived quality of personal information management, especially when they are applied during a longer time period.

However, there exist some significant conceptual differences between the Web and the desktop. First, in contrast to the World Wide Web, the desktop already has a well-established organization metaphor for data: *file systems*, which have been in use for decades. In consequence, the vast majority of personal information are stored in files, which are organized using hierarchical, labeled collections (*folders* or *directories*) or, to a far more limited extent, using metadata attached to or encoded within files. Therefore it is crucial for the Semantic Desktop to smoothly integrate with file systems in a way that allows for the annotation of files without breaking the behavior of existing desktop applications. A second major difference is the handling of broken links. While appearing and disappearing web resources are—to a certain extent—accepted on the Web, users rightfully expect their data on the desktop to remain consistent over time.

Since the RDF data model exposes a number of shortcomings that may cause problems for an efficient implementation of the Semantic Desktop, we propose the *sile model*, a data model that acts as an intermediate and integrative layer between file systems and Semantic Web technologies. This model allows users and applications to annotate and inter-relate file-like desktop resources. It is designed as an infrastructure on which applications and services can be built. One example of such a service, a virtual file system, is presented in this paper. Through this virtual file representation, the sile model can be used as a hierarchical file system and thus maintains full backwards-compatibility to existing systems and applications.

The sile model has been designed to be interoperable with vocabularies from the Semantic Web in order to establish a unified, homogeneous data space that encompasses the desktop and the Web. It enables tools and applications to operate on data both locally and globally, and data can be seamlessly exchanged between these two worlds. Hence we propose to use Web vocabularies for data representation wherever possible, and we support this requirement by using URIs—which may refer to Semantic Web resources—as identifiers for all annotations in our data model.

After an analysis on related work in the field of semantic file systems and Semantic Desktop technologies, this paper discusses the issues that arise when file systems and semantic technologies are integrated and presents the sile model as a data abstraction layer for the desktop. It discusses how the sile model can be used in applications, and proposes a set of already existing Semantic Web vocabularies for the annotation of desktop data. Finally, a prototypical implementation is presented, which has been evaluated under the assumption of realistic amounts of data.

Related Work

For a long time, file systems have been an interesting application field for metadata. The drawbacks and deficiencies of hierarchical file systems have been identified and described in various works (Boardman, 2001; Schandl & King, 2006; Sechrest & McClennen, 1992, Wills et al., 1995), which has lead to research and industry effort that aimed at integrating hierarchical file systems with metadata and semantic annotations. In this respect, we can observe two development lines: on the one hand, hierarchical file systems that can be found as part of common operating systems have been extended with support for file annotations and descriptions. On the other hand, a new class of file systems have been developed, which reduce the prominence of directory hierarchies in favor of a more metadata-centric approach. These systems often do not rely on a physically existing hierarchy, but instead virtually emulate it based on file annotations.

Extensions to Hierarchical File Systems. Originally, hierarchical file systems did not provide mechanisms to attach user- or application-defined metadata to files. Directory and file names were the only existing organization metaphor, and at most a limited pre-defined set of metadata attributes (such as date of creation and last update) was maintained. However, it has been recognized that a strict tree-based structure is not always appropriate for file management, and hence several mechanisms were introduced that allow files to appear in more than one directory, including *hard links* or *symbolic links*. While links solve a number of file categorization problems, they do not allow to further describe file characteristics in a structured manner, or to bilaterally relate files.

Modern file systems like *NTFS*, *HFS*, or *ext3* provide—in addition to directory hierarchies and links—support for different kinds of metadata. We can roughly distinguish between systems that provide *file forks*, which allow for storing additional content in separate data areas alongside the file content, and *file attributes*, which provide the means to attach structured name/value pairs to files. Table 1 gives an overview of modern file systems and the annotation features they support[3]. While file forks and file attributes provide sufficient means to attach meaningful metadata to files, they are still not expressive enough to express relationships between files in a stable and consistent manner, or to assign predefined types (classes, categories) to files. Works in this area are rooted in research on object-oriented data bases (e.g., Carey et al., 1986) and would have been integrated into WinFS (Grimes, 2004) whose development however halted in 2006.

Metadata-centric (Virtual) File Systems. Despite the support for file metadata provided by modern hierarchical file systems, hierarchical directory structures are still accentuated as the primary mechanism for file organization. A number of alternative approaches were proposed that raise the role of file metadata as the main file access method. Table 1 gives an overview on their most important features.

The Semantic File System (Gifford et al., 1991) uses structured name/value pairs, which are extracted from analyzing file contents, to establish a virtual directory hierarchy. The elements of a directory path represent a conjunction of search criteria. Gifford's system is, however, read-only since attribute values are derived only from extracting file features; support for write

Table 1. Comparison of metadata support and access mechanisms in hierarchical file systems and metadata-centric file systems

	Hard / Symbolic Links	Tags / Keywords	Attributes	Orthogonal Categories	Internal Relationships	External Relationships	Multiple Streams / Forks	Full Read and Write Support		Virtual File Hierarchy	API	Structured Query Language
FAT								✓		n/a		
NTFS	✓		✓				✓	✓		n/a	✓	
HFS	✓		✓				✓	✓		n/a	✓	
ext3 / ext4	✓		✓					✓		n/a	✓	
WinFS		✓	✓	✓	✓			✓		✓	✓	✓
SFS	✓		✓							✓		✓
AttrFS	✓	✓	✓					✓		✓		✓
Presto			✓			✓				✓	✓	✓
LISFS			✓	✓						✓		✓
TagFS	✓	✓	✓					✓		✓	✓	✓
libferris			✓					✓		✓	✓	✓
LiFS	✓		✓		✓		✓	✓		✓	✓	✓
SileFS	✓	✓	✓	✓	✓	✓		✓		✓	✓	✓

operations was introduced later in AttrFS (Wills et al., 1995). Presto (Dourish et al., 1999) follows a similar path by providing a virtual hierarchical view on annotated files. LISFS (Padioleau et al., 2006) extends the attribute-based virtual file system approach by interpreting paths as Boolean formulas over the file space. TagFS (Bloehdorn et al., 2006), which is built on a generic framework for semantic file systems, uses tags (keywords) instead of structured name/value pairs to simulate a directory hierarchy. libferris (Martin, 2006) focuses on the integration of different resources (like XML documents, plain files, or running applications) and represents them as a single unified virtual hierarchical file system; additional user-defined annotations are stored in a designated RDF store that is embedded in the platform. Finally, LiFS (Ames et al., 2006) represents relationships between files as virtual directories alongside the actual files, an approach also followed by LODFS (Schandl, 2009b) where remote Linked Open Data

sources (i.e., plain RDF graphs) are represented as virtual file systems.

The main problem with approaches that represent file metadata in the form of virtual directories is that they break some core characteristics of hierarchical file systems; however many file-based applications and services are implemented under the assumption of these characteristics. For instance, in a hierarchical file system an application can safely assume that a file is stored at exactly one location, and that different paths refer to different files (with the exception of symbolic or hard links): access in a hierarchical file system is based on *location*, not on *description*. If this assumption does not hold (as it is in the case of metadata-centric virtual file systems), software that crawls a file system (e.g., search engines) may run into problems because they are not able to determine whether two files are actually the same.

Moreover, virtual directory hierarchies do not provide *stable references* to external systems. In hierarchical file systems, the primary mechanism to refer to a file is its full path. It is clear for users and applications that file references become invalid if a file is moved or renamed. However, if the full path of a file contains metadata attributes (which, for instance, may be derived from the file contents or may reflect the user's opinion, which may change over time) these references become invalid when the file's metadata change; essentially this means that a modification of a file's content may cause its references to break.

Another problem with metadata-based virtual directory hierarchies is that in many cases the semantics of write operations is undefined. Consider, for instance, a virtual directory /(proj1,proj2,proj3) that contains files that are tagged with proj1, proj2, or proj3, or a combination thereof (Wills et al., 1995). While such virtual directories are helpful for search and retrieval, it is unclear how a file that is written into such a directory should be annotated. This restriction significantly reduces the benefit, convenience, and practical applicability of purely annotation-based virtual file systems.

Finally, it is unclear what the actual target audience and practical use cases of metadata-centric virtual file systems are. For applications that are based on hierarchical file systems, metadata-centric virtual directories are opaque since they do not understand the annotations' semantics, and therefore bring no additional benefit. For metadata-aware applications, the employment of a dedicated annotation model and an associated structured query language seems to be more practical. For end users, most approaches assume the usage of a command line to enter paths that represent search queries (usually via the cd and ls/dir commands). We doubt however that the typical end user will be sufficiently familiar with command line interfaces in order to efficiently work with this method: it requires one to memorize not only the required commands, but also the exact names of tags, attributes, and other annotations. Graphical, icon-based interfaces can be used in combination with virtual file systems although

these distinguish only between directories and files and are not aware of semantic file annotations. The formulation of more complex queries (as presented before) through graphical interfaces is often not possible at all; consequently the efficiency of navigation and browsing is reduced.

Semantic Desktop. The idea of the Semantic Desktop goes one major step further than semantic file systems do. The idea of this approach is not only to enrich file systems with expressive annotations, but also to integrate the entire information sphere of a user into a semantic network (Decker & Frank, 2004; Sauermann et al., 2005), which has the potential to significantly increase the quality of information work (Franz et al., 2009). This is accomplished either by providing services that maintain a layer of semantic descriptions that refer to actual resources like files, e-mails, and web pages, while users continue to work with their well-known applications, e.g., Nepomuk (Groza et al., 2007), Semex (Cai et al., 2005), or iMeMex (Blunschi et al., 2007), or by providing an integrated work environment that disbands the traditional application-centric paradigm of desktop computers in favor of a data- and annotation-centric work style, e.g., Haystack (Karger, 2007), DeepaMehta (Richter & Poelchau, 2008), or X-COSIM (Franz et al., 2007). As such, the Semantic Desktop can be considered as an orthogonal architecture that may embrace all kinds of storage mechanisms, including traditional as well as semantic file systems.

One significant outcome of Semantic Desktop research is the integration of semantic technologies into the *K Desktop Environment*[4] (KDE). An RDF database is now part of its standard distribution and enables the system-wide storage and retrieval of semantic annotations for files and other information items. References between the physical storage systems and the annotation store are maintained by using kernel notification services. Annotated files can be accessed transparently through virtual folders, which are supported by the system-provided dialogs for opening and

Table 2. Characteristics of user-driven, application-driven, and hidden file structures w.r.t. file and directory semantics

Characteristics	User-driven	Application-driven	Hidden
Application-defined semantics		✓	✓
Application-interpretable semantics		✓	✓
User-defined semantics	✓		
User-interpretable semantics	✓	✓	
Readable by applications	✓	✓	✓
Modifiable by applications		✓	✓
Readable by users	✓	✓	
Modifiable by users	✓		

saving files. However, this way of annotating files is restricted to tags that are derived from the names of virtual directories. More expressive annotations, like structured attributes or typed links, can only be accessed explicitly through the Nepomuk-KDE API. Although Nepomuk-KDE is not a semantic file system in the narrower sense, its increasing adoption by applications and users shows that there exists a significant need for more expressive file annotations.

Approaches in the field of the Semantic Desktop go far beyond the functionality and envisioned use cases of a metadata-enriched file system. However, semantically enriched file systems are highly complementary to semantic desktop approaches since they provide an integrated storage infrastructure for files and annotations without the need for additional synchronization mechanisms.

INTEGRATING FILE SYSTEMS AND RDF DESCRIPTIONS

The majority of personal information is stored within file systems, where we can observe three usage patterns. We denote the first one as *user-driven file structures*: a large number of applications do not use internal directory structures or file name conventions, but allow users to organize files in directories named and nested according to

their subjective needs. Examples for this group of applications include word processors, spreadsheet tools, or graphics suites. A second group establishes *application-driven file structures*, where directory hierarchies and files are managed entirely by applications, but still expose a certain meaning to end users. Examples of such applications are e-mail clients, which store email messages as files in a directory hierarchy and allow the user to manipulate these hierarchies through a dedicated interface, or media players, where the user has no influence on the handling of directories; here, the application uses file metadata (e.g., artist name or song title) as directory names. Typically, these applications do not operate on single files but on file collections, and interpret the directory hierarchies and file names in a semi-schematic manner. This pattern is also used for application-internal files that do not store user data; however the application requires certain files to be found in certain locations in order to work correctly. A third group of applications do not expose the semantics of file structures to the user, but rather operate on continuous data corpora; examples for this group include calendar applications that store appointments in one large file, or database-driven applications. We denote the data structures of such applications as *hidden file structures*, because in the end even these data are stored in file systems, although not semantically organized by the file system's means. Table 2 summarizes characteristics of these three groups of structures w.r.t. their application- and user-related semantics.

For all three classes of applications it is desirable to make information accessible in a semantically meaningful, application-independent way. This has two main benefits: first, it makes it possible to interrelate objects from different sources, which otherwise form disjoint structures in one's personal information space (Boardman, 2001); and second, it extends the possibilities provided by file systems with respect to search and retrieval (Sauermann & Heim, 2008). All three classes of applications, as described before, could benefit from such integration: user-driven file structures could be extended by more powerful and non-hierarchical annotation mechanisms that are orthogonal to the physical identification of files, like tags and typed relationships. Application-driven file structures could be disbanded in favor of explicit semantic annotations that ideally adhere to open vocabularies and therefore are interpretable by external entities. Finally, the internals of hidden file structures could be revealed and hence be integrated with other information sources.

The Gap to RDF. The RDF data model can be used to identify information units (*resources*) and to describe these units and the relationships between them using subject-predicate-object triples. Its successful usage in the context of Linked Open Data (Bizer et al., 2007) indicates that it is sufficiently expressive for a large number of applications, ranging from statistical data via geo information to descriptions of multimedia content. Certain RDF characteristics, however, are problematic in the context of the desktop. First, RDF does not consider the actual *content* of information items. The relationship between a resource identifier (a URI) and the resource itself has been explicitly left out of the scope of the RDF specification, which states, "[...] no assumptions are made here about the nature of resources; 'resource' is treated here as synonymous with

'entity', i.e. as a generic term for anything in the universe of discourse" (cf. Hayes, 2004, Section 1.2). In the open Web environment, broken links and unavailable resources are likely to occur; solutions to maintain data quality are still an open research issue (Bizer et al., 2009). However, on the desktop, applications must be enabled to rely on a consistent view on content objects and their annotations at any time; hence this integrity must always be ensured.

Another potentially problematic aspect of RDF is the Open World Assumption. Since RDF has been designed for the Web, incomplete or unknown information is accepted by RDF-based tools and applications by design. Again, for the closed environment of the desktop, incomplete information is not desirable; here, the Open World Assumption hinders the efficient realization of certain features, e.g., negated queries. Consequently, recent approaches to Semantic Desktop information modeling (e.g., Sintek et al., 2007a) have restricted the interpretation of RDF data to closed-world semantics.

As a third problematic issue, the application of certain RDF language elements (in particular collections, blank nodes, and reification) is being discouraged both in the context of the Web (cf. Bizer et al., 2007, Section 2.2) and the desktop (cf. Sintek et al., 2007b, Section 2.3.2). These features significantly increase the complexity of RDF processing, as well as representing RDF in user interfaces (Muñoz et al., 2007; Schmedding et al., 2007), but expose a very lightweight semantics. Hence it is questionable whether these elements are useful in the context of the desktop, where end users have only limited knowledge about the characteristics of the underlying data structures, and the available computing power is limited in comparison to large-scale database servers.

Recent Semantic Desktop projects (e.g., Blunschi et al., 2007; Groza et al., 2007; Karger, 2007) add an RDF layer on top of existing desktop infrastructures and refer to the actual content representation using local URIs. These URIs are often minted based on the characteristics of the underlying system. A URI that refers to a file on the user's hard drive, for instance, could be file:///data/semdav/semdav_description.doc. Such URIs, however, are not suitable as permanent identifiers for files (Schandl & Popitsch, 2010): first, they are *unstable* since they become invalid when files are renamed, moved to different directories, or deleted. Consequently, synchronization mechanisms are needed that propagate modifications to the metadata layer; however often it is difficult to track such modifications accurately. In the worst case, when such propagation is not possible, references to files become broken. Furthermore, path-based URIs are not *globally valid*, as they can be resolved only relative to the local system's context. This aspect is problematic when files are exchanged across machines, since the URIs may be no longer valid. Also they introduce the danger of creating different files with equal URIs, causing name clashes.

In the following, we present an alternative modeling approach that aims to solve the problems described before: we consider an item's content and its annotations as integral components, which are always processed together. Instead of adding a semantic layer on top of existing file structures and relying on unstable identifiers based thereon, we inject semantic annotations and globally valid, permanent identifiers into the core of the data representation structure. On top of this model a virtual, file system-like representation of the data stored therein is presented, which can be seamlessly accessed by existing tools and applications.

The Sile Model

Siles (*Se*mantic f*iles*) can be regarded as combinations of files and semantic annotations. A sile is always identified by a globally unique URI and consists of a (binary) string of arbitrary *content*, as well as an arbitrary number of *annotations*. In the context of siles, URIs are not used as URLs: while in the Semantic Web it is recommended that

the URI of a resource is at the same time a URL that can be de-referenced in order to retrieve the resource's representation (cf. Figure 1a), this is not necessarily the case for siles. In our model, URIs are solely used for identification purposes, and the sile identifier, the content, and the associated annotations are integral parts of the sile, as depicted in Figure 1b.

The sile model distinguishes between four types of annotations, which cover a large share of annotation needs in the desktop domain: *tags*, which are plain strings; *categories*, which refer to entities with machine-processable semantic interpretation (e.g., classes from a controlled vocabulary); *attributes* in the form of typed name/value pairs; and *slinks* (semantic links), i.e., directed typed relationships between siles. The names of categories, attributes, and slinks are URIs, which allow for an unambiguous interpretation of their semantics; however the formalism used for this purpose is out of the scope of the sile model. A category annotation, for instance, may refer to an OWL ontology class as well as to a table within a relational database schema. Figure 1b depicts a number of siles and their associated annotations, whereas different shapes and colors are used to indicate different annotation types.

Formal Model. Let *LIT* denote the set of all *string literals* which are finite sequences of characters from a *literal alphabet* α, and B the set of all *content literals* which are finite sequences of characters from a *content alphabet* β. Further, let *URI* denote the set of all *Uniform Resource Identifiers*. Let T denote the set of all *tags*, $T \subseteq LIT$, let C denote the set of all *categories*, $C \subseteq URI$, let A denote the set of all *attributes*, $A = URI \times LIT \times URI$, and let L denote the set of all *slinks*, $L = URI \times URI$. Let *ANN* denote the set of annotations, $ANN = T \cup A \cup C \cup L$.

Let Σ denote the set of all siles in the universe of discourse. Using the vocabulary defined before we can write a sile $s \subset \Sigma$ as a six-tuple $s = (u_s, b_s, T_s, C_s, A_s, L_s)$. $u_s \subset URI$ denotes the URI that

Figure 1. (a) RDF model: URIs refer to actual content; (b) Sile model: integrated view on content and annotations

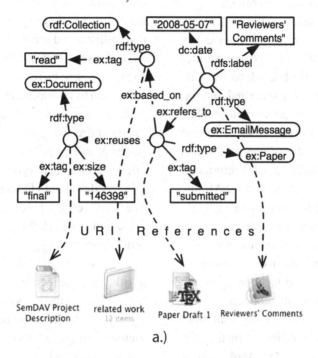

a.)

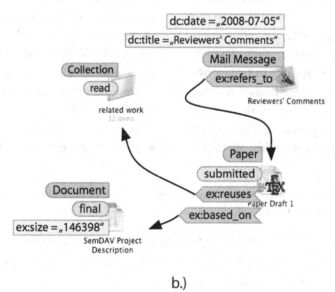

b.)

uniquely identifies sile s, $b_s \subset B \cup \bot$ denotes the sile's binary content, $T_s \subset T$ is the set of the sile's associated tags, $C_s \subset C$ is the set of the sile's associated categories, $A_s \subset A$ the set of the sile's

associated attributes, and $L_s \subset L$ is the set of the sile's associated slinks.

The sile model does not impose constraints on the structure or the nature of a sile's binary content. It neither defines rules that state how the content is to be interpreted, nor how annotations can be deduced by analyzing sile content.

Based on their annotations, siles can be accessed using operators from an abstract query algebra (Schandl, 2009a). This algebra provides annotation existence predicates, which indicate whether a given sile carries a specified annotation (e.g., $existsTag_\Gamma(s, t)$ returns whether sile s is annotated with tag t), as well as sile selection operators, which return sets of siles that fulfill certain criteria (e.g., $RelatedSiles_\Gamma(s)$ returns all siles that are related (linked) to sile s). All sile algebra operators are evaluated against a context Γ; for instance, a particular file system.

The sile model resembles characteristics from other data models, in particular from file systems and from the Semantic Web technology stack. Similar to files, it provides the concept of self-contained information units that carry content of unlimited length and undefined inner structure, but at the same time it avoids the problems of unstable references and the blending of identification and annotation by providing stable, globally unique identifiers for these information units. The sile model borrows from RDF the means to describe these information units using URI-based vocabularies, but it makes the semantics of these annotations more explicit by providing higher-level annotation concepts (tags, categories, attributes,

and slinks) instead of plain triples. Likewise it avoids aspects of RDF that are less frequently used, like blank nodes or reification, in favor of a simplified and more streamlined model.

Representing Directory Hierarchies. A basic file system can be represented without loss of information by an unordered tree having two types of nodes: directories and files. Directory nodes may have children, whereas file nodes are always leaf nodes. We map each node in the directory tree to a sile and represent its type by a category annotation (silefs:File or silefs:Directory $\subset C_s$, respectively). We reference an object's parent directory using a slink that refers to the parent object's URI (e.g., (silefs:parent, $U_{parent}) \subset L_s$).

By concatenating the labels of the nodes along a path, a unique identifier for each element (directory or file) of the file system can be constructed. However, when a path expression consists of many elements, traversal across a large fraction of the graph is required in order to locate the described file. To enable direct access to a file given its path, we additionally store the file's absolute path as a sile attribute (silefs:path, "/data/semdav/semdav-description.doc", xsd:string) $\subset A_s$). This leads to processing overhead when the file tree is modified, but significantly increases the performance of read operations. Figure 2 depicts a sile in its abstract notation. Here, the explicitly saved file

Figure 2. A file represented using the sile model. For the sake of readability we use CURIE notation (Birbeck & McCarron, 2009) to abbreviate URIs

```
s₁ =  (<urn:uuid:57207370-6880-11dd-ad8b-0800200c9a66>,
       "9j4AAQSkZJRgABAQEAYABgAAAoHBwgHBgoICAgLCgoLEYIx8l...",
       {"final","data","semdav"},{silefs:File},
       {(sile:creation-date, "2008-07-11T16:21:14", xsd:dateTime),
       (sile:update-date, "2008-07-11T17:32:02", xsd:dateTime),
       (sile:content-type, "application/msword", xsd:string),
       (sile:content-length, "146398", xsd:long),
       (silefs:path,"/data/semdav/description.doc", xsd:string)},
       {(dcterms:subject, <http://www.semdav.org>),
       (silefs:parent, <urn:uuid:60ad6a73-1b60-4553-9436-d09d395fc29c>)}
       )
```

path is also reflected by automatically generated tags, which are updated transparently when a file is created or moved.

Operations that involve a directory and its children (e.g., a directory listing) can be resolved by querying for silefs:parent relationships between siles. When a file or directory is renamed or moved, the steps to be taken depend on whether the file remains within its parent directory or not. In the former case, it is sufficient to update the sile's silefs:path attribute, while in the latter case the silefs:parent slink must additionally be updated to refer to the sile's new parent directory. However, the identity of this sile can be efficiently retrieved by querying for the directory sile's silefs:path attribute.

The representation of files using a graph-based model also enables us to represent hard or symbolic links by storing additional silefs:path attributes and silefs:parent relationships. The semantics of a link deletion can be simulated by checking whether a sile has more than one silefs:path attribute before deletion, and by only deleting the entire sile if it has only one such attribute. In the case of multiple silefs:path attributes, only the attribute and the silefs:parent slink are deleted.

We like to emphasize that, contrary to approaches that derive virtual directories from semantic file metadata (usually, tags or attributes), our approach uses *designated annotations* with well-defined names and semantics in order to explicitly represent a directory structure. Additional annotations can be derived from this information (e.g., the tags depicted in Figure 2). By doing so the danger of accidentally breaking file path references by changing file annotations is avoided. While our system in principle allows for metadata-based virtual directories, it would again lead to the undesired effects that common semantic file systems suffer from, as described before.

Annotating Files Using the Sile Model

Accessing Semantic Files. Using the mechanisms described in the previous section, we can now implement a common hierarchical file system that can be directly used by existing file-based applications. To read, write, and search for semantic annotations of files that are represented as siles, we have developed an Application Programming Interface (API) that is based on the formal specification of the sile data model as well as its associated query algebra. This API defines a type hierarchy for siles and annotations as well as corresponding access methods. To give the reader an idea, Figure 5 shows an excerpt of the class hierarchy for annotations, and Figure 3 shows a code example, which reproduces the

Figure 3. Sile API: write operations

```
// write data for one file
File docFile = new File("/data/semdav/semdav_description.doc");
docFile.write(...);
Sile docSile = SileFS.getSileForFile(docFile);
docSile.addAnnotation(SileFS.getCategory("nfo:PaginatedTextDocument"))
;
docSile.addAnnotation(SileFS.getTag("final"));

// write data for second file
File paperFile = new File("/data/papers/ijswis/paper.tex");
paperFile.write(...);
Sile paperSile = SileFS.getSileForFile(paperFile);
paperSile.addAnnotation(SileFS.getSlink("ex:based-on", docSile));
```

Figure 4. Sile API: search operations

```
// search all files tagged with "final" and linked to paperSile
Filter f1 = new TagFilter("final");
Filter f2 = new SileSlinkFilter(paperSile);
File[] results = SileFS.searchSiles(new AndFilter(f1, f2)).asFiles();
```

Figure 5. Sile API: annotation types

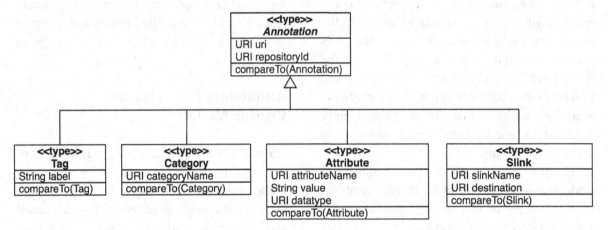

annotations depicted in Figure 1b: a category and a tag are attached to a file. Later, the application can easily retrieve the object by searching for these annotations by using a conjunctive filter, as shown in Figure 4.

The goal of this API is to allow application developers to easily integrate semantic annotations into their code. Assuming that files are stored on a sile-based virtual file system, one can retrieve the sile that represents a certain file by a single API call, and access or manipulate this sile's annotations. Additionally, the API allows an application to retrieve siles that match certain criteria and to determine the corresponding file paths. A word processing application, for instance, could be extended so that it stores metadata about created documents (e.g., author and title) as sile attributes, or a search operation could be used to retrieve files that are associated with a certain project.

We believe that our API, which tightly integrates files and semantic annotations, has the potential to significantly increase the proliferation of semantic technologies on the desktop. As described before, the majority of desktop applications operate directly on the file system. By transferring existing file hierarchies to a virtual, sile-based file system and by integrating semantic annotations into applications, the desktop can be extended using semantic technology while avoiding the need for fundamental architecture changes for single applications or entire operating systems.

Deriving Semantic Annotations for Files. Since siles are exposed as a virtual file system that emulates the behavior of a common hierarchical file system, they can be accessed by legacy applications and tools (e.g., file browsers) without changing any code. Other virtual file system views based on sile annotations (e.g., tags) can be additionally instantiated and therefore exposed to applications, under consideration of the problems imposed by this approach. Structured annotations can be extracted automatically from any file by applying content- or interaction-based feature extraction (e.g., Okoli & Schandl, 2009). Only applications that explicitly access file annotations and therefore follow their semantics, which may be defined e.g., using a formal schema, must be adapted to use the sile API.

We have shown in the previous section that the API for creating and retrieving sile annotations is easy to learn and straightforward to use. The question still remains why a developer of an application should make use of this API to store meaningful metadata associated to files. From the authors' perspective, the need for file metadata is obvious: the usage of desktop search engines, which usually provide mechanisms to index and retrieve structured file annotations, is very common. In the majority of cases these search engines rely on extraction plug-ins, which must be customized to file formats in order to extract semantically meaningful information for indexing.

Hence we can observe an encoding/decoding pattern: potentially relevant file metadata are written and encoded into file contents, and must later be decoded by metadata extractors for retrieval purposes, which introduces the danger of information loss. The sile model, its virtual file system representation, and its API close this gap by providing the infrastructure for storing, maintaining, and retrieving annotations in a format- and platform-independent manner. It abstracts over concrete metadata representation mechanisms that can be found in modern file systems, and it integrates with Semantic Web technologies. Thus, it can be considered as a step towards improved metadata interoperability in the domains of personal and social information management.

For all usage patterns outlined before, a semantically-enriched file system can bring significant benefit. User-driven file structures can be enriched (or even entirely replaced) by tagging structures, which avoid several problems of strictly hierarchical organization structures. Richer user interfaces to browse and search files can be realized using a metadata-centric approach, e.g., faceted browsing or tag clouds, while the traditional, well-known tree-based navigation metaphor can still be emulated. The same applies to application-driven and hidden file structures, which are anyway accompanied with application-specific metadata structures. By making hidden metadata explicit, but at the same time disassociating them from physical storage attributes, a flexible metadata-centric information space can be established. Since the different types of information can be separated orthogonally (e.g., by using sile category annotations) this space may encompass the entire information sphere of a user, which still can be efficiently managed due to its rich associated metadata.

Vocabularies for Desktop Data. Since the sile model uses URIs to identify annotations, it is obvious to reuse existing vocabularies and ontologies from the Semantic Web for interoperability purposes. Although—due to the open design of the sile model—applications may freely define terms, the usage of shared and commonly accepted vocabularies is strongly recommended. Shared vocabularies enable other applications—either on the same machine, or when siles are exchanged across systems—to interpret annotations in a semantically correct way. To establish that kind of interoperability, we propose the following strategy for sile annotation vocabularies:

1. Whenever possible, use terms taken from widely used vocabularies that are published on the Web in a structured, machine-readable format, i.e., RDFS or OWL.

2. If there is no such term that reflects the required semantics, reuse a semantically broader term by establishing e.g., an rdfs:subPropertyOf relationship, refine its semantics for the target application context within a new namespace, and publish it on the Web. This well-known procedure originating from the metadata area (Heery & Patel, 2000) allows one to create context-bound application profiles with clear and more specific semantic definitions.

3. If (1) and (2) are not feasible, create a suitable vocabulary and publish it on the Web in order to make it accessible also for other users and applications.

There already exist a number of widely used vocabularies, many of which are applicable for desktop data. Semantic search engines, such as Sindice (Oren et al., 2008) and Swoogle (Ding et al., 2004), or index sites for the Semantic Web5 are good starting points to search for existing vocabularies. Table 3 shows a representative set of Semantic Web vocabularies that are relevant for the desktop, grouped by their application domain. For each vocabulary we also indicate their base language as well as the number of concepts and properties they define.

Our analysis indicates that the Semantic Web already provides a large number of vocabularies, which cover a large share of the data we find on typical desktops. Many of the vocabularies included in this analysis are compact in terms of the number of classes and properties, and hence are relatively easy to understand and to implement. Moreover, a number of these vocabularies have been defined by re-using terms from other vocabularies. For instance, the Description of a Project (DOAP) vocabulary is based on Friend-of-a-Friend (FOAF) and therefore each application that understands FOAF is also enabled to interpret DOAP-based data to a certain extent.

The majority of the vocabularies presented in Table 3 are actually widely used, especially in the context of Linked Data (Bizer et al., 2009). Many data providers, both from scientific and commercial domains, make use of these vocabularies to expose data about millions of resources. Similarly, the NEPOMUK ontologies are already used by a

Table 3. Relevant Semantic Web vocabularies for the desktop

Vocabulary Name	Base	Concepts	Properties
General, Documents			
Dublin Core (DC)	RDFS	22	55
NEPOMUK Annotation Ontology (NAO)	RDFS	4	31
NEPOMUK File Ontology (NFO)	RDFS	47	60
Contacts, Communication			
Friend of a Friend (FOAF)	OWL	12	54
Semantically Interlinked Online Communities (SIOC)	OWL	11	53
NEPOMUK Contact Ontology (NCO)	RDFS	30	55
NEPOMUK Message Ontology (NMO)	RDFS	7	23
VCard Ontology	OWL	5	54
Calendar and Events, Project Management			
Description of a Project (DOAP)	RDFS	7	30
RDF Calendar Schema	OWL	14	48
NEPOMUK Calendar Ontology (NCAL)	RDFS	51	107
Location			
WGS84 Geo Positioning	RDFS	2	4
GeoNames Ontology	OWL	7	18
Multimedia			
Music Ontology	OWL	53	131

Figure 6. Virtual file system architecture

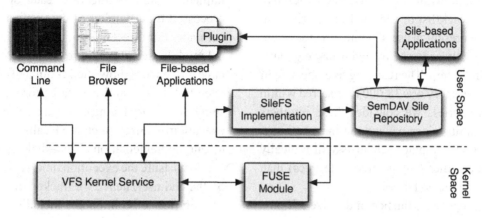

number of desktop applications that are built on top of the Nepomuk-KDE framework. Based on their concrete usage we can assume that they are suitable for their respective application domains.

Implementation

We have realized a sile-based file system on top of our SemDAV semantic repository[6], which implements the sile model and uses a combination of an RDF store (Jena, SDB, PostgreSQL) and plain files to persist siles and their annotations. It exposes the stored siles via a variety of protocols and interfaces (including XML-RPC, RMI, WebDAV, HTTP, and SPARQL). Additionally, siles and their annotations are exposed in a Linked Data-conforming way.

In addition to this repository implementation, we have developed a component that handles file system calls that are forwarded from the local machine's kernel and translates them to corresponding queries and operations on the sile model, according to the file system representation described before. To integrate the system with the local file system we have used the FUSE framework[7] and its Java binding FUSE-J[8]. FUSE defines a set of interfaces and data structures that describe files, their metadata structures, and operations thereon. Based on these frameworks we simulate a local file system that can be accessed

by applications and users as if it was a common file system; at the same time the files can also be annotated and queried through the sile API. Since all files in this virtual file system are persisted as siles in our repository and hence can be accessed only through the sile API or through the virtual file system, data consistency and completeness is ensured at all times. The architecture of this implementation is depicted in Figure 6.

Since file paths are represented as explicit sile annotations, it is straightforward to implement extensions or plug-ins for existing file-based applications: whenever an application operates on a file that is stored on a sile-backed file system, the corresponding sile can be easily retrieved, and vice versa.

Performance Evaluation

To evaluate the performance of our approach, we have analyzed the execution times of typical file system operations. To estimate a realistic amount of data, we crawled the home directories of our department's members, which includes scientific staff (7 persons) as well as technical and administrative staff (3 persons). We used only home directories in favor of scanning entire hard disks because personal data will be the target domain for a semantic file system, and there is little need to semantically annotate system- and application-internal file structures. We discarded files that were on a black list of files and directories that usually are present in users' home directories but are not directly accessed by end users; e.g.,.svn, desktop.ini, *.tmp. The resulting average size of the home directory was 38,000 files stored within 5,150 directories. We consider these numbers as upper limits, since we assume that the home directories of computer scientists will typically contain more files (e.g., source code trees) than those of average end users.

To estimate the influence of the size of home directories on our system's performance, we artificially created three test data sets, which are described in Table 4. To represent basic data about files and directories, nine triples per object were created. Note that this number does not include any additional descriptive triples (i.e., semantic annotations) since these were not considered in our performance evaluation. Our implementation also requires loading a set of core ontologies, which add another 700 triples to the database.

Virtual File System-Based Access. We have analyzed the runtime performance of typical file system access patterns: navigation between directories, listing of directory contents, deletion, moving, and renaming of files. We have carried out the experiments on a high-end consumer notebook (MacBook Pro, Core 2 Duo, with 2 GB RAM) running Mac OS X 10.5 and JVM 1.5. We have used the command shell (/bin/bash) to perform our measurements and used only standard commands (cd, ls, rm, and mv). Because of our implementation architecture, each operation is processed by a number of components that are not under our direct control (e.g., the FUSE kernel module; see also Figure 6. Hence we do not have influence on how shell commands are translated to file system driver calls; for instance, issuing a directory listing command (ls) causes the execution of four distinct FUSE calls being passed to our implementation. Nevertheless, our goal was to measure the execution time as experienced by the end user, hence we tracked the total processing time of commands, including overhead caused by the operating system and the FUSE kernel module.

The operations we have evaluated involve read-only access (directory navigation and directory listing) and read+write operations (deletion, moving, renaming). For the latter, the complexity of read and write operations differs: for a sile deletion, (*1*) the triples within the store that describe the object to be deleted have to be identified (read), and (*2*) these triples have to be removed from the store (write). Move and rename operations require in principle the same access operations, whereas a move across directories requires an additional read and write operation, namely the update of the relationship between the file and its parent directory. We did not evaluate the performance of operations that affect multiple siles (e.g., moving an entire file system subtree) since we are aware of the fact that the current modeling approach does not support such operations in a satisfying way. We plan to work on a more efficient support for

Table 4. Datasets for performance evaluation

Dataset #	1	2	3
Hierarchy Depth	2	3	4
Average no. of sub-directories per directory	5	6	7
Average no. of files per directory	12	15	15
Total number of siles (directories and files)	403	4,144	44,816
Total number of RDF triples	3,626	37,295	403,343
Total number of RDF triples incl. ontologies	4,361	38,030	404,078

such operations in the future. Further, we did not evaluate the performance of actual read and write operations on the file content: the modifications to metadata caused by these actions are comparable to those of a move operation (i.e., an update of the content-length and update-time properties), and the actual file content is provided by the underlying (physical) file system and hence is out of the scope of our performance measurements.

For our experiments, we executed every operation 10 times in random order, and repeated the entire experiment five times. The results of our experiments are depicted in Table 5. For the first two datasets (approx. 400 and 4,000 siles) we can observe very low execution times, which allow for uninterrupted interactive work with virtual file systems. For a dataset consisting of approx. 40,000 siles, the response times for simple operations (change directory, remove file) are still in a reasonable range, and even the operations that involve multiple, complex queries (directory listing, moving) can be performed in a time that is comparable to web browsing and acceptable for interactive use.

These results indicate that even a prototypical implementation of a virtual file system, based on our data model and built using an off-the-shelf RDF triple store without further optimization, provides acceptable performance for everyday usage on a typical consumer machine. A semantic file system based on a more efficient triple store that is better integrated into the operating system could achieve even better performance, since this would allow us to circumvent the rather inefficient architecture that we have chosen for the sake of implementation simplicity.

Metadata-Based Access. In addition to methods that are executed through the virtual file system interface, we also analyzed the execution runtime of typical queries that retrieve siles based on arbitrary combination of metadata. These queries cannot be directly executed through the virtual file system; instead, the sile API and a corresponding hierarchy of filters were used for these test runs. We extended the datasets from the previous section with sile annotations, whereas each sile was annotated with 20 annotations (tags, attributes, categories, and slinks) in average. These additional metadata amplified our test data sets up to 1.2 million triples for 40,000 siles. The requests were issued via our prototype's Java interface; each group of queries was repeated 10 times in random order.

The evaluated operations include search requests of varying complexity, ranging from searches for siles that are tagged with a single tag, to OR-combined search criteria. Additionally we tested calls that retrieved all annotations for a given sile, and operations that create and delete siles, respectively. The results (cf. Table 6) accentuate the performance overhead caused by the relatively complex architecture of our virtual file system, as described before. Operations that are executed directly against the sile repository are executed significantly faster than operations that are issued through the virtual file system.

Table 5. Virtual file system access operations: average execution times in seconds

Dataset #	1	2	3
Total number of siles	403	4,144	44,816
cd	0.029	0.048	0.107
rm	0.063	0.142	0.879
ls	0.258	0.464	1.547
mv within directory	0.254	0.488	2.488
mv across directories	0.296	0.688	3.238

Table 6. Metadata-based access operations: average execution times in seconds

Dataset #	1	2	3
Total number of triples	11,049	123,967	1,238,534
Search siles with a specific tag	0.271	1.084	2.008
Search siles with one out of three tags	0.734	1.182	2.304
Search siles related to a given sile	0.014	0.029	0.039
Retrieve all annotations for one sile	0.037	0.050	0.071
Create one sile	0.131	0.134	0.175
Add one tag to a sile	0.122	0.134	0.153
Delete one sile	0.044	0.051	0.071

This strengthens the need for a more efficient implementation of a virtual file system driver that is directly coupled to the sile repository, and thus avoids the indirection caused by our current prototypical architecture.

CONCLUSION

We discussed a number of issues regarding the integration of semantic technologies with file systems, which is a crucial requirement for a successful deployment of Semantic Desktop solutions. First, we showed that the RDF data model exposes a number of characteristics that may cause problems when used in the context of information management on the desktop. To overcome these limitations, we proposed the sile model, which combines characteristics from both the Semantic Web and file systems. Siles are digital objects that have a globally valid, immutable identity and can be annotated by tags, categories, and attributes; furthermore, they can be semantically related to each other. This model provides an integrated view on desktop resources and associated semantic annotations and is intended to serve as an intermediate layer between applications and the actual storage infrastructure. In conjunction with this model we presented an Application Programming Interface that allows developers to manipulate and retrieve siles and their annotations.

We also discussed our strategy for representing files and directories using siles and sile annotations. This allows us to simulate the behavior and characteristics of traditional, hierarchical file systems, which are used by a magnitude of applications. By providing a virtual file system view on a sile repository, users have the continuing ability to use the applications they are familiar with. In contrast to other semantic file systems, which expose semantic annotations as virtual directories, we employ designated attributes for this purpose. Therefore, we can simulate the behavior of file systems more accurately than other approaches since (virtual) file paths are not depending on semantic annotations, which may change over time and thus make path-based file references invalid. Still, the construction of metadata-based virtual directory views (e.g., based on tags) is possible.

The sile model is designed to be compatible with Semantic Web technologies. Therefore we also analyzed—as a further contribution—a representative set of vocabularies that can be used to annotate siles without further modification. These vocabularies cover a large fraction of the semantic definitions needed for desktop data. We proposed strategies how such vocabularies can be used in the desktop context in order to foster data interoperability on a global scale.

Finally, we presented our RDF-based implementation of the sile model and a virtual file system that is backed by our system. We analyzed the performance of typical file system operations under the consideration of realistic amounts of data that can be found on typical users' desktops, and demonstrated that the performance of such a virtual file system is acceptable for interactive usage. We also showed that the performance of metadata-based access to sile repositories is acceptable for typical desktop usage, even under the restrictions of a prototypical implementation.

ACKNOWLEDGMENT

This paper is an extended version of (Schandl & Haslhofer, 2009). Parts of this work have been funded by FIT-IT grants 812513 and 815133 from the Austrian Federal Ministry of Transport, Innovation, and Technology. The authors thank Stefan Pomajbik, Diman Todorov, and Arash Amiri for their support in the implementation of the system, and the anonymous reviewers for their helpful and inspiring comments.

REFERENCES

Ames, S., Bobb, N., Greenan, K. M., Hofmann, O. S., Storer, M. W., Maltzahn, C., et al. (2006). LiFS: An Attribute-Rich File System for Storage Class Memories. In *Proceedings of the 23rd IEEE / 14th NASA Goddard Conference on Mass Storage Systems and Technologies*.

Birbeck, M., & McCarron, S. (2009). *CURIE Syntax 1.0 — A Syntax for Expressing Compact URIs*. World Wide Web Consortium.

Bizer, C., Cyganiak, R., & Heath, T. (2007). *How to Publish Linked Data on the Web*. Berlin: Freie Universität Berlin.

Bizer, C., Heath, T., & Berners-Lee, T. (2009). Linked Data — The Story So Far. *International Journal on Semantic Web and Information Systems, 5*(3), 1–22.

Bloehdorn, S., Görlitz, O., Schenk, S., & Völkel, M. (2006). *TagFS – Tag Semantics for Hierarchical File Systems*. Paper presented at the 6th International Conference on Knowledge Management (I-KNOW'06).

Blunschi, L., Dittrich, J.-P., Girard, O. R., Karakashian, S. K., & Salles, M. A. V. (2007). A Dataspace Odyssey: The iMeMex Personal Dataspace Management System. In *Proceedings of the Third Biennial Conference on Innovative Data Systems Research* (pp. 114-119).

Boardman, R. (2001). Multiple Hierarchies in User Workspace. In *Proceedings of CHI '01 Extended Abstracts on Human Factors in Computing Systems* (pp. 403-404). New York: ACM Press.

Cai, Y., Dong, X. L., Halevy, A., Liu, J. M., & Madhavan, J. (2005). Personal Information Management with SEMEX. In *Proceedings of the 2005 ACM SIGMOD Conference on Management of Data* (pp. 921-923). New York: ACM Press.

Carey, M. J., DeWitt, D. J., Richardson, J. E., & Shekita, E. J. (1986). Object and File Management in the EXODUS Extensible Database System. In *Proceedings of the 12th International Conference on Very Large Data Bases* (pp. 91-100). San Francisco: Morgan Kaufmann Publishers Inc.

Decker, S., & Frank, M. R. (2004). *The Networked Semantic Desktop*. Paper presented at the WWW Workshop on Application Design, Development and Implementation Issues in the Semantic Web.

Ding, L., Finin, T., Joshi, A., Pan, R., Cost, R. S., Peng, Y., et al. (2004). Swoogle: A Search and Metadata Engine for the Semantic Web. In *Proceedings of the 13th ACM International Conference on Information and Knowledge Management* (pp. 652-659). New York: ACM Press.

Dourish, P., Edwards, W. K., LaMarca, A., & Salisbury, M. (1999). PRESTO: An Experimental Architecture for Fluid Interactive Document Spaces. *ACM Transactions on Computer-Human Interaction, 6*(2), 133–161. doi:10.1145/319091.319099

Franz, T., Scherp, A., & Staab, S. (2009). *Are Semantic Desktops Better? — Summative Evaluation Comparing a Semantic against a Conventional Desktop.* Paper presented at the Fifth International Conference on Knowledge Capture (K-CAP 2009).

Franz, T., Staab, S., & Arndt, R. (2007). The X-COSIM Integration Framework for a Seamless Semantic Desktop. In *Proceedings of the 4th International Conference on Knowledge Capture* (pp. 143-150). New York: ACM.

Gifford, D. K., Jouvelot, P., Sheldon, M. A., & O'Toole, J. W. (1991). Semantic File Systems. In *Proceedings of the 13th ACM Symposium on Operating Systems Principles* (pp. 16-25). New York: ACM Press.

Grimes, R. (2004). Code Name WinFS: Revolutionary File Storage System Lets Users Search and Manage Files Based on Content. *MSDN Magazine, 19*(1).

Groza, T., Handschuh, S., Moeller, K., Grimnes, G., Sauermann, L., & Minack, E. (2007). The NEPOMUK Project — On the Way to the Social Semantic Desktop. In *Proceedings of I-Semantics, 07*, 201–211.

Hayes, P. (2004). *RDF Semantics (W3C Recommendation 10 February 2004)*. World Wide Web Consortium.

Heery, R., & Patel, M. (2000). Application Profiles: Mixing and Matching Metadata Schemas. *Ariadne, September*(25).

Karger, D. R. (2007). Haystack: Per-User Information Environments Based on Semistructured Data. In Kaptelinin, V., & Czerwinski, M. (Eds.), *Beyond the Desktop Metaphor* (pp. 49–100). Cambridge, MA: Massachusetts Institute of Technology.

Martin, B. (2006). The World is a libferris Filesystem. *Linux Journal, 2006*(146).

Muñoz, S., Pérez, J., & Gutiérrez, C. (2007, June 3-7). Minimal Deductive Systems for RDF. In *Proceedings of the 4th European Semantic Web Conference,* Innsbruck, Austria (pp. 53-67).

Okoli, A., & Schandl, B. (2009). *Extraction of Contextual Metadata from File System Interactions.* Paper presented at the Workshop on Exploitation of Usage and Attention Metadata (EUAM 09).

Oren, E., Delbru, R., Catasta, M., Cyganiak, R., Stenzhorn, H., & Tummarello, G. (2008). Sindice.com — A Document-oriented Lookup Index for Open Linked Data. *International Journal on Metadata, Semantics, and Ontologies, 3*(1), 37–52. doi:10.1504/IJMSO.2008.021204

Padioleau, Y., Sigonneau, B., & Ridoux, O. (2006). Lisfs: A logical information system as a file system. In *Proceedings of the 28th International Conference on Software Engineering* (pp. 803-806). New York: ACM Press.

Richter, J., & Poelchau, J. (2008). DeepaMehta — Another Computer is Possible. In Rech, J., Decker, B., & Ras, E. (Eds.), *Emerging Technologies for Semantic Work Environments: Techniques, Methods, and Applications.* Hershey, PA: Idea Group.

Sauermann, L., Bernardi, A., & Dengel, A. (2005). Overview and Outlook on the Semantic Desktop. In S. Decker, J. Park, D. Quan, & L. Sauermann (Eds.), *Proceedings of the 1st Semantic Desktop Workshop*, Galway, Ireland. CEUR Workshop Proceedings.

Sauermann, L., & Heim, D. (2008). Evaluating Long-Term Use of the Gnowsis Semantic Desktop for PIM. In *Proceedings of the 7th International Semantic Web Conference* (pp. 467-482). Berlin: Springer.

Schandl, B. (2009a). *An Infrastructure for the Development of Semantic Desktop Applications*. Unpublished PhD thesis, University of Vienna, Department of Distributed and Multimedia Systems.

Schandl, B. (2009b). Representing Linked Data as Virtual File Systems. In *Proceedings of the 2nd International Workshop on Linked Data on the Web*, Madrid, Spain.

Schandl, B., & Haslhofer, B. (2009). The Sile Model – A Semantic File System Infrastructure for the Desktop. In *Proceedings of the 6th European Semantic Web Conference*, Heraklion, Greece.

Schandl, B., & King, R. (2006). The SemDAV Project: Metadata Management for Unstructured Content. In *Proceedings of the 1st International Workshop on Contextualized Attention Metadata: Collecting, Managing and Exploiting of Rich Usage Information* (pp. 27-32). New York: ACM Press.

Schandl, B., & Popitsch, N. (2010). *Lifting File Systems into the Linked Data Cloud with TripFS*. Paper presented at the 3rd International Workshop on Linked Data on the Web, Raleigh, NC.

Schmedding, F., Hanke, C., & Hornung, T. (2008). RDF Authoring in Wikis. In C. Lange, S. Schaffert, H. Skaf-Molli, & M. Völkel (Eds.), *Proceedings of the 3rd Semantic Wiki Workshop (SemWiki 2008)*. CEUR Workshop Proceedings.

Sechrest, S., & McClennen, M. (1992). Blending Hierarchical and Attribute-Based File Naming. In *Proceedings of the 12th International Conference on Distributed Computing Systems* (pp. 572-580). Washington, DC: IEEE Computer Society.

Sintek, M., van Elst, L., Scerri, S., & Handschuh, S. (2007a). Distributed Knowledge Representation on the Social Semantic Desktop: Named Graphs, Views and Roles in NRL. In E. Franconi, M. Kifer, & W. May (Eds.), *Proceedings of the 4th European Semantic Web Conference (ESWC 2007)*, Innsbruck, Austria (pp. 594-608). Berlin: Springer.

Sintek, M., van Elst, L., Scerri, S., & Handschuh, S. (2007b). *NEPOMUK Representational Language Specification (Technical Rep.)*. NEPOMUK Project Consortium.

Wills, C., Giampaolo, D., & Mackovitch, M. (1995). Experience with an Interactive Attribute-based User Information Environment. In *Proceedings of the 1995 IEEE Fourteenth Annual International Phoenix Conference on Computers and Communications* (pp. 359-365).

ENDNOTES

[1] http://esw.w3.org/topic/TaskForces/CommunityProjects/LinkingOpenData/DataSets

[2] http://esw.w3.org/topic/TaskForces/CommunityProjects/LinkingOpenData/CommonVocabularies

[3] Note that the actual naming of file system features differs; for instance, file forks are called *alternate data streams* in NTFS, while file attributes are called *extended attributes* in ext3/ext4.

[4] Semantic Desktop with KDE: http://nepomuk.kde.org

[5] e.g., http://pingthesemanticweb.com/stats/namespaces.php

[6] http://www.semdav.org

[7] http://fuse.sourceforge.net

[8] http://fuse-j.sourceforge.net

This work was previously published in International Journal of Semantic Web and Information Systems, Volume 6, Issue 3, edited by Amit P. Sheth, pp. 1-21, copyright 2010 by IGI Publishing (an imprint of IGI Global).

Chapter 5
Towards Controlled Natural Language for Semantic Annotation

Brian Davis
Digital Enterprise Research Institute, National University of Ireland, Ireland

Pradeep Dantuluri
Digital Enterprise Research Institute, National University of Ireland, Ireland

Siegfried Handschuh
Digital Enterprise Research Institute, National University of Ireland, Ireland

Hamish Cunningham
University of Sheffield, UK

ABSTRACT

Richly interlinked metadata constitute the foundation of the Semantic Web. Manual semantic annotation is a labor intensive task requiring training in formal ontological descriptions for the otherwise non-expert user. Although automatic annotation tools attempt to ease this knowledge acquisition barrier, their development often requires access to specialists in Natural Language Processing (NLP). This challenges researchers to develop user-friendly annotation environments. Controlled Natural Languages (CNLs) offer an incentive to the novice user to annotate, while simultaneously authoring his/her respective documents in a user-friendly manner. CNLs have been successfully applied to ontology authoring, but little research has focused on their application to semantic annotation. This paper describes two novel approaches to semantic annotation, which permit non-expert users to simultaneously author and annotate meeting minutes using CNL. Finally, this work provides empirical evidence that for certain scenarios applying CNLs for semantic annotation can be more user friendly than a standard manual semantic annotation tool.

DOI: 10.4018/978-1-4666-0185-7.ch005

INTRODUCTION

The Semantic Web endeavors to bring machine-processable meaning to the content of webpages. It envisions the Web as a universal medium for data, information and knowledge exchange, creating an environment where intelligent software agents can travel freely between web resources, carrying out sophisticated tasks for users[1]. In order for the Semantic Web to become a reality, we need, as a *primer inter pares*, semantic data. The process of providing semantic data is very often referred to as semantic annotation, because it frequently involves the embellishment of existing data, i.e. the text, with semantic metadata, which can subsequently describe the associated text. Hence semantic annotation is one of the core challenges for building the Semantic Web.

Manual semantic annotation however is a complex and labored task both time-consuming and expensive often requiring specialist annotators or the subsequent training of such annotators. This may require (an arguably unnecessary) exposure to formal ontological description. Such formal data representation can act as a significant deterrent for non-expert users or organizations seeking to annotate resources as part of their daily activity, thus allowing them to fully benefit from the adoption of Semantic Web technologies. While (Semi)-automatic annotation tools attempt to remove this constriction, which is commonly known as the *knowledge acquisition bottleneck*, their application often requires access to specialists who can combine Natural Language Processing(NLP)/ Machine Learning(ML) and Semantic Web ontology languages. Such specialists are costly and rare and furthermore the creation or acquisition of quality language resources to bootstrap such approaches may require significant investment, which for a small to medium enterprises may not be justifiable. Consequently, this challenges researchers to develop user-friendly manual annotation environments to support the knowledge acquisition process.

Controlled Natural Languages (CNLs) offer an incentive to the novice user to annotate, while simultaneously authoring, her respective documents in a user-friendly manner, yet at the same time shielding her from the underlying complex knowledge representation formalisms of ontology languages. "Controlled Natural Languages are subsets of natural language whose grammars and dictionaries have been restricted in order to reduce or eliminate both ambiguity and complexity."[2] The use of CNLs for ontology authoring and population is by no means a new concept and it has already evolved into quite an active research area (Smart, 2008). Furthermore, a natural overlap exists between tools used for both ontology creation and semantic annotation, for instance the Controlled Language for Information Extraction(CLIE)technology permits ontology creation and population by mapping both concept definitions and instances of concepts to a ontological representation using a CNL called CLOnE - Controlled Language for Ontology Editing (Funk et al., 2008). Despite such efforts, very little research has focused on applying CNLs to semantic annotation. The reader should note that there is a subtle *difference* between the process of ontology creation and population and that of semantic annotation. We describe semantic annotation as "a process as well as the outcome of the process". Hence it describes i) "the process of adding semantic data or metadata to content given an agreed ontology and ii) it describes the semantic data or metadata itself as a result of this process"(Handschuh, 2005). Of particular importance here is the notion of the *addition or association* of semantic metadata to *content*.

Latent Annotation

As with any annotation environment, a major drawback is that in order to create metadata about a document, the author must *first* create the content and *second* annotate the content, in an additional a posteriori, annotation step. In the context of our application of CNL to semantic annotation, we seek to merge both authoring and annotation steps into one. This process differs from classic *a-posteriori* annotation resulting in a new type of annotation which we call *latent* annotation. Latent comes from the Latin word with identical spelling who's etymology is derived from the Latin verb latere (lie hidden), a nod in respect to a-posteriori(later, what comes after)[3].

Towards a Definition of Controlled Language for Semantic Annotation

We hereby refer to the application of CNL to semantic annotation as controlled (natural language) annotation which reflects how traditional CNL intersects but also differs from our approach, whereby:

Controlled (Natural Language) Annotation or Controlled Annotation is the application of CNL technologies to the process of semantic annotation. Controlled annotation aims to reduce or eliminate ambiguity with respect to the semi-automatic/manual semantic annotation of textual resources. It may include the creation of semantic data or metadata from machine processable content as in traditional CNL or apply CNL techniques that act as an interface to associate semantic data or metadata with free or uncontrolled text. Unlike traditional CNL, content in controlled annotation can be independent of the process.

The above definition is clarified based on the following categories: **Provenance, Degree of Control, Comprehension, Ontology authoring, Task and Target User**. Each one is elaborated on below:

- **Provenance:** This refers to the creation of metametadata to record data about the metadata/knowledge which has been captured: i.e. Where an RDF statement has come from? Who made it? When was it created? Which document and where is it located in the original (textual) resource - position and offset within the document or webpage, the name of the resource, date of creation and author. Degree of Control: This refers to how *controlled* the language used to author and annotate content is. CNLs (although this may seem counterintuitive) in practice actually vary with respect to their degree of restriction on vocabulary and syntax. Usually a balance between ambiguity and user friendliness is sought. Controlled Annotation is similar in this respect in that a sentence may be syntactically constrained but may be more lenient with regards to the type of vocabulary that can be used i.e. (nouns or proper nouns), but CNL sentences or CNL snippets, (as we shall see in the section on design and implementation), may be embedded in free text. This overlaps with what Kaufmann (2007) describes as the Formality Continuum for Natural Language Interfaces and furthermore relates to Kuhn's (2010a) CNL design principle of *Clearness*.

- **Ontology authoring:** While CNLs usually focus on the creation of intensional, axiomatic or assertional knowledge statements, controlled annotation focuses on the creation of facts in the knowledge-base as well as the retention of provenance data and the maintenance of links or pointers to the original content. The creation of some intensional knowledge maybe permitted but this is reserved usually for the more confident or specialist user. In fact one may wish to prevent a casual user from altering an ontology at the class level as this could result in corruption of the ontology. On the other hand, one can argue that an annotation process with such ontology authoring features could serve as a quality assurance step for the ontology. In other words, if an ontology is truly well designed and representative of the domain vocabulary, there should be very little need to alter it at the class level. The creation of rules or axioms during annotation is not common practice. Consequently, in order to apply controlled annotation to a textual resource, the annotation environment must be pump primed with an ontology consisting, at minimum, of intensional or axiomatic knowledge.

- **Comprehension:** A subtle difference between traditional controlled annotation and CNL is that for controlled annotation content can be independent of the process. We argue that for content, to which controlled annotation has been applied too, is independent of any facts that have been captured from it. Consequently, controlled annotated content is arguably implicitly understood by the average human user regardless whether they are aware of whether or not the resource was annotated in a controlled manner. So a controlled annotated document will look reasonably like any other document on the Web, while on the other hand, a document written in CNL for ontology authoring is (although Â written in "natural language") would still read as a collection of knowledge statements in natural language can be counterintuitive to the casual user on the Web. Smart (2008) argues this point, in that despite the fact that knowledge statements can be described in CNL, users will still have the tendency to become "lost in logic". Although a user is shielded by the underlying formalisms of some logic notation, they will still require some minimal introduction to formal logic to comprehend certain knowledge statements in CNL. However, this is an inevitable consequence of attempting to author an ontology from scratch, in that knowledge statements at the class and rule level are necessary before instance population can proceed. Controlled Annotation is however, from a knowledge modelling perspective, a less complex task as it operates primarily at the instance level. This brings us to our next point.

- **Task and Target User:** Fundamentally, the tasks differ when considering controlled annotation and CNLs for ontology authoring. The purpose of annotation is to associate metadata to content, which will subsequently be discovered by a semantic agent active on the Web. The provenance metadata will point to the original resources from which it was derived. The agent will retrieve this content for the human user. In short, the final benefactor is the human. In contrast, with respect to CNL for ontology authoring, the human benefits more indirectly. Although CNLs act as a user friendly interface to the ontology, it is the semantic agent which exploits the CNL generated machine-processable vocabulary. Hence the ontology is applied to semantic metadata by the agent to perform reasoning and search over semantically annotated Web resources. With respect to controlled annotation we argue that the target user is a typical Social Web user who is comfortable with CMS systems or Wikis. No knowledge of semantic web formalisms is expected. In contrast, with respect to CNLs, the user is a domain expert who will require some basic foundation in ontologies and formal logic in order to author an ontology in CNL. Figure 1 describes the role of controlled annotation with respect to CNL. This visualization incorporates what Sure (2003) describes as the duality of ontology and metadata, in other words (i) the knowledge meta-process - the development of an ontology and (ii) the knowledge process - the subsequent creation of a knowledge base. CNLs for ontology authoring assign themselves to the role of the knowledge meta-process - the creation, continued extension and adaption of the ontology, while controlled annotation

Figure 1. Controlled annotation and the semantic web information food chain

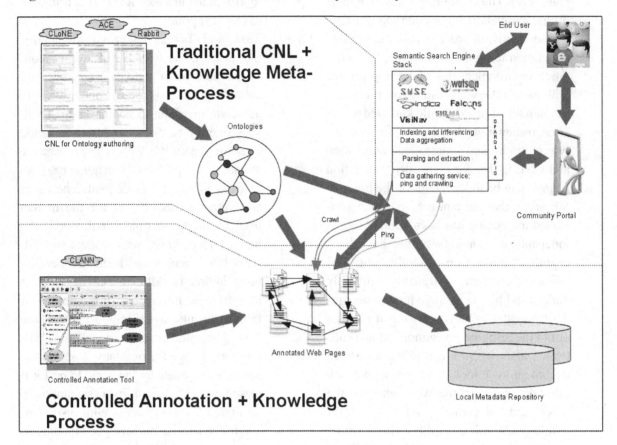

is concerned with the knowledge process - the steps for the creation and processing ontology based metadata. Figure 1 is also based on the *information food chain for the Semantic Web* described in (Decker, 2002).

Controlled Language ANNotation - CLANN

This manuscript describes the design and implementation of two user friendly approaches to applying CNL to Semantic Annotation, which we call CLANN - Controlled Language ANNotation, both of which are based on the CLOnE language (Funk et al., 2007). Both approaches to CLANN permit non-expert users to semi-automatically and simultaneously author and annotate meeting minutes and/or status reports using controlled

natural language. The motivation to develop two CLANN annotators was for exploratory purposes in order to assess which approach(or a combination of the two) would be more user friendly. Both CLANN annotators are essentially pathfinders to a final CNL annotator - CLANN III (see Conclusion and Future Work).

CLANN I is more automatic and aims to sacrifice expressiveness (wrt the controlling the manipulation and creation of metadata) over usability while in contrast CLANN II prioritizes expressiveness,(as in control over metadata manipulation), over usability. Uncovering the correct balance between expressiveness and usability is related to the *habitability* problem (Watt, 1968). A Natural Language Interface(NLI) is considered habitable if users can express everything needed to complete a task using language they would expect the system to understand. A second aspect of the habitability problem, an aspect sometimes overlooked within the CNL community itself, is that of Chomsky's (1965) distinction between competence vs performance. Human linguistic competence can be described as a set of strict rules of a language's grammar(in this case English grammar) while performance consists of the uses we make of competence. In simpler terms, *how information is written using the grammar* is a measure of competence and *what information can be written using the grammar* is a measure of performance. We argue that the design of CNLs is often driven by competence while the second aspect of habitability states that an NLI should also attempt to account for both. We will show how both CLANN annotators differ with respect to aspects of linguistic performance and what effect this has on usability.

Although the majority of work within the field of CNL for knowledge creation has focused on ontology authoring, as far as we are aware, no other work has sought to apply CNL to semantic annotation. This manuscript makes four original contributions:

1. An approach to manual annotation using CNL called Controlled Language ANNotation - CLANN.
2. We contribute to the semantic annotation field, proposing to move away from traditional a-posteriori annotation to *latent* annotation, by merging both authoring an annotations steps together.
3. Implementations for two types of CLANN annotator, both varying in expressiveness and usability in order to design a final optimal CLANN annotator based on the results of a user evaluation.
4. Empirical evidence to support the adoption of CNL for semantic annotation and evidence that for certain scenarios, CNL for semantic annotation or controlled annotation can be more user friendly than standard manual semantic annotation approach.

Building on previous methodology (Funk et al., 2007), we undertook a repeated-measures, task-based evaluation, comparing both types of CLANN annotator with each other. Furthermore we investigated issues of usability and habitability for each tool's respective CNL. We also included OntoMat[4], a standard manual semantic annotation tool. Our quantitative results demonstrate that controlled annotation can for certain use cases offer an attractive alternative to non experts over a standard manual annotation tool.

The remainder of this manuscript is organized as follows: the section CLANN: Design and Implementation discusses our use case and target domain and the design and implementation of both types of CLANN annotators and their corresponding CNLs. The section Evaluation presents our evaluation and discusses our quantitative findings. The section on Related Work discusses the current literature. The final section offers conclusions and future work.

CLANN: DESIGN AND IMPLEMENTATION

Use Case and Application Domain

The reader should note that controlled annotation cannot necessarily offer a panacea for manual semantic annotation as a whole since it is unrealistic to expect users to annotate every textual resource using CNL, however there are certain use-cases where CNLs can offer an attractive alternative as a means for manual semantic annotation, particularly in contexts, where controlled vocabulary or terminology is implicit such as health care patient records, business vocabulary and reporting. Our domain use case focuses on project administration tasks such as taking minutes during a project team meeting and writing weekly status reports. Very often such note taking tasks can be repetitive and boring. In our scenario the user is a member of a research group which is part of an integrated EU research project. We chose this domain because: (1) we observed the size of meeting minutes and status reports was quite limited and in addition sentences within such artifacts tended to be short, repetitious and more importantly tended to follow a subject, predicate, object pattern, making them good candidates from controlled annotation, and (2) we were able to construct our own small corpus of real-world meeting minutes and status reports generated over the three year period from the Nepomuk[5] project (271 reports).

One scenario could employ the use of pre-defined templates, whereby the user *simultaneously authors and annotates* his/her meeting minutes or status reports in CNL, using a semantic note taking tool - SemNotes[6], which is an application available for Nepomuk-KDE[7] - the KDE instance of the Social Semantic Desktop. The metadata is available for immediate use after creation for querying and aggregation. The scenario is not limited to the KDE Desktop or the semantic desktop. Other scenarios could involve integrating CLANN into a semantic wiki.

Both CLANN tools are bootstrapped via the Nepomuk Core Ontologies[8]. More specifically our domain is modeled using a meeting minutes/ status report ontology MEMO[9], which references the users Personal Information Model Ontology(PIMO) [10]. The MEMO ontology was initially engineered for the purpose of building both CLANN prototypes and was designed as a proof of concept. Since then we have begun to completely redesign and engineer our domain ontology in accordance with proper ontology engineering methodologies, specifically the METH-ONTOLOGY (Fernández-López, Gómez-Pérez, & Juristo, 1997) methodology.

We applied Word Smith Tools 5.0[11] to our corpus in order to identify common linguistic patterns and vocabulary which could be applied to both CLANN annotators but more specifically CLANN I. The results were not statistically significant due to the corpus size but our goal was not to provide empirical support for some particular linguistic phenomenon, but rather to apply the results of our corpus analysis to the design of CLANN I in conjunction with linguistic introspection - a common requirements analysis step within language engineering. In addition, recall that CLANN I seeks to address some aspects of linguistic performance. Hence a further justification for corpus analysis. This will be elaborated where appropriate in detail within the next sections.

CLANN I and II Overview

As mentioned earlier this work focuses on too approaches to Controlled Languages ANNotation - CLANN. Both CLANN annotators are implemented in GATE[12] and build on the existing advantages of the CLOnE(Funk et al., 2007) software and input controlled language and share the common features below:

1. Both annotators require only one interpreter or runtime environment, the Java 1.5 JRE.
2. As far as possible, CLANN I and CLANN II snippets are grammatically lax; in particular it does not matter whether the input is singular or plural (or even in grammatical agreement).
3. Both types of CLANN are relatively easy to learn by following examples and a small style guide, without having to study elaborate expressions of formal syntax.
4. Both CLANN annotators are a form of latent semantic annotation - merging both authoring and annotation steps.
5. Both annotators share a common template for meeting minutes.
6. Finally both CLANN annotators share a common Ontology API similar to CLOnE.

In our scenario each CLANN annotator is anchored to existing semi-structured data such as a AgendaTitle, Scribe or ActionItem based on predefined meeting minutes or status report templates described (See below). The templates were constructed based on linguistic introspection and and corpus analysis, which was conducted over the previously mentioned corpus of status reports and meeting minutes derived from the Nepomuk project. We choose to use a template for the CLANN prototypes for practical reasons, so the template could be easily applied to any note-taking environment or for instance emulated in a semantic wiki. For instance the application of extracting semantic metadata from wiki templates in Wikipedia was researched in (Auer & Lehmann, 2007). Furthermore, it would be inefficient to apply CLANN for creation of this template rather the focus here is the usage of CLANN for authoring and annotating natural language sentences contained within the following template (Figure 2).

CLANN I: Design and Implementation

The annotator architecture contains a standard GATE pipeline (see Figure 3) which includes the following language processing resources: The GATE English tokenizer, the Hepple POS tagger, a morphological analyzer, a gazetteer list component for recognizing useful key-phrases, such as structured elements from the templates and reserved CNL phrases. Any sentences for example, preceded by a Comment: element are considered candidates for controlled language

Figure 2. Template

Meeting Minutes Template for CLANN I and II

```
Meeting Date:<date>
Project Name:<project name>
Attendees:<attendee1>(,<attendee2>)+
Chair:<chair>
Scribe:<scribe>

Agenda Items:
Agenda Title:<title>
(Comment:<comment>.)+

RoundTable:
(Comment:<comment>.)+
```

parsing. Any remaining tokens from the CNL sentence which are not recognized as reserved CNL key-phrases are used as names to generate links to ontological objects. This is followed by a standard Named Entity(NE) transducer in order to recognize useful NEs, a preprocessing JAPE[13] finite state transducer(FST) for identifying quoted strings, chunking Noun Phrases(NPs) and additional preprocessing. A second gazetteer list lookup is applied to identify trigger phrases associated with NEs which intersect with quoted and unquoted NP annotation spans. Additional feature values are then added to the NP chunks to indicate the appropriate class to link an NP chunk as an instance to. The last FST parses the CNL from the text and generates the metadata. The current tool is bootstrapped via the Nepomuk Core Ontologies and currently the application populates a meeting minutes/status report ontology MEMO which references a user's Personal Information Model Ontology(PIMO), via the GATE Ontology API. Each meeting minute note follows a pre-defined template(shown above). The template is parsed initially to extract the inherent metadata about the meeting.

Each valid sentence in CLANN I matches exactly one syntactic rule and as mentioned earlier consists of reserved keyphrases (verb phrases, fixed expressions and punctuation marks) as well as *chunks* (which similar to noun phrases are used to name instances). Similar to CLOnE, the language has *quoted chunks*, a series of words which are enclosed in quotes (e.g. "the PhD proposal"). Quoted chunks permit the capture of multi-word expressions as instances. They also permit the use of reserved words that would other wise be detected by the reserved word gazetteer lookup.

An example syntactic rule is contained below:

<NP><VP>(<Prep>? <NP>)+

Figure 3. CLANN I pipeline

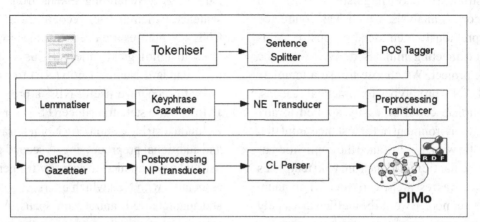

where <NP> corresponds to *chunk* or *quoted chunk* and <VP> corresponds to reserved verb phrases and paraphrases derived from corpus analysis. Furthermore <Prep> corresponds to any preposition annotated using the POS tagger. Finally (<Prep>? <NP>)+ matches one or more prepositional adjuncts i.e. "for the EU" or "in Work Package 3000". Hence the above rule would match the following sentences.

Comment: *Marco to visit "University of Karl-sruhe".*

Comment: *Dirk to complete paper by "Sunday 21st June" for "International Semantic Web Conference".*

The above rule extracts the instances as arguments. The reader should note that prior to this stage that standard NE transducer and post-processing NP transducer (see Figure 4) will have collected additional information about

Figure 4. CLANN I visualized in GATE

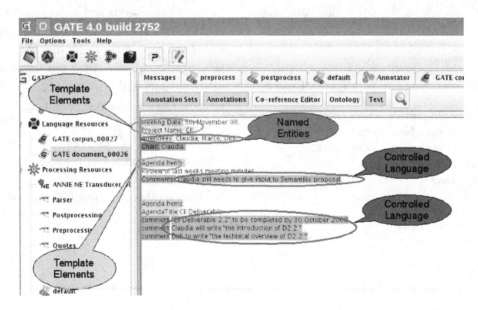

each chunk. So Marco and Dirk are associated to a *Pimo Person*, while "Sunday 21st June" will be recognized as a *Date*. Using similar techniques "University of Karlsruhe" would be recognized as an *Organization* and "International Semantic Web Conference" would be recognized as a *Conference*. The verb phrases to visit and to complete are then used to identify the relevant properties to link the instances recognized.

Other features of CLANN I include simple co-reference using the Alias: rule, which allows the user to express the same instance in varied forms. It also enables the usage of a *shorthand* by the user when taking minutes.

CLANN I also incorporates simple elements of language performance in order to make the controlled language more habitable. See the introductory section for a discussion on the term habitability. In order to engineer elements of linguistic performance into CLANN I we applied corpus analysis to generate lexicalisations for common properties within the MEMO ontology. These were then added to the the gazetteer list component within the CLANN I pipeline as CNL reserved phrases. We applied mutual information statistics to word frequencies within our corpus to assess the strength of collocation relationships within text. We used the output to generate lists of common trigger phrases which could be aligned to properties within the MEMO ontology. For example:

Comment: *Dirk to complete paper by "Sunday 21st June" for "International Semantic Web Conference".* can be paraphrased as:

Comment: *Dirk to finish up work on paper by "Sunday 21st June" for "International Semantic Web Conference".* or

Comment: *Dirk to wrap up paper by "Sunday 21st June" for "International Semantic Web Conference",*

where to finish up work on and to wrap up are lexicalisations of the property *toComplete*. On initial inspection, the reader may inclined to view such paraphrases as grammatically incorrect or stylistically inelegant, but recall that CLANN I is language performance driven and seeks to ease the user experience by incorporating such lexicalisations within the controlled language thus making it more habitable. In our evaluation section we will show how this design decision impacts favourably on user satisfaction. For additional examples of the CLANN I language and grammar, see Figure 5

Figure 5. Excerpt of CLANN I grammar with examples

Table 1: Excerpt of CLANN I grammar with examples

Sentence Pattern	Example	Parsed pattern
`<NP><VP><PP>+`	`Ambrosio to submit "her PhD Proposal" during "the next week".`	`(Ambrosia <NP>) (to submit <VP>) ((her PhD Proposal <NP>)<PP>) (during (the next week <NP>)<PP>).`
	`Dirk to work on "the E-Health Proposal" with Ambrosia`	`(Dirk <NP>) (to work <VP>) (on(the E-Health Proposal<NP>)<PP>) (with (Ambrosia <NP>)<PP>).`
ALIAS:`<`TEXT`>`;`<`ALIAS`>`	`Alias:<"CII Deliverable 6.7">;<"D6.7">`	Creates "D6.7"' as an alias for "CII Deliverable 6.7".

CLANN II: Design and Implementation.
The CLANN II architecture (see Figure 7 and Figure 8) is similar in design to CLANN I in that it shares the same language processing resources for tokenisation, sentence splitting, POS tagging and morphological analysis. CLANN II uses an identical template as CLANN I, however the Comment: element is non existent and furthermore sentences themselves are not written in controlled language. In CLANN II the user can write any sentence without restriction under the heading of an Agenda Item. What differs in CLANN II is that the user can use snippets of controlled language to associate metadata to a particular piece of text. Snippets of CNL are identified within square brackets using [....]. The CLANN II CNL snippets themselves are similar to the CLOnE language. A preprocessing finite state transducer(FST) similar to CLANN I is applied to extract values associated with template elements. In addition, text associated to the CNL snippets is also parsed at this stage. The final stage in the pipeline consists of a JAPE transducer which pulls the instances and properties to parse triples, ignoring the unassociated text. CLANN II shares the same API with respect to ontology manipulation as CLANN I and consults the ontology in similar manner. Similar to CLOnE and CLANN I, the language in CLANN II has *quoted chunks*, a series of words which are enclosed in quotes ("..."). This allows the user to associate metadata to more than one word. Example syntactic rules are shown below:

<Text>'['IS A CLASSNAME']'

where [IS A CLASSNAME] corresponds to a snippet of CNL. Hence:

Dirk[is a Person] to complete paper by "Sunday 21st June "[is a Date] for "International Semantic Web Conference"[is a Conference].

The rule below allows the user to simply embed a sentence in CNL in order to create relation metadata:

'['Chunk Property Chunk']'

This approach also allows users to handle adjuncts with much greater ease, such as associating the Date instance "Sunday 21st June" with paper i.e.

["to complete" same as toComplete].

Dirk[is a Person] to complete paper[is a Document] by "Sunday 21st June"[is a Date] for "International Semantic Web Conference"[is a Conference].

[Dirk "to complete" paper].

[Paper hasEndDate "Sunday 21st June"].

Note, that when creating instances of properties, the controlled language will recognize pre-existing annotations i.e. paper and "Sunday 21st June". In order to use a property in the CLANN II CNL, the user must either use the appropriate label for the property on inspection of the ontology (in this case *to complete* is a part of the ontology) or alternatively they can use the alias preprocessing command to create a more natural substitute for the property.

Another major difference between CLANN II and CLANN I is that the user can also create and manipulate classes, subclasses and class properties. Suppose the user is is unsatisfied with the association of paper to Document and would prefer to associate the text to instance of a non existent class ConferencePaper. CLANN II permits the creation of new classes on an ad hoc basis using the following rules:

'['<CHUNK> IS A SUBCLASS OF <CLASS-NAME>']'

resulting in the following:

["Conference Paper" is a subclass of Document]

Dirk[is a Person] to complete paper[is a "Conference Paper"] by "Sunday 21st June"[is a Date] for "International Semantic Web Conference"[is a Conference].

[Dirk to complete paper].

See Figure 6 for further examples of the CLANN II language.

Each CLANN annotator differs in the following ways:

- The CLANN II language is portable, while CLANN I must be re-targeted for a new domain. This is an inherent disadvantage of attempting to cater for some linguistic performance in CLANN I.
- CLANN I incorporates some linguistic performance while CLANN II does not. Linguistic Performance is the result of conducting basic simple corpus analysis(mentioned earlier).
- CLANN I cannot create terminological component(TBox) statements. This option

Figure 6. Excerpt of CLANN II grammar with examples

Table 2: Excerpt of CLANN II grammar with examples

Sentence Pattern	Example
<TEXT>'['IS A <CLASS>']'.	`Dirk[is a Person]` Creates an object of the class Person with label *Dirk*. Note the the label is taken from the document content.
<TEXT>'['IS A SUBCLASS OF <CLASS>']'.	`Proposal [is a subclass of Document]` or `[Proposal is a subclass of Document]` Creates a new class with label *Proposal* as a subclass of the class *Document*.
<TEXT>'['<PROPERTY> <OBJECT>']'.	`Dirk[to complete "PhD Proposal"]` or `[Dirk to complete "PhD Proposal"]` Creates a tripple which links the instances of *Dirk* and *PhD Proposal* with the property *toComplete*.

Figure 7. CLANN II pipeline

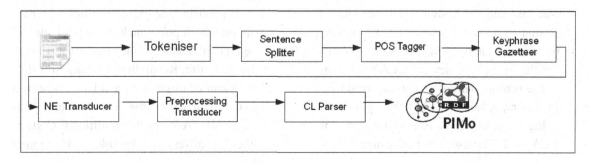

Figure 8. CLANN II visualized in GATE

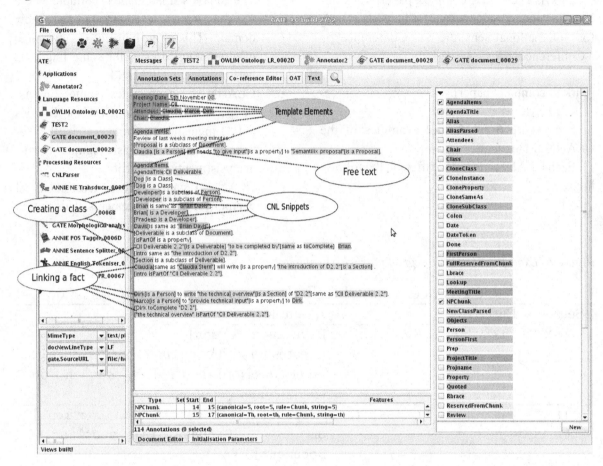

is available to CLANN II users. This raises interesting research questions: Should a proper annotation tool permit users to alter the ontology at the class level etc? Would annotators then invariably corrupt the ontology?

- CLANN II is more in line with the traditional spirit of semantic annotation. The CNL snippets act as the "glue" between free text and the knowledge base. This is similar to approach taken in some semantic wikis notably Semantic Media Wiki[14] but the we believe that the CLANN II language is more natural and human readable.

- In theory, CLANN II can be applied to a legacy text which is not the case for CLANN I. The user must be somewhat fa-

miliar with the ontology to use CLANN II, while the ontology is hidden in CLANN I.

Other points in relation to CLANN vs CNL:

- The reader may feel that CLANN I is simply applied CNL for fact creation, however the subtle but crucial distinction here is that CLANN I retains some provenance data regarding an extracted instance or relation which point back to original span of text and the name of the resource it was extracted from. Recall that we retain this data so it can be discovered at a later stage by a semantic agent on the Web. Provenance is arguably irrelevant for traditional CNL as the task differs and the role of the content is to interface with the ontology for authoring and population.

- The meeting minute is a human-readable account of a meeting and not merely CNL input for instance creation. Hence the annotated document when published on the Web should be implicitly understood by the casual user while as mentioned earlier in the introduction, in order for a casual user to completely understand traditional CNL knowledge statements, we would argue that such a user would require some introduction to modeling knowledge formally or ontologies to grasp the context.

EVALUATION

Research Questions

The aim of our evaluation is to answer the following research questions:

1. Can controlled annotation effectively substitute for standard manual semantic annotation tools in certain scenarios?
2. Is CLANN I more or less user friendly than CLANN II?
3. Is habitability in CLANN I preferred over expressiveness (with respect to metadata manipulation) in CLANN II?

Methodology

Our methodology is based on the criteria used to evaluate CLOnE(Funk et al., 2007), which has previously proven reliable. The methodology involves a *repeated-measures, task-based* evaluation: each subject carries out a similar list of tasks on all tools being compared. The evaluation material and results are available online for inspection[15]. The evaluation methodology involved the following:

- A pre-test questionnaire of 6 questions asking each subject to test their degree of knowledge with respect to semantic annotation tools, ontologies, and controlled natural languages. It was scored by assigning each answer a value from 0 to 2.
- A short document introducing ontologies, and the process of semantic annotation (partly inspired by Protégé's *Ontology 101* documentation (Noy & McGuiness, 2001) and (Handschuh, 2005) for semantic annotation respectively). Subjects were provided with reference guides and examples for both CLANN annotators and OntoMat. The reader should note the that both CLANN annotators were not integrated into a specialized interface, rather the texts containing their respective CNLs were loaded into GATE as documents. Our research goals are concerned with exploring the user reaction to using a controlled annotation languages while authoring as well measuring the comparison between our approaches and the standard manual annotation paradigm.
- A post-test questionnaire for each annotation tool, based on the *System Usability Scale* (SUS), which produces a score of 0-100 (Brooke, 1996).
- A comparative questionnaire similar to the one used in (Funk et al., 2007) was applied to measure each user's preference for each of the tools over the other. They were scored scored similarly to SUS so that for instance 0 would indicate a total preference for OntoMat, 100 would indicate a total preference for CLANN I, and 50 would result from marking all the questions *neutral*. Subjects were also given the opportunity to make comments and suggestions.
- Three equivalent annotation tasks in the form of a meeting minutes note, each consisting of the following subtasks:

Figure 9.Groups of subjects by source and tool order

Table 3: Groups of subjects by source and tool order

| Tool order | Background | | Total |
	Academia	Industry	
1-2-Ont	2	1	3
2-Ont-1	2	1	3
Ont-1-2	3	0	3
Ont-2-1	2	1	3
2-1-Ont	2	1	3
1-Ont-2	0	3	3
Total	11	7	18

- Create where necessary and associate instances within the text to classes,
- Create where necessary and associate instance properties within the text to instances.

For all three task lists, the same MEMO ontology was used. The same ontology was loaded into OntoMat for all three tasks. Again for both CLANN annotators the same ontology was used for all three tasks. See online for an example of all tasks. Note that the task texts contain no elements from either CLANN I or CLANN II. Templates elements were left partially incomplete across all three tasks.

OntoMat

OntoMat-Annotizer is a user-friendly interactive webpage annotation tool. It supports the user with the task of creating and maintaining ontology-based OWL-markups i.e. creating of OWL-instances, attributes and relationships. It includes an ontology browser for the exploration of the ontology and instances and a HTML browser that will display the annotated parts of the text. The intended user is the individual annotator. OntoMat allows the annotator to highlight relevant parts of a web page and create new instances via drag and drop interactions. It is representative of a conventional manual semantic annotation tool.

Sample Quality

We recruited 18 volunteers. The sample size ($n=18$) satisfies the requirements for reliable SUS evaluations (Tullis & Stetson, 2004). We recruited subjects with both industrial (I) and Academic (A) backgrounds. See Figure 9 for details.

- Research Assistants/Programmers/Post-Doctoral Researchers with an industrial background either returning (or new) to Academic Research respectively (I),
- Postgraduate Students who were new to the Semantic Web and unfamiliar with Ontology Engineering or Semantic Annotation (A),
- Researchers with no background in Natural Language Processing or Ontology Engineering (A) or
- Industrial Collaborators (I).

In all cases, we ensured that participants had limited or no knowledge of GATE or OntoMat. First, subjects were asked to complete the pre-test questionnaire, then they were permitted time to read the initial Ontology and semantic annotation guide, as well the reference guide for tool in question, and lastly they were asked to carry out each of the three annotation tasks with a different annotator. (A sixth of users(three users) carried out task document A with CLANN I, then document B with CLANN II and finally document C with

Figure 10. Summary of the questionnaire scores

Table 4: Summary of the questionnaire scores

Measure	min	mean	median	max	confidence interval[1]
Pre-test scores	0	4.28	4.5	10	2.7 - 5.8
CLANN 1 SUS rating	22.5	69.2	71.3	90	61.8 - 76.5
CLANN 2 SUS rating	5	55.6	61.3	85	46.6 - 64.5
Ontomat SUS rating	0	32.1	25	75	22.1 - 42.1
CLANN 1 Vs Ontomat Preference	42.5	67.5	65	100	60.1 - 74.9
CLANN 2 Vs Ontomat Preference	37.5	62.2	58.8	92.5	54.6 - 69.8
CLANN 1 Vs CLANN 2 Preference	30	54	56.3	80	47.8 - 60.3

OntoMat; the second group of three users undertook tasks A with OntoMat, then B with CLANN I and finally task C with CLANN II). The process of varying the tool order resulted in six permutations overall (see Figure 9). Each user's time for each task document was recorded. After each task the user completed the SUS questionnaire for the specific tool used, and finally a comparative questionnaire depending on the preceding tool. Comments and feedback were also recorded on the questionnaire forms.

Quantitative Findings

Figure 10 summarizes the main measures obtained from our evaluation. We used SPSS[16] to generate all our statistical results. In particular the mean CLANN I SUS score is above the baseline of 65--70% while the mean SUS score for OntoMat is well below the baseline (Bailey, 2006). In the CLANN I/OntoMat Preference scores, based on the comparative questionnaires, we note that the scores also favour on average CLANN I over OntoMat. Furthermore with respect to CLANN II the mean SUS score is relatively neutral. In addition, although the CLANN II/OntoMat preference score is high, it is not above the SUS baseline. Interestingly the CLANN I/CLANN II preference is neutral, indicating that users were undecided with regard to the preference of one CLANN tool over the other. Finally the mean Pre-test score is relatively neutral, indicating no particular bias with

respect to prior knowledge. Confidence intervals are also displayed in Figure 10.[17]

In addition, a one-way repeated measures ANOVA was conducted to compare SUS scores across each tool[18]. The results are displayed in Figure 11. There was a significant effect per tool ($p < .05$).

We also generated Pearson's coefficients (John & Phillips, 1996). Figure 12 displays the most important coefficients. The full listing of correlation coefficients is available online. We note the most important results.

There is a moderate correlation between the CLANN I SUS score and the CLANN I/CLANN II preference score, with an associated probability of 5%, however the value of the correlation itself is not particularly significant. There is also a moderate correlation between the CLANN II SUS score and the OntoMat SUS score, with an associated probability of 5%, however the value of the correlation itself is again not particularly significant. There is a relatively strong positive correlation between CLANN I task times and CLANN II task times and furthermore they are significantly related, $r = +.61$, $n = 18$, $p < .01$, two tails. Hence we can infer that non expert users tend to spend the equivalent time using either CLANN annotator to complete there annotation tasks. Finally there is a strong positive correlation between CLANN II/OntoMat preference scores and CLANN II/OntoMat preference scores and furthermore they are significantly related, $r = +.65$,

Figure 11. ANOVA scores per too

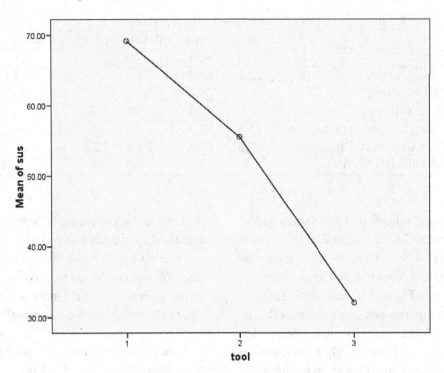

Multiple Comparisons
Dependent Variable: sus
LSD

(I) tool	(J) tool	Mean Difference (I-J) Lower Bound	Std. Error Upper Bound	Sig. Lower Bound	95% Confidence Interval Upper Bound	Lower Bound
1	2	13.61111(*)	6.36748	.037	.8279	26.3944
1	3	37.08333(*)	6.36748	.000	24.3001	49.8666
2	1	-13.61111(*)	6.36748	.037	-26.3944	-.8279
2	3	23.47222(*)	6.36748	.001	10.6890	36.2555
3	1	-37.08333(*)	6.36748	.000	-49.8666	-24.3001
3	2	-23.47222(*)	6.36748	.001	-36.2555	-10.6890

* The mean difference is significant at the .05 level.

Figure 12.Correlation coefficients

Table 5: Correlation coefficients

Measure	Measure	Pearson's	Correlation
CLANN 1 time	Ontomat time	-0.12	none
CLANN 2 time	Ontomat time	-0.19	none
CLANN 1 time	CLANN 2 time	0.61	strong +
CLANN 1 SUS score	CLANN 1 Vs Ontomat	-0.02	none
CLANN 1 SUS score	CLANN 1 Vs CLANN 2	0.49	moderate +
CLANN 2 SUS score	CLANN 2 Vs Ontomat	0.25	none
CLANN 2 SUS score	CLANN 1 Vs CLANN 2	-0.03	none
Ontomat SUS score	CLANN 1 Vs Ontomat	-0.43	weak −
Ontomat SUS score	CLANN 2 Vs Ontomat	-0.48	moderate −
CLANN 1 Vs Ontomat	CLANN 1 Vs CLANN 2	0.5	none
CLANN 2 Vs Ontomat	CLANN 1 Vs CLANN 2	-0.1	none
CLANN 1 Vs Ontomat	CLANN 2 Vs Ontomat	0.65	strong +

Figure 13.Comparison of SUS scores against backgrounds

Table 6: Comparision of SUS scores against backgrounds

Measure	Background	mean	median	standard deviation
Pre-test scores	Academia	3.3	2	3.3
	Industry	5.7	5	2.9
CLANN 1 SUS rating	Academia	67.3	70	18.9
	Industry	72.1	75	10.2
CLANN 2 SUS rating	Academia	52.5	50	22.7
	Industry	60.4	62.5	12.4
Ontomat SUS rating	Academia	28.4	22.5	20.4
	Industry	37.9	35	23.8
CLANN 1 Vs Ontomat Preference	Academia	64.3	62.5	14.8
	Industry	72.5	70	17.9
CLANN 2 Vs Ontomat Preference	Academia	63.4	60	16.4
	Industry	60.4	57.5	17.7
CLANN 1 Vs CLANN 2 Preference	Academia	48.9	52.5	10.7
	Industry	62.1	65	14.2

$n = 18$, $p < .01$, two tails. Hence, we can infer that users with little or no experience or knowledge of controlled languages, semantic annotation or ontologies who favour CLANN I over a standard manual semantic annotation tool will also tend to prefer CLANN II to a standard manual semantic annotation tool.

A comparison of SUS scores against user background is shown in Figure 13. Interestingly users with an industrial background scored CLANN I higher than academics by an additional 5 points. Furthermore, industry type users scored CLANN II higher than academics by an additional 8 points. With respect to the CLANN I/OntoMat preference scores, industrial users scored an extra 8 points higher than academics for CLANN I. Furthermore, users of an academic background scored 3 points higher than industry types in the CLANN II/Onto-Mat comparative questionnaire. Finally, the most interesting observation is the CLANN I/CLANN II

preference score, whereby industrial users scored their questionnaires roughly 13 points higher than academic users. More importantly, the relatively neutral CLANN I/CLANN II preference score of 48.9 is inconsistent with the high mean SUS score of 67.3 provided by academics for CLANN I. This implies that while academics liked using CLANN I, when asked to score preference of CLANN I and CLANN I, they were undecided. This was not the case for industrial users.

Finally, a comparison of tasks times against backgrounds is available in Figure 9. Academic users were in general slightly faster that industrial users with respect to both CLANN tools. In general users were 3-4 minutes faster using CLANN I, depending on their background, and in general OntoMat was the most time consuming tool averaging 23-25 minutes regardless of the user's background. The is due to the fact that 14 subjects requested to withdraw from their assigned

Figure 14. Comparison of task times against backgrounds

Table 7: Comparision of task times against backgrounds

Measure	Background	mean	median	standard deviation
CLANN 1 time	Academia	9	8	5.2
	Industry	9.9	4	8.5
CLANN 2 time	Academia	12.5	12	7.7
	Industry	14.3	14	5.7
Ontomat time	Academia	24.5	25	0.6
	Industry	23.4	25	3.7

annotation tasks due to waning interest. Consequently, we penalized the subjects by assigning them the maximum time of 25 minutes. We note that of the 14 subjects who withdrew, they did not completely annotate their respective task document. However, we ensured that they created sufficient metadata to complete the core tasks of creating or linking instances and instance properties. Of those 14 subjects that withdrew, 9 were academics and 5 were from an industrial background.

User Feedback

The test users also provided several suggestions/comments about both CLANN annotators:

- Many subjects requested a feature-rich graphical editor to assist the annotation process i.e. grammar correction, syntax highlighting and auto-completion. This, they argued would improve the speed of annotation and hence the usability of the tools.
- Most users requested features specific to the CLANN I editor include automatic template generation, auto-suggestion of verb phrases and instance labels and smart examples assiting the user.
- Most subjects requested features specific to the CLANN II editor included: automatic or assisted generation of snippets, machine learning capabilities to automatically recognise instances and an ontology visualization layer.

Discussion

Recall the goal of our evaluation has been to address the following research questions:

1. Can controlled natural languages for semantic annotation effectively substitute for

standard manual semantic annotation tools in certain scenarios?
2. Is CLANN I more or less user friendly than CLANN II?
3. Is habitability in CLANN I preferred over expressiveness (with respect to ontology manipulation) in CLANN II?

With respect to research question(1), our user evaluation consistently indicated that our subjects found CLANN I significantly more usable than OntoMat for annotation tasks. In addition novice users who preferred using CLANN I over OntoMat also tended to to prefer using CLANN II over OntoMat. Our data also revealed this relationship was also statistically significantly. This supports our hypothesis that for certain scenarios, CNLs can effectively substitute for manual semantic annotation and are also considered more user friendly.

Regarding research question(2), the relationship between task times for both CLANN annotators is significant. In our sample data, the tasks times of both CLANN annotators are positively correlated indicating that users spend the equivalent time to complete tasks with both CLANN tools. Although, CLANN I SUS scores were higher than CLANN II SUS scores, the CLANN I/CLANN II preference scores were scored as neutral and/or undecided and were inconsistent with the CLANN I SUS score. Hence, it is unclear which CLANN annotator was preferred by our sample users. However, interestingly, we noticed that industrial users in general had high usability scores for CLANN I consistent with CLANN I/CLANN II preference scores, which leads us to address (3). The reader should note that the ontology is completely hidden in CLANN I, requiring no interaction in order to create metadata. We suspect that industrial users appreciated CLANN I's tendency towards habitability because of its corpus driven design and subsequent language performance features. In contrast, though academics gave high usability scores for CLANN I, their CLANN 1/CLANN 2 preference scores were inconsistent with this, indicating that they were undecided with respect to which CLANN tool they preferred. Again recall that CLANN II is more expressive and powerful with regard to metadata creation and manipulation and is less habitable. The tool also requires inspection of the ontology. It is possible that academic users may have been conflicted with respect to deciding between a more formally expressive CNL and more a habitable CNL. Hence industrial users may favor habitability over expressiveness regarding metadata manipulation, while academics would perhaps rather sacrifice habitability for control over metadata and the ontology. We speculate that this may be also the case across industrial and academic groups within the true population of novice users, however our sample size is too small to make any statistical inferences in this regard.

Limitations of the Evaluation

We compared OntoMat with both CNL annotators, because OntoMat is a standard tool for manual semantic annotation. Furthermore OntoMat permits a user to easily import an external ontology. In addition, OntoMat was capable of emulating the structural annotation associated with the meeting minutes template used by both CLANN annotators. Another possible candidate was Semantic Media WiKi. However, firstly there are known issues with respect to importing external ontologies. Secondly and more importantly, Semantic Media Wiki associates metadata to wiki links and not text directly and was consequently not directly comparable to controlled annotation[19]. GATE was also a possible choice, but the Ontology Annotation Tool(OAT) in GATE is not as explicit as OntoMat with respect to annotating relational metadata[20] and in addition as CLANN is implemented in GATE, comparing it to OAT would have biased the evaluation.

With respect to the SUS questionnaire, we acknowledge that its high level nature makes the questionnaire quite general, however it is widely used, technologically agnostic and flexible, making it very suitable for general usability assessments. Although the majority of the participants were native speakers, we did not explicitly test for English proficiency among our sample users (as is the case in other work (Dimitrova et al., 2008). This is due to the fact that knowledge capture task is less complex than typical CNL tasks in that our users were not required to author axiomatic or intensional knowledge in CNL.

Efforts were made to exclude individuals with knowledge of ontologies and semantic annotation. One user had been exposed to GATE before, however our pretest scores were quite neutral. We argue that this was sufficient as a pilot study.

Annotation Metrics

It is important to understand that by comparing information extraction metrics across each tool, it results in an unfair comparison with respect to Ontomat. This is because CLANN I by its restricted nature, is deterministic and would always have 100% precision and recall. Hence the focus of our evaluation was on usability. The participants were given the meeting minutes in free text for all three tools. The sentences were examples taken from the aforementioned corpus we had gathered.

For both CLANN Tools in GATE: Where GATE indicated parsing errors in the message viewer, users were asked to rewrite the statements. We checked that the ontology was correctly populated after each user, which was the case. In the case of CLANN II: Since users were given some freedom with respect to CLANN II, we noticed that they sometimes linked to a super class rather than to the class instructed. For instance one user linked a chunk of text to the *Document* superclass instead of the class *Deliverable*. This is not incorrect rather inexact. The above mentioned "error" occurred with 40% of users. Finally, with respect to Ontomat: 14 out 18 participants requested to stop their task, usually after 5-10 minutes. We ensured that for each user who withdrew, they

Figure 15. Summary for the Precision and Recall scores for each tool

Table 8: Summary of the Precision and Recall scores for each tool

Precision	Recal	F-measure	
CLANN I	1	1	1
CLANN II	.9	1	.94
Ontomat	1	.53	.69

completed at least 7/18 annotations, correctly. The other remaining 4 participants created their annotations correctly. Figure 15 summarises the standard precision and recall metrics for each tool.

RELATED WORK

A plethora of tools exist for the manual or (semi-) automatic semantic annotation of free text. To our knowledge, however, very little research exists involving the application of CNL to semantic annotation. Our related work focuses on controlled natural languages for knowledge creation but for a thorough survey of manual and (semi-)automatic semantic annotation tools and platforms, we refer the reader to (Uren et al., 2006). In addition, the idea of *latent annotation*, blurring the lines between authoring and annotation, has its origins in (Handschuh & Staab, 2002) as part of the CREAM(CREAting Metadata) framework for (semi-automatic)semantic annotation. However, the implemention is simplistic and implies dragging an RDF Label for a given concept from the ontology viewer and essentially pasting the label into the document.

"Controlled Natural Languages (CL)s are subsets of natural language whose grammars and dictionaries have been restricted in order to reduce or eliminate both ambiguity and complexity" (Schwitter, 2007). They have also found favour in large multi-national corporations, usually within the context of machine translation and machine-aided translation of user documentation (Schwitter, 2007; Adriaens & Schreurs, 1992).

The application of CNLs for ontology authoring and instance population is an active research area (Smart, 2008). *Attempto Controlled English*[21] (ACE) (Fuchs & Schwitter, 1996), is a popular CNL for ontology authoring. It is a subset of standard English designed for knowledge representation and technical specifications, and is constrained to be unambiguously machine-readable DRS - Discourse Representation Structure, a form of first-order logic. It can also be re-targeted to other formal languages (Fuchs et al., 2006). The Attempto Parsing Engine (APE) consists principally of a definite clause grammar, augmented with features and inheritance and is written in Prolog (Hoefler, 2004). ACE OWL, a sublanguage of ACE, proposes a means of writing formal, simultaneously human- and machine-readable summaries of scientific papers (Kaljurand & Fuchs, 2006; Kuhn, 2006)

ACEView is a plugin for the Protégé editor[22] (Kaljurand, 2008). It empowers Protégé with additional interfaces based on the ACE CNL in order to create, browse and edit an ontology. The user can also query the ontology using ACE questions to access newly asserted facts from the knowledge base. A recent development with respect to ACE is the translation of a complete collection of pediatric guideline recommendations into ACE (Shiffman et al., 2010).

The Rabbit CNL is a another well known implementation (Hart, Johnson, & Dolbear, 2008). It is similar to CLOnE in its implementation but is much more powerful with respect to grammar expressiveness and ontology authoring capabilities. Rabbit was developed by the national mapping agency of Great Britain - Ordnance Survey. Rabbit can be converted in OWL[23] to provide natural language support for ontology authoring. OWL development is not the primary objective of Rabbit and not all Rabbit expressions can be mapped into OWL. It is primarily a vehicle for capturing, representing and communicating knowledge in a form that is easily understood by domain experts.

In (Engelbrecht, Hart, & Dolbear, 2009), the authors undertake a paraphrase-based evaluation to assess whether domain experts without any ontology authoring development can author and understand declaration and axiom sentences in Rabbit. The experiment included 21 participants from the ordnance survey domain and a Rabbit language expert. The participants were given a text that describes a fictional world and were asked to make knowledge statements which were then compared to equivalent statements created by the Rabbit expert. The sentences produced by non-experts were analyzed for correctness (with regard to the knowledge captured) by independent experts and were compared to those produced by the Rabbit expert. Interestingly, on average 51% of the sentences generated at least one error. Furthermore, the most common error was the omission of the quantifier "every" at the beginning of a sentence. This observation was of statistical significance. Other user errors included: confusing instances with subclass declarations, a tendency to omit intensional information as well difficulties modeling knowledge under the open world assumption. The work of Hart et al. (2008) and Engelbrecht et al. (2009) is important in the context of CNL evaluation in that we see the advent of the paraphrase-based approach to evaluating CNL's.

ROO (Dimitrova et al., 2008), developed by the University of Leeds, is an open source java based plugin to Protege which supports a domain expert to create and edit ontologies using Rabbit. The tool is based on the experiences of the Ordnance Survey(OS) agency with creating large-scale geospacial ontologies. The OS identified a number of factors based on their experiences, such as: (1) the difficulty in expressing knowledge constructs in a formal language, (2) the lack of appropriate methodology for capturing the knowledge of domain experts and (3) the poor usability of existing ontology editing tools. The ROO interface is based on the manipulation of Rabbit statements and not OWL constructs. The technical details of OWL are hidden from the end user. The design of the ROO interface is based on Ordnance Survey's proposed ontology development methodology called *Kanga*. ROO monitors user activity as well as the state of the underlying knowledge base. It provides the appropriate contextual suggestions and assistance to user in the forms of ontology construction feedback, syntax highlighting of Rabbit statements and error messages. An evaluation study of ROO was conducted against ACEView (Kalijurand, 2008) where participants from the domains of geography and environmental studies were asked to create ontologies based on hydrology and environmental models respectively. Both ontology creation tasks were designed to resemble real tasks performed by domain experts at OS. Controls were put in place to eliminate bias and ontologies for both domains were also produced by the OS to compare against the ROO generated ontologies. The quantitative results were favourable. Although ACEView users were more productive (not in the statistically significant sense), they tended to create more errors in the resulting ontologies. Furthermore with respect to ROO users, their understanding of ontology modelling improves significantly in comparison to ACEView. Interestingly, but not surprisingly, none of the ontologies produced were usable without post editing. Even though one could argue that the user experience is significantly improved with either ACE or ROO over a non CNL supported standard ontology editing tool, users would still require some formal training knowledge modelling techniques to author quality ontologies.

Other work involves integrating Rabbit(as well as support for ACE) into Semantic Media Wiki[24], the purpose of which is user friendly collaborative ontology authoring using multiple CNLs and template based language generation capabilities (Bao, Smart, Barnes, & Shadbolt, 2009).

With respect to evaluation frameworks, Kuhn (2010b) describes an evaluation framwork for CNLs based on *Ontographs*. Ontographs are a graphical notation to enable tool independent and reliable evaluation of the human understanding of a given knowledge representation language. The author categorises CNLs evaluations into (1) task-based, whereby users are provided with a specific task to complete and (2) paraphrase-based which are are concerned with testing the understandability of the CNL. Ontographs serve as a common basis for testing and comparing the understandability of two different formal languages and facilitate the design of tool-independent and reliable experiments. The author claims that Ontographs are simple and intuitive. They are useful for representing simple logical forms but they do not cater for functions and are restricted to unary and binary predicates. In short, Ontographs serve to test the relative understanding of the core logic for two different formal languages.

A recent addition to the CNL field is GF - Grammatical Framework (Angelov & Ranta, 2009) and (Ranta, 2004), which is an implementation framework which the authors claim can cope with a variety of CNLs as well as boost of the development of new ones. In their paper, the authors reverse engineer ACE for GF in order to demonstrate how portable CNLs are to the GF framework as well as how CNLs can be targeted to other natural languages. In this case ACE is ported from English to five other natural languages. In short, the core advantage of GF is its multilingualism in that its primary task is domain specific knowledge based Machine Translation (MT) of controlled natural languages. GF follows the functional programming paradigm and began as an experimental system in 1998 at XEROX Europe[25] (Dymetman, Lux, & Ranta, 2000) The GF framework uses a logical framework based on

Martin Loef's type theory (Nordstrom, Petersson, & Smith, 1990) for building semantic models of languages. It adds a syntax formalism to the logical framework which defines realisations of formal meanings as concrete linguistic expressions. The semantic model is called the *abstract syntax* while the syntactic realisation functionality is called *concrete syntax*. A substantial amount of linguistic competence and domain expertise is needed to define a concrete syntax for a given source/target language. Consequently the authors developed a collection of GF resource libraries to provide a language engineering solution to this issue. The GF libraries now contain a collection of wide coverage grammars for over 15 natural languages. One could view GF as a general framework for developing and extending controlled languages, similar to NLP architectures such as GATE. Although the work is very impressive, one should bare in mind that no results to our knowledge have been reported with respect to the quality of the translated output of GF.

The most closely related technologies to controlled annotation (specifically the CLANN II syntax) are semantic wikis, which have become a somewhat popular way of adding semantics to user generated wiki pages. The term semantic wiki often implies either ontology authoring or the semantic annotation of wiki content. A traditional wiki creates links between pages without defining the kind of linkage between pages. Semantic Media Wiki (Krötzsch, Vrandečić, & Völkel, 2006) allows a user to define the links semantically, thereby adding meaning to links between pages. Each concept or an instance has a page in Semantic Media Wiki(SMW), and each outgoing link from this page is annotated with well-defined properties as links. However this kind of approach differs to the kind of semantic annotation that we aim for. The Semantic Media Wiki model forces the users to use the wiki pages for content creation and to create a new page for each instance.[26] Moreover, the relational meta-data represented in a Semantic Media Wiki always has the corresponding page as its subject, thereby restricting the creation and description of other relevant entities.

With respect to user evaluation, the authors describe observations regarding SMW usage. The authors state first and foremost that the "majority of users will neglect annotation as it does not bear immediate benefit" (Krötzsch, Vrandečić, & Völkel, 2006). This is understandable given any annotation context, whereby the benefits of annotation are not recognised until the semantic search stage. In addition, they argue that "without conclusive studies on the usage of wikis in general, any prediction on the effect of introducing semantics in the (wikipedia) environment lacks justifications". In (Krötzsch, Vrandečić, & Völkel, 2006), the authors base their wiki usage experiments on ontoworld.org, which is itself maintained by the authors. The site's function is to collect information about semantic web researchers, events and projects. The authors record 930 registered users, the majority of which have contributed little to the total recorded 37,880 edits. The semantic knowledge base of ontoworld.org, at the time, counted 17,562 property annotations for 808 property edits. The majority of the properties have a page in the wiki, while 50% are of type Page and are used to annotate hyper-links. With respect to the usage of properties, they noted that 5% of the properties accounted for over 74% of the annotations, whereas the least used 80% of the properties accounted for less than 9% of all semantic statements. The authors state that these results have very similar power-law distributions to those of Wikipedia's categories (Krötzsch, Vrandečić, & Völkel, 2006). In conclusion, they argue that SMW features are at least equivalent to Media WiKi functionality, however as the authors themselves state "one cannot conclude whether or not the requested (annotation)functions are actually considered useful for a given purpose" and that additional research is needed to obtain definitive results. While the research is very important in that it records observations with respect to SMW usage over a large user populations, one

cannot conclude any specific user satisfaction rating with respect to the users and further more the user group is arguably extremely biased to that of the semantic web community.

In (Pfisterer, Nitsche, Jameson, & Barbu, 2008), the authors report better results, but it is in the context of the interface extensions to SMW by AIFB[27] in collaboration with Ontoprise GmbH[28]. The interface enhancements include: (1) a factbox which summarises all facts, linked to a given article, (2) a semantic query interface with strong auto-completion features, (3) an ontology browsing interface and (4) a Semantic Tool-Bar, which seeks to ease the semantic annotation process, but a classical a posteriori fashion and not at the editing/authoring stage. The Semantic Tool-Bar, which is enabled by software derived from the HALO[29] project, allows users to add/change annotations, whereby the changes are written directly to the wiki source text. They conducted two evaluations, whereby the shared scenario is the creation of a scientific Semantic Wikipedia. They recruited seven test subject matter experts consisting of two experts in physics, three in chemistry and two in biology. The experts had little or no familiarity with semantic wikis and had never edited a Wiki article before the evaluation. They participated in the design and development of the enhanced SMW over a period of seven months. With respect to both evaluations, they are more aligned to usability testing rather than being able to make and statistically significant inferences about the general target user population regarding the usability of their Wiki. A SUS (Brooke, 1996) questionnaire was administered to the group, once before and once after user feedback had been integrated into the enhanced Wiki. The user satisfaction was low prior to the enhancements and high, upon re-administration of the questionnaire. The sample size, at seven, was too small to make any statistically significant claims. More importantly, as the authors note, there are flaws in the evaluation in that a portion of first questionnaire group intersected with the second questionnaire group. This portion had been exposed to the enhanced SMW for a few months, so the high user satisfaction observed is inaccurate.

With respect to the second of the two afore-mentioned user evaluations, forty-two students from an introductory human-computer interaction class served as the sample user population. Each subject, after being provided introductory material, were asked to annotate a random wiki page in the enhanced SMW. In addition, after completing this task they were asked to formulate a number of queries to the SMW. This was followed by a SUS usability questionnaire. The resulting user satisfaction score was below the SUS baseline at 54.8%. In addition, on average each student created 4.2 annotations and only 50.3% were fully correct. Errors were caused primarily by unrecognised characters or date formats, which are rectifiable. The speed of the systems reaction accounted for a large amount of negative feedback. However, performance limitations in speed were undoubtably caused by over 20 users editing the SMW at the same time. This would invariably have had an impact on user satisfaction scores. Nevertheless, no statistical tests are performed on the SUS results and no inferences are made about the general target population. Despite the weak empirical results, the work presented in (Pfisterer, Nitsche, Jameson, & Barbu, 2008) is very important in that in represents a shift towards proper user evaluation and user centered design within the the semantic wiki community. The authors themselves acknowledge that there is still a need to provide more "concrete examples" with respect to application of user centered design to semantic wikis.

Other flavours of semantic wikis include IkeWiki[30] (Shaffert, 2006) and KiWi[31] One could argue that Semantic Wikis are only usable by the Semantic Web community and retain a significant formal barrier to a casual user or even an IT pro-fessional in the industry. ACEWiki (Kuhn, 2008)

attempts to circumvent this using the CNL ACE in combination with a predictive editor as an interface to a Semantic Wiki. However the task here is collaborative ontology authoring and not (controlled) annotation, which seeks to provide wiki content with a semantic backbone.

CONCLUSION AND FUTURE WORK

The research contributions of this article can be summarized as follows:

1. The description of a new approach to manual annotation using CNL called controlled annotation.
2. Our concept of latent annotation, by merging both authoring an annotations steps together.
3. We also implemented two types of CLANN (Controlled Language ANNotation) annota-tors, both varying in expressiveness and usability.
4. Empirical evidence to support the adoption of controlled annotation and evidence that for certain scenarios, controlled annotation can be more user friendly than standard manual semantic annotation tool.

Based on the results of our evaluation, we are merging best practices of both CLANN annotators into a hybrid annotator - CLANN III. Although the JAPE parsing process is quite robust, the parsing error messaging provided in GATE is insufficient. Clearly, it is evident that a proper interface is re-quired to improve the usability of both CLANN annotators as they are quite prototypical. CLANN III is being implemented in link grammar[32]. GATE is ideal for rapid prototyping in this context but the JAPE language has disadvantages inherent to finite-state parsing. Link grammar will provide us with more power(particularly due to its context free parsing capabilities allowing us to model the reification of triples properly) and furthermore it will provide CLANN III with free predictive parsing/editing capabilities to improve usability.

One could argue that our notion of latent annotation is not novel. Semantic Media Wiki also merges both authoring and annotation steps. However we believe that an annotation syntax (particularly in the context of CLANN II) should be as close to natural language as possible. So one could view the comparison as an annotation syntax problem. We argue that, for semantic wikis, the use of a formal syntax to link to facts to wiki pages represents a significant barrier to non-semantic users. This is supported by the weak results of user studies reported in the section on related work. Furthermore, in the context of the enhanced Semantic Media Wiki presented in (Krötzsch, Vrandečić, & Völkel, 2006), the "latent annotation" approach or standard semantic annotation syntax of the Wiki, is essentially abandoned for a Semantic Tool-Bar, which takes a traditional drag and drop a posteriori approach similar to a standard manual annotation tool. The purpose of this is to shield users from the formal annotation syntax of the Wiki. Despite this, the user satisfaction results are not favourable. In summary, there are still open questions with regard to the usability of Semantic Media Wiki, particularly in the context of creating annotation either at the authoring stage or following content creation.

We intend to integrate CLANN III into Semantic Media Wiki. We plan to conduct a user evaluation of CLANN III, comparing it either against the baseline Semantic Media Wiki[33] or the Enhanced Semantic Wiki co-developed by AIFB and Ontoprise (Pfisterer, Nitsche, Jameson, & Barbu, 2008). Hence, it remains to be seen whether controlled annotation can make an attractive alternative to conventional semantic wiki annotation approaches.

REFERENCES

Adriaens, G., & Schreurs, D. (1992). From CO-GRAM to ALCOGRAM: Toward a controlled English grammar checker. In *Proceedings of the Conference on Computational Linguistics (COLING '92)*, Nantes, France (pp. 595-601).

Angelov, K., & Ranta, A. (2009). Implementing controlled languages in gf. In *Proceedings of CNL* (pp. 82-101).

Auer, S., & Lehmann, J. (2007). What have Innsbruck and Leipzig in common? extracting semantics from wiki content. In *Proceedings of Eswc* (pp. 503-517).

Bailey, B. (2006). *Getting the complete picture with usability testing*. Washington, DC: U.S. Department of Health and Human Services. Retrieved December 16, 2010, from http://usability.gov/articles/newsletter/pubs/030106news.html

Bao, J., Smart, P., Braines, D., & Shadbolt, N. (2009, March). *A controlled natural language interface for semantic media wiki using the rabbit language*. Paper presented at the Workshop on Controlled Natural Language (CNL'09).

Brooke, J. (1996). SUS: a "quick and dirty" usability scale. In P. Jordan, B. Thomas, B. Weerdmeester, & A. McClelland (Eds.), *Usability evaluation in industry*. London: Taylor and Francis. Retrieved December 16, 2010, from http://www.usabilitynet.org/trump/documents/Suschapt.doc

Chomsky, N. (1965). *Aspects of the theory of syntax*. Cambridge, MA: MIT Press.

Decker, S. (2002). *Semantic web methods for knowledge management*. Unpublished doctoral dissertation, University of Karlsruhe, Germany.

Dimitrova, V., Denaux, R., Hart, G., Dolbear, C., Holt, I., & Cohn, A. (2008). Involving Domain Experts in Authoring OWL Ontologies. In *Proceedings of the 7th International Semantic Web Conference (ISWC 2008)*, Karlsruhe, Germany.

Dymetman, M., Lux, V., & Ranta, A. (2000). Xml and Multilingual Document Authoring: convergent trends. In *Proceedings of the 18th Conference on Computational Linguistics* (Vol. 1, pp. 243-249). Morristown, NJ: Association for Computational Linguistics.

Engelbrecht, P. C., Hart, G., & Dolbear, C. (2009). Talking rabbit: A user evaluation of sentence production. In *Proceedings of CNL* (pp. 56-64).

Fernández-López, M., Gómez-Pérez, A., & Juristo, N. (1997, March). Methontology: from ontological art towards ontological engineering. In *Proceedings of the AAAi97 Spring Symposium* (pp. 33-40).

Fuchs, N., & Schwitter, R. (1996). Attempto Controlled English (ACE). In *CLAW96: Proceedings of the First International Workshop on Controlled Language Applications*, Leuven, Belgium.

Fuchs, N. E., Kaljurand, K., Kuhn, T., Schneider, G., Royer, L., & Schröder, M. (2006). *Attempto Controlled English and the semantic web* (Deliverable No. I2D7). Retrieved December 16, 2010, from http://rewerse.net/deliverables/m24/i2-d7.pdf

Funk, A., Tablan, V., Bontcheva, K., Cunningham, H., Davis, B., & Handschuh, S. (2007). Clone: Controlled language for ontology editing. In *Proceedings of ISWC/ASWC* (pp. 142-155).

Handschuh, S. (2005). *Creating ontology-based metadata by annotation for the semantic web.* Unpublished doctoral dissertation, University of Karlsruhe, Germany

Handschuh, S., & Staab, S. (2002). Authoring and annotation of web pages in cream. In *Proceedings of WWW* (pp. 462-473).

Hart, G., Johnson, M., & Dolbear, C. (2008, June). Rabbit: Developing a control natural language for authoring ontologies. In *Proceedings of the 5th European Semantic Web Conference (ESWC2008)* (pp. 348-360).

Hoefler, S. (2004). *The syntax of Attempto Controlled English: An abstract grammar for ACE 4.0* (Tech. Rep. No. Ifi-2004.03). Zurich, Switzerland: Department of Informatics, University of Zurich. Retrieved December 16, 2010, from http://www.ifi.unizh.ch/attempto/publications/papers/hoefler2004theSyntax.pdf

Kaljurand, K. (2008, October 26-27). ACE View — an ontology and rule editor based on Attempto Controlled English. In *Proceedings of the 5th OWL Experiences and Directions Workshop (OWLED 2008)*, Karlsruhe, Germany.

Kaljurand, K., & Fuchs, N. E. (2006, June). Bidirectional mapping between OWL DL and Attempto Controlled English. In *Proceedings of the 4th Workshop on Principles and Practice of Semantic Web Reasoning.*, Budva, Montenegro.

Kaufmann, E. (2007). *Talking to the semantic web: natural language query interfaces for casual end-users.* Unpublished doctoral dissertation, University of Zurich.

Krötzsch, M., Vrandečić, D., & Völkel, M. (2006). Semantic MediaWiki. In *The semantic web - Iswc 2006* (LNCS 4273, pp. 935-942).

Krötzsch, M., Vrandečić, D., Völkel, M., Haller, H., & Studer, R. (2007). Semantic Wikipedia. *Journal of Web Semantics*, 5(4), 251–261. doi:10.1016/j.websem.2007.09.001

Kuhn, T. (2006, March). Attempto Controlled English as ontology language. In F. Bry & U. Schwertel (Eds.), *Proceedings of the REWERSE Annual Meeting 2006.*

Kuhn, T. (2008). AceWiki: Collaborative Ontology Management in Controlled Natural Language. In *Proceedings of the 3rd Semantic Wiki Workshop*. CEUR Workshop Proceedings.

Kuhn, T. (2010a). *Controlled English for knowledge representation*. Unpublished doctoral dissertation, University of Zurich. Retrieved December 10, 2010, from http://attempto.ifi.uzh.ch/site/pubs/

Kuhn, T. (2010b). An evaluation framework for controlled natural languages. In N. E. Fuchs (Ed.), *Proceedings of the Workshop on Controlled Natural Language (CNL 2009)* (LNCS 5972, pp. 1-20).

Nordstrom, B., Petersson, K., & Smith, J. M. (1990). *Programming in Martin-Löf's Type Theory: An Introduction*. New York: Oxford University Press.

Noy, N. F., & McGuinness, D. L. (2001, March). *Ontology development 101: A guide to creating your first ontology* (Tech. Rep. No. KSL-01-05). Stanford, CA: Stanford Knowledge Systems Laboratory. Retrieved December 5, 2009, from http://protege.stanford.edu/publications/ontologydevelopment/ontology101-noy-mcguinness.html

Pfisterer, F., Nitsche, M., Jameson, A., & Barbu, C. (2008). User-Centered Design and Evaluation of Interface Enhancements to the Semantic MediaWik. In *Proceedings of the Semantic Web User Interaction Workshop at CHI 2008: Exploring HCI Challenges*. CEUR Workshop Proceedings.

Phillips, J. L. (1996). *How to think about statistics*. New York: W. H. Freeman and Company.

Ranta, A. (2004). Grammatical Framework: A Type-Theoretical Grammar Formalism. *Journal of Functional Programming*, *14*(2), 145–189. doi:10.1017/S0956796803004738

Schaert, S. (2006). *Ikewiki: A semantic wiki for collaborative knowledge management*. Paper presented at the 1st International Workshop on Semantic Technologies in Collaborative Applications (STICA06).

Schwitter, R. (2007). *Controlled natural languages*. Retrieved, July 15, 2008, from http://www.ics.mq.edu.au/rolfs/controlled-natural-languages

Shiman, R. N., Michel, G., Krauthammer, M., Fuchs, N. E., Kaljurand, K., & Kuhn, T. (2010). Writing clinical practice guidelines in controlled natural language. In N. E. Fuchs (Ed.), *Proceedings of the Workshop on Controlled Natural Language (CNL 2009)* (LNCS 5972, pp. 265-280).

Smart, P. R. (2008). *Controlled natural languages and the semantic web*. Southampton, UK: School of Electronics and Computer Science, University of Southampton.

Sure, Y. (2003). *Methodology, tools and case studies for ontology based knowledge management*. Unpublished doctoral dissertation, University of Karlsruhe, Germany.

Tullis, T. S., & Stetson, J. N. (2004, June). *A comparison of questionnaires for assessing Website Usability*. Paper presented at the Usability Professionals' Association Conference, Minneapolis, MN.

Uren, V. S., Cimiano, P., Iria, J., Handschuh, S., Vargas-Vera, M., & Motta, E. (2006). Semantic annotation for knowledge management: Requirements and a survey of the state of the art. *Journal of Web Semantics*, *4*(1), 14–28. doi:10.1016/j.websem.2005.10.002

Watt, W. C. (1968). Habitability. *American Documentation*, *19*, 338–351. doi:10.1002/asi.5090190324

ENDNOTES

1. Herman, Ivan (2008-03-07). "Semantic Web Activity Statement". W3C. http://www.w3.org/2001/sw/Activity.html. Retrieved 2008-03-13.
2. http://www.ics.mq.edu.au/rolfs/controlled-natural-languages/
3. http://www.myetymology.com/latin
4. http://annotation.semanticweb.org/ontomat/index.html
5. http://www.semanticdesktop.org
6. http://smile.deri.ie/projects/semn
7. http://nepomuk.kde.org/
8. http://www.semanticdesktop.org/ontologies/
9. http://ontologies.smile.deri.ie/2009/02/27/docs/
10. http://www.semanticdesktop.org/ontologies/2007/11/01/pimo/
11. http://www.lexically.net/wordsmith/version5/index.html
12. General Architecture for Text Engineering, See http://gate.ac.uk/
13. Java Annotations Pattern Engine
14. http://semantic-mediawiki.org/wiki/Semantic_MediaWiki
15. http://smile.deri.ie/evaluation/2009CNLSem
16. SPSS 15.0, http://www.spss.com
17. A data sample's *95% confidence interval* is a range 95% likely to contain the mean of the whole population that the sample represents [20].
18. **Tool 1** represents CLANN I, **Tool 2** represents CLANN II and **Tool 3** represents OntoMat
19. At the time evaluation, the SMWriter API had not been developed. See http://semantic-mediawiki.org/wiki/Help:SMWWriter
20. This has improved in GATE 6.0
21. http://www.ifi.unizh.ch/attempto/
22. http://protege.stanford.edu/
23. http://www.w3.org/TR/owl-features/
24. More information about Semantic MediaWiki can be found at http://semantic-mediawiki.org/wiki/Help:Introduction_to_Semantic_MediaWiki
25. http://www.xrce.xerox.com/
26. At the time of evaluation, the SMWriter API had not been developed. http://semantic-mediawiki.org/wiki/Help:SMWWriter.
27. Institut für Angewandte Informatik und Formale Beschreibungsverfahren (AIFB) http://www.aifb.kit.edu
28. http://www.ontoprise.de/
29. http://www.projecthalo.com/
30. http://ikewiki.salzburgresearch.at/
31. http://www.kiwi-project.eu/
32. http://www.link.cs.cmu.edu/link/
33. This has been made more feasible with the recent development of the SMWriter API

This work was previously published in International Journal of Semantic Web and Information Systems, Volume 6, Issue 4, edited by Amit P. Sheth, pp. 64-91, copyright 2010 by IGI Publishing (an imprint of IGI Global).

Chapter 6

A Tool Suite to Enable Web Designers, Web Application Developers and End-Users to Handle Semantic Data[1]

Mariano Rico
Universidad Autónoma de Madrid, Spain

Óscar Corcho
Universidad Politécnica de Madrid, Spain

José Antonio Macías
Universidad Autónoma de Madrid, Spain

David Camacho
Universidad Autónoma de Madrid, Spain

ABSTRACT

Current web application development requires highly qualified staff, dealing with an extensive number of architectures and technologies. When these applications incorporate semantic data, the list of skill requirements becomes even larger, leading to a high adoption barrier for the development of semantically enabled Web applications. This paper describes VPOET, a tool focused mainly on two types of users: web designers and web application developers. By using this tool, web designers do not need specific skills in semantic web technologies to create web templates to handle semantic data. Web application developers incorporate those templates into their web applications, by means of a simple mechanism based in HTTP messages. End-users can use these templates through a Google Gadget. As web designers play a key role in the system, an experimental evaluation has been conducted, showing that VPOET provides good usability features for a representative group of web designers in a wide range of competencies in client-side technologies, ranging from amateur HTML developers to professional web designers.

DOI: 10.4018/978-1-4666-0185-7.ch006

INTRODUCTION

Web application development is becoming increasingly difficult, especially when focusing on designing attractive and reusable web applications. Web application developers need to be skilled in a wide set of client-side technologies (e.g., HTML, Javascript, CSS, DHTML, Flash, AJAX) and server-side ones (e.g., JSP, ASP, .NET), addressing an extensive number of programming languages (e.g., Java, Python, Ruby, PHP). The fast and divergent development of client-side technologies, which have formed the basis for the emergence of the Web 2.0 concept (O'Reilly, 2005) and attitude (Davis, 2005), has increased the importance of having experts in this type of technologies. In this paper, we refer to these client-side experts as web designers. This heterogeneity and complexity converts web designers in skilled programmers, as pointed out by Rochen, Rosson, and Pérez (2006), and increases the development cost of such applications.

The situation becomes even more complex when Web application developers want to incorporate Semantic Web data in their applications. Although many domains have a lack of ontologies, semantic technologies are mature enough and there is an increasing number of ontologies publicly available. According to d'Aquin et al, in 2007 there were around 23,000 ontologies available on the Internet (d'Aquin et al., 2007), and this number is growing quickly, especially due to the Linked Open Data initiative (Bizer, Heath, & Berners-Lee, 2009).

Therefore, this wealth of information still remains hidden to most Web application developers and end-users. On the one hand, semantic web technology experts are not usually focused on producing attractive and reusable web applications what makes it difficult for end-users to access this information (Macías & Castells, 2007). For example, early work on Semantic Web portals showed that usability aspects were not well considered in general in semantic web portal technologies (Lausen et al., 2005). From our experience with semantic web portals (Corcho, López-Cima, & Gómez-Pérez, 2006), we did conclude that such portals required very skilled people to maintain them, and demanded more flexible frameworks in order to create complex applications combining traditional web development and semantic data management. On the other hand, Web application developers need to improve their skills with those for the understanding and management of ontologies and semantic data, in order to produce semantically-enabled web applications (Oren, Heitmann, & Decker, 2008; d'Aquin et al., 2008).

Our approach aims at hiding much the complexity of semantic web technologies to the parties responsible for bringing the Semantic Web to end-users. In our previous work (Rico, Camacho, & Corcho, 2008) we divided the skills required to create a semantically-enabled web application into different groups of competencies, identifying the roles (profiles) involved. Two of these roles were identified as developers. The first of them had competencies in semantic web technologies and was low-skilled in web application development. The second developer profile had minimal skills in semantic web technologies but high competencies in web application development. For the first developer profile we built a wiki-based framework named *Fortunata* (Rico, Camacho, & Corcho, 2010), which allows semantic web application developers to create, configure and activate pieces of code that run on top of the framework, in a collaborative way. The experimental evaluation of this framework showed that the development cost and the required competencies for handling this framework were lower when compared to traditional technologies. We measured the usability of Fortunata from the developer's perspective by means of early-prototypes of Fortunata-based application, and that information was useful to identify usability pitfalls and successfully solve most of them, as well as to create a "Fortunata-based-application developers guide".

For the second developer profile, the most common currently available, we provide them with a programming-language independent mechanism (based in HTTP messages) to use 'semantic templates'. These templates are created by web designers by using a Fortunata-based application named *VPOET* (Rico et al., 2008), which plays a key role between the two developer profiles described.

The novelty of this paper is the description of the final version of VPOET, and the analysis of VPOET from the perspective of its users.

VPOET lets web designers create semantic templates to present and edit semantic data, even if they are low skilled in semantic web technologies. VPOET may have been implemented with any traditional combination of the aforementioned server-side and client-side technologies. However, the advantage of using Fortunata as a basis for the development of VPOET is that, as we said previously, this framework simplifies the development of semantically-enabled web applications.

To support some of the tasks required by VPOET's users we have also implemented another Fortunata-based tool called *OMEMO*. This application is aimed at web designers with no knowledge about ontology languages. Instead of opening the ontologies in specialized tools, non-skilled users can browse ontology components (classes and properties) by means of a set of wiki pages that are automatically generated whenever an RDFS or OWL ontology is included in the system. This application is similar to those provided for ontology developers by ontology edition tools like Protégé, SWOOP or NeOn Toolkit, or those provided as on-line services, like OWLDoc. However we considered it interesting to have this ontology visualizer highly coupled with VPOET, since understanding the structure of a given ontology component is one of the major tasks to be accomplished by a web designer who is designing a presentation template for an ontology component.

Our hypothesis is that web designers with no previous knowledge about semantic technologies, but skilled in client web technologies in the range from low to experts, can create easily VPOET templates.

To prove the validity of our hypothesis we carried out a usability and user satisfaction evaluation with a representative group of web designers, ranging from low-skilled to advanced. In this evaluation, all these web designers had a common objective: to create a presentation template for a specific ontology component. Once this objective was accomplished each of them had to answer a detailed set of questionnaires. The analysis of their answers revealed good values for usability and user satisfaction in the whole representative range of web designers, validating our hypothesis.

In the rest of this article we start with a brief description of VPOET architecture. Then the focus of the paper is centred in the two perspectives of VPOET: the one provided to web designers and the one provided to web developers. The next section shows the experimental evaluation of the usability and user satisfaction concerning VPOET. Then, a section showing related work is given, and we finish with conclusions and further work.

VPOET ARCHITECTURE AND ROLES INVOLVED

Fortunata[1] is a Java library built on top of the JSP-Wiki wiki engine. The main features of this engine are its support for the management of forms and its extensibility capabilities by means of plugins. Fortunata simplifies the creation of semantically-enabled web applications by delegating to the underlying wiki engine the client-side presentation and server-side publication of semantic data. The creation of pages is done with a wiki-based syntax, which has predefined constructs to create links, sortable tables, tables of contents, etc. The publication of semantic data is done automatically by the system.

Figure 1. VPOET architecture and actors involved

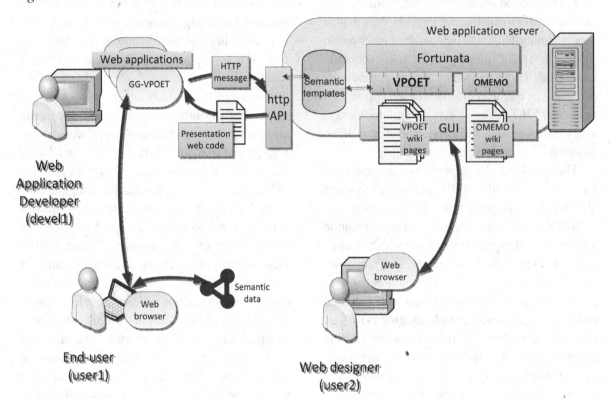

A Fortunata-based application consists of a set of wiki pages that contain regular wiki code intertwined with calls to Fortunata plugins (F-plugins). For instance, VPOET is a Fortunata-based application that consists in four interrelated wiki pages and seven F-plugins. Figure 1 shows the architecture of VPOET and the roles involved.

Table 1 provides details about these roles, focusing on the activities that they perform, the skills required to perform such activities, and the benefits achieved by this approach. In summary the roles are these:

- **Web application developer (devel1)** creates semantically-enabled web applications by using the templates stored in VPOET. This role only requires basic HTTP management skills in any programming language in order to make a simple HTTP call to get a visualization for the se-

Table 1. Description on the roles involved in VPOET

Role	Activities	Requirements	Benefits
devel1	Web application developer. Integrates VPOET templates in any web application in order to create semantically-enabled web applications	HTTP management skills in **any** programming language	No client technologies skills are required
user2	VPOET user. Uses VPOET to design web templates	Web design skills	No semantic web technologies skills are required
user1	VPOET Google Gadget end-user. Uses the VPOET Google Gadget to visualise semantic data	HTML basics (cut & paste simple generated code)	No client or semantic technologies skills are required

mantic data specified. Playing this role we have created an application oriented to end-users, based in Google Gadgets technology, which enable end-user to handle semantic data in their web pages. This application, named GG-VPOET, is described later.

- **Web designer (user2)** uses VPOET to create templates to present semantic data (output templates), or request data to the user that will be converted to semantic data (input templates). This role requires skills in web design (HTML, CSS, AJAX, etc.).
- **End-user (user1)** uses his/her web browser to use the application created by devel1. In this case, by using the VPOET Google Gadget (GG-VPOET) end-users can handle semantic data in their own pages or any Google product such as Google Docs, Google Pages, or iGoogle.

VPOET FOR WEB DESIGNERS: ENHANCING THE PRESENTATION AND CAPTURE OF SEMANTIC DATA

VPOET enables web designers (*user2* in Figure 1), also known as "Template Providers", to create web templates for a set of ontology components. There are two types of VPOET templates: output templates are intended to present semantic data, input templates are intended to request data from users. For example, let us imagine that we want to create output and input templates to render and create, respectively, semantic data for the concept Person, belonging to the FOAF ontology, one of the most popular concepts in the Semantic Web with 60 million instances available[2]. Output templates can be used to render any data source containing instances (individuals) of this class, or any subclass if there are no more specialized templates for them. Input templates are intended to present a form to request data that will be converted to an instance of Person.

VPOET is focused on web designers, who should be able to author attractive designs capable of handling semantic data. Hence, VPOET only requires basic skills in client-side technologies (e.g., HTML, Javascript). As described in following sections, the most difficult task to be performed by web designers is to embed some semantic data management macros in the client-side web code. Hence there is little training needed to start creating templates (a 30-minute online tutorial[3] is enough, as demonstrated in our evaluation).

Although it will be described in the next section, Web application developers can use the templates stored in VPOET in their own web applications. From the point of view of end-users who browse semantic data sources through the visualizations generated by output templates or who have to introduce data through input templates, a VPOET-enabled application is like any other Web application, with information shown in simple tables or advanced client-side elements such as Flash.

In the following subsections we will describe the process to be followed in order to create VPOET output and input templates, how to reuse output templates, and we will also provide some additional information about the related Fortunata-based tool OMEMO which can be also used in this process.

Creation of VPOET Output Templates

The process to create an output template starts with the selection of the corresponding ontology component to be visualized. As an example we show the steps to be followed to create an output template for the concept Person from the FOAF ontology:

1. Getting information about the structure of the targeted component. The VPOET user needs to know the structure of this component: its properties, sub-components, etc. Although

this information can be obtained by directly analyzing the corresponding ontology in its implementation language (e.g., RDFS, OWL) or by using ontology visualization tools, typical VPOET users are not skilled to achieve this task. We have developed an specific tool named OMEMO (described later) to achieve this task. Figure 7 shows a snapshot of the information provided by OMEMO for the class FOAF:Person.

In this case, the VPOET user can see that FOAF:Person comprises properties such as first-Name or interest, as well as firstName is a Literal belonging to the rdfs ontology. The link in Literal will open the web page for this element.

2. Authoring a web design (with any web authoring tool) where semantic data will be inserted. Figure 2 shows a initial example of a web design. The left-most column shows the HTML code, whereas the right-most one shows how it is rendered in a web browser.
3. Choosing an identifier for the template, which will generate the corresponding wiki page in the system with information about the template, as described in step 8.
4. Cutting & pasting the web design code into the appropriate VPOET form fields, with the appropriate HTML, CSS and Javascript code. If the code includes references to files (e.g., images), these can be uploaded into the VPOET or any web server.
5. Replacing any absolute paths in the web design code (e.g. path to images or Javascript files) by the macro OmemoBaseURL, which expands into the appropriate URL at runtime, depending on the URL of the server where the system is running. A list with the available macros can be found in Table 2. Our experience has shown that this small set is enough to cover the most common needs for the creation of VPOET templates.
6. Replacing any dummy semantic values in the web design code by specific macros that insert the actual property values at runtime. For example, the dummy text "this is the name" in Figure 2 should be replaced by the macro OmemoGetP, which gets the values of the property indicated. The result of this

Figure 2. Initial output template example. Left: initial HTML code. Right: template rendered in a web browser.

```
Code
<table style='background: #F0F0F0; padding: 1px;
border: thin solid #DDDDDD; margin-left: 1em'>
<tr> <td>Name:</td><td>this is the name</td>
</tr>
<tr> <td>Given Name:</td><td>this is the
givenname</td>
</tr>
<tr> <td>Family name:</td><td>this is the
family_name</td>
</tr>
<tr> <td>Home page:</td><td><a
href='http://somewhere.com'>http://somewhere.com</a
></td>
</tr>
<tr> <td>Depiction:</td><td><img
src='http://somewhere.com/mi_image.gif'></td> </tr>
<tr> <td>Knows:</td><td>list of known people</td>
</tr>
</table>
```

Rendering

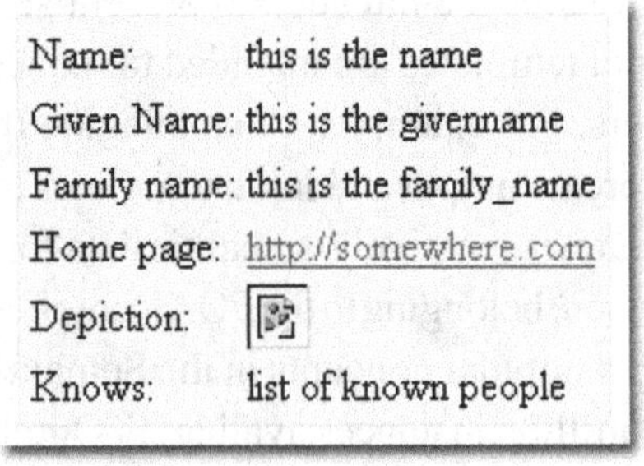

Name: this is the name
Given Name: this is the givenname
Family name: this is the family_name
Home page: http://somewhere.com
Depiction:
Knows: list of known people

Figure 3. Placing the source code in VPOET. Some code is replaced by macros.

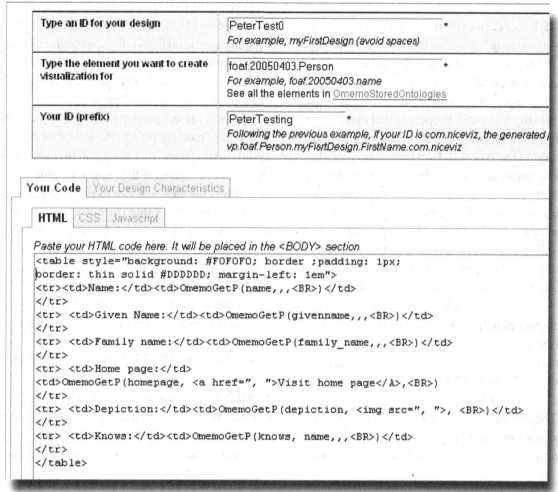

replacement is shown in Figure 3. Other macros like OmemoConditionalVizFor and OmemoGetLink allow reusing existing VPOET templates, and are described later.

7. Testing the design with semantic-data sources (typically external to VPOET) that contain instances of the targeted component. Figure 3 shows the kind of results that can be achieved when a given output template is tested with data from a given data source (in this case http://ishtar.ii.uam.es/fortunata/foaf.rdf) which contains some instances of the class FOAF:Person.

8. Describing the designed template with the following information: template type (input or output), behavior in case of changes to the font size, sizes (preferred, minimum and maximum), code-type (HTML, Javascript, CSS), and dominant colors. This information is included in the corresponding template wiki page, and is useful to discover at runtime the most appropriate template for a given user or interaction device, as described in the conclusions and future work section.

Reusing Templates in VPOET

VPOET users can exploit two macros that allow reusing existing VPOET output templates belonging to him/her or to any other template provider, so that it is possible to create compositions of templates and hence more modular designs. This is normally used with properties that connect an individual with another individual (e.g., with the relation FOAF:knows). However, it may be also used to reuse specific templates for some types of property values. For example, if a VPOET output template for visualizing e-mails with Javascript obfuscation to avoid SPAM has been created and is available in the system, we may reuse this template when a class contains a property showing the e-mail address of a person or organization. This can be used as well to hide details in order to get a compact visualization. Clicking in a small icon can expand or substitute the visualization area to display details. These expand and/or contraction features require AJAX knowledge or third parties javascript libraries.

The first macro, OmemoGetLink (see Table 2), specifies a property that is substituted at runtime by a link that points to the VPOET communica-tion servlet, with the appropriate parameters, for rendering the destination instance. For example, the property FOAF:knows establishes a relation between an origin (FOAF:Person in this case) and a destination (another FOAF:Person). If we use this macro for this property, we get a link capable of rendering any "known" person.

When a given property has no value, the macro OmemoGetP returns the string "N.A.". To avoid this effect, the macro OmemoConditionalVizFor checks if the property value exists and, if it is the case, uses an existing template to show the property value (in this case, a simple text renderer). This is also applicable with relations that link the instance with other instances.

The code requited to create the template shown in Figure 4 is shown in Figure 4. Macros are framed within a thick rectangle, and reused templates are framed within a thin stroke.

Creation of VPOET Input Templates

VPOET input templates are HTML forms that convert the entered values into semantic data (RDF). As in output templates, an input template is intended for an ontology component (which usu-

Table 2. Main set of macros available for VPOET template providers

Macro	Arguments	Explanation
OmemoGetP	propName	It is replaced by the property value propName. As most properties can be multivalued, the next version is used.
OmemoGetP	propName, prefix, posfix, separator	Indicated for multivalued properties, it is replaced by the whole set of values, starting with the code specified in prefix, finishing with the code in posfix, and placing the code in separator between each property value. See an application example in Figure 3, in the code placed in the HTML tab.
OmemoGetP	relation, propPref, prefix, posfix, separator	Indicated for relations, it shows the value(s) of the property propPref (preferred) of the entity target of the relation. See an application example in Figure 3.
OmemoBaseURL	No arguments	It is replaced by the URL of the server where VPOET is running. See an application example in Figure 5
OmemoConditionalVizFor	propName, designerID, designID	It renders the property propName only if it has a value, using the template indicated by designerID and designID.
OmemoGetLink	relationName, designerID, designID	It is replaced by a link capable of displaying components of the type pointed by the relation relationName using the template indicated by designerID and designID. See an application example in Figure 5

Figure 4. Testing a sample output template against a given semantic data source. The balloons show different individuals, even anonymous. Non anonymous individuals can be rendered individually if the link in the right side of the balloon is clicked.

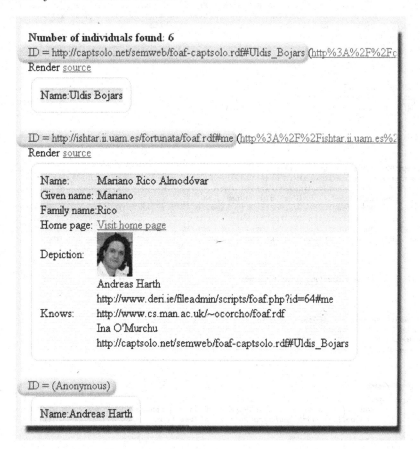

ally comprises a set of ontology sub-components). For example, an input template for the ontology component FOAF:Person must provide a form with input fields for firstName, knows, etc. The process to create an input template is similar to the one required to create output templates. The main differences are the following:

- The template source code does not contain macros, although it must follow some conventions: (1) the HTML code must contain an HTML form with the action attribute pointing to an specific servlet provided by VPOET, (2) the form must contain a hidden input field named "ontoelem", whose

value is the name of the ontology component for which this template has been created, (3) the HTML form controls (i.e. input fields, radio buttons, etc.) must have an attribute name that corresponds to the corresponding component (e.g., property) in the ontology. This can be referenced to with the following notation: ontologyAlias.version.elem (this is the OMEMO syntax, described in the next subsection), or with the corresponding URI.

- The test phase does not use external semantic data sources. However, as the VPOET servlet generates semantic data, this source can be rendered by a VPOET output tem-

Figure 5. Advanced example showing macros (thick rectangles) and templates reuse (thin rectangles)

```
<tr>
   <td background="OmemoBaseURL/attach/Mra68Graphics/bg_hlines_gray.gif">Depiction:</td>
   <td background="OmemoBaseURL/attach/Mra68Graphics/bg_hlines_gray.gif">
      OmemoGetP(depiction, <img src=", ">, <BR>)</td>
</tr>

<table border="0" cellpadding="0" cellspacing="0">
  <tr>
    <td><img src="OmemoBaseURL/attach/Mra68Graphics/xample_body_esi.gif"></td>
    <td background="OmemoBaseURL/attach/Mra68Graphics/xample_body_upper_pat.gif"></td>
    <td><img src="OmemoBaseURL/attach/Mra68Graphics/xample_body_esd.gif"></td>
  </tr>
  <tr>
    <td background="OmemoBaseURL/attach/Mra68Graphics/xample_body_left_patt.gif" ></td>
    <td>

<table border="0" cellpadding="0" cellspacing="0">
<tr><td colspan=2>OmemoConditionalVizFor(title, mra68,
SimpleFOAFOutput.title)OmemoConditionalVizFor(name, mra68, SimpleFOAFOutput.name)</td></tr>
<tr><td colspan=2>OmemoConditionalVizFor(givenname, mra68, SimpleFOAFOutput.givenname)</td></tr>
<tr><td colspan=2>OmemoConditionalVizFor(family_name, mra68, SimpleFOAFOutput.family_name)</td></tr>
<tr><td colspan=2>OmemoConditionalVizFor(homepage, mra68, SimpleFOAFOutput.homepage)</td></tr>
<tr><td colspan=2>OmemoConditionalVizFor(depiction, mra68, SimpleFOAFOutput.depiction)</td></tr>
<tr><td colspan=2>OmemoConditionalVizFor(knows, mra68, AdvancedFOAFOutput.knows)</td></tr>
</table>

</td>
    <td background="OmemoBaseURL/attach/Mra68Graphics/xample_body_right_patt.gif"></td>
  </tr>
  <tr>
    <td width="17" style="font-size: 2px"><img
src="OmemoBaseURL/attach/Mra68Graphics/xample_body_eii.gif"> </td>
    <td background="OmemoBaseURL/attach/Mra68Graphics/xample_body_bottom_pat.gif"></td>
    <td width="17" style="font-size: 2px"><img
src="OmemoBaseURL/attach/Mra68Graphics/xample_body_eid.gif"> </td>
  </tr>
</table>

<tr>
   <td background="OmemoBaseURL/attach/Mra68Graphics/bg_hlines_gray.gif">Knows:</td>
   <td background="OmemoBaseURL/attach/Mra68Graphics/bg_hlines_gray.gif">
      <A href ="OmemoGetLink(knows)">OmemoGetP(knows, name,,,<BR>) </A></td>
</tr>
```

plate. Therefore, it is recommended to create an output template for each input template, for testing proposes. Typical errors such as wrong property names can be detected with this strategy.

Figure 6 shows an example of a VPOET input template for the ontology class FOAF.20050403. Person. The figure shows a "plus sign" on the right of some fields. This is automatically generated by VPOET when a property can have multiple values. Similarly the icon on the right of the property knows is also automatically generated by VPOET. When a user clicks on it, it opens an "instance browser", a web page that allows end-users to select a set of instances from the corresponding target class. These instances may be available in the system (and then the system shows them in the list) or the end-user may write their URI directly, if they are in a external semantic data source.

As such, input templates are very similar to what has been traditionally done in semantic portals for the introduction of semantic data according to a given ontology model. Hence there is not much innovation on this side, apart from the fact that semantic portals are usually more rigid and do not allow using properties for an individual that are not connected to the class that the individual belongs to. This is something that can be done easily in VPOET.

Figure 6. An example of VPOET input template in action

OMEMO: Wiki-Based Documentation of Ontologies

OMEMO is another Fortunata-based application. It stands for "Ontologies for MEre MOrtals", and it is aimed at users with no skills in ontology languages, as mentioned in the introduction. With OMEMO users can find out which components (classes and properties) are defined in a set of ontologies.

OMEMO generates a set of wiki pages that describe any given OWL or RDF Schema ontology. An ontology may have different versions, which can be distinguished from one another by its publication date or, as proposed in the current OWL 2 working draft (OWL, 2009), by specific versioning properties. In the following example, we consider the FOAF ontology 20050403.

OMEMO only requires the URL of a given ontology, and the generation process results in a page for the ontology and another page per each

class and property. Carrying on with the example, Figure 7 shows a section of the wiki page generated for the class Person (version 20050403). Point 4 indicates that other versions of the same ontology exist and lets us access those pages through those links. Property interest has type FOAF:Document (point 3), and property firstName (point 1) has type RDFS:Literal (point 2). These solid links indicate existing component wiki pages; otherwise, links will be underlined by a dotted-line.

It is worth mentioning that the pages generated by OMEMO are automatically indexed by JSPWiki using the Lucene engine, as it happens with any other wiki page generated manually. Hence search facilities provided by JSPWiki include the text in these pages. Besides, any manually-created wiki page can link to any of these automatically-generated pages.

Figure 7. Snapshot of the OMEMO wiki page for class Person (version 20050403) of the FOAF ontology

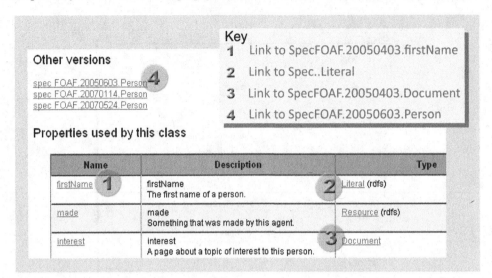

VPOET FOR WEB APPLICATION DEVELOPERS: INCLUDING VPOET TEMPLATES IN WEB APPLICATIONS

As shown in Figure 1, Web application developers (represented by *devel1*) can exploit VPOET templates in order to create easily semantically-enabled web applications.

For example, a web page about the city of Madrid would include the usual HTML code to show the text, multimedia objects and links to internal or external URLs. We can also include additional calls to VPOET templates that link some of those pieces of text, multimedia objects and links with the visualization of semantic data available in the system or in any other external semantic data source. From this description, this configuration may seem to be similar to that of semantic wikis. However, in these systems the visualization of semantic data is done always by reference to internal semantic data and by means of predefined tables, which is not the case with the use of applications exploiting VPOET.

Now we describe how to include VPOET templates into any web application. Developers can use VPOET templates by means of an ad-hoc communication servlet that lets clients make HTTP GET/POST requests with variable parameters in order to facilitate queries like "render the semantic data at URL Z by using the output template X created by designer Y". This request is codified as http://URL-to-servlet/VPoetRequestServlet? action=renderOutput&designID=X&prov ider = Y&source=Z. In this example, the semantic data are referenced by means of the source parameter (GET message), but can be included in the HTTP message (POST message). The complete syntax of these requests is shown in Table 3.

Semantic data can be included or not in the parameters of the HTTP message. SPARQL end-points[4] provide a similar functionality, but they are oriented to much more specialized developers (those capable of writing the SPARQL queries that must be specified in the HTTP message). As we aim at a wider audience with little or no knowledge about Semantic web technologies, we preferred to provide the current syntax.

HTTP messages with the specified syntax, can be sent to the VPOET communication servlet by other programs written in any programming language, or by Javascript applications executed in a web browser. However, browsers are more limited

Table 3. Parameters accepted in the HTTP GET/POST request

Parameter	Value	Explanation/Example
action	renderOutput	Request a visualisation for the components object in the data source given in parameter source
	renderInput	Request a visualisation to request data for the component object from the user
object	prefix.class[.ver]	Example: foaf.Person
	prefix.relation[.ver]	Example: foaf.firstName
source (GET only)	URL	URL of the semantic data source
[provider]	ID	Identifier of the visualization provider. For example: user3.test
outputFormat	HTML	Default value
	XHTML	XHTML is used by WAP 2.0 mobile phones

than other applications because they suffer security limitations due to the fact that communication is restricted to the server which holds the web application. This is the case for Tabulator (Berners-Lee et al., 2006), which requires reducing the security restrictions of the browser. Our approach does not have this problem because communications between the end-user and the different semantic data sources are centralised by VPOET.

VPOET Google Gadget (GG-VPOET)

Besides the previous HTTP-based mechanism, and aimed at decreasing even more the required skills needed to use VPOET templates, we have created a Google Gadget called GG-VPOET[5]. By using this gadget, any developer or end-user can render easily a semantic data source or provide a web interface to create semantic data. GG-VPOET, as any other Google Gadget, can be inserted into an ordinary web page or in Google products such as iGoogle, Google Desktop or Google Pages.

This gadget is configured by end-users by providing simple parameters such as the template ID or the web designer ID, which can be obtained reading the VPOET "designs list" wiki page. Figure 8 shows this gadget in action using a given output template for the ontology component foaf:Person. The left-most window shows how this gadget can be inserted in a web page (and

how it is configured), whereas the right-most one shows this gadget in a proprietary tool such as Google Pages.

EXPERIMENTAL EVALUATION

The evaluation of our work has focused on providing evidence that supports our principal aim concerning ease-of-use and expressiveness of VPOET. As we have shown, VPOET has two faces, the first one intended for web designers and the second one intended for web application developers. The first is provided through a web application and the second is provided through an HTTP API. Although both faces can be evaluated, we have focused on the first one. The HTTP API was informally discussed with some developers, and they did applaud the simplicity of the HTTP calls and the high functionality provided. Although there are techniques to measure the quality of object oriented APIs (Bansiya & Davis, 2002), we do not have any reference on quality metrics for HTTP APIs. Therefore, we trust in the informal evaluation of the VPOET API and focus our study in measuring quality features of web designers using VPOET, specifically usability clues and user satisfaction with the user interface.

In this context, usability is defined as "the ease of use and acceptability of a system for a particu-

Figure 8, Using GG-VPOET in different application oriented to end-users. Left: a personal page. Right: Google Pages lar class of users carrying out specific tasks in a specific environment"(Holzinger, 2005).

Description of the Experiment

In order to have a real feeling about VPOET users' perception, we selected fifteen postgraduate students to carry out this experiment. Some of them had basic technical background and knowledge about client-side web languages such as HTML, CSS or Javascript. Some other had large experience in web design.

We provided all of them with a 30-minute talk about the task that they had to accomplish playing the role of web designers, giving a general overview of VPOET and OMEMO. The talk used an online tutorial in which concepts such as class, instance, value, property, relation, were explained with practical examples. More advanced concepts such as conditional rendering or templates reusing also were covered by the online tutorial and were used by the participants. After this introductory talk, we explained them the main objective of the evaluation: creating a VPOET output template for the class Person defined in the ontology FOAF (version 20050403). We made explicit that the time needed to perform this task was not going to be evaluated, so they could take as long as needed, but emphasizing that the objective was to create attractive visualizations of the ontology component specified. Links to existing semantic data sources were supplied in the wiki in order to help them test their designs.

Some of the common errors that they made were those related to the wrong display of multi-valued properties such as Person.knows, or to the incorrect visualization of missing values for properties such as Person.title. Once every user finished and tested his/her template, each participant filled in a detailed questionnaire[6] of 49 questions comprising different features such as (a) skills in client-side technologies, (b) usability concerning VPOET, and (c) user's satisfaction concerning the User Interface of VPOET. Most of these questions were based on standard questionnaires from Perlman site[7].

Evaluation

Choosing the Number of Participants

To achieve a 95% confidence level for a given mean with error less than 1%, it is required to take 15 measurements at least (Efron & Tibshirani, 1986). This assumes intervals based on a normal population distribution for mean.

$$n = (z^* \cdot \sigma / m)^2.$$

In this equation, is the upper $(1-C)/2$ critical value for the standard normal distribution (C is the confidence level), σ stands for the standard distribution (sample mean), and m stands for the margin of error.

Evaluation of Skills in Client-Side Technologies

The user's skills were calculated as the sum of the numerical values freely auto-assigned by each user (depending on his/her level of competence, from 0 to 5) on the client side issues described in the questionnaire. These issues are shown in Table 4. An additional question to measure the level of competencies in semantic web technologies was removed from the results due to none of the participants had competencies in this topic.

Evaluation of Usability

The questions about the usability of VPOET were taken from a standard test called "Practical Heuristics for Usability Evaluation" (Perlman, 1997). This test includes 13 questions ranging from 1 (bad) to 5 (good), which provides a useful measure of the user's perceived usability. The results of this test are shown in Figure 10a and Figure 9a. Figure 10a shows that three types of

Table 4. Topics in the skills questionnaire

ID	Client-side web technologies
Q1	HTML
Q2	CSS
Q3	DHTML (Javascript + DOM)
Q4	AJAX Basics (Javascript + asynchronous invocation + DOM)
Q5	Advanced AJAX Level 1 (AJAX basics+management of XML/JSON)
Q6	Advanced AJAX Level 2 (AJAX basics+API's usage = mashups)
Q7	Flash basics
Q8	Advanced Flash (XML data exchange and/or communication with Java/ Others)

Figure 9. Mean value of the user's responses in the questionnaire (circles). Thin bars show standard deviation. Thick bars show the 90% confidence interval of the mean. Dark dotted line shows the average usability value, and light dotted lines show standard deviation bounds.

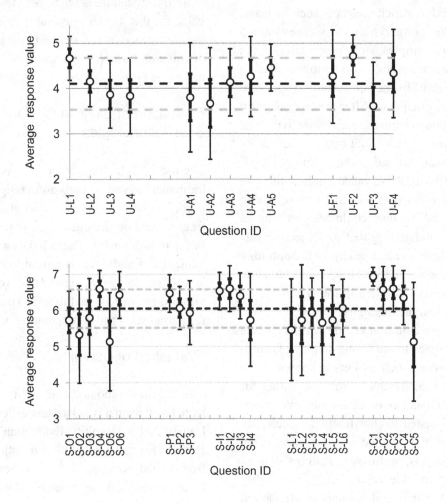

Figure 10. Usability and satisfaction as a function of user's skills in client-side technologies grouped by skills. Bars show standard deviation.

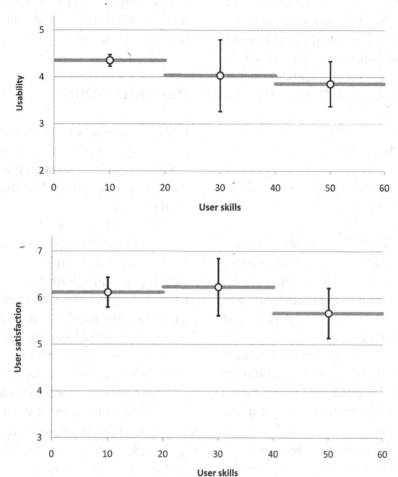

users can be identified: those with basic skills (range 0-20, with 5 users), medium (20-40, with 7 users), and advanced (greater than 40, with 3 users). Figure 9a shows the average value assigned by the participants to the questions related to usability in the questionnaire.

The analysis of usability was based on the average value assigned in this test, which was 4.1, with a standard deviation of 0.595. This shows high usability values for the whole range of participants, although the most skilled users assign slightly lower usability values. A possible explanation is that skilled users are more demanding, and this results in slightly lower evaluations, but even these advanced users provide high usability

values. These results confirm that VPOET is a useful tool even for less skilled designers.

Evaluation of User's Satisfaction

In order to evaluate the user's satisfaction concerning the VPOET user interface, we used a slightly modified version of the standard test "User Interface Satisfaction" (Chin, Diehl, & Norman, 1988). The standard version includes 27 questions, but it was reduced to 24 due to overlaps with the usability test described previously. Valid responses to these questions were positive integers ranging from 0 (not satisfied at all) to 7 (completely satisfied). The results are shown in Figure 10b and Figure 9b.

The average value for user satisfaction was 6.06, with a standard deviation of 0.53. Besides, the results show the dependency between the user's satisfaction and his/her skills. It is worth noting that the user satisfaction depends on the user skills in the same way that usability, that is, higher-skilled users assign a slightly lower value to satisfaction.

Treats to Validity

The next list summarises the context in which these results must be considered:

- The justification for the number of participants assumes intervals based on a normal population distribution for mean.
- The task proposed to the participants was the creation of a simple template, and many complex elements such as transitive relationships, axioms and constraints were not considered. Therefore the validity of this evaluation is restricted to the creation of presentation templates for simple ontology components.
- The effects of the underlying framework (Fortunata) impose several restrictions to the web application user interface. These restrictions have an effect in the web designer perception so that, these results must be considered in the context of Fortunata-based applications. A new version of VPOET, built with traditional web technologies, although more expensive in terms of development cost, could result in a tool better evaluated by web designers.

Analysis Results

In summary, from the experimental evaluation with 15 participants, we can conclude that VPOET provides good average values for usability (8.2 in a 0-10 range) and user satisfaction concerning the user interface (8.7 in a 0-10 range) for a wide range of user competencies, what confirms our main hypothesis, that is, VPOET is a usable tool for web designers in a wide range of client-side technologies skills.

RELATED WORK

Our approach has some relationships with work performed in the context of semantic wikis, semantic portals, semantic pipes and semantic-web browsers, as well as End User Development (EUD).

Semantic Wikis (Oren, Delbru, Moller, Volkel, & Handschuh, 2006) are collaborative web applications that allow creating semantic data (e.g., RDF triples) and publish it in a wiki-like fashion, normally combined with natural language text. These systems require users trained in the annotation of natural language text and knowledge about the annotation terms to be used (ontologies terms). The wiki pages generated by these systems normally show both the natural language text and the semantic information in a predefined way. Although some systems provide users with templates, there is a one-to-one relation between an ontology term and a template. That is, the template for an ontology term is used to render all the ontology term individuals. VPOET externalizes this functionality, providing ways to access the templates and allowing a one-to-many relation between ontology terms and templates. Wikis can exploit VPOET templates easily (Rico, Camacho, & Corcho, 2009b).

Users can also handle semantic data in a *non-explicit* way, i.e. navigating through a web application as usual, but where semantic data are generated under the hood. This is the case for *Semantic Portals* (Lausen et al., 2005). These portals normally present data in table-based representations and request data to users by means of forms. Both of them are configured by portal developers with ad-hoc scripting languages. VPOET follows this non-explicit approach, allowing forms to request data from users (input templates) and a template based way to render semantic data (output templates) instead of scripting languages. The concept of semantic templates can be found in pOWL (Auer, n.d.), which provides users with a concept similar to VPOET templates, but much simpler; and Rhizome (Souzis, 2006), in which the ZML language is defined, but it is oriented to programmers instead of web designers with no skills in programming or semantic web technologies, as is the case for PEGASUS (Macías & Castells, 2007), that also require technically skilled users.

A very recent approach close to both Semantic Wikis and Semantic Portals is the one from *Semantic Pipes* (Le-Phuoc, Polleres, Hauswirth, Tummarello, & Morbidoni, 2009). It provides a friendly web interface for users who want to handle semantic data, allowing the creation of semantically-enabled web applications as workflows that connect the inputs and outputs of different semantic data services. These applications can be contributed by others to be used under a philosophy very close to VPOET templates. However, unlike VPOET they are not focused on the presentation/request of data but only on its transformation. In this sense, VPOET is complementary to Semantic Pipes, and could be added to them as a visualization service of the intermediate or final results. A detailed comparison between VPOET templates and those from Semantic Media Wiki, Fresnel, and Rhizome can be found at (Rico, Camacho, & Corcho, 2009a).

In summary, VPOET aims at combining the advantages of semantic wikis (allowing collaborative features to create templates), semantic portals (allowing forms to enter user's data that will be converted to semantic data) and semantic pipes (allowing semantic data transformation), minimizing their drawbacks (uncontrolled edition of semantic data in semantic wikis, difficult transformation of user's input in semantic portals and lack of focus on presentation in semantic pipes).

Our approach can be also compared to some of the efforts in the Semantic Web area on the development of browsers that are able to show or that allow users navigating through semantic data. These browsers are normally called *Semantic-Web browsers* (Quan & Karger, 2004). These features are used by VPOET web designers and GG-VPOET end-users. Web designers take advantage of these features during the "testing loop", i.e., when web designers have to test the output template against a set of semantic sources to discover pitfalls in the template. GG-VPOET users exploit these features each time the Google Gadget renders a given semantic data component due to the browsing facilities provided. It must be noticed that these "browsing facilities" are different from the ones provided by semantic-web browsers because browsing is limited to a given type of semantic individuals (the one of the selected output template). The extension to support the renderization of heterogeneous data will be studied in the near future.

Concerning the architecture of these browsers, two main groups exists: browser-centered and server-centered. Tabulator (Berners-Lee et al., 2006) belongs to the former group. DISCO (Bizer & Gauß, 2007) belongs to the latter group, and the same applies to VPOET templates. Browser-centered applications create some security problems, only solved by reducing the browser security level. Server-centered browsing does not have this limitation because browsing is indeed done by the server. Compared to DISCO, VPOET templates work with both URIs and URLs, however DISCO works only with URIs. Tabulator and DISCO render semantic data sources in a specific and non changeable way.

Many other semantic data visualization tools and languages exist, but are intended for professional users with high or medium skills on semantic web technologies. The most remarkable tools are IsaViz (Pietriga, 2001), which renders graphics in SVG[8] format, or ClusterMaps (Fluit, van Harmelen, & Sabou, 2002). Some proposed visualization specifications are Graph-StyleSheets (GSS[9]), used by IsaViz; or Fresnel (Bizer, Lee,

& Pietriga, 2006), used by Haystack (Quan & Karger, 2004) and PiggyBank (Huynh, Mazzocchi, & Karger, 2005). Fresnel requires advanced technical skills, so that it is not designed for web designers or common users. Although one of the features of PiggyBank is Semantic-Web browsing, it renders semantic data in a predefined way (determined by Fresnel) as the aforementiones semantic-web browsers. Compared to these systems, the main benefit of VPOET is that VPOET macros are simple and allow web designers with no technical knowledge about semantic web technologies a simple and efficient way to handle semantic data sources.

Another close related research field is End User Development (EUD), specifically in the area of mash-ups (Huynh, Miller, & Karger, 2008), where conceptual frameworks such as meta-design (Fischer & Giaccardi, 2006; Fischer, Giaccardi, Ye, Sutcliffe, & Mehandjiev, 2004) are well-defined and different types of users and developers have been identified. Although our approach is close to EUD, we consider a more traditional separation between the end users of our tools and the developers of semantic web applications.

CONCLUSION AND FUTURE WORK

In this paper we have presented VPOET, a semantically-enabled web application designed to lower the adoption barrier of semantic data for web designers and common web application developers. VPOET allows web designers with no knowledge about semantic web technologies to create web templates capable of handling semantic data. VPOET *output* templates can render a given semantic component from a given semantic data source. VPOET *input* templates provide a web interface to request data from users, creating or updating a semantic data source. All these templates can be easily exploited by third parties by using simple HTTP calls. As an example of this, a Google Gadget has been created, which can be easily inserted into any user web page, providing a simple tool to handle semantic data sources.

VPOET have been built by using the Fortunata framework, a wiki-based infrastructure that joins the benefits of wiki systems and an ontology management system. As the creation of semantic templates is the cornerstone of VPOET, for the widest audience, from amateur to professional, an experimental evaluation have been carried out. The evaluation shows that VPOET is considered as highly usable by web designers in a wide range of skills. It also shows that users are satisfied with VPOET user interface in the same skills range.

Our future work will be mainly focused on adaptivity, which involves the adaptation of the user interface to a user's profile (device used, user impairments, and aesthetic preferences). Another research line is the creation of renders capable of displaying heterogeneous semantic data, and renders specialised in displaying dozens, hundreds or thousands semantic data. Some web designers have also identified missing useful macros that should be implemented, as well as some needs such as communication between templates that would allow communicating two GG-VPOET templates located in the same web page.

ACKNOWLEDGMENT

This work has been partially funded by the Spanish Ministry of Science and Innovation under the projects HADA (TIN2007-64718), METEORIC (TIN2008-02081) and DEDICON (TIC-4425).

REFERENCES

Auer, S. (n.d.). *Powl – a web based platform for collaborative semantic web development.* Retrieved from http://powl.sourceforge.net/overview.php

Bansiya, J., & Davis, C. (2002). A hierarchical model for object-oriented design quality assessment. *IEEE Transactions on Software Engineering*, 4–17. doi:10.1109/32.979986

Berners-Lee, T., Chen, Y., Chilton, L., Connolly, D., Dhanaraj, R., Hollenbach, J., et al. (2006, November). Tabulator: Exploring and analyzing linked data on the semantic web. In *Proceedings of the 3rd International Semantic Web User Interaction Workshop (SWUI)*, Athens, GA. Retrieved from http://swui.semanticweb.org/swui06/papers/Berners-Lee/Berners-Lee.pdf

Bizer, C., & Gauß, T. (2007). *Disco - hyperdata browser*. Retrieved from http://sites.wiwiss.fu-berlin.de/suhl/bizer/ng4j/disco/

Bizer, C., Heath, T., & Berners-Lee, T. (2009). Linked data - the story so far. *International Journal on Semantic Web and Information Systems*, 5(3), 1–22.

Bizer, C., Lee, R., & Pietriga, E. (2006). Fresnel: A Browser Independent Presentation Vocabulary for RDF. In *Proceedings of the Second International Workshop on Interaction Design and the Semantic Web* (pp. 158-171).

Chin, J. P., Diehl, V. A., & Norman, K. L. (1988, June 15-19). Development of an instrument measuring user satisfaction of the human-computer interface. In E. Soloway, D. Frye, & S. B. Sheppard (Eds.), *Interface Evaluations: Proceedings of ACM CHI'88 Conference on Human Factors in Computing Systems*, Washington, DC (pp. 213-218).

Corcho, O., López-Cima, A., & Gómez-Pérez, A. (2006). A platform for the development of semantic web portals. In *Proceedings of the 6th International Conference on Web Engineering (ICWE2006)* (pp. 145-152). New York: ACM Press.

d'Aquin, M., Baldassarre, C., Gridinoc, L., Angeletou, S., Sabou, M., & Motta, E. (2007). Characterizing Knowledge on the Semantic Web with Watson. In *Proceedings of the 5th International Workshop on Evaluation of Ontologies and Ontology-Based Tools (EON2007), ISWC/ASWC* (Vol. 329, pp. 1-10). CEUR Workshop Proceedings. Retrieved from http://sunsite.informatik.rwth-aachen.de/Publications/CEUR-WS/Vol-329

d'Aquin, M., Motta, E., Sabou, M., Angeletou, S., Gridinoc, L., & Lopez, V. (2008). Toward a New Generation of Semantic Web Applications. *IEEE Intelligent Systems*, 23(3), 20–28. doi:10.1109/MIS.2008.54

Davis, I. (2005). *Talis, web 2.0 and all that*. Retrieved from http://iandavis.com/blog/2005/07/talis-web-20-and-all-that?year=2005&monthnum=07&name=talis-web-20-and-all-that

Draft, W. W. (2009). *Owl 2 web ontology language* (Tech. Rep.). Retrieved from http://www.w3.org/TR/owl2-overview

Efron, B., & Tibshirani, R. (1986). Bootstrap methods for standard errors, confidence intervals, and other measures of statistical accuracy. *Statistical Science*, 1(1), 54–75. doi:10.1214/ss/1177013815

Fischer, G., & Giaccardi, E. (2006). Meta-design: A framework for the future of end-user development. In Lieberman, H., Paternò, F., & Wulf, V. (Eds.), *End User Development: Empowering people to flexibly employ advanced information and communication technology* (pp. 427–457). Berlin: Springer.

Fischer, G., Giaccardi, E., Ye, Y., Sutcliffe, A., & Mehandjiev, N. (2004). Meta-design: a manifesto for end-user development. *Communications of the ACM*, 47(9), 33–37. doi:10.1145/1015864.1015884

Fluit, C., van Harmelen, F., & Sabou, M. (2002). Ontology-based information visualisation. In Geroimenko, V. (Ed.), *Visualising the Semantic Web* (pp. 36–48). Berlin: Springer Verlag.

Holzinger, A. (2005). Usability engineering methods for software developers. *Communications of the ACM, 48*, 71–74. doi:10.1145/1039539.1039541

Huynh, D., Mazzocchi, S., & Karger, D. (2005). Piggy bank: Experience the semantic web inside your web browser. In *Proceedings of the International Semantic Web Conference (ISWC)*(LNCS 3729, pp. 413-430).

Huynh, D., Miller, R., & Karger, D. (2008). Potluck: Data mash-up tool for casual users. *Web Semantics: Science. Services and Agents on the World Wide Web, 6*(4), 274–282. doi:10.1016/j.websem.2008.09.005

Lausen, H., Ding, Y., Stollberg, M., Fensel, D., Lara, R., & Han, S.-K. (2005). Semantic web portals: state-of-the-art survey. *Journal of Knowledge Management, 9*(5), 40–49. doi:10.1108/13673270510622447

Le-Phuoc, D., Polleres, A., Hauswirth, M., Tummarello, G., & Morbidoni, C. (2009). Rapid prototyping of semantic mash-ups through semantic web pipes. In *WWW '09: Proceedings of the 18th International Conference on World Wide Web* (pp. 581-590). New York: ACM.

Macías, J., & Castells, P. (2007). Providing end-user facilities to simplify ontology-driven web application authoring. *Interacting with Computers, 19*(4), 563–585. doi:10.1016/j.intcom.2007.01.006

O'Reilly, T. (2005). *What is web 2.0. Design patterns and business models for the next generation of software.* Retrieved from at http://oreilly.com/web2/archive/what-is-web-20.html

Oren, E., Delbru, R., Moller, K., Volkel, M., & Handschuh, S. (2006). Annotation and navigation in semantic wikis. In *Proceedings of the ESWC Workshop on Semantic Wikis.* Retrieved from http://ftp.informatik.rwth-aachen.de/Publications/CEUR-WS/Vol-206

Oren, E., Heitmann, B., & Decker, S. (2008). Activerdf: Embedding semantic web data into object-oriented languages. *Web Semantics, 6*(3), 191–202.

Perlman, G. (1997, April 18-23). Practical usability evaluation. In *CHI '97: Extended Abstracts on Human Factors in Computing Systems,* Los Angeles (pp. 168-169). New York: ACM.

Pietriga, E. (2001). *Isaviz: A visual authoring tool for rdf.* Retrieved from http://www.w3.org/2001/11/IsaViz

Quan, D., & Karger, D. (2004). How to Make a Semantic Web Browser. In *Proceedings of the 13th International Conference on the World Wide Web. Session: Semantic Interfaces and OWL Tools.* ISBN:1-58113-844-X

Rico, M., Camacho, D., & Corcho, Ó. (2008). VPOET: Using a Distributed Collaborative Platform for Semantic Web Applications. In C. Badica, G. Mangioni, V. Carchiolo, & D. Burdescu (Eds.), *Intelligent Distributed Computing, Systems and Applications: Proceedings of the 2nd International Symposium on Intelligent Distributed Computing (IDC'2008)* (pp. 167-176). Berlin: Springer. ISBN: 978-3-540-85256-8

Rico, M., Camacho, D., & Corcho, Ó. (2009a). Macros vs. scripting in VPOET. In *Proceedings of the 5th Workshop on Scripting and Development for the Semantic Web (SFSW2009),6th Annual European Semantic Web Conference (ESWC).* (Vol. 449). CEUR Online Proceedings.

Rico, M., Camacho, D., & Corcho, Ó. (2009b). VPOET Templates to Handle the Presentation of Semantic Data Sources in Wikis. In *Proceedings of the 4th Workshop on Semantic Wikis: The Semantic Wiki Web (SemWiki2009), 6th Annual European Semantic Web Conference (ESWC)* (Vol. 464, pp. 186-190). CEUR Online Proceedings.

Rico, M., Camacho, D., & Corcho, Ó. (2010). A Contribution-based Framework for the Creation of Semantically-enabled Web Applications. *Journal of Information Science, 180*(10), 1850–1864. doi:10.1016/j.ins.2009.07.004

Rochen, R., Rosson, M., & Pérez, M. (2006). End user Development of Web Applications. In Lieberman, H., Paternò, F., & Wulf, V. (Eds.), *End-User Development* (pp. 161–182). Berlin: Springer.

Souzis, A. (2006, June 12). Bringing the wiki-way to the semantic web with rhizome. In M. Völkel & S. Schaffert (Eds.), *SEMWIKI 2006: Proceedings of the First Workshop on Semantic Wikis,* Budva, Montenegro. Retrieved from http://www.ceur-ws.org/Vol-206/paper19.pdf

ENDNOTES

[1] More details can be found at http://ishtar.ii.uam.es/fortunata.

[2] Data from http://esw.w3.org/TaskForces/CommunityProjects/LinkingOpenData/DataSets/Statistics, accessed in july 2010

[3] The VPOET tutorial is available at http://ishtar.ii.uam.es/fortunata/Wiki.jsp?page=VPOETTutorial

[4] The SPARQL protocol is available at http://www.w3.org/TR/rdf-sparql-protocol/

[5] The VPOET Google Gadget (GG-VPOET) is available at the Google Gadgets Directory (http://www.google.com/ig/directory?q=vpoet&type=gadgets)

[6] The questionnaire is available at http://ishtar.ii.uam.es/fortunata/Wiki.jsp?page=UsabilityAndUserSatisfactionOfVPOET

[7] Web-based user interface evaluation with questionnaires is available at http://oldwww.acm.org/perlman/question.html

[8] SVG is available at http://www.w3.org/Graphics/SVG

[9] GSS is available at http://www.w3.org/2001/11/IsaViz/gss/gssmanual.html

This work was previously published in International Journal of Semantic Web and Information Systems, Volume 6, Issue 3, edited by Amit P. Sheth, pp. 38-60, copyright 2010 by IGI Publishing (an imprint of IGI Global).

Chapter 7
Adaptive Hybrid Semantic Selection of SAWSDL Services with SAWSDL–MX2

Matthias Klusch
German Research Center for Artificial Intelligence (DFKI), Germany

Patrick Kapahnke
German Research Center for Artificial Intelligence (DFKI), Germany

Ingo Zinnikus
German Research Center for Artificial Intelligence (DFKI), Germany

ABSTRACT

In this paper, the authors present an adaptive, hybrid semantic matchmaker for SAWSDL services, called SAWSDL-MX2. It determines three types of semantic matching of an advertised service with a requested one, which are described in standard SAWSDL: logic-based, text-similarity-based and XML-tree edit-based structural similarity. Before selection, SAWSDL-MX2 learns the optimal aggregation of these different matching degrees off-line over a random subset of a given SAWSDL service retrieval test collection by exploiting a binary support vector machine-based classifier with ranking. The authors present a comparative evaluation of the retrieval performance of SAWSDL-MX2.

INTRODUCTION

Semantic service selection is commonly considered key to the discovery of relevant services in the semantic Web, and there are already quite a few matchmakers available for this purpose and different formats like OWL-S, WSML and SAWS-DL (Klusch, 2008). As a W3C recommendation

DOI: 10.4018/978-1-4666-0185-7.ch007

dated August 28, 2007, the SAWSDL[1] (Semantic Annotations for WSDL) specification proposes mechanisms to enrich Web services described in WSDL[2] (Web Service Description Language) with semantic annotations. Among others, one goal of these additional descriptions is to support intelligent agents in automated service selection, a task which is hard to accomplish using pure syntactic information of service profiles based mainly on XML Schema definitions. Typical application scenarios that require or benefit from a service matchmaking component include for example negotiation and coalition forming among agents and automated or assisted service composition. The first hybrid semantic service matchmaker SAWSDL-MX1 for semantic services in SAWSDL (Klusch & Kapahnke, 2008) adopted the ideas of our hybrid matchmakers OWLS-MX and WSMO-MX (see Klusch, Fries, & Sycara, 2009; Kaufer & Klusch, 2006) for semantic services in OWL-S, respectively, WSML.

However, SAWSDL-MX1 focuses on semantic annotations of the signature but not on the XML structure of the Web service as a whole. This is taken into account by the WSDL-Analyzer tool presented in (Zinnikus et al., 2006) by means of measuring the XML tree edit distances between given pair of services through XML type compatibility, token-based text and lexical similarity measurements. Besides, SAWSDL-MX1 combines logic-based and text-similarity-based matching in a fixed manner: It applies five logical matching filters and ranks service offers that share the same logical matching degree with respect to a given request according to their text similarity value. The hybrid variant SAWSDL-M0+WA does the same as SAWSDL-MX1 except that its ranking of services with the same logical matching degree is according to their structural similarity value as computed by the WSDL-Analyzer.

Finally, the adaptive hybrid matchmaker variant SAWSDL-MX2 computes three kinds of semantic matching, logical, text and structural similarity-based. In addition, it learns the optimally weighted aggregation of these different types of semantic matching to decide on the semantic relevance of a service to a given request.

One major advantage of this off-line learning is that it renders SAWSDL-MX2, in principle, independent from any given service test collection or future extensions with other matching filters. In fact, the configuration of any non-adaptive matchmaker such as SAWSDL-MX1 would have to be manually retuned by the developer of the matchmaker to reflect such changes.

Whether this adaptation feature may even improve the precision of non-adaptive variants in practice has been checked by us against the only publicly available SAWSDL service retrieval test collection SAWSDL-TC1 consisting of more than 900 SAWSDL services from different application domains. The results of our experiments show that all hybrid semantic service matchmaker variants outperform the single matching type variants (logic-based or text similarity or structural XML similarity only) in terms of precision, while all SAWSDL matchmaker variants available today, whether adaptive or not, do not significantly differ from each other in terms of their precision with respect to this collection SAWSDL-TC1.

The remainder of the paper is structured as follows. After a brief introduction to SAWSDL in the following section, the SAWSDL service matching approach of the non-adaptive matchmaker SAWSDL-MX1 is recapitulated. The subsequent section presents the structural matching of Web services in WSDL performed by the WSDL-Analyzer tool, followed by an illustration of the application of all three matching filters by example. The adaptive aggregation of different matching results based on an off-line learned binary Support Vector Machine (SVM) classifier with ranking by the adaptive matchmaker SAWSDL-MX2 is described thereafter. We briefly present implementation details and then report the results of our experimental evaluation over the public test collection SAWSDL-TC1 in terms of macro-averaged recall/precision, average precision and average query response time. Eventually, we comment on related work on SAWSDL service matchmaking and conclude. This paper is an extended version of (Klusch et al., 2009).

SERVICE DESCRIPTIONS IN SAWSDL

SAWSDL is designed as an extension of WSDL enabling service providers to enrich their service descriptions with additional semantic information.

Figure 1. SAWSDL extensions of WSDL service interface components

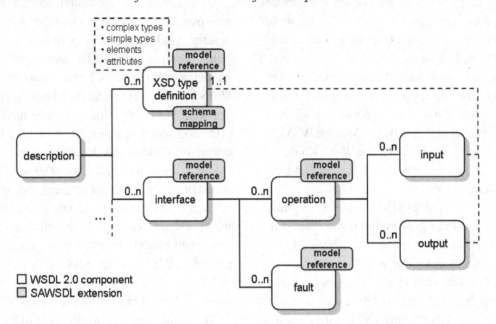

For this purpose, the notions of *model reference* and *schema mapping* have been introduced in terms of XML attributes (tags) that can be added to already existing WSDL service description elements including XML Schema definitions for message parameters as depicted in Figure 1.

Semantic Annotation of WSDL Services

More precisely, the following extensions are used for semantic annotations of WSDL services:

modelReference: A *modelReference* points to one or more concepts with equally intended meaning expressed in an arbitrary semantic representation language. They are allowed to be defined for every WSDL and XML Schema element, though the SAWSDL specification defines their occurrence only in WSDL interfaces, operations, faults as well as XML Schema elements, complex types, simple types and attributes. The purpose

of a model reference is mainly to support automated service discovery.

liftingSchemaMapping: Schema mappings are intended to support automated service execution by providing rules specifying the correspondences between semantic annotation concepts defined in a given ontology (the "upper" level) to the XML Schema representation of data actually required to invoke the Web service (the "lower" level), and vice versa. A *liftingSchemaMapping* describes the transformation from the "lower" level in XML Schema up to the ontology language used for semantic annotation.

loweringSchemaMapping: The attribute *loweringSchemaMapping* describes the transformation from the "upper" level of a given ontology to the "lower" level in XML Schema.

However, the current specification of SAWSDL model references poses quite some problems for semantic service matchmaking as follows.

No uniform, formal ontology language. Unlike OWL-S or WSML, the specification of SAWSDL does not restrict the developer to any uniform, formal ontology language like OWL or as defined as part of WSML. As a result, any mean of automated semantic service selection has to cope with the semantic interoperability problems of heterogeneous domain ontologies and ontology languages. While this problem could be resolved in some cases by means of syntactic and semantic transformations - such as for OWL-DL and WSML-DL - it remains hard in general.

Multiple references to different ontologies. The same holds especially for references to different kinds of ontologies like plain or structured text files, annotated image archive, or logic theories. In fact, SAWSDL allows multiple references to different kinds of ontologies for annotating even the same service description element. How shall any semantic service matchmaker know how to process them to understand the semantics of that single element? Are its annotations meant to be complementary or equivalent[3]? If complementary, how to aggregate them, if equivalent, which one to select best for further processing? This opens up a wide range of differing pragmatic solutions for SAWSDL service matching.

Top-level vs bottom-level annotations. According to the SAWSDL specification, semantic annotation by means of so-called *top-level annotation* and *bottom-level annotation* shall be considered both independent from each other and applicable at the same time. While *top-level annotation* refers to the annotation of a complex type or element definition of a message parameter by means of a model reference as a whole, any *bottom-level annotation* focuses only on a single (atomic) XML element. Unfortunately, it remains unclear how to evaluate a matching *between* top-level and low-level annotated parameters, or which one to prefer if both levels of annotation are available for a complex service description element. In addition, element and type definition specifying a message component can be annotated at the same time.

Pragmatic assumptions for SAWSDL service matching by SAWSDLMX. Regarding the above mentioned problems of SAWSDL service matching, the following pragmatic assumptions, illustrated in Figure 2, were made for using all members

Figure 2. Example of pragmatic assumptions for service selection by SAWSDL-MX

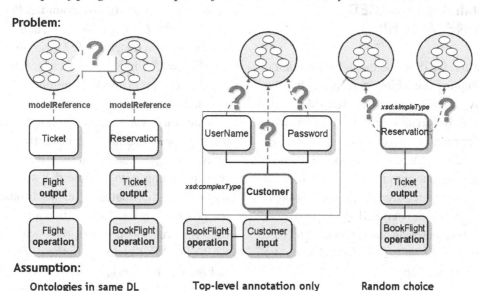

of our SAWSDL-MX matchmaker family, that is the non-adaptive matchmakers SAWSDL-MX1, its variant SAWSDL-M0+WA, and the adaptive matchmaker SAWSDL-MX2 each of which we will describe in subsequent sections.

References to formal ontologies in description logics only. The current implementation of SAWSDL-MX performs reasoning on logic-based annotations in OWL-DL[4] but is not restricted to it: It supports other description logics (DL) if they are translated into the standard DIG 1.1[5] interface representation format.

Only top-level semantic annotations of service parameters are considered for service matching. Direct top-level annotation of a WSDL message part has priority over the top-level annotation of the respectively referenced (and annotated) XML Schema element or type.

In case of multiple annotations of a single element at the same level, one of them is selected uniformly at random. Only semantic annotations of service (IO) parameters are considered, but not annotations of entire operations or interfaces. However, the proposed matching variants could easily be adopted for this purpose.

SAWSDL-MX1: LOGIC AND TEXT SIMILARITY-BASED SIGNATURE MATCHING

In this section, we describe the hybrid semantic service signature matching performed by the non-adaptive matchmaker SAWSDL-MX1. Its logic-based only variant is called SAWSDL-M0. Since service requests and offers are presumed to be formulated in SAWSDL, each of their interfaces comprising one or multiple operations with semantically annotated signatures, we first present the way in which SAWSDL-MX1 performs hybrid semantic matching on the service interface level based on the results of its hybrid semantic matching of pairs of operations.

Hybrid Service Interface Matching

For each pair of service offer O and service request R, the matchmaker SAWSDLMX1 first determines their semantic similarity by evaluating every combination of their operations in terms of logic-based only (SAWSDL-M0) and text similarity-based only operation matching. These processes of logic-based and text similarity-based (service) operation matching are described in more detail below.

To determine an injective mapping between service offer and request operations that is optimal regarding their matching degrees, SAWSDL-MX1 applies bipartite operation graph matching. Nodes in the graph represent the operations and the weighted edges are built from possible one-to-one assignments with their weights derived from the computed degree of (logical/text/hybrid) operation match. If there exists such a mapping, then it is guaranteed that there exists an operation of the service offer for every requested operation, disregarding the quality of their matching at this point.

For example, consider the service request and service offer given in Figure 3. Every request operation RO_i (with $i \in \{1, 2\}$) is compared to every advertisement operation O_j (with $j \in \{1, 2, 3\}$) with respect to logic-based filters defined in the next section. In this example, RO_1 exactly matches with O_1, but fails for O_2 and O_3. O_3 is a weaker plug-in match for RO_2 (the subsumed-by match of RO_2 with O_2 is even weaker than a plug-in match). The best (max) assignment of matching operations is $\{<RO_1,O_1>, <RO_2,O_3>\}$.

One conservative (min-max) option of determining the matching degree between service offer and request based on their pairwise operations matching is to assume the worst result of the best operation matching results. In other words, we guarantee a fixed *lower* bound of similarity for *every* requested operation - which is what SAWSDL-MX1 is doing. In the example shown in Figure 3, the service offer is considered a *plug-in* match for the request. Other not yet imple-

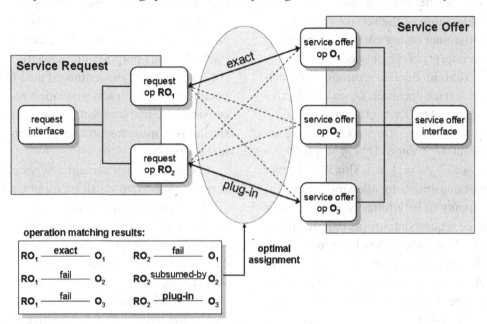

Figure 3. Interface level matching of SAWSDL-MX1 for logic-based semantic similarity

mented possibilities would be to merge the operation matching results based on their average syntactic similarity values and to provide more detailed feedback to the user on the operation matchings involved.

Logic-Based Operation Matching

The logic-based operation matching by SAWSDL-MX1 bases on the successive application of the following four filters of increasing degree of relaxation to a given pair service offer operation O_O and service request O_R: *Exact*, *Plug-in*, *Subsumes* and *Subsumed-by*. These filters have been originally developed for the matchmaker OWLS-MX but extended with bipartite concept graph matching to ensure an injective mapping between I/O concepts of service offer and request, whenever possible. As an overview to description logic and DL reasoning, we refer to (Baader et al. 2003). The sets $lgc(C)$ and $lsc(C)$ contain the least generic concepts of C (direct parent) and the least specific concepts of C (direct child), respectively.

Exact match: Service operation O_O *exactly* matches service operation $O_R \Leftrightarrow (\exists$ injective assignment M_{in}: $\forall m \in M_{in}$: $m_1 \in in(O_O) \wedge m_2 \in in(O_R) \wedge m_1 \equiv m_2) \wedge (\exists$ injective assignment M_{out}: $\forall m \in M_{out}$: $m_1 \in out(O_R) \wedge m_2 \in out(O_O) \wedge m_1 \equiv m_2)$. There exists a one-to-one mapping of perfectly matching inputs as well as perfectly matching outputs. Assuming that an operation fullfills a requesters need if every input can be satisfied and every requested output is provided, the assignments only require to be injective (but not bijective), thus additional available information not required for service invocation and additional provided outputs not explicitly requested are tolerated.

Plug-in match: Service operation O_O *plugs into* service operation $O_R \Leftrightarrow (\exists$ injective assignment M_{in}: $\forall m \in M_{in}$: $m_1 \in in(O_O) \wedge m_2 \in in(O_R) \wedge m_1 \} m_2) \wedge (\exists$ injective assignment M_{out}: $\forall m \in M_{out}$: $m_1 \in out(O_R) \wedge m_2 \in out(O_O) \in m_2 \in lsc(m_1))$. The filter relaxes the constraints of the exact matching filter by additionally allowing input concepts of the service offer to be arbitrarily more general than those of the service request, and advertisement output concepts to be direct child concepts of the queried ones.

Subsumes match: Service operation O_O *subsumes* service operation $O_R \Leftrightarrow (\exists$ injective assignment $M_{in}: \forall m \in M_{in}: m_1 \in in(O_O) \wedge m_2 \in in(O_R) \wedge m_1 \} m_2) \wedge (\exists$ injective assignment $M_{out}: \forall m \in M_{out}: m_1 \in out(O_R) \wedge m_2 \in out(O_O) \in m_1 \} m_2)$. This filter further relaxes constraints by allowing service offer outputs to be arbitrarily more specific than the request outputs (as opposed to the *plug-in* filter, where they have to be direct children). Thus, a *plug-in* can be seen as special case of a *subsumes* match resulting in a more fine-grained view at the overall service ranking.

Subsumed-by match: Service operation O_O is *subsumed by* service operation $O_R \Leftrightarrow (\exists$ injective assignment $M_{in}: \forall m \in M_{in}: m_1 \in in(O_O) \wedge \mu_2 \in in(O_R) \wedge m_1 \} \mu_2) \wedge (\exists$ injective assignment $M_{out}: \forall m \in M_{out}: m_1 \in out(O_R) \wedge m_2 \in out(O_O) \in m_2 \in lgc(m_1))$. The idea of the *subsumed-by* matching filter is to determine the service offers that the requester is able to provide with all required inputs and at the same time deliver outputs that are at least closely related to the requested outputs in terms of the inferred concept classification.

The matching degree of *fail* is true if and only if none of the matching filters defined above succeed. As a result, services are ranked according to their matching degree in the following decreasing order: *exact* > *plug-in* > *subsumes* > *subsumed-by* > *fail*.

Text Similarity-Based Operation Matching

The hybrid variants of SAWSDL-MX1 also perform a complementary text similarity-based matching by means of classical token-based text similarity measures *Loss-of-Information*, *Extended Jaccard (Tanimoto)*, *Cosine* and *Jensen-Shannon* as implemented, for example, in Sim-Pack[6]. For this purpose, the semantic signatures (i.e., the semantic annotations of the I/O message parameters) of both service request and offer are considered as text such that the degree of semantic similarity is measured in terms of their averaged text similarity.

Concretely, each semantic service signature is transformed into a pair of weighted keyword vectors for input, respectively, output according to the classical vector space model of information retrieval. For this purpose, each input concept is logically unfolded in the shared ontology (as defined for standard tableaux reasoning algorithms) and concatenated with all others to a complex logical expression containing only primitive components and logical operators. This expression is treated as a mere text string which is being processed to a TFIDF weighted keyword vector; the same is done with service output concepts. The TFIDF term weighting values are computed over two distinct text indices depending on whether service inputs or outputs are compared.

The motivation for applying the above mentioned text similarity measures, originally intended for natural language document comparison, is the experimentally evidenced observation that the primitive (concept and role) components or terms that are used to describe more complex concepts logically keep to *Zipf's Law*. That is, taking into account all *documents* derived from the logical description of the semantic service signatures provided by services taken from the public SAWSDL service retrieval test collection SAWSDL-TC1 (this also holds e.g. for the public OWL-S service test collection OWLS-TC2), the observed distribution of terms is as follows:

$$f(k, s, N) = \frac{1}{k^s} \bigg/ \sum_{n=1}^{N} \frac{1}{n^s}$$ with k being the

observed rank, N the number of ranks and s a given parameter to characterize the distribution.

Figure 4. Term distribution for service signature text documents (SAWSDL-TC1)

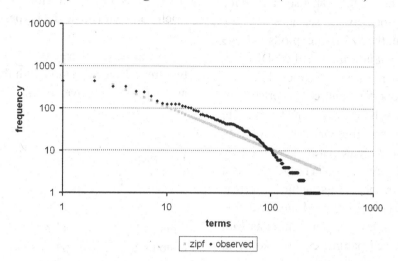

For natural language text, $s \approx 1$ is usually assumed, reducing the formula to a normalized variant of $1/k$, i.e. the term at rank 1 occurs two times as often as the term at rank 2, three times as often as rank 3 and so on.

Figure 4 scatterplots (logarithmically scaled) one of the term indices. In fact, the term distributions for both service signature (service input, respectively, output concepts) indices support the proposition that the data generated for text similarity matching as described above resemble natural language text.

Non-Adaptive SAWSDL-MX1 Algorithm

To summarize, the hybrid semantic service match-maker SAWSDL-MX1 first applies both logical matching and text matching to each pair of operations of each pair of advertised and requested SAWSDL service interface. It then determines the degrees of both logical and text matching for the given service pair on the interface level by means of two respective bipartite graph matchings based on these results which eventually leads to the hybrid semantic service matching degree denoted as a 2-tuple (logic-based semantic service matching degree, text similarity-based service matching

value). Finally, it ranks those service offers with the same logical matching degree (i.e., the first part of the hybrid matching degree) with respect to the given request according to their text similarity values (i.e., the second part of their hybrid matching degree) in decreasing order.

SAWSDL-M0. The logic-based only match-maker variant SAWSDL-M0 of SAWSDLMX1 only performs the logic-based semantic service matching as described above, and ranks service offers that share the same logical matching degree with respect to the given request uniformly at random.

WSDL-ANALYZER: STRUCTURAL SERVICE MATCHING

The WSDL-Analyzer (WA) tool introduced in (Zinnikus et al., 2006) performs a structural only matching of WSDL 1.1 services. That is, it ignores the semantic annotations of SAWSDL service descriptions, hence treats any SAWSDL service as a mere WSDL service. The WA tool detects similarities and differences between WSDL files to find a list of non-logic-based semantically relevant Web services. Since its similarity algorithm inherently produces a mapping between WSDL service descriptions, the tool can also be used for supporting mediation between services.

More concrete, the WA tool exploits various types of XML schema information of WSDL operation signatures such as element names, datatypes and structural properties, and characteristics of data instances, as well as background knowledge from dictionaries and thesauri. The similarity algorithm recursively calculates the similarity between the XML structures of a requested and a candidate service, respects the structural information of complex datatypes involved, and is flexible enough to allow for a relaxed matching as well as matching between parameters that come in different orders in service parameter lists.

WSDL-Analyzer Algorithm

The structural matching of two WSDL services is a multi-step process. It starts off with (1) comparing the operation sets of both services on interface level, which is based on (2) the comparison of the structures of the operation signatures, that is their input and output messages, which, in turn, is based on (3) the comparison of the XML Schema data types of the objects communicated by these messages. This recursive structural matching of two XML-based WSDL service descriptions is performed as follows.

A WSDL description is represented as a labeled tree where leaf nodes are the basic built-in data types provided by the XML schema specification[7]. Let $L = \{l_1, l_2, ..., l_n\}$ be a set of labels. A *labelled tree* $T = (N, E, root(T), \varphi)$ is an acyclic, connected graph with:

$N = \{n_1, n_2, ..., n_n\}$ is a set of nodes.

$E \subset N \times N$ is a set of edges.

$root(T)$ is the root of the tree.

$\varphi: N \to L$ is a function which assigns a label to each node with basic data types $D \subset L$.

The process of calculating the similarity of two trees T_1 and T_2 starts with the roots $root(T_1)$ and $root(T_2)$, and traverses these trees recursively: For $a \in N_{T1}$ and $b \in N_{T2}$ do compute

$$sim(a,b) = \begin{cases} \omega_n \cdot sim_n(\varphi(a), \varphi(b)) + \omega_s \cdot \max\{\oplus_{i,j}(sim(n_i, m_j))\} & , \varphi(a), \varphi(b) \notin D \\ sim_t(\varphi(a), \varphi(b)) & , \varphi(a), \varphi(b) \in D \end{cases}$$

where $(a, n_i) \in E_{T1}$, $(b, m_j) \in E_{T2}$ and $\oplus_{i,j}(n_i, m_j)$ denotes the sum of pairs $sim(n_i, m_j)$ for $1 \le i \le card(n)$ and $1 \le j \le card(m)$ such that each n_i and m_j occur at most once in the sum. If $card(n) \ne card(m)$, some of the nodes cannot be matched. Weights ω_n and ω_s are used to either increase or decrease the effect of element (label) name or structural similarity.

The computation of type similarity sim_t bases on a given type compatibility table, that assigns a similarity value to each combination of the considered basic data types. The similarity of names (labels) sim_n can be calculated with different measures such as string edit distance, substring containment or WordNet[8] similarity (semantic proximity). In order to improve the mapping results, we used substring matching and WordNet. Experiments showed that especially in rather standardized areas the results are better than with pure data type mapping.

Hybrid Semantic Matchmaker SAWSDL-M0+WA

The hybrid semantic service matchmaker SAWSDL-M0+WA performs (a) logic-based semantic matching and (b) ranks service offers that share the same logical matching degree with respect to a given request according to their degree of structural similarity as computed by the WSDL-Analyzer.

SERVICE MATCHING EXAMPLE

In the following, we demonstrate the application of the three different semantic service matching approaches, that is logic-based, text similarity-based and structural service matching by example. Suppose a user is searching for a Web service that returns a map for a given location as input. The main parts of the description of the desired service in SAWSDL are as follows:

The requested service offers exactly one operation which returns the reference to an appropriate map given a GPS position as input. As usual, the message data types of the operation signature are semantically annotated using SAWSDL model references that point to appropriate ontologies in which the semantics of the used annotation concepts are defined. In this example, the operation (service) input is claimed to conform to the concept *GPSPosition* while the output is a *Map*, both concepts described in OWL. Besides, there is a service offer (registered at the matchmaker) which provides similar functionality:

During the matching process, this offer is compared to the request using one or more variants as proposed in this paper. For the logic-based and text similarity matching, the interface level matching is examined at first. Since the request only consists of a single operation, the bipartite graph matching problem is trivial and omitted here. We just assume that the second operation of the service offer provides different functionality and thus is not part of the final assignment.

Logical Service Matching

For the logic-based semantic service operation matching, the following concept definitions are assumed (written in the more compact standard DL notation instead of the normative RDF syntax of OWL-DL):

Map μ *Image* * ∃*hasScale.Scale* * ∃*contains. GeographicalEntity*

RoadMap μ *Map* * ∃*contains.Road*

Location μ *GeographicalEntity* * ∃*hasParameter.GPSPos*

GPSPos μ ∃*hasLongitude.FPNum* * ∃*hasLatitude.FPNum*

Sequential application of the different logic-based matching filters for this example results in a *fail*, which can be considered as *false negative*. Although the fact *RoadMap* μ *Map* holds for the outputs, there does not exist an inclusion for the concepts *Location* and *GPSPos*. Thus, the example exposes one of the main problems with this standard matching technique. Both concepts are strongly related to each other, but logic-based concept subsumption reasoning fails to recognize that. One possibility to deal with such cases is the usage of text similarity approaches as described previously in this paper.

Text Similarity-Based Matching

The unfolded concept definitions are used as input for a text similarity measure based on the vector space model utilizing TFIDF weights over a given (service) document corpus. In this example, the matchmaker applies the common *Loss-of-Information* similarity measure which just takes the two service documents into account:

$$LOI(R,S) = 1 - \frac{|R \cup S| - |R \cap S|}{|R| + |S|},$$

where R is the set of terms of the request document and S the set of terms of the service offer. Since the proposed text similarity approach is *structured*, distinct values are computed for inputs and outputs respectively.

For example, the set of terms of inputs of the request after unfolding and stopword elimination is $R_{in} = \{hasLongitude, FPNum, hasLatitude\}$ while the corresponding set for the service offer is S_{in} = {*Location, GeographicalEntity, hasParameter, hasLongitude, FPNum, hasLatitude*}. The partial similarity result restricted to these service inputs then is $LOI(R_{in}, S_{in}) \approx 0.66$, which indicates a moderate textual similarity (in contrast to the logic-based *fail*). For the outputs, the similarity value is computed as $LOI(R_{out}, S_{out}) \approx 0.92$, which indicates high similarity (only the single term *Road* distinguishes both sets). The overall structured textual similarity of both services R and S is the average of both values, that is $LOI(R, S) = 0.75$, which is clearly in the upper part of the similarity function range, thus compensates the logic-based *false negative*.

Structural Service Matching

To illustrate the functionality of the structural WSDL matching described in Section 4, the similarity computation of the two operations in question is exemplified here. Please note, that the actual similarity computation of the WSDL Analyzer (WA) involves the whole document structure, but this is an analogous process omitted here for reasons of simplicity.

Basically, the WA algorithm recurs into the lower level WSDL tree representation nodes of both service descriptions until a leaf node containing a basic data type occurs. If this is also the case for the other service at the same time, the data type similarity is looked up in a predefined table. If a basic data type occurs on one hand but some complex structure at the other hand, the system tries to find the best matching simple type contained in the complex type. Recursion takes place at every pair of nodes to compare structures that are not leaf nodes in the corresponding WSDL trees. At this step, the label similarity is computed for these nodes and the *maximum* of possible similarities for subnode recursion is added to the overall similarity.

For our example of service request and offer (cf. Figures 5 and 6, Figure 7), the operation

similarity (sub-) computation involves comparing *GPSType* to *LocationType*. Since *GPSType* is a complex type and *LocationType* a leaf node, simple types contained in *GPSType* are checked for type similarity resulting in 0.8 as stated in the lookup table (both simple subtypes in question are *float* and for the offer *string* was found).

By comparing their labels using WordNet, a relationship is discovered. Also, upper level nodes have a high textual similarity in most cases for the example, e.g. *getMapRequest* and *getMAPRequest*. For the output part of the operation, the algorithm ends up in comparing the two leaf nodes labeled *MapType* in both cases. Both also share the same simple datatype *anyURI*, thus these branches add a high similarity value to the overall structural similarity value.

Table 1 summarizes all similarity computations of the WA assuming that both weighting parameter values (ω_n, ω_s) are equal to 1. For computing the name similarity, WA applies a simple token-based string comparison in combination with WordNet matching. The token matching adds a value of 1 for each matched token to the overall similarity, WordNet matching ranges to an interval [0, 1], and both results are added for the overall sim_n value. The given lookup table for data type matching (sim_t) assigns similarity values in [0, 1] where equal types have a similarity value of 1.

As can be seen from the bottom line of Table 1, the overall result for the example request and service offer pair is 20.3, which is normalized by the maximum obtainable structural matching value of 28 to 0.73. Obviously, each of the different semantic matching approaches above has its pros and cons. While logic-based semantic matching takes advantage of formal semantic definitions of concepts and roles, it may be mislead in some cases as for the concepts *GPSPos* and *Location*. The additional use of text IR techniques and structural matching may overcome this problem in this example: Text similarity of 0.75 and structural similarity of 0.73 are both sufficiently high enough

Figure 5. Service Request

```
<types><schema ...>

  <complexType name="GPSType" modelReference="http://...#GPSPos">

    <sequence>

      <element name="longitude" type="float"/>

      <element name="latitude" type="float"/>

    </sequence>

  </complexType>

  <simpleType name="MapType" modelReference="http://...#Map">

    <restriction base="anyURI"/>

  </simpleType>

</schema></types>

<message name="getMapResponse">

  <part name="_Map" type="MapType"/> </message>

<message name="getMapRequest">

  <part name="Location" type="GPSType"/> </message>

<portType name="PositionMapInterface">

  <operation name="getMAP">

    <input message="tns:getMapRequest"/>

    <output message="tns:getMapResponse"/>

  </operation>

</portType>
```

to indicate semantic relevance. However, as noted for example in (Klusch et al., 2009), each of these non-logic-based semantic matching approaches can, in principle, introduce misclassifications on their own.

SAWSDL-MX2: ADAPTIVE MATCHING AGGREGATION

As mentioned above, the logic-based filters of SAWSDL-MX1 have been complemented by text similarity matching in a fixed, that is, in a non-

adaptive way. In particular, services were ranked according to their logical matching degree first and then (within the same logical matching class) according to their signature text similarity. Obviously, there are some problems with this approach. The first problem is the tedious search for a text similarity threshold parameter value for arbitrary pairs of service offers and requests. Second, more general, how to best combine different semantic service matching filters such as those described in previous sections to obtain a reasonable retrieval performance in terms of precision and recall? In particular, how to achieve this in a way that

Figure 6. Service Offer

```
<types><schema ...>

  <simpleType name="LocationType" modelReference="http://...#Location">

    <restriction base="string"/>

  </simpleType>

  <simpleType name="MapType" modelReference="http://...#RoadMap">

    <restriction base="anyURI"/>

  </simpleType>...

</schema></types>

<message name="getMAPResponse">

  <part name="MapPart" type="MapType"/> </message>

<message name="getMAPRequest">

  <part name="LocationPart" type="LocationType"/> </message>

<portType name="LocationMapInterface">

  <operation name="createMAP">

    <input message="tns:getMAPRequest"/>

    <output message="tns:getMAPResponse"/>

  </operation>

  <operation ...>...</operation>

</portType>
```

Figure 7. Structural WSDL service operation matching example

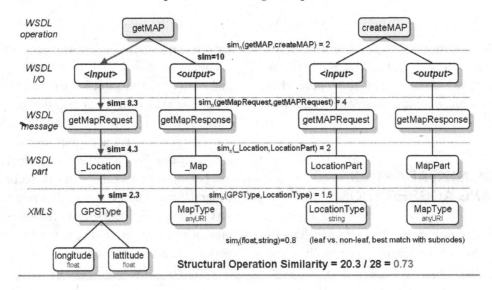

Table 1. Structural similarity values computed by the WSDL-Analyzer (WA)

Similarity	$w_n \cdot sim_n$	$w_s \cdot \max\{\oplus_{i,j}\}$
sim(GPSType, LocationType)	1.5	sim_l(float, string) = 0.8 (leaf/non-leaf)
sim(_Location, LocationPart)	2	2.3
sim(getMapRequest, getMAPRequest)	4	4.3
sim(<input>, <input>)	0 (no names)	8.3
sim(MapType, MapType)	3	sim_l(anyURI, anyURI) = 1
sim(Map, MapPart)	2	4
Sim(getMapResponse, getMAPResponse)	4	6
sim(<output>, <output>)	0 (no names)	10
sim(getMAP, createMAP)	**2**	**18.3**

renders the matchmaker independent from any service collection in principle?

One option to resolve these issues is to let the matchmaker learn how to do it rather than finding a solution by hand. Inspired by the work of (Joachims & Radlinski, 2007) and (Kiefer & Bernstein, 2008) on off-line adaptive search, we developed an off-line adaptive hybrid semantic matchmaker for SAWSDL services, called SAWSDL-MX2, that simply learns how to optimally solve the just mentioned problems with fixed hybrid matchmaking by means of a support vector machine-based classifier that is trained and cross-validated over a given test collection and then applied to the selection process for a service request at hand.

SAWSDL-MX2 Overview

In short, the SAWSDL-MX2 matchmaker returns a ranked list of relevant services *S* for a given request *R* in SAWSDL based on the aggregated results of separately performed logical, text and structural similarity-based matching. Each of these different matching filters has been described above for SAWSDL-MX1 and the WSDL-Analyzer tool. Their aggregation by SAWSDL-MX2 is optimal with respect to average classification accuracy according to its binary SVM-classifier that has been learned over a given training set previously.

In the following, we describe the training (off-line learning) phase and the subsequent use of the learned SVM-classifier for hybrid semantic service selection by SAWSDL-MX2 in more detail.

Off-Line Learning of SVM Classifier

The problem of classifying a given service *S* with respect to its semantic relevance to a given request *R* can be re-formulated as the problem of learning a binary support vector machine-based classifier. That is to find a separating hyperplane in a given feature space *X* such that for all positive and negative training samples with minimal distances (these particular samples are also called support vectors) to it, these distances are maximal.

In case of SAWSDL-MX2, we consider a 7-dimensional feature space $X = \{0, 1\}^5 \times [0, 1] \times [0, 1]$, where each of the first five binary dimensions corresponds to the occurrence of one out of five different logical matching degrees (*exact, plug-in, subsumes, subsumed-by, fail*) followed by the two real-valued dimensions for text, respectively, structural similarity-based matching degrees. For example, the feature vector $x_i = (0, 0, 1, 0, 0, 0.6, 0.7)$ ($i \leq N$, *N* is the size of the training set of positive and negative samples) indicates that the matching results for the service offer/request pair (*S, R*) that corresponds to the training sample (x_i, y_i) (with $y_i = 1$ if *S* is relevant to *R* according to the binary relevance sets defined in the test collection SAWSDL-TC1, else $y_i = -1$) yields a logical *subsumes* match, a text similarity of 0.6, and structural similarity of 0.7.

For the training set $\{(x_1, y_1), \ldots, (x_N, y_N)\}$, we randomly selected 2325 samples in total derived from SAWSDL-TC1 with equal quantities of positive and negative samples. This amounts to around 10% of the complete search space of samples (which size is the number of requests times the number of services in the used collection) over which the binary SVM classifier for service relevance is learned.

The SVM classification problem is defined as the following optimization problem:

$$\text{minimize in } w, b, \xi : \frac{1}{2} w^T w +$$

$$C \sum_{i=1}^{N} \xi_i \text{ subject to } \forall 1 \leq i \leq N : y_i(w^T \phi(x_i) + b)$$
$$\geq 1 - \xi_i, \xi_i \geq 0$$

where w and b define the optimally separating hyperplane as the set of points satisfying $w^T\varphi(x) + b = 0$. Furthermore, w is the *normal vector* which specifies the orientation of the plane, b is called *bias* and indicates the offset of the hyperplane from the origin of the feature space X. The error term $C \sum_{i=1}^{N} \xi_i$ is introduced to allow for outliers in a non-linear separable training set, where the error penalty parameter C must be specified beforehand. The predefined function φ maps features into a higher, possibly infinitely dimensional space in which the SVM finds an optimal hyperplane that allows the classification of non-linear separable data (more precise with respect to the original dimension of X)[9].

Since $w = \sum_{i=1}^{N} y_i a_i \phi(x_i)$ is a linear combination of training sample feature vectors the dual formulation of the SVM classification problem that is actually solved by SAWSDL-MX2 is as follows:

$$\text{maximize in } a : \frac{1}{2} \sum_{i,j=1}^{N} y_i y_j a_i a_j K(x_i, x_j) - \sum_{i=1}^{N} a_i$$

$$\text{subject to } \sum_{i=1}^{N} y_i a_i = 0, \forall 1 \leq i \leq N : 0 \leq a_i \leq C$$

The kernel function $K(x_i, x_j) = \varphi(x_i)^T\varphi(x_j)$ implicitly defines φ in the scalar product. The problem is solved by finding a set of Lagrange multipliers φ_i representing the hyperplane for which training samples x_i with $\varphi_i \neq 0$ are called support vectors (of the hyperplane). For SAWSDL-MX2, we choose the RBF Kernel (Radial Basis Function) as suggested in (Hsu et al. 2007):

$$K(x_i, x_j) = e^{-y\|x_i - x_j\|^2}.$$

Unlike polynomial kernels, it only introduces a single parameter y which keeps the complexity of model selection low. Besides, for specific parameter settings it can behave like a linear or sigmoid kernel.

The searching of a SVM parameter setting (C, y) that is optimal with respect to its average classification accuracy has been done through means of grid search and 6-folded cross-validation. Binary classification of samples $x \in X$ for service pair (S, R) with the above parameters is defined as follows: $d(x) = \sum_{i=1}^{N} y_i a_i K(x_i, x) + b$ with bias b satisfying the Karush-Kuhn-Tucker condition (Chang & Lin 2001), such that S is classified as relevant if and only if $d(x) > 0$. Please note, that w is not a direct output of the dual optimization but computed using the objective value o of the dual optimization and the coefficients α_i based on the relation between the primary and dual problem:

$$\|w\|^2 = w^T w = \sum_{i,j=1}^{N} y_i y_j a_i a_j K(x_i, x_j)$$
$$= 2 \cdot \left(o + \sum_{i=1}^{N} a_i\right)$$

For more details on SVM in general and on the dual problem solving in particular, see Hsu et al. (2007).

Figure 8 illustrates the functioning of a linear SVM classifier (i.e. $K(x_i, x_j) = x_i^T x_j$) in a two-dimensional example for adapting the aggregation of two service matching variants (structural + text) forming a linearly separable 2D feature space $[0,1] \times [0,1]$. The parameters of both problem formulation variants for this case are shown: the normal vector w specifies the orientation of the resulting hyperplane and b the offset from the origin for the primal formulation. The dual parameters α_i characterize the support vectors (labeled SV in the figure), which lie exactly on the planes with maximum margin computed by the SVM optimization problem solver.

Using Learned SVM Classifier with Ranking for Service Selection

Once the matchmaker SAWSDL-MX2 has finished its training phase over the given test collection, it can apply the learned SVM classifier to any new service pair (S, R) with a new request R that is not known in the training set to compute the hybrid semantic matching degree. More concrete, it just applies its learned binary classifier d to the corresponding feature vector x of (S, R) as described above. That is, service S is relevant to R, if and only if $d(x) > 0$, otherwise it is classified as irrelevant. Finally, the matchmaker SAWSDL-MX2 then ranks the service S according to the distance $dist(x) = d(x)/|w|$ of its feature vector x to the learned hyperplane. Eventually, it returns the computed hybrid semantic matching degree for the pair (S, R) as the tuple $(d(x), dist(x))$.

The off-line learning of SAWSDL-MX2 renders it, in principle, independent from any given test collection, in particular any set of services registered at the matchmaker (it just has to learn over the respectively modified test collection in case of changes) as well as any set of different matching filters that the developer would like to use in combination in future versions of SAWSDL-MX2. In this case it just automatically re-learns off-line how to best aggregate them for the actual service collection at hand. That is particularly in

Figure 8. Illustration of SVM classification for training set of linear separable 2D samples

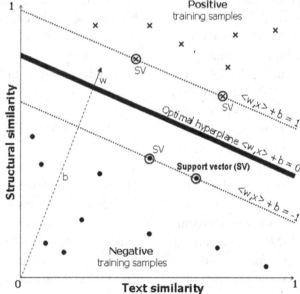

Figure 9. Architecture of the adaptive hybrid semantic matchmaker SAWSDL-MX2

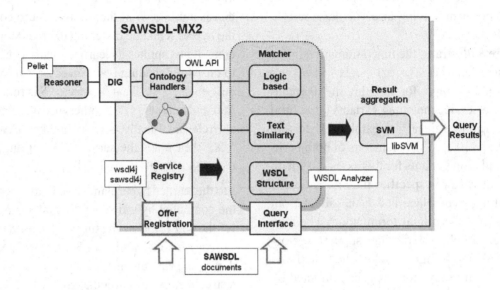

line with the off-line adaptive search engine Striver (Joachims & Radlinski, 2007) and the adaptive OWL-S matchmakers OWLS-MX3 (Klusch & Kapahnke, 2009) and OWLS- iMatcher2 (Kiefer & Bernstein, 2008).

IMPLEMENTATION

We implemented the SAWSDL matchmaker variants described in previous sections in Java. In particular, we used the sawsdl4j[10] API (handling SAWSDL for WSDL 1.1) to parse SAWSDL documents, the OWL API[11] for accessing OWL ontologies used for annotation, the DIG 1.1 standard interface to handle OWL-DL (SHOIQ) knowledge base queries, and the OWL-API/ Pellet[12] reasoner as OWL-DL inference engine for logic-based semantic matchmaking. The binary SVM-classifier with ranking as used by the SAWSDL-MX2 has been implemented with the public libSVM[13] software.

Figure 9 provides an overview of the components of the SAWSDL-MX2 matchmaker architecture. The implementation of both the non-adaptive SAWSDL-MX1 and the adaptive

SAWSDL-MX2 is publicly available at the portal semwebcentral.org.

The semantic service selection tool called SAWSDL-MX offers both matchmakers with an integrated graphical user interface (see Figure 10).

The functionality of this tool covers all steps of semantic service selection ranging from the selection of given test collection, configuration of the selected matchmaker variant, and the display of not only its answer set for a particular request but also the results of applying different selected retrieval performance evaluation measures which can be conveniently saved in form of an evaluation summary report in PDF.

PERFORMANCE EVALUATION

For evaluating the retrieval performance of the different non-adaptive and adaptive SAWSDL service matchmakers described in previous sections, we conducted a comparative evaluation experiment based on the only publicly available SAWSDL service retrieval test collection SAWS-DL-TC1 and the classical retrieval performance measures macro-averaged recall/precision, aver-

Figure 10. Graphical user interface of the semantic service selection tool SAWSDL-MX

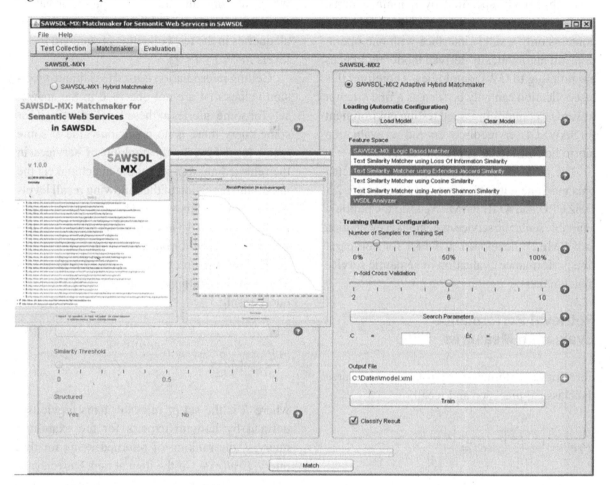

age precision and average query response time. For checking the statistical significance of the evaluation results for different matching variants, we used the standard Friedman test.

In the following, we focus on the comparative retrieval performance evaluation of the non-adaptive matchmakers SAWSDL-M0+WA and SAWSDL-MX1, and the adaptive matchmaker SAWSDL-MX2. For more detailed results on SAWSDL-MX1 alone, we refer to (Klusch & Kapahnke, 2008).

Evaluation Setup

The experimental evaluation of service retrieval performance is based on the first SAWSDL test collection SAWSDL-TC1. It is semi-automatically derived from OWLS-TC 2.2[14] using the OWLS-2WSDL[15] tool, as there is currently no other standard test collection for SAWSDL available. OWLS2WSDL transforms OWL-S service descriptions (and concept definitions relevant for parameter description) to WSDL through syntactic transformation. Top-level annotations taken from the original OWL-S descriptions have been added for XML Schema type definitions used to describe message inputs and output.

The collection SAWSDL-TC1 consists of around 900 Web services covering different application domains: education, medical care, food, travel, communication, economy and weaponry. It also includes a set of queries and binary relevance sets subjectively specified by domain experts. As one result, each service in SAWSDL-TC1 contains only a single interface with one operation. All automatically derived model references are pointing to OWL ontologies. Therefore, this test collection can only be seen as a first attempt towards a commonly agreed testing environment for SAWSDL service discovery and our evaluation has to be considered as preliminary.

The performance tests have been conducted on a machine with Windows XP 32b, Java 6, 2.8 GHz CPU and 4 GB RAM. We used the publicly available semantic service matchmaker evaluation tool SME2[16] developed at DFKI for comparative performance evaluation of semantic service matchmakers.

Retrieval Performance Evaluation Measures

For retrieval performance evaluation, we measured the classical precision and recall:

$$Prec = \frac{|A \cap B|}{|B|}, Rec = \frac{|A \cap B|}{|A|},$$

where A is the set of all relevant documents, and B the set of all retrieved documents for a request. Further, we measured the *macro-averaged precision at standard recall levels*:

$$Prec_i =$$
$$\frac{1}{|Q|} \cdot \sum_{q \in Q} \max\{P_O \mid R_O \geq Rec_i \wedge (R_O, P_O) \in O_q\}$$

where O_q denotes the set of observed pairs of recall/precision values for query q when scanning the ranked services in the answer set for q stepwise for true positives in the relevance sets of the test collection. For evaluation, the answer sets are the sets of all services registered at the matchmaker which are ranked with respect to their (totally ordered) matching degree. In other

words, we computed the mean of precision values for answer sets returned by the matchmaker for all queries in the test collection at standard recall levels Rec_i $(0 \leq i < \lambda)$.

Ceiling interpolation is used to estimate precision values that are not observed in the answer sets for some queries at these levels; that is, if for some query there is no precision value at some recall level (due to the ranking of services in the returned answer set by the matchmaker) the maximum precision of the following recall levels is assumed for this value. The number of recall levels from 0 to 1 (in equidistant steps n/λ, $n = 1, ..., \lambda$) we used for our experiments is $\lambda = 20$.

The *Average Precision* (AP) measure produces a single-valued rating of a matchmaker for a single query result:

$$AP = \frac{1}{|R|} \sum_{r=1}^{|L|} isrel(r) \frac{count(r)}{r},$$

where R is the set of relevant items previously defined by domain experts for the examined query, L the ranking of returned items for that query, $isrel(r) = 1$ if the item at rank r is relevant and 0 otherwise and $count(r)$ the number of relevant items found in the ranking when scanning top-down, i.e. $count(r) = \sum_{i=1}^{r} isrel(i)$. Please note that the AP measure is independent from the way and size of ranking.

Statistical Significance Test

In general, differences in performance evaluation results can be shown to be statistically significant or insignificant by means of the so-called Friedman test. This is a non-parametric test for simultaneously analyzing ranked result sets of at least two different (service matching) methods and has been shown in (Hull, 1993) to be a vital explanatory component of a comparative retrieval performance evaluation.

We are using the Friedman Test variant proposed in (Iman & Davenport, 1980) as $F_N = MSR/MSE$, where MSR is the mean-squared difference between the different matching variants and MSE the mean-squared error. The resulting value can be compared to the F-distribution with $m - 1$ and $(n - 1)(m - 1)$ degrees of freedom, where n is the number of queries and m the number of tested matching variants. The resulting p-value indicates, if there is a significant difference between the variants which one cannot interpret as being an implication of the *null hypothesis*, i.e. that variations of the matchmaker rankings per query are insignificant. As a threshold value for p, we rely on $\alpha = 0.05$, which is frequently used for tests like this. To produce the rankings for the test, averaged AP values have been used.

Performance Evaluation Experiments

As a first experiment, we compared the retrieval performance of SAWSDLM0+WA to that of both approaches applied solely. This experiment was conducted mainly to check, whether even such a simple hybrid combination of logic-based and non-logic-based semantic matching as in SAWSDL-M0+WA can improve upon the performance of each of both (SAWSDL-M0 and Text-IR) individually.

As shown in Figure 11(a), the combination of both performs best at almost every recall level except towards full recall. This is in perfect line with our experimental results on SAWSDL-MX1 reported in (Klusch & Kapahnke, 2008). As we already pointed out there, ontologies currently found in the Web are merely inclusion hierarchies or taxonomies rarely making use of elaborated logical concept definitions for service annotation, which still dampens the benefit of any logic-based semantic matching approach.

To compare the performance of the adaptive hybrid matchmaker SAWSDLMX2 (logic, text, structural similarity) with that of the non-adaptive variants SAWSDL-M0+WA (logic and structural

similarity) and SAWSDL-MX1 (logic and text similarity), we conducted a second evaluation experiment. As shown in Figure 11(b), the adaptive SAWSDL-MX2 performs better than SAWSDL-M0 (logic-based only) and at least as good as the non-adaptive variant SAWSDL-MX1 utilizing logic-based matching and extended Jaccard (Tanimoto) text similarity-based matching. This is mainly due to the fact, that text similarity computation as described introductorily is closely related to structural matching when applied to mere is-a ontologies (inclusion hierarchies, taxonomies).

In fact, for the given test collection, where SAWSDL files have been semi-automatically derived from OWL-S and the XML Schema parameters origin from OWL concept definitions, the WSDL-Analyzer (WA) indirectly performs both structural and text similarity-based concept matching which makes it partly redundant to SAWSDL-MX2 in such cases. Nevertheless, for the general case, the adaptive approach of SAWSDL-MX2 enables an easy and well-defined integration of arbitrary matching mechanisms to improve result rankings in the future.

Table 2 summarizes the average precision (AP) and query response time (AQRT) of SAWSDL-MX1 and SAWSDL-MX2 as well as other available SAWSDL matchmakers developed elsewhere, that are non-adaptive COM4SWS, URBE and adaptive SAWSDL-iMatcher3; we will comment on these relevant matchmakers in the next section. The results of their performance evaluation over the same test collection SAWSDL-TC1 (and same publicly available evaluation tool SME2[17]) are taken from the summary report of the 2009 edition of the international semantic service selection contest (S3 2009).

The average precision values for the individual service matching variants, that are logic-based matching (SAWSDL-M0), structural matching by WSDL-Analyzer (WA) and text matching with TFIDF-Cosine (IR) are 0.53, respectively, 0.44, respectively, 0.46. Their average

Figure 11. Macro-averaged precision/recall of SAWSDL service matchmaking variants. (a) Logical (SAWSDL-M0) vs. structural (WSDL-Analyzer/WA) vs. hybrid (SAWSDL-M0+WA) semantic service selection.(b) Non-adaptive hybrid (SAWSDL-M0+WA & SAWSDL-MX1) vs. adaptive hybrid (SAWSDL-MX2) semantic service selection.

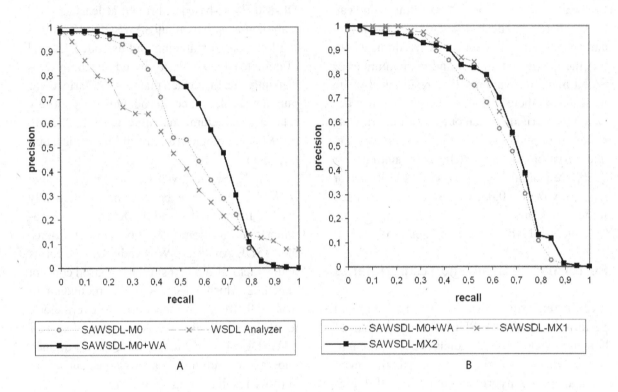

Table 2. Average precision and query response time (in seconds) of SAWSDL-MX matchmaker variants compared to other SAWSDL matchmakers URBE, COM4SWS and SAWSDL-iMatcher3

	SAWSDL-MX1	SAWSDL-MX2	COM4SWS	URBE	SAWSDL-iMatcher3
AP	0.7	0.68	0.68	0.73	0.63
AQRT	3.1s	7.9s	6.14s	20s	.75s

query response times are 1.7, respectively, 3, respectively 1.4 seconds. The differences between their precision values are not statistically significant. It is noteworthy that the text matching did outperform neither pure logic-based nor structural matching. The latter is partly due to redundant text similarity measurement of unfolded I/O concepts by the WA and IR since the XML schema parameter definitions of SAWSDL services in SAWSDL-TC were automatically derived

from respective I/O concept definitions for corresponding OWL-S services in the collection OWLS-TC2 by the publicly available conversion tool OWLS2WSDL [18].

The hybrid semantic SAWSDL matchmaker variants SAWSDL-M0+WA (logic + structural) and SAWSDL-MX1 (logic + text) outperformed the individual filters (SAWSDL-M0, WA, IR) in terms of AP 0.61, respectively, AP 0.68. For example, the statistical significance test for macro-averaged recall/precision results for SAWSDL-M0+WA (logic + structural matching) compared to the structural only matching by the WSDL-Analyzer (WA) and the logic-based only matchmaker variant SAWSDL-M0 yielded $p = 0.026$, respectively, $p = 0.0028$ both of which below threshold α. That is, the hybrid combination significantly outperformed the individual ones at 5% level. This is in perfect line with experimental evaluation results for hybrid semantic service matchmakers reported elsewhere (Klusch et al., 2006, 2009; Klusch, Fries, et al., 2009).

RELATED WORK

All SAWSDL matchmakers listed in Table 2 did perform equally well, that is with reasonable and statistically insignificant differences between their average precision ($p = 0.331$ at 5% level), but with unacceptably high query response times for many applications. For the given test collection SAWSDL-TC1, no performance gain resulted from using adaptive SAWSDL matchmakers like SAWSDL-MX2 (SVM classifier) or SAWSDL-iMatcher3 (linear regression) instead of non-adaptive ones like SAWSDL-MX1, COM4SWS and URBE manually optimized with respect to the collection.

However, as mentioned above, the automated optimal aggregation of different kinds of selection results through machine learning renders the respectively adaptive matchmakers independent from changes of considered service collections as well as newly added or modified matching filters. In case of non-adaptive matchmakers, this would require a tedious manual (re-) tuning of their individual and aggregated matching processes to (again) keep up with the precision of adaptive ones. The off-line learning time of SAWSDL-MX2 over its training subset of SAWSDL-TC1 was 31 minutes of which 5 minutes were devoted to feature space building for 2325 samples (cf. page 15). In addition, most non-adaptive matchmak-

ers use linearly weighted aggregation functions while SAWSDL-MX2 automatically learns such aggregation even for non-linear separable feature spaces.

It is noteworthy that the only other adaptive SAWSDL service matchmaker SAWSDL-iMatcher3 trained over the full test collection of the contest by their developers using a linear regression model was slightly outperformed by SAWSDL-MX2 which was only trained over a random 10% subset using SVM-based classification. The extremely fast query response time of SAWSDL-iMatcher3 is due to its essentially pre-computed answer sets for this collection.

In any case, we emphasize that the above results of our experimental evaluation strongly depend on the only publicly available SAWSDL service retrieval test collection SAWSDL-TC1. In this regard, the reported results are preliminary until a more comprehensive standard SAWSDL test collection (like the TREC collections in the information retrieval domain) becomes available in the future.

The first search engine for WSDL-S services has been Lumina (Li et al. 2006) developed in the METEOR-S project[19]. It follows an approach similar to FUSION based on mapping WSDL-S (the predecessor of SAWSDL) to UDDI but performs non-logic-based semantic matching in terms of structural ontology-based (path lengths between terms in shared ontology) and simple keyword-based service matching scores only.

The URBE matchmaker (developed by Pierluigi Plebani in 2008 at the Politecnico di Milano, Italy) performs non-logic-based semantic SAWSDL service matching (Plebani & Pernici, 2009). In particular, it performs text similarity matching of property-class and XSD I/O message data types as well as structural ontology-based I/O concept similarity in terms of worst-case path length between concepts in a shared ontology. There is no logical reasoning involved. Like SAWSDL-MX1 and SAWSDL-MX2, URBE performs bipartite graph-matching of service operations and ranks services based on weighted aggregation of structural and text matching scores. Remarkably, URBE won the special track for SAWSDL service selection of the international S3 (semantic service selection) contest editions 2008 and 2009 in terms of average precision (0.72). Though, the differences to the adaptive SAWSDL matchmakers SAWSDL-MX2 and SAWSDL-iMatcher3 were statistically not significant, and its average query response time was worst (20 sec) compared to that of its next ranked competitors.

The COM4SWS matchmaker (developed by Stefan Schulte and his colleagues at the Technische Universität Darmstadt, Germany) is also a hybrid semantic SAWSDL service matchmaker: It performs non-logic-based clustering (FarthestFirst, syntactic distance) of service descriptions in the vector space model and checks for logic-based mutual coverage of (subclasses of) I/O concepts. Matching of service components from a service offer and a service request is based on the Hungarian algorithm (i.e., bipartite service signature graph matching) while ranking values are computed as weighted similarity values from all service abstraction levels. No further information is available on COM4SWS yet. It is noteworthy, that it performed close to the next ranked adaptive SAWSDL-MX2 in terms of average precision (0.681) but slightly faster in average (6.14 sec) at the 2009 edition of the S3 contest.

The SAWSDL-iMatcher3 (developed by Dengping Wei and Avi Bernstein in 2009 at the University of Zurich, Switzerland) is most relevant to SAWSDL-MX2 with respect to adaptive selection of SAWSDL services. It partially applies the selection process performed by the OWL-S matchmaker iMatcher developed by the same group (Kiefer & Bernstein, 2008) to the case of SAWSDL service selection. In particular, SAWSDL-iMatcher3 is hybrid in the sense that it performs logical matching based on output concept subsumption and text similarity-based matching of service names, if they are provided in the respective SAWSDL descriptions. For the latter

purpose, it applies different token- and edit-based text similarity measures. Like SAWSDL-MX2 it learns how to best select services off-line but applies a linear regression model with ranking and does perform neither text matching of logically unfolded I/O concept definitions nor WSDL structure matching.

(Syeda-Mahmood et al., 2005) present a hybrid semantic service matchmaking approach for WSDL-S with annotations in OWL based on the combination domain-independent knowledge aquired from the WordNet thesaurus and domain-dependent semantic scoring. In contrast to SAWSDL-MX2, it relies on a fixed scoring schema that is adapted manually to valuate different types of concept relations. Hybrid result aggregation is also fixed by considering the minimum result as overall ranking score, whereas our approach automatically adapts the overall aggregation strategy including different degrees of logical match using SVM training. Apart from the matching procedure itself, a redundant storage strategy named attribute hashing is presented to improve retrieval performance in large service repositories.

The adaptive and hybrid semantic service matchmaker OWLS-MX3 (Klusch & Kapahnke, 2009) is similar to SAWSDL-MX2 in that it performs the same SVM-based off-line learning and is restricted to semantic annotations in OWL-DL. However, both matchmakers significantly differ in various aspects of their selection process such as the way of how they perform structural matching. While SAWSDL-MX2 performs structural matching on the WSDL files of SAWSDL service descriptions ignoring the semantic annotations, OWLS-MX3 ignores the grounding of semantic services in WSDL completely. Another differing aspect is the definition of the logic-based filters. While SAWSDL-MX2 applies bipartite graph matching at operation level to compute the optimal one-to-one parameter assignment for request and service offer, OWLS-MX3 allows multiple assignments for a parameter mapping, thus producing false positives caused by parameters that subsume more than one parameter of its counterpart.

For a comprehensive survey of semantic service matchmakers in general, we refer the interested reader to (Klusch, 2008). A survey of approaches to WSDL service signature or behavior (message-based conversation) matching such as WXplorer (Stroulia & Wang, 2004) or Woogle (Dong et al., 2004) is out of the scope of this paper but provided, for example, in (Plebani & Pernici, 2009). Taking a broader view, the task of semantic service retrieval can be interpreted as finding compositions of services that fulfill given requirement specifications, as for example in SEMAPLAN (Akkiraju et al., 2006), which applies semantic service matching in a cost function to guide an AI planner in generating favorable service compositions, or Opossum (Toch et al., 2007), which introduces the notion of service networks to represent service dependencies as basis for approximated retrieval of service composition. However, integration of SAWSDL-MX2 in such a system is out of the scope of this paper.

CONCLUSION

We discussed different hybrid SAWSDL service matchmakers each of which outperform the individual types of semantic service signature matching that they combine. Among others, the comparative experimental performance evaluation showed that the combined use of logical and non-logic-based structural matching may indeed outperform logic-based only matching but not the combination of logical with text similarity-based matching by SAWSDL-MX1.

Further, the adaptive combination of all three types of matching by SAWSDL-MX2 performed as well as the non-adaptive hybrid variant in terms of average precision. This experimental result appears somewhat disappointing at first glance but, apart from that it depended on the only available test collection SAWSDL-TC1, the major benefit

of the offline learning capability is that it renders SAWSDL-MX2 independent from any manual adjustment to other or updated test collections and matching filters in the future. In fact, if services or ontologies change or new filters shall be used or integrated into a given non-adaptive matchmaker, the optimal configuration of its filters with respect to precision would have to be sought by the developer in time-consuming experiments and analysis otherwise.

REFERENCES

Akkiraju, R., Srivastava, B., Ivan, A.-A., Goodwin, R., & Syeda-Mahmood, T. (2006). SEMAPLAN: Combining Planning with Semantic Matching to Achieve Web Service Composition. In *Proceedings of the 6th International Conference on Web Services (ICWS)*. Washington, DC: IEEE Computer Society.

Baader, F., Calvanese, D., McGuinness, D. L., Nardi, D., & Patel-Schneider, P. F. (2003). *The Description Logic Handbook: Theory, Implementation, and Applications*. Cambridge, UK: Cambridge University Press.

Chang, C.-C., & Lin, C.-J. (2001). *Libsvm: a library for support vector machines*. Retrieved from http://www.csie.ntu.edu.tw/ cjlin/libsvm

Dong, X., Madhavan, J., & Halevy, A. (2004). Mining Structures for Semantics. *ACM Special Interest Group on Knowledge Discovery and Data Mining Explorations Newsletter, 6*(2).

Hsu, C.-W., Chang, C.-C., & Lin, C.-J. (2007). *A Practical Guide to Support Vector Classification*.

Hull, D. (1993). Using statistical testing in the evaluation of retrieval experiments. In *Proceedings of the 16th ACM SIGIR Conference on Research and Development in Information Retrieval*.

Adaptive Hybrid Semantic Selection of SAWSDL Services with SAWSDL-MX2

Iman, R. L., & Davenport, J. M. (1980). Approximations of the critical region of the Friedman statistic. *Communications in Statistics, A9*(6), 571–595. doi:10.1080/03610928008827904

Joachims, T., & Radlinski, F. (2007). Search Engines that Learn from Implicit Feedback. *IEEE Computer, 40*(8), 34–40.

Kaufer, F., & Klusch, M. (2006). WSMO-MX: A Logic Programming Based Hybrid Service Matchmaker. In *Proceedings of the 4th IEEE European Conference on Web Services (ECOWS 2006)*, Zurich, Switzerland. Washington, DC: IEEE Computer Society.

Kiefer, C., & Bernstein, A. (2008). The Creation and Evaluation of iSPARQL Strategies for Matchmaking. In *Proceedings of the 5th European Semantic Web Conference (ESWC)* (LNCS 5021).

Klusch, M., Fries, B., & Sycara, K. (2006). Automated Semantic Web Service Discovery with OWLS-MX. In *Proceedings of the 5th International Conference on Autonomous Agents and Multi-Agent Systems (AAMAS)*, Hakodate, Japan. New York: ACM Press.

Klusch, M., Fries, B., & Sycara, K. (2009). OWLS-MX: A Hybrid Semantic Web Service Matchmaker for OWL-S Services. *Web Semantics, 7*(2), 121–133.

Klusch, M., & Kapahnke, P. (2008). Semantic Web Service Selection with SAWSDL-MX. In *Proceedings of the 2nd Workshop on Service Matchmaking and Resource Retrieval in the Semantic Web (SMR2)*, Karlsruhe, Germany. CEUR.

Klusch, M., & Kapahnke, P. (2009). OWLS-MX3: An Adaptive Hybrid Semantic Service Matchmaker for OWL-S. In *Proceedings of the 3rd International Workshop on Semantic Matchmaking and Resource Retrieval (SMR2) at ISWC*. CEUR.

Klusch, M., Kapahnke, P., & Zinnikus, I. (2009). SAWSDL-MX2: A Machine-Learning Approach for Integrating Semantic Web Service Matchmaking Variants. In *Proceedings of the IEEE 7th International Conference on Web Services (ICWS)*, Los Angeles. Washington, DC: IEEE Computer Society.

Kourtesis, D., & Paraskakis, I. (2008). Combining SAWSDL, OWL-DL and UDDI for Semantically Enhanced Web Service Discovery. In *Proceedings of the 5th European Semantic Web Conference (ESWC)* (LNCS 5021).

Li, K., Verma, K., Mulye, R., Rabbani, R., Miller, J. A., & Sheth, A. P. (2006). Designing Semantic Web Processes: The WSDL-S Approach. In Cardoso, J., & Sheth, A. (Eds.), *Semantic Web Services, Processes and Applications*. New York: Springer. doi:10.1007/978-0-387-34685-4_7

Plebani, P., & Pernici, B. (2009). URBE: Web Service Retrieval Based on Similarity Evaluation. *IEEE Transactions on Knowledge and Data Engineering, 21*(11), 1629–1642. doi:10.1109/TKDE.2009.35

Schumacher, M., Helin, H., & Schuldt, H. (Eds.). (2008). *CASCOM – Intelligent Service Coordination in the Semantic Web*. Berlin: Birkhäuser Verlag. doi:10.1007/978-3-7643-8575-0

Stroulia, E., & Wang, Y. (2004). Structural and Semantic Matching for Assessing Web-Service Similarity. *Cooperative Information Systems, 14*(4).

Toch, E., Gal, A., Reinhartz-Berger, I., & Dori, D. (2007). A semantic approach to approximate service retrieval. *ACM Transactions on Internet Technology, 8*(2).

Zinnikus, I., Rupp, H.-J., & Fischer, K. (2006). Detecting Similarities between Web Service Interfaces: The WSDL Analyzer. In *Proceedings of the 2nd International Workshop on Web Services and Interoperability (WSI 2006)*.

ENDNOTES

1. http://www.w3.org/TR/sawsdl/
2. http://www.w3.org/TR/wsdl/ and http://www.w3.org/TR/wsdl20/
3. The W3C recommendation for SAWSDL does not define a logical relationship among multiple model references for a single element.
4. http://www.w3.org/2004/OWL/
5. http://dig.sourceforge.net/
6. http://www.ifi.uzh.ch/ddis/research/semweb/simpack/
7. http://www.w3c.org/TR/xmlschema-2/
8. http://wordnet.princeton.edu/
9. The fraction ½ is introduced for computational reasons only, and does not affect the classification result.
10. http://knoesis.wright.edu/opensource/sawsdl4j/
11. http://owlapi.sourceforge.net/
12. http://pellet.owldl.com/
13. http://www.csie.ntu.edu.tw/~cjlin/libsvm/
14. http://projects.semwebcentral.org/projects/owls-tc/
15. http://projects.semwebcentral.org/projects/owls2wsdl/
16. http://projects.semwebcentral.org/projects/sme2/
17. SME2: Semantic Service Matchmaker Evaluation Tool. Available at projects.semwebcentral.org/projects/sme2/
18. OWLS2WSDL converter. Available at projects.semwebcentral.org/projects/owls-2wsdl/
19. http://lsdis.cs.uga.edu/projects/meteor-s/

This work was previously published in International Journal of Semantic Web and Information Systems, Volume 6, Issue 4, edited by Amit P. Sheth, pp. 1-26, copyright 2010 by IGI Publishing (an imprint of IGI Global).

Section 3
Semantic Applications

Chapter 8
Enhancing Folksonomy–Based Content Retrieval with Semantic Web Technology

Rachanee Ungrangsi
Shinawatra University, Thailand

Chutiporn Anutariya
Shinawatra University, Thailand

Vilas Wuwongse
Asian Institute of Technology, Thailand

ABSTRACT

While Flickr, a widely-known photo sharing system, allows users to describe their own photos with tags (aka. folksonomy tags) for indexing purposes, its tag-based photo retrieval function is severely hampered by the inherent nature of folksonomy tags. This paper presents SemFlickr, an application which enhances the search in Flickr with its semantic query suggestion feature. SemFlickr employs SQORE, an ontology retrieval system, to retrieve relevant ontologies from the Semantic Web and then derives query term suggestions from those ontologies. To ensure that the highly related photos will appear at the top of the results, SemFlickr takes the ontological relations among the given query terms to assign tag scores and then generates its ranked results. Experimental outcomes are encouraging and reveal a number of useful insights for developing applications that integrate the Semantic Web and Web 2.0 together.

1 INTRODUCTION

Flickr – http://www.flickr.com (20092009Yahoo! Inc., 2009!!) is one of the very first successful and widely-used Web 2.0 applications. It allows users to freely upload, tag and share photos and videos with others. With its self-tagging mechanism, different users can annotate the same resource with different tags depending on the social communities they belong to, their background, their perception and areas of expertise, etc. To date, there are approximately at least 3 million items uploaded per day with 20 million unique users visiting Flickr per month. In spite of its rapid

DOI: 10.4018/978-1-4666-0185-7.ch008

growth and (meta) data richness, its users are experiencing increasing difficulties of searching for a particular photo or video.

Consider, for example, that Flickr currently has more than 2 million photos tagged with the term baby whereas its full-text search engine returns approximately 6 million photos relevant to the term baby. Simply searching Flickr with the query term baby will not return only the photos of very young children, but also those about baby-related products, toys, young animals, pregnant women and even adults. Unlike a concept defined in an ontology, the semantics of a particular tag is ambiguous, and may carry more than one specific meaning depending on each user's viewpoint and context. This can answer why Flickr's most interesting photos of baby contain a lot of animal photos (See Figure 1). Therefore, users must put an extra effort to think of additional precise query terms to clarify a search and obtain the

desired results. Assisting the searching process by providing users with query suggestions can help reduce the searching effort and improve the search's precision.

This paper, therefore, presents the *SemFlickr* application which employs Semantic Web technologies to enhance the search in Flickr with its query suggestion feature. In particular, SemFlickr is a prototype semantics-driven photo retrieval application that supports the user during a photo search by suggesting additional query terms derived from on-line ontologies available in the Semantic Web. Its search interface is designed to enable the user who has limited knowledge about the searching domain to explore more related query terms and search results. It is available on-line at URL: http://research.siu.ac.th/SemFlickr. In addition, to improve the retrieval performance, a semantics-based ranking mechanism is also proposed. A comparison of Flickr's and Sem-

Figure 1. Top twelve most interesting Flickr's photos tagged with "Baby" (retrieved on 27 July 2009)

Flickr's search results has been conducted and shows that SemFlickr can yield better search results. Furthermore, a user-based evaluation implies clear benefits of semantic query suggestion and indicates a few issues which require careful consideration in Semantic Web application development.

The paper is organized as follows. Sect. 2 reviews related works. Sect. 3 introduces *SQORE*, the exploited ontology retrieval engine. Sect. 4 describes SemFlickr and its underlying mechanism for deriving semantic query suggestions and ranking the search results. Sect. 5 and 6 discuss the two conducted experiments and their results. Conclusions and future works are presented in Sect. 7 and followed by acknowledgement in Sect. 8. Finally, Appendix provides a glossary of important technical terms used in the paper.

2 RELATED WORK

This section reviews Flickr's search functions, the Semantic Web and ontologies, recent approaches to integrating ontologies and Folksonomy and existing approaches to enhancing a search in Flickr.

Flickr's Search Functions

Flickr offers two search functions: text-based and tag-based. The former retrieves photos having the query terms contained in their titles or descriptions, while the latter returns photos having tags that match with the given query terms. Due to the nature of social tags, users are often not able to obtain the photos they are looking for. As revealed by many research results, tags in social tagging systems can be inaccurate because free tagging allows inconsistencies and contraries to exist (Peterson, 2006). The problems include ambiguity, lack of synonymy and discrepancies in granularity. Thus, it is difficult for a user to retrieve all the desired resources unless he knows all the possible variants of the tags that may have

been used. In addition, the title, description and tags of a photo provided by the owner based on his point of view may not match with others'.

In Flickr, the returned results can be sorted either by their *published dates* (most recent) or by *interestingness* (most interesting). The interestingness property of each photo is defined by taking the following elements into account: i) where the click-throughs come from (pages that users visited before entering the current page); ii) who comments on it and when; iii) who marks it as a favorite; iv) its tags and resources. With all these continuing activities, a photo's interestingness changes over time. However, the experimental results, to be discussed in details in this paper, show that the two aforementioned sorting criteria (i.e. most recent and interestingness) are not much useful for users. In addition, to facilitate users during tag-based search, Flickr provides two additional features: *tag clusters* and *related tags*, which are created by means of a clustering technique and tag co-occurrence statistics, respectively. Clusters are groups of similar tags and one tag may appear in more than one cluster.

Semantic Web and Ontologies

The *Semantic Web* vision was introduced by Berners-Lee et al. (2001) as an extension of the Web with semantics in order to provide a means for exchanging, accessing and processing data and information from distributed and heterogeneous sources on the Web. A key technology underlying this vision is *ontology*—shared, domain-specific conceptualization. Nowadays, the Semantic Web is getting closer to the reality with the effort of its community in producing and consuming on-line semantic information. To date, there are a large number of ontologies publicly accessible on the Web and covering a wide range of knowledge domains. The current statistics of *Watson* (http://watson.kmi.open.ac.uk/)—a Semantic Web gateway which provides an access point to on-line semantic contents—indicate that it has indexed a few million RDF documents describing millions of entities through billions of statements. In addition, based on the ontologies collected for an automatic ontology metadata generation application, namely *OMEGA* (Ungrangsi & Simperl, 2008), the Semantic Web currently has more than 26,000 ontologies and widely covers the top 17 topics in the *Open Directory project* (DMOZ, 1998), as shown in Figure 2. Note that in this analysis, an ontology may fall into more than one DMOZ topic if its key concepts appear in several topics.

An increasing number of available Semantic Web knowledge resources have driven the development of new knowledge-intensive applications in various areas including the academic world, medicine, digital libraries, automobile and telecommunication industries. Existing Semantic Web applications can be classified into: *first-generation*

and *next-generation* (Motta & Sabou, 2006; d'Aquin et al., 2008). The former ones typically employ a single pre-defined domain ontology selected at the design time to support their tasks. A widely-known example is *CS AKTive Space* (Shadbolt, Gibbins, Glaser, Harri, & Schraefe, 2004), which combines data about UK computer science research from various sources and lets users explore the data through an interactive portal. The latter ones, on the other hand, aim to exploit the whole Semantic Web as a large-scale, heterogeneous semantic source, and are typically multi-domain applications that retrieve (either single or multiple) relevant ontologies automatically and dynamically at runtime. Examples include *PowerMagpie* (Gridinoc & Guidi, 2007)— a Semantic Web browser that uses the publicly available semantic data to help users interpret arbitrary Web page content.

Figure 2. Comparison of the number of public ontologies in the top 17 topics in DMOZ's taxonomy classified by OMEGA

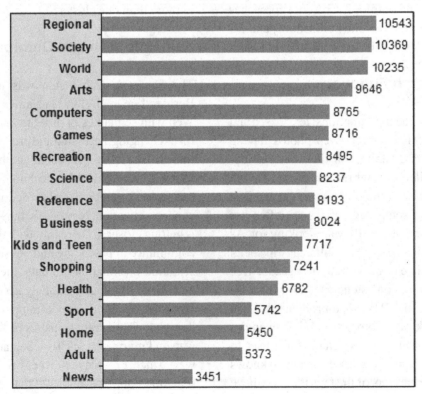

Regional	10543
Society	10369
World	10235
Arts	9646
Computers	8765
Games	8716
Recreation	8495
Science	8237
Reference	8193
Business	8024
Kids and Teen	7717
Shopping	7241
Health	6782
Sport	5742
Home	5450
Adult	5373
News	3451

'Ontology search engines are crucial to enable Semantic Web applications to find and reuse Web-accessible ontologies efficiently. Several of such systems have been developed in the past few years, e.g., *Swoogle* (Ding et al., 2004), *OntoKhoj* (Patel, Supekar, Lee, & Park, 2003), and *OntoSearch* (Zhang, Vasconcelos, & Sleeman, 2005). However, these systems mainly focus on automatically crawling the Web for collecting ontologies, and employ traditional keyword search mechanisms to retrieve relevant ontologies. As a result, they fail to capture the structural and semantic information about the user's desired domain concepts and relations. Furthermore, they usually return a large number of ontologies, but cannot guarantee query coverage which is a mandatory requirement for *automatic ontology reuse* in Semantic Web applications. Therefore, a few ontology retrieval systems have recently been constructed for dealing with such requirements, such as Watson (d'Aquin et al., 2007) and SQORE (Ungrangsi, Anutariya, & Wuwongse, 2007). The application developed in this paper employs SQORE as a key component to generate query suggestions because it is the very first ontology retrieval system that can determine ontology combination and guarantee full query coverage. Sect. 3 briefly introduces SQORE.

Integrating Ontologies and Folksonomy

To date, a number of computer scientists have focused on integrating the Semantic Web and Web 2.0 together. This idea was initiated by Gruber (2007), who introduced the term *"Ontology of Folksonomy"* which applies the Semantic Web to the data of Web 2.0. Gruber also developed *TagOntology*, a common ontology for tagging. This ontology is about identifying and formalizing a conceptualization of the activity of tagging, and

building technology that conforms to the ontology at the semantic level.

Interestingly, there have been a number of proposed approaches to identifying relations between tags in order to construct clusters, a taxonomy or an ontology. Most recent works consider tag co-occurrences for organizing related tags and creating appropriate clusters. For example, Schmitz (2006) constructed an ontology based on a subsumption-based model, derived from the co-occurrence of tags. Begelman, Keller, and Smadja (2006) organized the tag space as an undirected graph, representing co-occurring tags as vertices, weighting the edges between them according to their co-occurrence frequency, and applying a spectral clustering algorithm to refine the resulting groups. Mika (2005) used co-occurrence information to build graphs which take tags, users and resources as their nodes and create edges between tags and users or between tags and resources. Then, he applied techniques of network analysis to discover sets of clusters of semantically related tags. Lastly, Specia, and Motta (2007) clustered tags and attached formal semantics to tags by deriving from online ontologies in order to construct an ontology.

In several approaches, *WordNet* (Miller, 1995) has become a semantic lexical source to identify the meaning of tags. For example, Maala, Deiteil, and Azough (2007) identified the meaning of tags in order to enrich relevant resources with RDF descriptions. This work uses WordNet and other knowledge resources to organize tags into six predefined conceptual categories of tags in Flickr, and then enriches Flickr photos with RDF triples created from each of those tag categories. Another interesting example is *FLOR* (Angeletou, Sabou, & Motta, 2008), which takes a set of tags as input and automatically relates them to relevant semantic entities defined in online ontologies and WordNet.

Enhancing Flickr's Search Functions

Here, recent approaches to enhancing Flickr's search functions are reviewed as follows.

Lerman et al. (2007) developed a method to personalize image search results on Flickr based on a user's interests extracted from his social network and tags he used for annotating his own images. To personalize search results for a particular user, first, the results from Flickr are restricted to those created by the user's contacts. Then, this method uses a probabilistic model to discover latent topics in the search results and selects ones on topics that are of interest by the user. Li et al. (2008) proposed an image retrieval mechanism that employs an algorithm to find the relevance of a tag with respect to the visual content it is describing. Intuitively, if different persons annotate similar images using the same tags, these tags are likely to reflect the objective aspects of the visual content. The relevance level of a tag is computed from the number of votes on that tag from visually similar images (neighbors) of a given image. The visual similar neighbors are images that have similar visual patterns (e.g., color and texture) to the given image. Later, Liu et al. (2009) presented an approach to rank the tags of each image according to their relevance to the image content. It estimates an initial relevance score of each tag by using a probability density estimation, and then uses the random walk model to refine the score.

Findr (http://www.forestandthetrees.com/findr), is a Web application that retrieves images and tags from Flickr. It allows a user to refine his search by comparing and displaying the related tags that appear in all last three queries together with the corresponding image results from Flickr. *T-ORG* (Abbasi, Staab, & Cimiano, 2007) is an example of using a user-selected ontology to organize Flickr photos into a set of predefined categories according to the annotating tags. The *TagPlus* system, presented by Lee and Yong (2007), uses WordNet (Miller, 1995) to disam-biguate the senses of Flickr tags by performing a two-step query. First, a user looks for a tag, then the system returns all the possible WordNet senses defining the tag, and the user selects the sense that can best describe his search goal. Finally, the system retrieves all Flickr photos tagged with the given tag and its synonym, derived from the selected sense.

In order to improve the retrieval performance of Flickr, the above review shows that most of the existing approaches mainly focus on developing a technique to re-rank or group the search results. Although TagPlus addressed another possible technique, which is to assist Flickr's users to precisely formulate queries that can well capture their search goals, there exist certain limitations. Firstly, it only supports the extension of a user-given query term in the context that is defined by WordNet (its reference lexical source). For instance, the term jaguar can refer to either a car or an animal in the real world. However, WordNet only defines it with the meaning of an animal. As a result, the user is able to retrieve only animal photos. Secondly, when a user is unfamiliar with the search domain, he may start with a query term that does not precisely describe his interest. For example, assume that a user wants a photo of clownfish. He knows what the clownfish looks like, but he does not know its name. When he performs a search, he may simply enter the term fish. In this situation, TagPlus can only suggest general fish photos from the most related sense, since it lacks a mechanism to continue assisting the user to explore his search to other directions by suggesting semantics-broader terms, semantics-narrower terms or semantics-related terms. Therefore, devising a semantic query suggestion algorithm to enhance a search in Flickr, by retrieving the most relevant ontologies from the Semantic Web and then deriving query term suggestions from those ontologies, is the focus of this paper.

Figure 3. SQORE's framework

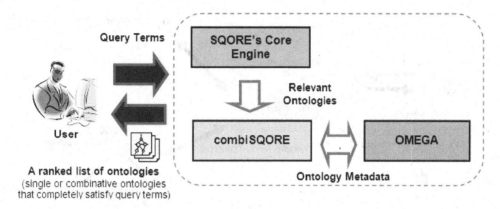

3 SQORE ONTOLOGY RETRIEVAL SYSTEM: AN INFORMAL INTRODUCTION

Figure 3 illustrates the framework of the SQORE ontology retrieval system which consists of the follwing three key elements:

- **SQORE's core engine** (Ungrangsi, Anutariya, & Wuwongse, 2009): the core retrieval engine which semantically performs a user query on its ontology database and returns a ranked list of matching ontologies. To support reasoning capabilities and enhance the matching results, SQORE uses an ontology reasoner and employs also a semantic lexical database in the query evaluation process. As an example, SQORE could yield an ontology defining the concept infant as a relevant ontology to the given query term baby;
- **combiSQORE** (Ungrangsi, Anutariya, & Wuwongse, 2008): a greedy algorithm that determines the most relevant and minimal (irreducible) sets of ontologies that completely satisfy the query; and
- **OMEGA** (Ungrangsi & Simperl, 2008): an algorithm that automatically generates ontology metadata of a given ontology by using data-mining techniques and by re-

ferring to trustworthy ontology metadata libraries. Its metadata elements are useful for evaluating the ontology in various aspects and for computing ranking measures.

Basically, the SQORE system works as follows: Upon receiving a set of query terms from a user (or a software agent), the system employs its core engine to semantically evaluate the query terms against its ontology database (currently containing more than 26,000 ontologies) and compute a ranked list of relevant ontologies. The combiSQORE algorithm then uses such ranked list of relevant ontologies to find the sets of single or combinative ontologies which can entirely cover the given query terms. Each of these single or combinative ontologies is then evaluated according to the following criteria, in order to determine the final rankings and return the ranked results to the user:

1. **semantic similarities:** between the query and the ontology;
2. **query coverage:** the number of query terms which are semantically defined by the ontology;
3. **combinative ontology quality:** the quality of the combinative ontology by considering various properties of all ontology members

Figure 4. SemFlickr's system architecture

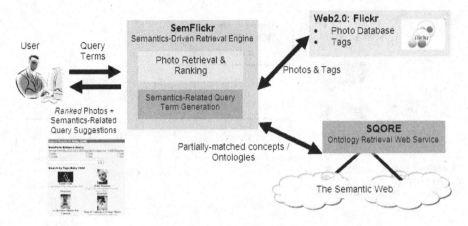

in the combination, such as their sizes and languages used; and

4. **ontology modification (integration) costs:** estimating the cost of integrating all ontology members in a combinative ontology by determining their overlapping concepts.

Note that, when computing the *combinative ontology quality*, the system uses several ontology properties or metadata, which is, however, absent in many ontologies. Therefore, the OMEGA algorithm is employed to automatically generate the missing ontology metadata elements.

Since the SQORE system comprises three components, its overall computation complexity is the sum of each component's complexity, which can be further reduced to the one with the highest-order complexity, that is combiSQORE. Hence, for m: the number of the given query terms and n: the size of an ontology database, the system's computation complexity is $O(mn^2 \log n)$, which is $O(n^2 \log n)$, when $m \ll n$. The detailed explanation of the complexity analysis can be found in Ungrangsi, Anutariya, and Wuwongse (2008).

4 SEMFLICKR: SEMANTIC PHOTO RETRIEVAL SYSTEM BASED ON FLICKR

This section first explains the overall process of using SemFlickr to search for photos in Flickr. Then, it describes the way SemFlickr generates semantic query suggestions and ranks its results.

SemFlickr's System Architecture

Figure 4 illustrates SemFlickr's architecture, comprising the following three key components: 1) *semantics-driven retrieval engine*, 2) *SQORE's ontology retrieval Web service*, and 3) *Flickr's Web service*. The semantics-driven retrieval engine has two main functions: 1) *photo retrieval & ranking function*, and 2) *semantics-related query term generation function*. The first function retrieves photos from Flickr via its Web service interface according to the given user query, and then ranks them according to the query-photo relevance. The second function dynamically generates semantic query suggestions from the user query based on available ontologies in the Semantic Web by means of SQORE's Web services (Ungrangsi, Anutariya, & Wuwongse, 2009).

To start a photo search in SemFlickr, a user simply inputs the query term(s) into the search

Figure 5. SemFlickr's interfaces: (a) SemFlickr's home page with five options for suggesting semantics-related query terms (b) SemFlickr's result of searching with the query term "baby". Assuming that the user chooses to include partially-matched concepts found in the Semantic Web for suggesting additional semantics-related query terms, the upper pane lists those suggested terms. The lower pane shows the top twelve relevant Flickr's photos of the query "baby".

(a)

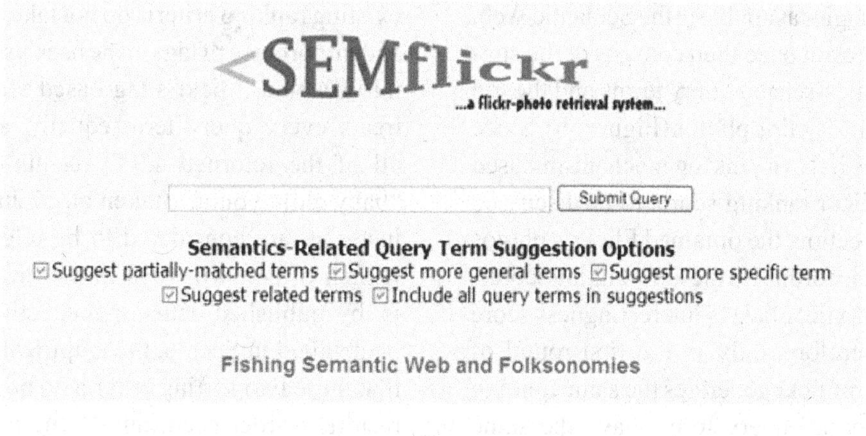

(b)

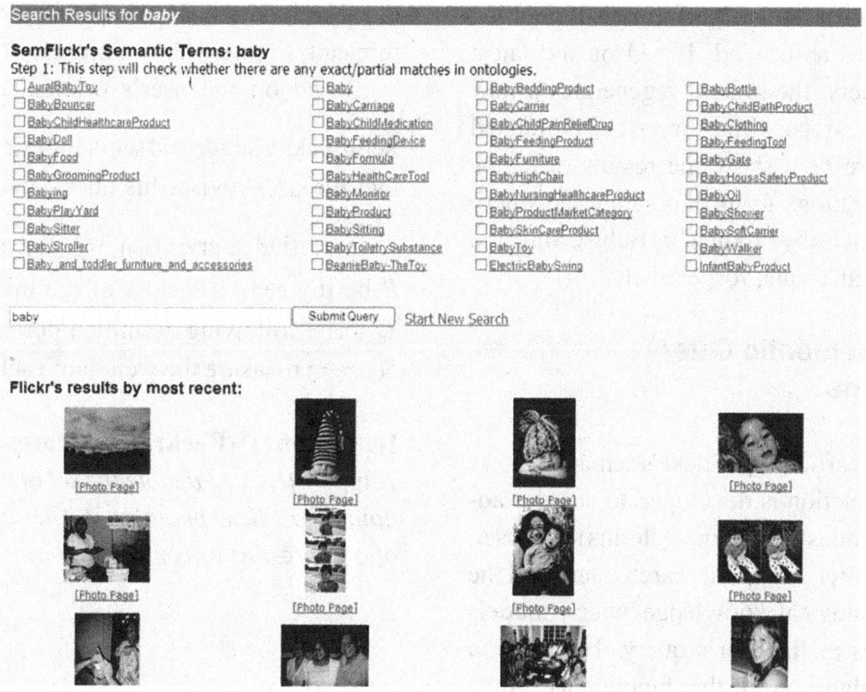

box (see Figure 5a). With the five options underneath, the user can specify how he/she wants SemFlickr to help suggest additional semantics-related query terms: i) whether or not to include partially-matched concepts, ii) broader, iii) narrower, or iv) semantically related concepts, or v) to guarantee that all the input query terms appear in the retrieved ontological knowledge. SemFlickr then passes the user's query to Flickr in order to obtain Flickr's photos. At the same time, it determines additional semantics-related query terms to suggest the user based on the original user's query terms, the selection of the five search options and the relevant knowledge provided by multiple ontologies available in the Semantic Web. The returned result page then consists of the suggested semantics-related query terms and the top twelve relevant Flickr's photos (Figure 5b). Since SemFlickr has its own ranking mechanism based on the SemFlickr ranking score, to be discussed in a later subsection, the obtained Flickr's photos are reordered according to the new ranking scores. In the event of a tie, Flickr's interestingness score breaks it. Therefore, only in the first round of searching, SemFlickr generates the same ranking as Flickr since all query terms have the same weight.

SemFlickr lets the user perform (re-)searching as many times as needed. Based on the latest submitted query, the system regenerates a new set of semantics-related query terms and the ranked results. Figure 6a-c show the results of a few searching iterations using the suggested query terms: i) Infant Baby Product, ii) Baby Child, and iii) Baby Child Young, respectively.

Deriving Semantic Query Suggestions

As discussed earlier, SemFlickr's semantic query generation function is developed to suggest additional semantics-related query terms to the user, based on the user's original search query and the relevant ontological knowledge which models the semantics of the user's query. This section devises the algorithm of this function as shown in Figure 7.

Let m denote the size of a given user query and n the size of an ontology database. The computation complexity of this semQuerySuggestion algorithm can be analyzed by considering its primary computing steps (Table 1) as follows.

Thus, when $m \ll n$, the overall computation complexity is $O(n^2 log\, n)$.

SemFlickr's New Ranking Method

Another important problem of Flickr is that its existing ranking criteria do not take the semantics and importance of tags in the user's search context into account. Flickr's tag-based search function treats every query term equally, and therefore all of the returned 4,947 results of the query "baby child young" (taken on 27 July 2009), for instance, are considered to be relevant equally. It then offers two ways to sort the results, that is, by published dates or interestingness. As to be detailed in Sect. 6, the empirical results show that these two sorting criteria do not yield a good resulting order according to the user's interest. That is, some photos which are not relevant to the search criteria appear before those which are relevant. Figure 8 shows this example.

Based on the user's original query Q and SemFlickr's suggested semantic query $\overline{Q}$, assume that the user revises his query, which results in the modified query $Q' Q \bigcup \overline{Q}$. Let a set of photos P be the search results of the modified query Q'. The following definition defines *Flickr Tag Score* to measure the weight of each Flickr's tag.

Definition 1 *(**Flickr Tag Score: TScore**) Let Tag(p) ={$t_1, ..., t_l$} denote the set of tags which annotated a Flickr photo p∈P. The score or weight of a tag t∈ Tag(p) is measured by:*

$$TScore(t) = \begin{cases} w_o & :if\, t \in Q, \\ w_p & :else\, if\, t \in Q' \cap Q\, and\, \exists q \in Q\big(partialMatch(t,q)\big) wrt.ODB, \\ w_b & :else\, if\, t \in Q' \cap Q\, and\, \exists q \in Q\big(parent(t,q)\big) wrt.OntoQ, \\ w_n & :else\, if\, t \in Q' \cap Q\, and\, \exists q \in Q\big(child(t,q)\big) wrt.OntoQ, \\ w_r & :else\, if\, t \in Q' \cap Q\, and\, \exists q \in Q\big(directlyRelate(t,q)\big) wrt.OntoQ, \\ 0 & :otherwise. \end{cases}$$

Figure 6. SemFlickr's results of a few searching iterations: (a) SemFlickr's results of "Infant Baby Product" (b) SemFlickr's results of "Baby Child" (c) SemFlickr's results of "Baby Child Young".

Figure 7. Semantics-related query term suggestion algorithm

```
Algorithm semQuerySuggestion

Input:     Q: a user query,
           ODB: an ontology database,
           includePartiallyMatchedConcepts: an input option indicating
                   whether or not a user wants to include partially-
                   matched concepts in the returned semantic query
                   suggestions,
           includeParentConcepts: an input option indicating whether or not
                   a user wants to include parent concepts (superclass)
                   in the returned semantic query suggestions,
           includeChildConcepts: an input option indicating whether or not a
                   user wants to include child concepts (subclass) in
                   the returned semantic query suggestions,
           includeSemanticallyRelatedConcepts: an input option indicating
                   whether or not a user wants to include concepts that
                   have a direct relation to the given concept in the
                   returned semantic query suggestions,
           guaranteeQueryCoverage: an input option indicating whether the
                   retrieved ontologies (to be used as a reference
                   knowledge source) must completely cover the input
                   query or not.

Output:    Q̄: the semantic query suggestion
```

Step 1: $\overline{Q} = \varnothing$ // Initialize $\overline{Q}$ to be the empty set.

Step 2: if $(includePartiallyMatchedConcepts)$

         for-each query term q in Q

             $\overline{Q} = \overline{Q} \cup getPartiallyMatchedConcepts\,(q, ODB)$

/* If the option *includePartiallyMatchedConcepts* is checked, then find the concepts from **ODB** that partially match with a user query term *q*. */

Step 3: $OntoQ = getSetOfBestOntologies(Q, ODB, guaranteeQueryCoverage)$

/* Find the set of single or combinative ontologies that can best model the user query *Q* by calling the SQORE ontology retrieval engine. */

Step 4: if $OntoQ \neq \varnothing$

         for-each query term q in Q

          $\overline{Q} = \overline{Q} \cup getRelevantConcepts(q, OntoQ, includeParentConcepts,$

                 $includeChildConcepts, includeSemanticallyRelatedConcepts)$

/* Get all concepts that are relevant to each user query term *q* from the retrieved ontologies in **OntoQ**, based on the three options: *includeParentConcepts*, *includeChildConcepts* and *includeSemanticallyRelatedConcepts*. */

Step 5: return $\overline{Q}$

Table 1.

Computation	Complexity
Step 1: Initiating the semantic query suggestion as an empty set	$O(1)$
Step 2: Retrieving all partially-matched concepts	$O(mn)$
Step 3: Finding the set of best single or combinative ontologies that can fully cover the given query by means of the SQORE system	$O(n^2 \log n)$
Step 4: Retrieving relevant concepts from the ontologies found in Step 3	$O(mn)$

Figure 8. Ranking photos: An example

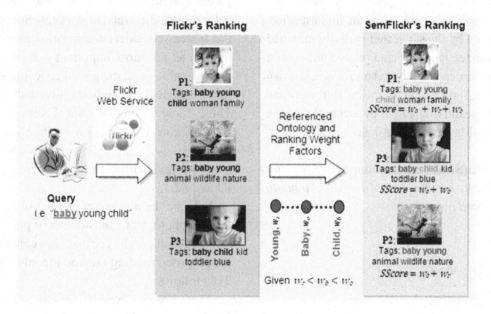

where

- w_o: the weight factor for the *original* query term (given by the user at the first step);
- w_p: the weight factor for a semantic query term (suggested by the system) that *partially* matches with one of the original query terms;
- w_b: the weight factor for a semantic query term that is the parent concept of the original query term (its semantics is *broader*);
- w_n: the weight factor for a semantic query term that is the child concept of the original query term (its semantics is *narrower*);

- w_r: the weight factor for a semantic query term that has direct semantics *relation* to the original query term;
- *partialMatch*(t,q): the tag t partially matches with the query term q;
- *parent*(t,q): the tag t is the parent concept of the query term q;
- *child*(t,q): the tag t is the child concept of the query term q; and
- *directlyRelate*(t,q): the tag t is related to the query term q. ❑

The weight factors play an important role in *TScore* to differentiate the importance of each tag according to the semantic relation defined in the

Table 2.

Computation	Complexity
Step 1: Compute Flickr tag score for each tag of each photo result	$O(xy)$
Step 2: Compute SemFlickr ranking score of each photo	$O(y)$
Step 3: Rank the results	$O(y \log y)$

retrieved ontology. In practice, the weight factor setting should be $w_o \geq w_p \geq w_b \geq w_n \geq w_r \geq 0$. That is, the original user query terms have the highest priority, followed by the suggested partially-matched terms, broader, narrower and related terms, in a decreasing order. Thus, based on *TScore*, one can measure the similarity between the user query and each photo result from Flickr by accumulating the weights of all tags annotating this photo, as follows.

Definition 2 (SemFlickr Ranking Score: *SScore*)
The similarity between a user query and a photo p is measured by

$$SScore\left(p\right) = \sum_{i=1}^{l} TScore\left(t_i\right),$$

where $t_i \in Tag(p)$. ❑

Figure 8 depicts an example when a user first enters a query term baby, and then selects two additional suggested query terms young and child, which implies that the user's context is a small child. Suppose that there are three photos returned by Flickr according to the interestingness: P1 (a child), P2 (a squirrel) and P3 (a child), respectively. One can see that P3 should have a higher rank than P2 because P3 is more relevant. SemFlickr then re-ranks those results according to its new ranking score, *SScore*, which mainly focuses on the semantic closeness between the query and the folksonomy tags annotating the photos. By referring to SQORE's dynamic ontological knowledge (i.e. by selecting the best ontology that models

the concept baby), it finds that child is the baby's parent (broader) concept whereas young is a baby's semantics-related concept. Suppose that the system considers the original user's query term(s) as the most important (i.e., w_o has the highest value), and the parent concepts are more important than the semantics-related concepts. Thus, *TScore(baby)*=w_o, and *TScore(child)*=w_b > w_r=*TScore(young)*. As a result, *SScore(P1)*= $(w_o+w_r+w_b)$>*SScore(P3)*=(w_o+w_b)>*SScore(P2)* =w_o+w_r), and hence SemFlickr's rankings is P1, P3 and P2.

Let x be the maximum number of tags annotating a photo, and y the number of photos in the returned results. The computation complexity of the proposed ranking method is analyzed (Table 2) as follows:

Therefore, the overall computation complexity of the new ranking method is $O(y \log y)$, when $x \ll y$.

5 EXPERIMENT I

This experiment aims to compare SemFlickr's semantic query suggestion feature with the two existing tag suggestion features in Flickr: *related tags* and *clusters*. Firstly, four tags (i.e., mushroom, fruit, beverage and mammal) were selected from food and animal species domains, which are the well-covered domains in the Semantic Web, as suggested by Angeletou et al. (2007). Then, Flickr's related tags, Flickr's clusters and SemFlickr's semantics-related terms were retrieved and compared. Table 3 presents the result summary.

Table 3. Comparison of Flickr's related terms, clusters and SemFlickr's semantics-related terms

Query Terms	Topics of Tags			The Ratios indicating how many of SemFlickr's semantics-related terms were found as Flickr's tags	
	Flickr's related tags	Flickr's clusters	SemFlickr's semantics-related terms	Compound words	Single words
Mushroom	• plant • nature • photo jargon • color	• plant • food • colors • scientific names	• food • plants • scientific names	4:14	20:20
Fruit	• colors • nature • photo jargon	• yellow fruits • red fruits • green fruits • fruits and markets	• plants • events • places • food • animal • action	53:84	89:92
Beverage	• food • drinks • drink containers	• mixes of drinks and containers • soft drinks	• types of beverages • occupations • processing • equipments	14:35	39:39
Mammal	• animals • nature • cute	• domestic mammals • marine mammals	• types of mammals • scientific names • organs • biology jargons	27:54	69:73

The results reveal that a number of tags returned from Flickr's related tags are not useful for searching because they are too general. For instance, the related tags comprise tags about locations (i.e., nature, forest), seasons (i.e., autumn), and actions (i.e., cooking). Moreover, since Flickr is a photo-sharing application, tags about colors (i.e., red, brown, white) and photo jargons (i.e., macro) are commonly used for describing photo contents. Given a tag, SemFlickr offers more varieties of topics (depending on the domain coverage in the Semantic Web and the user's selections) comparing to Flickr's clusters.

Intuitively, a semantics-related term suggested by SemFlickr is considered to be useful for searching in Flickr, if it is also used to tag a photo in Flickr. Therefore, in the experiment all terms suggested by SemFlickr were submitted to Flickr for testing. Table 3 (right-most column) shows the ratios indicating how many of SemFlickr's semantics-related terms (either compound or single words) were found as Flickr's tags. The results imply that semantics-related terms generated by SemFlickr mostly appear in Flickr, and a Flickr's tag is more likely to be a single word rather than a compound one.

6 EXPERIMENT II

To evaluate the practicability of SemFlickr and its underlying mechanism, a user-based experiment with 30 participating users was conducted. It used 145 Flickr's *all time most popular tags*, depicted in Figure 9, as an initial set of query terms used in the experiment. From these 145 tags, 104 of them (72%) were terms defined in the ontology database, while the other 41 tags were not defined as concepts nor properties in the database. These terms included city/country names, adjectives, photo jargon and abbreviations, such as Barcelona, Berlin, bw, de, la, cute, fun, geotagged, Germany, China, Nikon, etc.

Figure 9. Flickr's all time most popular tags (retrieved on 19 December 2008)

The ontology database employed in the experiment comprises approximately 26,000 ontologies retrieved from the Semantic Web. The twelve tags randomly selected for the experiment were Baby, Band, Dog, Fall, Flower, Food, Holiday, Light, Ocean, Rock, Snow and Wedding. Initially, each participant arbitrarily selected 5 out of 12 query terms, and then specified his search goal represented by each particular term. Next, the participant used both Flickr and SemFlickr to search for the photos corresponding to each search goal. Then, he analyzed the results and answered the questionnaire. With this experimental setup, each query term was evaluated by at least 10 participants, and the ranking weight factors used were: $w_o=1.0, w_p=1.0, w_b=0.8, w_n=0.6$, and $w_r=0.4$.

Precision Improvement

To examine the retrieval performance of Sem-Flickr, all participants were asked to count the number of *relevant* photos returned by Flickr and SemFlickr. In this experiment, from a participant's point of view if the content of a photo matches his search goal defined for a particular query then that photo is relevant to the query. Note that only the top twelve results were considered by the participants to prevent drop-out during the experi-

ment. Table 4 compares Flickr's and SemFlickr's average precision values for each query, where the precision value for a query is calculated as the ratio of the retrieved photos that are relevant to the query to the total number of retrieved photos, by considering only the top twelve results. The results show that SemFlickr has higher precision values over Flickr for almost all query terms and also for the overall average value. These results imply that SemFlickr can assist users to search and retrieve practically well, and its ranking scores give better results comparing to the existing ranking mechanisms in Flickr.

Usability Study

To evaluate the usefulness of SemFlickr, when compared to Flickr, the 30 participants were asked to complete a questionnaire and rate a few aspects of both systems regarding the search environment and their performance by selecting: *Excellent, Good, Fair* or *Bad*.

In the study, about half of the participants indicated that Flickr's related tag suggestion feature, and the interestingness and most recent sorting criteria were not helpful for their search. From the participants' point of view, 40% of Flickr's related tags were usable for their search context.

Table 4. Performance comparison between Flickr's and SemFlickr's search functions

Query terms	Average Precision		
	Flickr's Most Recent	**Flickr's Most Interesting**	**SemFlickr**
Baby	0.52	0.18	0.61
Band	0.50	0.41	0.71
Dog	0.76	0.71	0.83
Fall	0.29	0.35	0.44
Flower	0.45	0.49	0.51
Food	0.43	0.20	0.58
Holiday	0.33	0.49	0.60
Light	0.13	0.42	0.44
Ocean	0.49	0.65	0.63
Rock	0.30	0.26	0.51
Snow	0.48	0.46	0.56
Wedding	0.49	0.39	0.44
OVERALL AVERAGE	**0.43**	**0.42**	**0.57**

In addition, about 60% of the participants agreed that using the search box and thinking of additional query terms are difficult. Most participants (~92%) agreed that additional search assistance is needed, and they also like to have a query suggestion function (87%) as well as a query auto-completion feature (50%) in Flickr.

On the other hand, more than 70% of the participants rated *Good* to *Excellent* for SemFlickr's results and the usefulness of the semantic query suggestion. For instance, a participant explained that when she searched for a particular breed of dog, the name of which she could not exactly remember. From the ontologies retrieved from SQORE, the system could suggest a list of semantics-related query terms which include the names of dog breeds. This becomes the critical shortcut for her search.

However, some participants were unsatisfied with the system's response time and some were overwhelmed by a large number of suggested terms. The Internet connection was the main cause of the slowness because SemFlickr's semantics-driven retrieval engine relies on a number of Web services. Moreover, the recommended tags were sometimes confusing because they were irrelevant to the participants' search goals. For instance, consider a search using the term rock, having stone as the search objective; the system additionally suggested the term university which was confusing. In addition, a few users were not able to obtain better results from SemFlickr because their query terms did not exist in the available ontologies; hence, the system could not suggest additional useful query terms.

Since the semantic query suggestion function is an additional feature available in SemFlickr, it is interesting to see the effect of this function to the users' search activities. Table 5 compares Flickr and SemFlickr, considering the number of query terms and search iterations that the participants performed in the experiment. The result indicates that on average, the participants used 2.11 query terms and performed 2.25 search iterations in Flickr. On the other hand, they slightly used fewer query terms and fewer search iterations in SemFlickr (1.91 query terms and 1.71 iterations, respectively). In particular, SemFlickr could significantly reduce the number of steps and query terms when the participants searched for holiday, light, snow and wedding. This finding implies that the semantic query suggestion function in

Table 5. Flickr vs. SemFlickr – User search behaviors

Query terms	Average number of query terms		Average number of search iterations	
	Flickr	SemFlickr	Flickr	SemFlickr
Baby	1.75	2.00	2.00	1.83
Band	2.56	1.78	2.22	1.78
Dog	1.82	1.55	1.64	1.36
Fall	1.71	2.00	1.86	1.71
Flower	1.62	1.92	2.08	1.85
Food	2.14	2.79	2.79	2.21
Holiday	2.45	1.82	2.64	1.82
Light	3.00	1.83	2.92	1.58
Ocean	1.45	1.55	1.70	1.45
Rock	2.33	2.82	2.64	2.00
Snow	2.33	1.22	2.22	1.33
Wedding	3.11	2.11	2.56	1.56
OVERALL AVERAGE	**2.11**	**1.91**	**2.25**	**1.71**

SemFlickr does not put more burden on users during their search activities, and sometimes it even speeds up the search process.

7 CONCLUSION

This paper aims to demonstrate how Semantic Web technology can complement Web 2.0 applications by developing SemFlickr, a semantics-based photo retrieval application. By employing Flickr as its photo database and SQORE as its ontology retrieval engine, SemFlickr can support a user during a photo search by dynamically suggesting additional semantics-related terms derived from online ontologies available in the Semantic Web. Its search interface offers an easy yet flexible mechanism to add or modify query terms, which reduces the searching effort and improves the search's precision. In addition, to ensure that the most relevant photos will appear at the top of the results, SemFlickr takes the ontological relations among user query terms to assign tag scores and then generates its ranked results, while Flickr's interestingness scores are occasionally used to break the tie.

The user evaluation has implied a number of benefits for semantic query suggestion, and a few issues regarding its current mechanism and implementation have arisen, and hence require careful consideration. Firstly, the retrieval performance of SemFlickr greatly relies on the knowledge richness in the Semantic Web. Although there are a larger number of publicly available ontologies nowadays, they are inadequate to support all possible user queries in diverse domains. Secondly, Semantic Web applications tend to employ a number of Web services, and so does SemFlickr. Thus, network infrastructure and Web service integration become critical factors during the application design and implementation in order to maximize the system performance and reliability. Thirdly, the limitation of user-based evaluations may not provide an extensive IR performance comparison. Therefore, conducting a more comprehensive experiment using an annotated dataset such as the MIRFLICKR-25000 (Huiskers & Lew, 2008)—a collection of 25,000 annotated images selected from Flickr, which is freely redistributable for research purposes—is planned. Despite the three mentioned issues, the experiments show encouraging results.

ACKNOWLEDGMENT

The authors are grateful to the panel of reviewers for their valuable comments which helped improve the quality of the paper. Special thanks are given to Reviewer #3 for his/her detailed reviews and suggestions.

REFERENCES

Abbasi, R., Staab, S., & Cimiano, P. (2007). Organizing Resources on Tagging Systems using t-org. In *Proceedings of the 4th European Semantic Web Conference* (pp. 97-110). Heidelberg, Germany: Springer.

Angeletou, S., Sabou, M., & Motta, E. (2008). Semantically Enriching Folksonomies with FLOR. In *Proceedings of the 1st International Workshop on Collective Semantics; Collective Intelligences & the Semantic Web at the 5th European Semantic Web Conference,* Tenerife, Spain (pp.65-79).

Angeletou, S., Sabou, M., Spacia, L., & Motta, E. (2007). Bridging the Gap Between Folksonomies and the Semantic Web: An Experience Report. In *Proceedings of the Workshop: Bridging the Gap between Semantic Web and Web 2.0, European Semantic Web Conference*, Vienna, Austria.

Begelman, G., Keller, P., & Smadja, F. (2006). Automated Tag Clustering: Improving Search and Exploration in the Tag Space. In *Proceedings of the Collaborative Web Tagging Workshop at the 15th WWW Conference,* Edinburgh, Scotland.

Berners-Lee, T., Handler, J., & Lassila, O. (2001, May). The Semantic Web. *Scientific American,* 28–37.

d'Aquin, M., Motta, E., Sabou, M., Angeletou, S., Gridinoc, L., & Lopez, V. (2008). Toward a New Generation of Semantic Web Applications. *IEEE Intelligent Systems, 23*(3), 20–28. doi:10.1109/MIS.2008.54

d'Aquin, M., Sabou, M., Dzbor, M., Baldassarre, C., Gridinoc, L., Angeletou, S., et al. (2007). Watson: A Gateway for the Semantic Web. In *Proceedings of the Poster Session of the 4th European Semantic Web Conference,* Vienna, Austria.

Ding, L., Finin, T., Joshi, A., Pan, R., Scott, R., Peng, Y., et al. (2004). Swoogle: A Search and Metadata Engine for the Semantic Web. In Proceedings of *the 13th ACM International Conference on Information and Knowledge Management* (pp. 652-669). New York:ACM Press.

DMOZ. (1998). *ODP - The Open Directory Project.* Retrieved February 2008 from http://dmoz.org

Gridinoc, L., & Guidi, D. (2007). *PowerMagpie- a Semantic Web Browser.* Retrieved February 2008 from http://powermagpie.open.ac.uk

Gruber, T. (2007). Ontology of Folksonomy: A Mash-up of Apples and Oranges. *International Journal on Semantic Web and Information Systems, 3*(2), 1–11.

Huiskes, M. J., & Lew, M. S. (2008). The MIR flickr retrieval evaluation. In *Proceedings of the 1st ACM Int'l Conference on Multimedia Information Retrieval*, Vancouver, Canada (pp. 39-43).

Lee, S., & Yong, H. (2007). Tagplus: A Retrieval System using Synonym tag in Folksonomy. In *Proceedings of the International Conference on Multimedia and Ubiquitous Engineering*, Seoul, Korea (pp. 294-298).

Lerman, K., Plangpoasopchok, A., & Wong, C. (2007). Personalizing Image Search Results on Flickr. In *Proceedings of the AAAI 5th Workshop on Intelligent Techniques for Web Personalization*, Vancouver, Canada.

Li, X., Snoek, C. G. M., & Worring, M. (2008). Learning Tag Relevance by Neighbor Voting for Social Image Retrieval. In *Proceedings of the 1st ACM Int'l Conference on Multimedia Information Retrieval,* Vancouver, Canada (pp. 39-43).

Liu, D., Hua, X., Yang, L., Wang, M., & Zhang, H. (2009). Tag Ranking. In *Proceedings of the 18th International World Wide Web Conference*, Madrid, Spain (pp. 351-360).

Maala, M., Deiteil, A., & Azough, A. (2007). A Conversion Process from Flickr tags to RDF descriptions. In *Proceedings of the 10th International Conference on Business Information Systems*, Poznan, Poland.

Mika, P. (2005). Ontologies are us: a Unified Model of Social Networks and Semantics. In *Proceedings of the 4th International Semantic Web Conference* (pp. 522-536). Heidelberg, Germany: Springer.

Miller, A. (1995). WordNet: A Lexical Database for English. *Communications of the ACM, 38*(11), 39–41. doi:10.1145/219717.219748

Motta, E., & Sabou, M. (2006). Next Generation Semantic Web Applications. *The 1st Asian Semantic Web Conference* (pp. 24-29). Heidelberg, Germany: Springer.

Patel, C., Supekar, K., Lee, Y., & Park, E. (2003). OntoKhoj: A Semantic Web Portal for Ontology Searching, Ranking, and Classification. In *Proceedings of the 5th ACM International Workshop on Web Information and Data Management*, USA (pp. 58-61).

Peterson, E. (2006). Beneath the Metadata: Some Philosophical Problems with Folksonomy. *D-Lib Magazine, 12*(11). doi:10.1045/november2006-peterson

Schmitz, P. (2006). Inducing Ontology from Folksonomy tags. In *Proceedings of the Collaborative Tagging Workshop at the 15th International WWW Conference*, Edinburgh, Scotland.

Shadbolt, N., Gibbins, N., Glaser, H., Harri, S., & Schraefe, M. (2004). CS AKTive Space, or How We Learned to Stop Worrying and Love the Semantic Web. *IEEE Intelligent Systems, 19*(3), 41–47. doi:10.1109/MIS.2004.8

Specia, L., & Motta, E. (2007). Integrating Folksonomies with the Semantic Web. In *Proceedings of the 4th European Semantic Web Conference* (pp. 624-639). Heidelberg, Germany: Springer.

Ungrangsi, R., Anutariya, C., & Wuwongse, V. (2008). combiSQORE: A Combinative-ontology Retrieval System for Next Generation Semantic Web Applications. *IEICE Transactions on Information and Systems. E (Norwalk, Conn.), 91-D*(11), 2616–2625.

Ungrangsi, R., Anutariya, C., & Wuwongse, V. (2009). SQORE: An Ontology Retrieval Framework for the Next Generation Web. *Concurrency and Computation, 21*(5), 651–671. doi:10.1002/cpe.1385

Ungrangsi, R., Anutariya, C., & Wuwongse, V. (n.d.). *SQORE Web Services*. Retrieved June 2009 from http://research.shinawatra.ac.th:8080/sqore

Ungrangsi, R., & Simperl, E. (2008). OMEGA: An Automatic Ontology Metadata Generation Algorithm. In *Proceedings of the 16th International Conference on Knowledge Engineering and Knowledge Management* (pp. 239-254). Heidelberg, Germany: Springer.

Yahoo. Inc. (n.d.). *Flickr APIs*. Retrieved June 2009 from http://www.flickr.com/services/api/

Yahoo. Inc. (n.d.). *Flickr- Photo Sharing*. Retrieved June 2009 from http://www.flickr.com

Zhang, Y., Vasconcelos, W., & Sleeman, D. (2005). OntoSearch: An Ontology Search Engine. In *Proceedings of the 24th SGAI International Conference on Innovative Techniques and Applications of AI*, UK (pp. 58-69).

APPENDIX: GLOSSARY

Term	Definition
Concept	A concept defined in an ontology to formally define a class of a type of objects in a domain of interest.
Combinative ontology	A set of ontologies, suggested by the combiSQORE algorithm, that can fully satisfy the user-given ontology requirements.
Full query coverage	An ontology (either single or combinative) is said to guarantee *full query coverage*, if all query terms of the given query are semantically defined by the ontology.
Latent topic	Topics (or semantic concepts) that are recovered from a collection of words (documents) based on a reference corpus by using a probabilistic model.
Partially-matched concept	A concept defined by an ontology which contains a user-given query term as its substring.
Query coverage	The proportion indicating the number of query terms in a given query which are semantically defined by a particular ontology.
Query term	A term given by a user to represent his search goal.
Self-tagging mechanism	A kind of tagging rights in Web 2.0 applications, which allows only the owners of resources to tag their own contributions.
Semantics-related query term	A term that has a semantic (ontological) relation to a user-given query term.
Sense	A term defined by WordNet (Miller,1995) which means the meaning of a word
Tag	A single or group of words that is given by a user to annotate and categorize a resource.

This work was previously published in International Journal of Semantic Web and Information Systems, Volume 6, Issue 2, edited by Amit P. Sheth, pp. 17-35, copyright 2010 by IGI Publishing (an imprint of IGI Global).

Chapter 9
Semantic Search on Unstructured Data:
Explicit Knowledge through Data Recycling

Alex Kohn
Roche Diagnostics GmbH, Germany

François Bry
University of Munich, Germany

Alexander Manta
Roche Diagnostics GmbH, Germany

ABSTRACT

Studies agree that searchers are often not satisfied with the performance of current enterprise search engines. As a consequence, more scientists worldwide are actively investigating new avenues for searching to improve retrieval performance. This paper contributes to YASA (Your Adaptive Search Agent), a fully implemented and thoroughly evaluated ontology-based information retrieval system for the enterprise. A salient particularity of YASA is that large parts of the ontology are automatically filled with facts by recycling and transforming existing data. YASA offers context-based personalization, faceted navigation, as well as semantic search capabilities. YASA has been deployed and evaluated in the pharmaceutical research department of Roche, Penzberg, and results show that already semantically simple ontologies suffice to considerably improve search performance.

INTRODUCTION

Nowadays most data produced in business is captured electronically and stored in computer systems. Search engines are of key importance in making this "hidden" information visible to the employees. Spoiled by the improvements in Web search, experts expect now a similar search performance in their intranet environment. However, current state-of-the-art enterprise search engines underperform (Feldman & Sherman, 2004). In effect, search for information becomes a central problem in companies.

DOI: 10.4018/978-1-4666-0185-7.ch009

A particularity of enterprise search is the lack of scientific publications. In case of commercial products, the information provided in booklets or white papers give only a vague picture of the applied algorithms. An aggravating factor is that the methods' effectiveness in improving information retrieval in enterprise search is barely empirically investigated. Indeed, published methods often restrict to synthetic evaluations. Further, scientific publications often describe methods which are optimized for the Web but not for intranet environments. Lastly, papers addressing intranet search are often focused on the intranet web, ignoring the fact that file shares, e-mails, databases, applications, etc. are also part of an intranet which needs to be searched.

We conclude that search for information in intranet environments is theoretically and practically disappointing. The rising question is: why is search for information in the enterprise such a challenge?

Many reasons can be given (Fagin et al., 2003; Hawking, 2004): Heterogeneous data sources and formats, complex security permissions, less user observations, few or missing metadata, growing amounts of data, etc.

The World Wide Web is dominated by the hypertext protocol. This is in contrast to intranets, where only a small portion of the data is in a Web accessible format. This *heterogeneity* makes data integration a difficult task, as large portions of the intranet are not search engine friendly. Further, ranking of search results is made more difficult due to a different or missing linkage structure (Xue et al., 2003).

The *complex security permissions* present in companies are a mixed blessing. On the one hand side the information landscape is fragmented into many silos, i.e. any employee can only see a small subset of all data. On the other hand, ranking of search results is eased as only a subset of all data needs to be sorted by relevance. The degree of fragmentation depends of course on the company's philosophy of information sharing across departments.

Observing a *user's search behavior* enables search engines to detect the context of a user, which ultimately leads to personalization services (Micarelli et al., 2007). Such services are already part of the leading Web search engines. Offering personalization services in the enterprise however, is a difficult task due to the lack of feedback data: a few users are facing a lot of data.

Being confronted with *barely explicit metadata* at hand and mostly unstructured free-text documents represents another challenge. Therefore, it is difficult to offer semantic search capabilities – a problem, well known from the Internet.

Considering the mentioned challenges, the problem is how to improve search for information in the enterprise. Could integration, i.e. federated search, make the information landscape accessible? Could the ranking of search results be improved by applying facetted navigation or personalized search? Could high-quality metadata be obtained by applying automatic information extraction? Could domain knowledge (e.g., organizational charts, project databases, etc.) be used to set the searcher as well as the results in context?

Technically, we contribute by compiling and developing several approaches for facing the listed challenges, namely role-based adaptation, guided navigation, and incorporation of domain knowledge. The approaches are implemented into YASA (Your Adaptive Search Agent). YASA is deployed in the pharmaceutical research department of Roche in Penzberg.

Scientifically, we contribute by conducting an empirical evaluation of the applied methods in a real world setting. In particular, we analyze whether the ranking of search results can be improved by our role-based adaptation method. We investigate how useful faceted navigation is for finding information. Further, we analyze whether automatic metadata extraction can help improve information acquisition. Last, we determine whether search for information can be improved by including domain knowledge into the search process. These aspects have previously only insufficiently been investigated or not all.

Figure 1. Usage of search engines linked from the Pharma Research Penzberg website

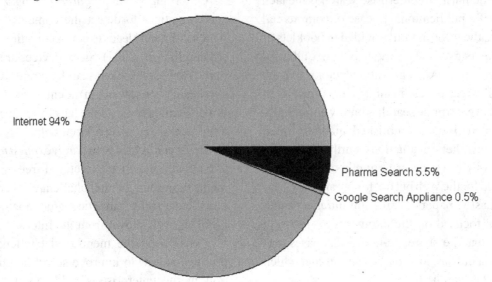

This paper focuses on the scientific contributions, and is structured as follows. First, we discuss the initial situation in the investigated division. Second, we introduce our concept for a professional search tool. We discuss which material could be recycled, we present our recycling methodology, we show several recycling examples, and we outline how the recycled data helps to improve search for information. Third, we present the evaluation of the investigated methods and discuss the results. Finally, we conclude the work.

RESEARCH ENVIRONMENT

In 2007 two in-house studies were conducted in the Pharma Research division of Roche in Penzberg, with the aim to identify issues and characteristics of information acquisition (Mühlbacher, 2008; Maßun, 2008). Their key finding is, that search for internal information is a tedious task. A third study was conducted by us with the aim to measure the usage of search engines linked from the local Pharma Research website – the default start page for approximately 400 employees. The usage analysis was conducted using log data, collected over a period of one month in 2007. We collected a total of 30.000 log entries (Figure 1).

The results match Mühlbacher's questionnaire regarding the fact that most queries are transmitted to the Internet. We were surprised that the Google Search Appliance was barely used, even though it used to index a local file share which is part of the daily work. The file share contains over 700.000 documents and over 100.000 folders. Its content includes lab experiments, studies, meeting notes, presentations, etc. The low usage of the search tool suggests that employees prefer to access the data by means of the file explorer. We concluded that employees are not satisfied with intranet search tools.

AN ONTOLOGY-BASED INFORMATION RETRIEVAL APPROACH FOR PROFESSIONAL SEARCH

As indicated previously, our approaches of recycling data and exploiting them in a search engine are particularly focused on file shares. Nonetheless, the ideas and concepts introduced in the subsequent sections could be mapped to other data sources, such as document management systems or intranet portals.

Recyclable Materials on File Shares

The most common document representation and indexing approach in keyword-based search engines, is the Vector Space Model (VSM) (Salton et al., 1975). In the past decades, the VSM was the foundation for various improvement and extension points. Indeed, most advances were achieved by hybrid approaches which combine the traditional VSM with additional knowledge. Next, we give two examples of how the VSM was improved.

One of the first issues which caught the attention of researchers was the VSM's inability to deal with synonymy and polysemy. An early approach to cope with these was query expansion. Typically, query expansion is based on the addition of terms from a thesaurus (e.g., WordNet) to a query and on relevance feedback (Rocchio, 1971). A more recent method is Latent Semantic Indexing (Furnas et al., 1988) – an extension of the traditional Vector Space Model, which captures the semantic associations between terms, documents, as well as terms and documents.

Another example is search on the Web. It was not until the recycling of the Web's linkage structure by Page and Brin in the late 90s, that search on the Web could be improved tremendously (Brin & Page, 1998). Indeed, the conversion of hyperlinks into popularity votes and their combination with the relevancy scores obtained by traditional retrieval models was unique.

We expect that search in intranets could also benefit from hybrid approaches. In particular, we propose to recycle neglected data into useful information. The problem is though, to find materials which are worth the recycling effort. A difficult issue because file shares have no linkage structure as seen in the Web and the amount of available metadata is in general low. So, what kind of data could possibly be recycled?

Document Header: The most obvious place to look into is the document's header. Typically, a header contains information such as "Author", "Title", and "Category", which might be well used for semantic search purposes. Unfortunately, our experience at Roche shows that these fields are in general of poor quality and thus not useful. People do not take care of the fields' content. In effect, observing values such as "new document", "template" or "unknown" is the norm.

Path Name: Folders are usually structured and labeled in such a way, that the content beneath is described well. The incentive is obvious: the more organized the file share is, the easier it is to re-find information. Indeed, file shares at Roche are usually well structured. Most notably, the first level typically contains the folders "organization" and "project". The "organization" branch is structured according to the organizational structure. The "projects" branch, on the other hand, is flat and contains project related subfolders, where data from several departments is consolidated.

We could thus recycle folder names and transform them into new explicit knowledge, namely the projects and departments a file is associated with. The feasibility of doing so depends on the file share's structure. As long as folder names are shared and the schemas are re-used, recycling should be easy. However, the moment a branch uses different structures, synonyms or syntactic variants, the task is not trivial anymore.

Security Groups: Administrative databases are used amongst other to manage security groups. The groups are used to control access to file shares, web portals, applications, etc. Access control is typically enabled by matching the security groups of the source (e.g., a file located in a file share) to the groups the employee is a member of. Security

Figure 2. Recycling documents

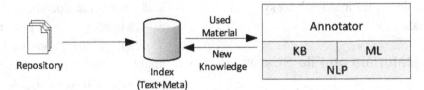

groups are of special value, because they are not created randomly but are usually well structured.

Groups are for instance created to hold all members of a department, a project or users of an application. In case the semantics of the groups are known, we could recycle the data into explicit knowledge. In effect, semantic queries such as "show me all files belonging to the bioinformatics department and belonging to the project fermentation" would become possible.

Full-Text Content: While the full text content describes what a document is about, it is also the most difficult to process. One could rely on natural language processing in order to extract facts and relationships from the text. A well known example is the extraction of protein-protein-interactions from medical abstracts. Another recycling option would be to do text categorization, i.e., to associate topics with the document. The latter could be used to browse documents by certain topics.

The next section gives details about the recycling methods applied in YASA.

Recycling Methodology

An automatic conversion of a document's full-text content as well as its associated properties (path, security groups, etc.) into a conceptualized ontology is an almost impossible task in general (Reeve & Han, 2005). Therefore, rather than conducting a complete recycling, we merely do a partial conversion, i.e. we restrict to the extraction of a few relevant concepts.

The concepts are extracted by means of an annotator, which scans the files and extracts new knowledge based on pre-defined or learned rules. We use natural language processing (NLP) (Nadeau & Sekine, 2007), machine learning (ML) (Mitchell, 1997), and a knowledge base (KB) (Levesque & Lakemeyer, 2001) so as to partially convert used material into explicit metadata (Figure 2).

Parts of the index structure are modeled in a classification ontology (Figure 3). The central class of the classification ontology is *Document*. A *Document* is identified by its *URI* (the document's location). Because we are in a corporate environment, we also include access control lists (*ACL*; expressing access rights) in the model. The *hasACL* property thus tells which groups are allowed to view the document. Beside this fundamental information, a *Document* is described by several relations to concepts of the domain ontology: *Entity*, *Project*, *Department*, and *Classification*. The links to these concepts are inferred by annotators using the fundamental information (i.e., *URI*, *FileType*, *ACL*, and full-text) of a *Document*.

The methods used to infer the new knowledge (i.e., a document's relations to concepts of the domain ontology) are summarized in Table 1. The detection of a file's association to projects or departments is accomplished by a combination of regular expression and rules. In order to determine the topic of a document as well as named entities occurring in the full-text content, natural

Figure 3. Classification Ontology. The facts of the domain ontology (white concepts) are obtained from existing company databases. Notice that the instances of the domain ontology might be hierarchical (e.g., organizational diagram in case of Department)

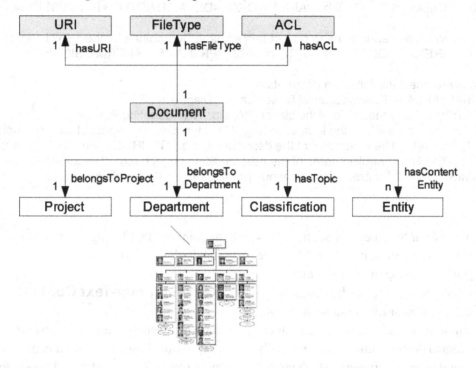

Table 1. Recycling methodologies

Source	Recycling Method	Target
URI (Path)	Regular Expressions + Rules	Project / Department
ACL	Regular Expressions + Rules	Project / Department
Full-text content	Natural Language Processing / Knowledge Engineering / Machine Learning	Named Entities / Topic

language processing and either knowledge engineering or machine learning is used.

The next section outlines how YASA applies regular expressions and rules on ACLs in order to determine a file's context in terms of projects and departments. The subsequent section then discusses how the full-text content is recycled into useful metadata.

Recycling Access Control Lists

Knowing the syntax of the access control list's name enables us to infer its semantics – here: whether the group refers to a department or a project (Figure 4). Further, if we know that a group is about a certain project / department, we also know the associations of the respective file. This could be expressed in a rule such as: "If the security group of the file contains the infix '_ORG_' and if the permissions suffix denotes

Figure 4. ACL syntax in the investigated division

```
# Structure encoding permissions to departmental data. Determined by the "_ORG_" infix.
<GLOBAL_AREA>_<LOCATION>_<AREA>_ORG_<DEPARTMENT>_<PERMISSION>

# Structure encoding permissions to project related data. Determined by the "_PRJ_" infix.
<GLOBAL_AREA>_<LOCATION>_<AREA>_PRJ_<PRJNAME>_<PERMISSION>

# The tags represent the following information
# <GLOBAL_AREA>: "Pharmaceutical Research" or "Diagnostics"
# <LOCATION>: The mnemonic of the city or site, e.g., "PZ" denoting Penzberg
# <AREA>: The mnemonic of the local area, e.g., "TR" denoting "Pharmaceutical Research",
# <DEPARTMENT>: The mnemonic of the department, e.g., "TR-IB" denoting "Bioinformatics"
# <PRJNAME>: The controlled name of the new medicine project, e.g., "Herceptin"
# <PERMISSION>: "C" representing a change permission, or "R" denoting a read only permission
```

a change permission 'C', then extract the <DEPARTMENT> and associate it with the file". The rule for projects is analogous. Notice, that in the rule we explicitly refer to groups denoting change permissions. The reason for doing so is simple. A read permission only tells us that a department has read access to the file – this could potentially apply to several other departments which are not related to the file. Change permissions however, are in general only given to the creators of the file. Thus, the ontological data extracted from the ACLs are based on the assumption that change permissions reflect ownerships. Experience has shown that this assumption is acceptable in the considered case.

In order to express such rules we use the OntoBroker implementation of F-Logic (Kifer et al., 1995), a frame-based language which supports the semantic web standards. The benefit of using F-Logic over OWL axioms is its ability to use variables as well as the possibility to extend the logic language by means of built-ins. This is particularly useful for doing text processing – a task which is not well suited for logic programming. Another difference to OWL is that F-Logic uses the closed world assumption, i.e., negation as failure. While this assumption might be unfavorable in the Internet, it is very well suited for intranet environments. Last, we want

to point out that F-Logic is not an official W3C standard.

Recycling Full-Text Content

Having discussed the recycling of ACLs, we now outline how the full-text content of a document can be processed in order to determine its topic. We compare two paradigms: Knowledge-engineering (KE) and machine learning (ML). In KE, a set of rules is defined which encode an expert's knowledge on how to classify a document into a specific category. In ML, an inductive process automatically builds a classifier by learning from a set of pre-classified documents (Mitchell, 1997; Sebastiani, 2002). We are aware that ML has become the state-of-the-art method in text categorization. However, the availability of semantic technologies makes the application of KE interesting. Having explicit classification rules defined, enables users to understand why a document was classified into a certain class of the ontology. Further, adjustments can be easily applied by simply updating the rules. Therefore, we investigate whether KE is feasible and how it performs compared to ML. The rules of the KE approach are also expressed by means of F-Logic in OntoBroker. ML is conducted with support vector machines (SVM) (Cortes & Vapnik, 1995)

Figure 5. Text categorization using machine learning and knowledge engineering

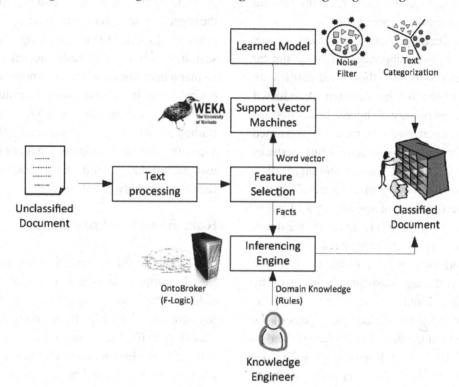

in WEKA. SVMs are capable of handling well a high-dimensional and sparse input space as is the case in text classification (Joachims et al., 1998).

The first step of text categorization is to process the full-text content (Figure 5). Passing an input text through a chain of different analyzers reduces complexity and redundancy. Notice that text processing and feature selection is different for ML and KE.

In case of ML, text is represented as a word vector, where terms are weighted using the term frequency measure. A combination with the inverse document frequency is omitted because it did not yield any significant improvement for us. The word vectors are going through tokenization, lower case filtering, stop word removal, and named entity expansion. Finally, the vector's dimensionality is reduced by filtering irrelevant terms. Feature expansion is the only step which adds information to the input data by annotating the words' types: person, date, time, and tags (special

keywords such as "agenda", "start time", "participants", etc.). Annotation, i.e., named entity recognition, is done with UIMA using regular expressions and dictionaries. Notice, that we do not apply stemming as its benefit of reducing word density does not outweigh the loss of potentially relevant information. The reason is that our corpus contains mixed languages (German and English). Thus, applying e.g., the porter stemmer (Porter, 1980) on documents containing German text may result in conflating unrelated words. A language detector may be applied to mitigate this issue. However, we did not investigate this option due to time constraints.

The final word vectors are then passed to the classification models. The first model separates noise (documents which do not belong to any of the pre-defined categories) from signal. The second model categorizes the signal into the learned classes. Using two models reduces the complexity for the individual learner. Further, the models can be fine-tuned for their specific task.

In case of KE, the output is a set of facts. Hence, while the text processing steps might be similar to the ML approach, only the named entities are considered at the end. Classification is conducted by applying the rules, which have been encoded by a domain expert, on the extracted facts (named entities). Working with entities not only reduces the number of terms but also the amount of rules. For instance, by referring to the entity *Time* in a rule we save the work of specifying all kind of variants like 10:00, 11:00, etc. In case of the document type "minutes", a rule might read as follows: "if the tag 'agenda' appears within the first 100 words, and if the tag 'start-time' is followed by an entity 'time', and if the tag 'participants' is followed by at least 5 subsequent entities of the type person then the document is categorized as an 'agenda' document". Even though such rules might seem rough, they turned out to be quite satisfying in the considered cases.

ON THE USAGE OF THE RECYCLED MATERIAL

Having shown how unstructured data can be recycled into new metadata, the rising question is how to use it? In YASA, recycled material is used for the following purposes: semantic search, faceted search, and adaptation of search results based on the working context.

Semantic Search and Navigation

The recycled information can be used to enable simple semantic search capabilities. For instance, we could ask the search engine YASA for documents in the category "Pre-Clinical Study Report" written by the author "Smith" which are part of the department "TR-I". In case of the departments we have additionally the possibility to extend search results to sub- and super-department. This is made possible by exploiting the "is-a" relationship of the organizational chart, which is also stored in an ontology. In order to ease the usage of semantic search, we offer additionally faceted navigation, so that a user does not need to know the specific query syntax in order to create complex queries. Rather, a search and browse style is applied for finding information. Semantics could thus enable a comprehensible navigation experience to the user as it could exploit and display all kind of relationships between the objects

Role-Based Adaptation

The recycled information can also be used to adapt search results. In just the same manner as we are able to extract the context of a file, we are able to extract and determine the working context of a user (Figure 6). The knowledge about the ACLs' semantics enables us to model the interest of a user into certain organizational areas. We could thus state that users are interested in the projects in which they are involved, i.e., we can create a rule which filters the ACLs encoding an interest into a project. The reasoning engine can thus determine the preferred ACLs, which in effect are associated to a set of documents, of which we assume the user is interested in.

This kind of adaptation does not require storing any person related information so that it is particularly suited for companies. Indeed, laws and the work council often prohibit the explicit storage and processing of person related data, as they could be misused to track an employee's activities.

We capture the pre-defined user interests (i.e., the user model) in an ontology. The interests are expressed by means of rules which denote specific interest strengths for documents belonging to specific security groups. The interest strengths are incorporated as boosting factors into the query. The rules applied by us, i.e. the search stereotypes, are sketched in Figure 7.

Figure 6. Inferring a user's assumed interests

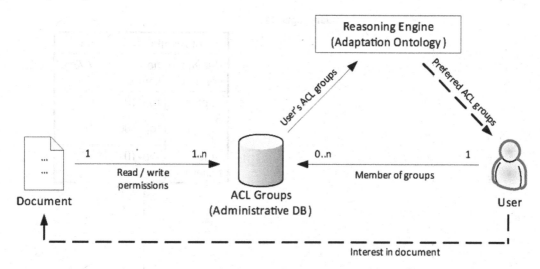

Figure 7. Pre-defined stereotypes

Let P be the current searcher, then the following rules are applied.

Rule 1: P is interested in files from his department (e.g., Fermentation)
Rule 2: P is interested in files from his area (e.g., Pharma Research)
Rule 3: P is interested in files belonging to projects he is involved.

The interest strengths were obtained by trial and error and may differ for other companies. Therefore, we omit showing the interest weights.

Next, we discuss the influence of role-based adaptation on the ranking of search results (Figure 8). For this purpose we use the query term "Agenda" which is submitted from a searcher in the research informatics department. The query returns a total of 5.177 results from all kind of working contexts (departments, projects, etc.). It is thus ideally suited to illustrate how our approach works. The scores of the top-50 documents returned by the baseline ranking (VSM) are almost identical and not a single document originating from the searcher's context is in the top-10, i.e., the text similarity measure is unable to discriminate their importance to the searcher's information need. In contrast, role-based ranking is able to discriminate the documents relevant to

the searcher's context, i.e., the top-10 contains only documents from the searcher's context.

EVALUATION

The goal of the evaluation presented in this chapter is to provide an answer to the following questions: Does the full-text classification perform well and more importantly which method does provide the best performance? Is role-based ranking of search results outperforming the baseline ranking? Is facetted navigation useful? How do the users rate the implemented methods? How is the usage statistic of YASA compared to other search engines in the intranet?

In order to answer these questions we conduct controlled experiments, user studies, and online log analysis.

Figure 8. Effect of role-based adaptation

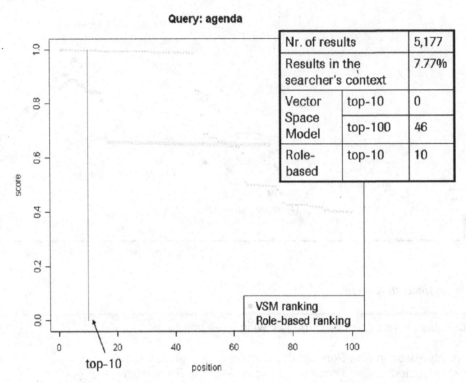

Nr. of results		5,177
Results in the searcher's context		7.77%
Vector Space Model	top-10	0
	top-100	46
Role-based	top-10	10

Two Full-Text Classification Methods Compared

In this section we investigate how feasible the two classification paradigms knowledge engineering (KE) and machine learning (ML) are.

In text categorization, optimization and performance evaluation is usually conducted on two distinct data sets (Mitchell, 1997): a training set and a test set, consisting of an input vector (full-text) and an answer vector (topic). Performance on the training set tells us that the applied method is able to memorize the given examples. It is not an indicator for the performance on unseen data. Therefore, the separate test set is supplied. Notice, that sampling is done in such a way, so that the relative proportions of each class are the same in both sets, i.e., the sets are stratified (Table 2).

Table 2. Size of the training set and the test set

	Category	Training Set	Test Set
Step 1	Signal	1835	130
	Noise	714	49
Step 2	Agenda	625	35
	Minutes	275	13
	Memo	321	12
	Portfolio	46	6
	SOP	243	14
	Pre-Clinical Study Report	453	20

Table 3. Text classification methods compared

		Knowledge Engineering		Machine Learning	
		Precision	Recall	Precision	Recall
Step 1	Signal	1.0	**0.72**	0.99	0.96
	Noise	0.58	1.0	0.91	0.98
Step 2	Agenda	1.0	**0.72**	0.92	0.97
	Memo	0.92	1.0	0.92	0.92
	Minutes	1.0	**0.62**	1.0	0.77
	Portfolio	1.0	1.0	1.0	1.0
	SOP	-	-	0.93	1.0
	Pre-Clinical Study Report	-	-	1.0	1.0

In step 1 (noise filtering), both approaches yield very good precision levels for detecting signal (Table 3). However, the recall levels differ significantly. While, the ML method has a recall value of 0.96, the KE method has a recall level of only 0.72.

In step 2 (topic classification), we observe again the tendency of KE to have a high precision at the cost of a lower recall (Table 3). In detail, for the topic "Agenda" the ML method provides the better harmonic mean of precision and recall. In contrast, the topic "Memo" is better categorized by the KE approach. In just the opposite manner, the ML approach provides a better performance for the topic "Minutes". The topic "Portfolio" is classified perfectly by both paradigms. In case of the categories "SOP" and "Pre-clinical study" the ML method gives a very good performance. KE was not considered for those due to the difficulty of detecting common terms.

Misclassifications mostly revolved around the topics "Minutes", "Memo" and "Agenda". The reason is their similar structure and the synonymous usage of the terms "Agenda" and "Minutes". Indeed, even a human annotator has sometimes difficulties in distinguishing between them.

Wrapping it up, the applied SVMs provide in average the better performance compared to KE, especially due to the recall levels. This result was expectable because the rules have been engineered very strictly, so that false positive hits are minimized. It is also due to the fact that we can not express per se fuzziness in the rules – something which is done implicitly in case of ML by weighting the importance of a term's frequency.

We conclude that KE is the method of choice if topics have a precise structure, if precision is more important than recall, and if understanding why a topic was assigned is relevant. Otherwise, ML should be chosen as it requires fewer efforts and more importantly, it executes considerably faster than our KE approach.

PERFORMANCE OF ROLE-BASED ADAPTATION

In this section we analyze whether the adaptation of search results based on the working context is preferred by the users in the investigated Roche department over the baseline ranking, i.e. Lucene's (lucene.apache.org) implementation of the vector space model (VSM).

A performance comparison based on expert judgment is related with high efforts. Therefore, we apply an unobtrusive method for comparing the ranking algorithms (Joachims, 2003). The experiment is conducted online without the user's

Table 4. Goal, question, methods, and metrics used in the user study

Goal	Question	Method	Metric
A significant improvement in satisfaction of the scientists' information need	How effective can users complete the tasks?	Objective	Success rate
	How efficient can users complete the tasks?	Objective	Execution time, mouse movement
	How satisfied are users with the systems?	Subjective	Questionnaire

awareness. Instead of showing the user the original result list, a combined result list is presented. The list is obtained by merging the individual result lists of the compared algorithms using a round-robin approach. Based on recorded click-through logs, we can determine an item's position in the original ranking and thus deduce which algorithm is preferred.

The statistical significance of such a preference is determined by us, using the McNemar test (McNemar, 1947) and the Wilcoxon signed rank test (Wilcoxon, 1945). These are suitable for discrete and ordinal data as obtained in our experiment. The null hypothesis H_0 is defined as "no preference towards a ranking algorithm". The alternative hypothesis H_1 is defined as "there is a preference towards one of the ranking algorithms". Further, we use a 95% confidence level for verifying / falsifying a hypothesis.

The experiment was conducted over a period of three weeks in May '09. A total of 568 click-through entries originated from 293 queries are recorded. Thus, we encountered in average 1.93 clicks per query, suggesting that correct answers were found rather fast.

The Wilcoxon signed-rank test returns a p-value of 0.832 and the McNemar test returns a p-value of 0.23. Therefore, at a 0.95 confidence level we can not conclude that H_1 holds and thus H_0 can not be declined. In other words, no statistical significant preference towards any ranking algorithm can be detected.

We conclude that the applied stereotypes are too coarse. For instance, Rule 3 (Figure 7) does only apply to group and department leaders, as they are members of various projects.

USER STUDY

In order to evaluate various aspects of YASA we use the goal question metric paradigm (Basili et al., 1994): a top-down approach which allows evaluating the quality of specific processes and products of a software system (Table 4). First, a goal is defined for an object which can be product deliverables, product specifications, processes, or resources. Then, a set of questions are formulated, which characterize the object of measurement. Finally, a metric is associated with every question in order to get a quantitative measurement. The data on which the metrics are applied can be objective or subjective.

The evaluation process consists of three phases, which are designed to be completed within 30 minutes. In the first phase (*briefing*) the test person is introduced to the test system. In the second phase (*observation*) we determine whether the participants solve the objective tasks more efficiently using YASA or conventional tools (any tool except YASA). In order to exclude a potential bias we decided to split the participants into two groups. The first group begins solving the tasks using conventional tools and then YASA, while the second group uses the tools in reverse order. In the third phase (*feedback*), the user is given a questionnaire whose purpose is to capture

Table 5. List of tasks. *: Baseline task. #: A gene name not to be disclosed

TaskID	Description
1*	Find a Wikipedia article about Herceptin
2	Find the location and phone number of the company's medical doctor at Roche in Penzberg
3	Get the full text of a publication named: A Breast Cancer Risk Haplotype in the Caspase-8 Gene
4	Find a location with literature (publications, presentations, posters) about YASA (Your Adaptive Search Agent)
5	Find the main folder on the PRPZ-Share where literature (studies, reviews, etc.) about MyGene# (also known as ---) is consolidated
6	Find the intranet homepage of the application "Prous Integrity"

the subjective opinion about the prototype's applied principles.

We asked 20 persons of the Roche Pharma Research department of Penzberg to participate in our evaluation. The persons were selected so that a representative distribution is achieved. Among the 20 participants, there were 19 employees (including 6 group leaders) and one student. The highest academic degrees distribute as follows among them: a bachelor degree is owned by 1 person, a diploma by 3 persons, and a Ph.D. by 15 persons. The majority of the participants, i.e., 16 persons, had used YASA before while the others used YASA during the evaluation for the first time.

We compiled a total of six different tasks for the observation phase (Table 5). The tasks are retrieval tasks, i.e., the test persons have to look up information. Depending on the task one or more

answers can be valid. Notice that these tasks do not aim to evaluate the ranking algorithm – which was done in the previous section – but to determine how efficiently answers can be given with YASA (due to features such as integration and faceted navigation) compared to conventional search tools. Therefore, these tasks are generic, i.e., they are not context-specific for any of the participants.

In addition to the six objective tasks we also ask the test persons to participate in a questionnaire. While the tasks were used to compare the performance of YASA to conventional tools, the questionnaire aimed at determining quality characteristics which can not be captured well by mere numbers. Therefore, we asked 14 questions which cover the quality of the objective tasks, various aspects of search, and several details about YASA (Table 6). The questionnaire is conducted using

Table 6. List of questions used in the questionnaire

QID	Question	QID	Question
1	The previous tasks correspond to task types that I also need to do for my work	8	The refine search options (facets) help me to find the information I need
2	Search results in YASA are relevant to my query	9	The *my files* facet is helpful
3	I prefer search results from my department	10	The *file format* facet is helpful
4	I often use YASA to find documents of other groups or departments in Pharma Research	11	The *year* and *month* facets are helpful
5	I immediately find what I am looking for	12	The *project* facets are helpful
6	Would you like to be able to search other areas such as Pharma Technical Development as well?	13	The *department* facet is helpful
7	It is useful to have access to internal & external information from one search tool	14	The *category* facet is helpful

the IsoMetrics (Gediga & Hamborg, 1999) usability inventory which is a summative as well as formative approach in software evaluation. Each question is assessed using a 5 point rating scale, starting from 1 ("predominantly disagree") to 5 ("predominantly agree"). In addition a "no opinion" field is supplied to reduce arbitrary answers.

Our test system is build on top of a regular Roche desktop computer. The only difference to an out-of-the-box system is the installed application for conducting the evaluation and monitoring purposes. On the one hand side the application provides the objective tasks of the second phase (observation) to the user. On the other hand it monitors the user's performance. The tasks are presented sequentially to the current user. He has to press start when he starts processing a task and he has to press stop when he has finished a task. Task processing is unidirectional.

RESULTS OF THE OBSERVATION PHASE

The results of the observation phase are summarized in Table 7. In case of the internet tasks (task 1 and task 3), all users were able to give the correct answer. However, answers have been provided faster with conventional tools in case of task 3. In case of the intranet web retrieval tasks

(task 2 and task 6) the users conducted slightly less errors using YASA. More interestingly, the retrieval of the correct answer of task 6 was considerably faster using YASA. The last two tasks (task 4 and task 5) aimed at comparing the performance when searching the file shares. In both cases, participants were able to provide more accurate answers using YASA. Further, answers were provided significantly faster using YASA.

The observed execution time can be thought of as a random sample of a larger population. Our observation is thus a reflection of the unobservable underlying probability density function, according to which a large population is distributed. Using statistics, we are able to estimate the density function based on the observed data, so that we can plot the probability of obtaining a certain performance value. The density function shows that there are considerably more tasks which are answered faster with YASA than with conventional tools (Figure 9). At about 500 seconds, there is a small peak due to the wrong answers which pile-up at the cut-off value.

Considering these results, we conclude that YASA provides the better search performance for intranet retrieval tasks. Further, YASA offers an integrated search. Hence, using YASA is advantageous if a user does not know well the information landscape and if several sources need to be queried simultaneously.

Table 7. Results of the observation phase. A relative time performance below one means, the task was answered faster using YASA. A relative time performance above one means that the task was answered faster using conventional tools

Task ID / Description	Target	Relative time performance	% errors using YASA	% errors using Conventional
1 / Herceptin	Wikipedia	1.08	-	-
3 / Publication	PubMed	1.25	-	-
2 / Med. Doctor	SharePoint (FAST)	1.01	15%	15%
6 / Application	SharePoint (FAST)	0.57	-	5%
4 / Literature	File Share	0.65	30%	35%
5 / Literature	File Share	0.40	20%	60%

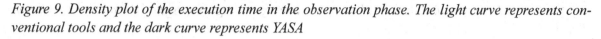

Figure 9. Density plot of the execution time in the observation phase. The light curve represents conventional tools and the dark curve represents YASA

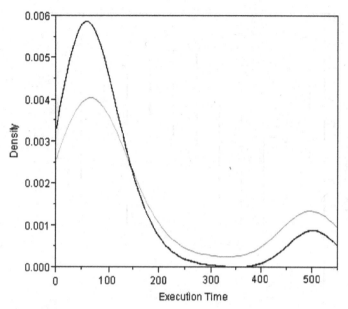

RESULTS OF THE FEEDBACK PHASE

The results of the feedback phase are summarized in Figure 10. Participants agree that the tasks correspond to task types that they typically do in their work (QID 1; short for Question ID 1). Regarding the quality of search results in YASA, the participants strongly agree that search results are relevant to their query (QID 2; QID 5). QID 3 and QID 4 are coupled as the first one asks whether the user prefers search results from the department he is working in and the second one asks whether he often searches for information in other departments. The average answers for both questions suggest that people slightly prefer to search in other departments than in their own. However, the standard deviation is rather high suggesting a controversial point of view.

Considering the usage of facets, the analysis shows that people strongly agree that facets help them to find information faster with YASA (QID 8). The importance of the individual facet is disputed. The "my files" facet (QID9; restricts results

to documents the searcher has created) and "year / month" (QID 11) facets are mediocre and have a high standard deviation. The "file format" facet (restricts results to a certain document format) is considered as highly relevant (QID 10). The "project", "department", and "category" facets are all agreed to be important having a relatively low standard deviation (QID 12, 13, and 14).

Given these results we conclude that faceted navigation is an important feature of enterprise search engines. Another conclusion is that the applied role-based adaptation of search results needs more fine-granular rules.

Usage Statistics

In this section we investigate two aspects of YASA, namely the usage of facetted navigation within YASA and the usage of YASA compared to other search tools. In both cases the analysis is conducted by means of log data which was collected over a period of 6 month in 2009.

The usage of facetted navigation is considerable. Indeed, users are refining search results

Figure 10. Results of the questionnaire showing the average rating (points) and the standard deviation (lines)

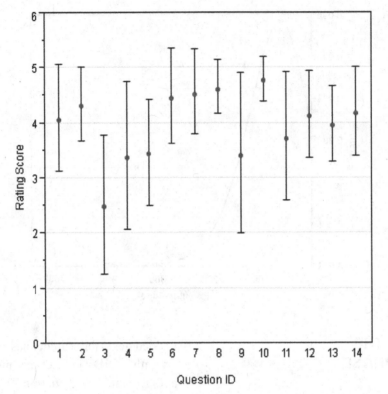

by means of guided navigation in 10.2% of the searches (Figure 11). The facet *Department* is used considerably (28%). The usage of the facet *Project* might seem low at first (2.2%). However, we must consider that the facet *Project* is only relevant to employees having leadership responsibility, i.e. group and department leaders. Because they are outnumbered by the majority of the employees it is only natural that the facet *Project* is used less

compared to the facet *Department*, which is useful to all employees. The facet *Category* (the document class obtained by full-text classification), has a low usage (2.6%). However, this numbers might change as this facet was only introduced towards the end of the log analysis period.

Next, we investigate how the usage of search engines advanced since 2007 (cf., cp. "Research Environment"). Notice that two changes were

Figure 11. Usage of facets

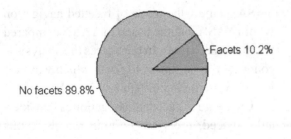

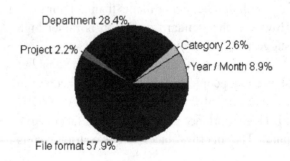

Figure 12. Usage of search engines linked from the Pharma Research Penzberg website

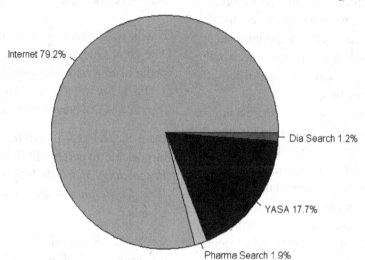

made since then. First, the search engine indexing the diagnostics division was incorporated. Second, the Google Search Appliance was discontinued due to its poor performance and replaced by YASA. The conducted analysis

The results show, that YASA has a usage ratio of 17.7% (Figure 12) – a considerable amount. The usage of the intranet web search engines, Pharma Search and Dia Search, are low with a ratio of 1.9% and 1.2%, respectively.

We conclude that YASA is a well established search engine. Further, we conclude that YASA is favored by the users – YASA has a significantly higher usage compared to the Google Search Appliance (0.5% in 2007; Figure 1).

CONCLUSION

At the beginning of this research project we started empty-handed: No formal ontology modeling the knowledge domain of Pharma Research was available. In fact, there was not even a taxonomy-like structure which described frequently used concepts and their relationships. For that reason, we had to build upon unstructured free-text documents. This is a serious issue, because the

ability to extend search by symbolic knowledge representation approaches such as those of the semantic web (RDF/S, OWL, F-Logic) is limited by the quality of the indexed content. This was the case in this research project.

Interestingly, our results show that this widespread limitation can be compensated to a large degree by using automatic recycling techniques. Indeed, we were able to extract large quantities of explicit metadata from a file's content and attributes. Amongst others, we can extract the department to which a file belongs, the project to which it is related, and a range of topics. We are aware that such an automatic extraction does not yield optimal quality: extracted metadata may be erroneous and more importantly, the metadata is not semantically rich. Indeed, the ontologies describing the metadata are not complex but have large similarities to taxonomies. These "sparse semantics" might even be seen as a flaw in our approach. However, our results show that professional search already benefits from "sparse semantics". Therefore, it seems to be worthwhile to intensify research on including even more semantics.

A key message of the experiences obtained with YASA, is that all information lying on a data server of a company is potentially useful for improving search. We have shown that even data such as a file's or a user's security groups contain useful domain knowledge – knowledge which is typically ignored by current state-of-the-art enterprise search solutions.

This work made use of statistics, logical inference, and heuristics in order to recycle "garbage" data such as a file's or a user's security settings into useful knowledge. However, these methods share a common drawback. They do not automatically adjust to changing environments as encountered in companies: projects change, departmental hierarchies are undergoing steady adjustments due to internal re-structuring, existing document topics shift their focus, new topics are added due to new trends in research, etc. In effect, the characteristics of each category undergo steady changes so that the classification models and rules must be adjusted. The required adjustments may vary greatly depending on the considered class. In case of departments for instance, it would suffice to simply update the organizational hierarchy in the ontology. In case of topic classifications on the other hand, new training data must be provided potentially causing a considerable effort.

Without a doubt, keeping the extracted metadata up-to-date, poses a challenge if context-based search is to be applied on the corpus of large corporations. It remains to be seen if other approaches, possibly based on human computation (Von Ahn & Dabbish, 2004) in which the computational ability of humans solve problems computers cannot, could mitigate the issue. For the time being we have enough to do by coping with those problems for which approaches exist, that at least look promising. Hopefully, this paper is a useful contribution towards solving some of these issues.

We conclude, that already a small bit of semantics goes a much longer way than one would have expected.

REFERENCES

Basili, V., Caldiera, G., & Rombach, H. D. (1994). The Goal Question Metric Paradigm, Encyclopedia of Software Engineering. In Marciniak, J. J. (Ed.), *Encyclopedia of Software Engineering* (pp. 528–532). New York: John Wiley & Sons.

Brin, S., & Page, L. (1998). The anatomy of a large-scale hypertextual Web search engine. In *Proceedings of the 7th International World Wide Web Conference* (pp. 107-117). Amsterdam: Elsevier.

Cortes, C., & Vapnik, V. (1995). Support-Vector Networks. *Machine Learning*, 20, 273–297. doi:10.1007/BF00994018

Fagin, R., Kumar, R., McCurley, K. S., Novak, J., Sivakumar, D., Tomlin, J. A., et al. (2003). Searching the workplace web. In *Proceedings of the International World Wide Web Conference* (pp. 366-375). New York: ACM.

Feldman, S., & Sherman, C. (2004). The High Cost of Not Finding Information. *KM World, 13*.

Furnas, G. W., Deerwester, S., Dumais, S. T., Landauer, T. K., Harshman, R. A., Streeter, L. A., et al. (1988). Information retrieval using a singular value decomposition model of latent semantic structure. In *Proceedings of the Annual ACM Conference on Research and Development in Information Retrieval* (pp. 465-480). New York: ACM.

Gediga, G., & Hamborg, K. C. (1999). IsoMetrics: An usability inventory supporting summative and formative evaluation of software systems. In *Proceedings of the 8th International Conference on Human-Computer Interaction* (pp. 1018-1022). Hillsdale, NJ: Lawrence Erlbaum Associates Inc.

Hawking, D. (2004). Challenges in enterprise search. In *Proceedings of the ACM International Conference Proceeding Series* (Vol. 52, pp. 15-24). Darlinghurst, Australia: Australian Computer Society, Inc.

Joachims, T. (2003). Evaluating retrieval performance using clickthrough data. In Franke, J., Nakhaeizadeh, G., & Renz, I. (Eds.), *Text Mining* (pp. 79–96). New York: Springer.

Joachims, T., Nedellec, C., & Rouveirol, C. (1998). Text categorization with Support Vector Machines: Learning with many relevant features. In *Proceedings of the 10th European Conference on Machine Learning*. Berlin: Springer.

Kifer, M., Lausen, G., & Wu, J. (1995). Logical foundations of object-oriented and frame-based languages. *Journal of the ACM, 42*, 741–843. doi:10.1145/210332.210335

Levesque, H. J., & Lakemeyer, G. (2001). *The Logic of Knowledge Bases*. Cambridge, MA: MIT Press.

Maßun, M. (2008). *Collaborative Information Management in Enterprises*. Regensburg, Germany: University of Regensburg.

McNemar, Q. (1947). Note on the sampling error of the difference between correlated proportions or percentages. *Psychometrika, 12*, 153–157. doi:10.1007/BF02295996

Micarelli, A., Gasparetti, F., Sciarrone, F., & Gauch, S. (2007). Personalized search on the World Wide Web. In Brusilovsky, P., Kobsa, A., & Nejdl, W. (Eds.), *The Adaptive Web: Methods and Strategies for Web Personalization* (pp. 195–230). Berlin: Springer.

Mitchell, T. (1997). *Machine Learning*. New York: McGraw-Hill.

Mühlbacher, S. (2008). *Scientific Information Literacy in Enterprises*. Regensburg, Germany: University of Regensburg.

Nadeau, D., & Sekine, S. (2007). A survey of named entity recognition and classification. *Linguisticae Investigationes, 30*, 3–26. doi:10.1075/li.30.1.03nad

Porter, M. (1980). An Algorithm for Suffix Stripping Program. *Program, 14*, 130–137.

Reeve, L., & Han, H. (2005). Survey of semantic annotation platforms. In *Proceedings of the Symposium on Applied Computing* (pp. 1634-1638). New York: ACM.

Rocchio, J. J. (1971). Relevance feedback in information retrieval. In Salton, G. (Ed.), *The SMART Retrieval System - Experiments in Automatic Document Processing* (pp. 313–323). Englewood Cliffs, NJ: Prentice-Hall.

Salton, G., Wong, A., & Yang, C. S. (1975). A vector space model for automatic indexing. *Communications of the ACM, 18*, 613–620. doi:10.1145/361219.361220

Sebastiani, F. (2002). Machine learning in automated text categorization. *ACM Computing Surveys, 34*, 1–47. doi:10.1145/505282.505283

Von Ahn, L., & Dabbish, L. (2004). Labeling images with a computer game. In *Proceedings of the Conference on Human Factors in Computing Systems* (pp. 319-326). New York: ACM.

Wilcoxon, F. (1945). Individual comparisons by ranking methods. *Biometrics Bulletin*, 80–83. doi:10.2307/3001968

Xue, G. R., Zeng, H. J., Chen, Z., Ma, W. Y., Zhang, H. J., & Lu, C. J. (2003). Implicit link analysis for small web search. In *Proceedings of the Annual ACM Conference on Research and Development in Information Retrieval* (pp. 56-63). New York: ACM.

This work was previously published in International Journal of Semantic Web and Information Systems, Volume 6, Issue 2, edited by Amit P. Sheth, pp. 17-35, copyright 2010 by IGI Publishing (an imprint of IGI Global).

Chapter 10
Ontology–Enhanced User Interfaces:
A Survey

Heiko Paulheim
SAP Research CEC Darmstadt, Germany

Florian Probst
SAP Research CEC Darmstadt, Germany

ABSTRACT

Ontologies have been increasingly used in software systems in the past years. However, in many of those systems, the ontologies are hidden "under the hood". While a lot of useful applications of ontologies on the database and business logic layer have been proposed, the employment of ontologies in user interfaces has been gaining comparatively little attention so far. For providing a deeper understanding of that field as well as assisting developers of ontology-enhanced user interfaces, the authors give an overview of such applications and introduce a schema for characterizing the requirements of ontology-enhanced user interfaces. With this article, a state of the art survey of approaches is presented along with promising research directions.

INTRODUCTION

During the past years, ontologies have been used in information sources for numerous purposes, such as annotating resources for better information retrieval, integrating data from different sources and systems, and automatically coupling intelligent agents. In most of those fields, ontologies are

used on the information source and the business logic layer, and thus hidden "under the hood".

One of the most complete surveys of using ontologies in software engineering is probably given by Ruiz and Hilera (2006). The authors have analyzed more than 50 possibilities of employing ontologies in software engineering, only two of which target at user interfaces. Heitmann, Kinsella, Hayes, and Decker (2009) have presented a survey on applications using semantic web technology and, not much surprisingly, they found out that

DOI: 10.4018/978-1-4666-0185-7.ch010

more than 90% of those applications come with a user interface. The survey, however, contains only little information about *how* the employment of semantic web ontologies influences the provided user interfaces.

In this article, we want to shed light at this area and take a closer look at the various possibilities of enhancing user interfaces with ontologies. We have reviewed various projects and identified a number of purposes for which ontologies can be used on the user interface layer, e.g., adapting UIs to a user's needs, or providing input assistance. Each of those purposes poses particular requirements to the ontologies and their use in the application. So far, no structured review of those requirements and approaches has been performed. To summarize these approaches, we prefer the more general notion *ontology-enhanced user interface* instead of *ontology-driven user interface*, as sometimes used (e.g., Paton et al., 1999; Visser & Schuster, 2002), since ontologies may also be employed to provide one single functionality in a larger user interface (and thus *enhance* the user interface) without being the key element *driving* the user interface. We propose the following definition:

Defintion: An *ontology-enhanced user interface* is a user interface whose visualization capabilities, interaction possibilities, or development process are enabled or (at least) improved by the employment of one or more ontologies.

According to this definition, we have looked at projects where the development process and/or the usability of a user interface has been improved by employing ontologies. Applications such as pure ontology editors or viewers thus are out of scope here, since the ontologies do not improve the user interface in these cases – in these applications, ontology engineering itself is the *purpose*, not a *means to enhance* the user interface's capabilities.

While this definition is quite broad, it does not encompass every application using an ontology. There are many applications that use ontologies in-ternally – e.g., for integrating different information sources, or for enabling information exchange with other systems – where the fact that an ontology is used in a particular place does *not* have any effect on the application's user interface. Furthermore, there are applications providing functionality which are implemented with ontologies, and the applications' user interfaces grant access to that functionality – however, in these cases, the user interface as such is not directly influenced (let alone improved) by the employment of an ontology. In contrast, we concentrate on applications of ontologies that *directly* improve user interfaces or their development.

We have carefully studied the current state of the art of improving user interfaces with ontologies. To that end, we have looked at numerous projects which use ontologies in the development of user interfaces. From that overview, we have derived a number of criteria for both the ontologies and the mode of their employment which are relevant for characterizing ontology-enhanced user interfaces. This characterization serves two purposes: it allows for a better understanding ontology-enhanced user interfaces, and it supports developers who want to use ontologies for a certain purpose in a user interface by pinpointing the relevant requirements. Furthermore, the survey in this article helps identifying new interesting research directions. The survey of approaches we present is purely descriptive, as a detailed discussion of whether each of the improvements addressed could also or even better be achieved without ontologies is out of scope of this article.

The rest of this article is structured as follows. The next section outlines existing classifications of ontologies in software systems in general. Based on these classifications, we present our own characterization framework, which is especially tailored to ontology-enhanced user interfaces. Next, we present a representative selection of approaches and apply our framework to discuss their characteristics. Following our definition, these approaches are classified in three categories: *improving the user interface's appearance, improving the interaction with the user interface*, and *improving the development process of the user interface*. We conclude with a summary and a discussion in which we point to possible future trends by identifying research areas within ontology-enhanced user interfaces that are currently underrepresented.

EXISTING CLASSIFICATIONS OF ONTOLOGIES IN SOFTWARE SYSTEMS

Although no classification of ontology-enhanced user interfaces and of the use of ontologies in user interfaces has been proposed so far, a number of classifications for using ontologies in software systems and in software engineering *in general* exist, which may to a certain degree be applied to the area of ontology-enhanced user interfaces.

An often-cited classification schema (Heijst, Schreiber, & Wielinga, 1997; Gómez-Pérez, Fernández-López, & Corcho, 2004) distinguishes the domain modeled in an ontology and the ontology's complexity. It distinguishes four types of domains (domain, application, representation, and generic ontologies) which vary in their level of detail and reusability within a domain and across domains, and three levels of complexity (lexicons, information ontologies, and knowledge modelling ontologies).

Guarino (1998) proposes a classification for using ontologies in information systems. This classification distinguishes three levels of generality (top level, domain/task level, and application level), two types of usage time (development and run time), and three system layers in which the ontologies are used (database, application logic, and user interface). While there are some examples for using ontologies in user interfaces, such as directly browsing an ontology for a certain domain or improving textual input, no further detailed analysis is performed.

Happel and Seedorf (2006) introduce a classification schema more targeted at using ontologies in software engineering, which is a blend of the two schemas above. The authors distinguish two types of domains: the real world domain for which the software is built (e.g., banking, travel, etc., confusingly called *software* in their work), and the domain of software systems (called *infrastructure* in their work). In addition, they distinguish between using the ontology at development time and and run time of the software system.

Gruninger and Lee (2002) identify three relevant categories for the usage of ontologies in computer systems in general. Ontologies may be used for *communication* (between people, between systems, and between people and systems.), for *inter-operability* (between systems), and for *improving the development process*. This is one of the most comprehensive descriptions of what ontologies can be used for in computer systems (not necessarily only software systems). Improving the user interface is covered by communication between people and systems. Approaches for improving the development of user interfaces can be subsumed in the last category.

Uschold and Jasper (1999) give a more detailed classification, using criteria such as the role of the ontology (used for operational data (L_0), for classification of that data (L_1), or as a language for defining other ontologies (L_2)), the actors working with it (ontology author, data author, application developer, application user, and knowledge worker), the supporting technology (i.e., languages, programming frameworks, etc.) and the maturity level of the ontology (from experimental to commercially used). The approaches in this article most often deal with L_0 and L_1 ontologies. The ontology users are implicitly reflected in our classification of approaches: improving the appearance and interaction of user interfaces target at application users, improving UI development targets at application developers.

The already mentioned survey by Ruiz and Hilera (2006) distinguishes various cases of using ontologies in software engineering, based on the traditional phases of the software engineering process. For each phase, they list different possibilities of how ontologies may be employed, and suggest ontologies that may be used for that purpose.

All of those classifications contain valuable criteria to characterize the use of ontologies in user interfaces. However, as they do not concentrate on user interfaces in particular, they are often too general for that specific area. In the following section, we propose a set of criteria suitable for analyzing ontology-enhanced user interfaces.

CHARACTERISTICS OF ONTOLOGY-ENHANCED USER INTERFACES

As discussed, there are various classifications of ontologies and their employment, each following a certain purpose and thus having a particular bias. We adopt some of the criteria proposed in those works and enhance them with criteria which are useful for categorizing user interfaces.

Since the development of user interfaces is a sub-area of software engineering, we follow Happel and Seedorf (2006) and take the ontologies' domain and the time of its employment into account. Furthermore, we adopt the ontology complexity criterion from Heijst et al. (1997) and Gómez-Pérez et al. (2004), as this is a useful criterion for tackling the requirements when it comes to decide for an ontology language and a matching programming framework.

We augment these three criteria by two additional ones that target specifically at user interfaces, based on the fact that user interfaces usually serve two main purposes: a) presenting information to the user, and b) allowing interaction with a system. For ontologies in user interfaces, we therefore propose the following two additional criteria: a) how the ontology is presented to the user, and b) how the user can interact with the ontology.

Thus, we end up at a characterization schema comprising five criteria, as depicted in Figure 1. In the rest of this section, we discuss each of those criteria in detail.

Figure 1. Characterization schema for ontology-enhanced user interfaces

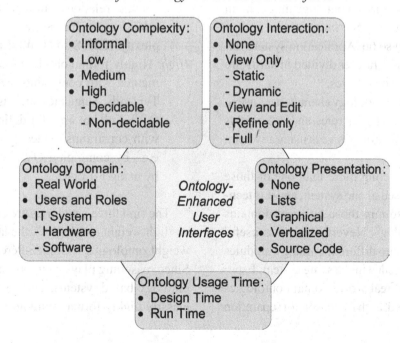

Criterion 1: What Domain is the Ontology About?

The first criterion regards the ontology's domain, i.e., what the ontology is about. Happel and Seedorf (2006) distinguish two types: the real world domain for which the software is build, and the domain of software systems. We introduce a third domain, namely users and the roles they have (Kagal, Finin, & Joshi, 2003). Roles are most often roles a person takes in the real world. However, roles may also affect the way that person can interact with a system (e.g., whether that person has certain rights within a system) or is supposed to perform certain tasks. Thus, they cannot be clearly assigned to any of the two domains introduced by Happel and Seedorf. Therefore, we propose users and roles as a domain of its own, ending up with the following three domains:

Real world: The ontology characterizes a part of the real world, typically the one that the application is used in (e.g., banking, travel, etc.). The goal is to identify the central concepts and their relations.

IT system: The IT system itself is formalized in the ontology. Such an ontology may contain categories such as SOFTWARE MODULE, WEB SERVICE, and so on. Application system ontologies can be further divided in hardware and software ontologies.

Users and roles: The ontology characterizes users, their preferences, their roles, and/or the rights and possibilities they have in using a system.

Ontologies covering more than one of those domains can be used in one system, and it is technically possible to mix those different domains in the same ontology. Nevertheless, it is useful to separate them into different ontology modules even if they are needed in the same system. Especially system and real world domain ontologies should be separated, both for reasons of separation of concerns and of flexibility when reusing the ontologies (Klien & Probst, 2005).

Criterion 2: How Complex is the Ontology?

Ontologies come in various complexities, starting from simple glossaries up to sets of logical statements and constraints (Smith & Welty, 2001; Uschold & Gruninger, 2004; Rebstock, Fengel, & Paulheim, 2008). For each degree of complexity, different languages may be used. For our purpose, we distinguish the following degrees of complexity:

Informal: Informal ontologies are collections of definitions which have no further structure, such as a glossary. Such ontologies do not require any sophisticated language, they can be expressed, e.g., in XML, XML Schema, or RDF.

Low: Ontologies of low complexity consist of class hierarchies and subclass relations. Such ontologies are typically expressed in RDF-S or OWL Lite.

Medium: Ontologies of medium complexity also contain relations other than the subclass relation. Like for ontologies with low complexity, RDF-S and OWL Lite can be used.

High: Highly formal ontologies are further augmented with constraints, rules, and so on. Typically, languages such as OWL DL and OWL Full are used for defining ontologies with constraints. Rules can be expressed, e.g., by combining OWL with SWRL, or by using F-Logic.

The first three categories are often referred to as "lightweight ontologies", the latter as "heavyweight ontologies" (Gómez-Pérez et al., 2004). Since reasoning plays an important role in many ontology-based systems, it is beneficial to further classify highly formal ontologies into decidable and non-decidable ontologies (Antoniou, Franconia, & van Harmelen, 2005).

Criterion 3: When is the Ontology Used?

When developing user interfaces, ontologies may be used at different points of time in the development process. Following Happel and Seedorf (2006), we distinguish the following two:

Design time: Ontologies are used while developing the system.
Run time: Ontologies are used when the system is executed.

In the first case, the ontologies typically are not a part of the user interface which is developed, and they are used to assist the developer. In the second case, the ontologies most often become a part of the user interface and fulfil a certain function in that user interface.

Criterion 4: How is the Ontology Presented to the User?

In ontology-enhanced user interfaces, the ontologies used and the information contained therein may be, at least partially, presented to the user. Therefore, the question *how* the ontology is presented is particularly interesting.

No presentation: The ontology is completely hidden.
Lists: Lists of categories from the ontology are shown without making relations between those categories visible. Those lists may be actual selection lists as well as the names of single concepts from the ontology appearing as text blocks in some places of the user interface.
Graphical: Relations between concepts are visualized, e.g., in form of trees (most often showing the taxonomy) or graphs (including

non-taxonomic relations). A detailed survey of ontology visualization techniques is given by Katifori, Halatsis, Lepouras, Vassilakis, and Giannopoulou (2007), encompassing various graphical representations in 2D and 3D.
Verbalized: A textual representation of the axioms contained in the ontology is provided.
Source code: The ontology's source code, e.g., in OWL or F-Logic, is shown to the user.

At first glance, it may be questionable whether we are still talking about ontology-enhanced user interfaces if those ontologies are completely hidden, or whether the ontologies are rather used in the business logic or data layer when they are not visible in the user interface. However, we will show some examples in the next chapter where hidden ontologies can directly influence the user interface and thus conform to our definition.

Criterion 5: How can the User Interact with the Ontology?

There may be different types of interaction with the ontologies used in an ontology-enhanced user interface. In some cases, the ontologies may only be viewed, in others, the user can also extend and alter them. We distinguish three types of interaction with ontologies:

No Interaction: The user cannot interact with the ontology.
View Only: The user can view the ontology or selected parts thereof. The view can be static (e.g., in form of pictures) or dynamic (i.e., allowing to browse between concepts, zoom in and out, etc.)
View and Edit: The user can modify the contents of the ontology. Such modifications can either be limited to refining the ontology (i.e., adding new subcategories or relations), or allow full modification, such as changing and deleting existing concepts.

In most cases where ontologies may be altered, this functionality is only accessible by a selected group of users, such as administrators.

In summary, the five criteria in the characterization schema presented in this section are mostly independent from each other, although some cross-dependencies exist. For example, graphical visualization requires at least a taxonomy of categories, and extending and altering ontologies is only possible when ontologies are not invisible, at least for the group of users who can perform these tasks.

Other Criteria

Besides the criteria above, there is a number of others which could be used, but which we do not consider relevant for characterizing ontology-enhanced user interfaces for the following reasons:

Storage: Ontologies can be stored centrally or distributed, locally or on the web, in flat files or triple stores. This is an engineering decision which does not affect the user interface.

Free floating vs. Grounded: Ontologies are often grounded in foundational ontologies such as DOLCE (Masolo, Borgo, Gangemi, Guarino, & Oltramari, 2003). This allows engineers to better understand those ontologies and compare different ontologies. For the end user, this distinction is often not particularly relevant.

Modularity: Likewise, ontologies can be built as a single large ontology or as a number of interconnected small ontologies. Although we strongly encourage the use of modular ontologies, this is merely an engineering decision without any direct impact on the user interface.

Size: Ontologies can significantly vary in size, ranging from a dozen categories to a few million. As we have found no examples where a certain minimum or maximum size is required for a certain application, we have

decided to neglect this criterion as well. However, size is an important issue when it comes to the performance and scalability of an ontology-based application.

SURVEY OF PURPOSES AND APPROACHES

Following our initial definition, there are three main purposes for which ontologies can be employed in ontology-enhanced user interfaces, namely

1. Improving the visualization capabilities,
2. Improving the interaction possibilities, and
3. Improving the development process

of a user interface. Based on this categorization, we will give an overview on approaches for pursuing these purposes and present some *representative examples* for each approach.

Each of those approaches is analyzed and characterized based on the schema introduced in the previous chapter, and the relevant requirements for implementing the approaches are pointed out. A table at the end of the chapter will compare and summarize the approaches and give hints for the identification of interesting research gaps.

Using Ontologies for Improving the Visualization Capabilities

Ontologies may be used for improving the appearance of the user interface, i.e., the way information is presented to the user. This means that given a set of information items, the transformation into visual items on the screen is influenced by ontologies. The determination of the initial set of information items, however, is not a task performed in the user interface, but in the underlying business logic. Therefore, approaches such as ontology-based information filtering are out of

Table 1. Characterization of examined information clustering approaches

Ontology domain:	Real World
Ontology complexity:	Low or higher
Ontology visualization:	Lists of graphs
Interaction with the ontology:	View only
Ontology usage time:	Run time

scope here, unless combined with an ontology-enhanced user interface.

Information Clustering: When retrieving information, it is possible that a large number of information items is returned. Therefore, the user may want some assistance in handling the query results. One possible approach is *information clustering*: Here, information items are subsumed to groups which stand for a set of single items. Each of these groups is represented by one visual item on the screen (Herman, Melançon, & Marshall, 2000).

One example for ontologies-based information clustering is the *Cluster Map* project (Fluit, Sabou, & Harmelen, 2003). In Cluster Map, search results (e.g., from a web or database search) are visualized as connected sets (painted as balloons), which contain small dots representing the individual results. The user can navigate the ontology and get an idea of the number of results in each category. The *Courseware Watchdog* project (Tane, Schmitz, & Stumme, 2004), an e-learning resource management system, uses ontologies to provide an intuitive way to access e-learning resources. Here, taxonomic and non-taxonomic relations between classes can be displayed as well, allowing the user a flexible way of navigating through the set of resources. In the *SWAPit* project (Seeling & Becks, 2003), clusters of documents are computed from the metadata assigned to them, and the documents belonging to different categories in a domain ontology are marked in different colours in those clusters. In each of those cases,

ontologies help finding resources by creating new visualizations apart from simple lists.

Ontologies can be used for information clustering at run-time to provide the groups and their labels for information clustering. By subsuming each information item to a class in the ontology's class hierarchy, those items can be clustered, and the classes are visualized on the screen (Table 1). Thus, the ontology is characterizing the real world domain that the information items refer to, and it has to consist of at least a class hierarchy (although additional relations may be visualized as extra guidance). Both lists and graphical visualizations are possible, where in the latter case, the user may also navigate through the visualization interactively.

Text Generation: Information contained in ontologies is usually encoded in machine-readable languages that only experts can understand. When trying to make that information available to the user, it can be beneficial to transform it into a language that can be understood by the end user. To that end, different ontology verbalizing algorithms have been developed (Kaljurand & Fuchs, 2007).

An example for using verbalized ontologies is the *MIAKT* project (Bontcheva & Wilks, 2004): in this project, information about medical cases gathered from an information base in the form of RDF triples is turned into human-readable reports. The RDF triples and the definitions from

Table 2. Characterization of examined text generation approaches

Ontology domain:	Real world
Ontology complexity:	Medium or higher
Ontology visualization:	Verbalized
Interaction with the ontology:	View, edit is possible
Ontology usage time:	Design and run time

the corresponding ontology are verbalized and turned into a small text describing a medical case.

There are other examples where not full text, but only text fragments are generated from information contained in ontologies. One promising strategy is to use texts that already exist and augment them with additional information taken from ontologies. In the *COHSE* project (Carr, Hall, Bechhofer, & Goble, 2001), text documents are augmented with links to related documents and categories as lists of links added to the texts. Here, ontologies defining the documents' domain of discourse can help identifying the correct anchor terms in the document, and ontology-based information retrieval may be one step in finding relevant documents to link to the anchor terms. Depending on whether the documents are directly linked to the anchor terms or link lists based on categories from the ontologies are generated, the ontologies are either invisible or visualized as lists. One appealing vision of applying this approach is to have a large information base, such as Wikipedia, interlinked and enhanced by using ontologies (Völkel, Krötzsch, Vrandecic, Haller, & Studer, 2006). In this scenario, the user can even enhance and alter the ontology in a collaborative setting.

For verbalizing knowledge with ontologies, those ontologies have to be at least fairly complex, otherwise, no reasonably interesting text can be produced (only short sentences such as "a cat is an animal" can be generated from less complex ontologies). Reasoning over more complex ontologies can also be useful to provide better natural language representation, since statements which are not explicitly contained in the ontology can

also be added to the text (Carr et al., 2001). Text generation may be performed both at design-time (in cases where a set of documents is compiled prior to using the system) as well as run-time (in cases where reports etc. are produced on demand) (Table 2). Although editing verbalized ontologies in collaborative settings is possible, most approaches only foresee viewing ontologies.

Adapation of User Interface Appearance: Apart from the information displayed in a user interface, the appearance of the parts of a user interface itself may also be directed by ontologies. Most commonly, the user interface is adapted to the user's needs. If both the user interface elements and the user's profile are defined by using highly formal ontologies, a reasoner can determine the appearance which fits the user's needs best and thus personalize the user interface.

One particularly interesting application is the adaptation of user interfaces for users with special needs, such as in the *Semantic Life* project (Karim & Tjoa, 2006) or the W3C's *WAI ARIA* initiative (W3C, 2009). Such adaptation includes adjusting font size, colours (for partly colour-blind people), and the organization of contents on the screen. In the Semantic Life project, the ontology models users' impairment and appropriate visualizations, i.e., it covers parts of the user as well as the system domain, so a reasoner can determine appropriate visualizations. In WAI ARIA, only the system parts are modeled in an ontolgy, and the selection of appropriate visualizations is left up to an agent (which is not specified any further). In both approaches, the underlying ontologies are evaluated at run-time for adapting the user interface, but they are not visible to the user.

Ontologies may not only be used for software adaptation, but also for *hardware adaptation*. One example is the *Context Studio* application developed by Nokia (Korpipää, Häkkilä, Kela, Ronkainen, & Känsälä, 2004). Here, the user may define rules how mobile devices are supposed to provide information to the user in given situations (e.g., "if the display is turned down, do not ring aloud"). To this end, an ontology of the mobile phone and context situations is defined, which can be utilized by the user to create rules on how they want their mobile devices to behave (and thus extend the underyling ontology). The ontology is presented to the user when defining rules in the form of selection lists (although graphical assistance in defining those rules would also be possible), but is invisible outside the rule definition mode. In the case of mobile phones, the user's context may additionally be acquired, e.g., from GPS sensors of the mobile device, thus allowing adaptation of mobile applications based on the user's spatial context (Lee, 2010).

Another approach for hardware adaptation is shown in the *MaDoE* project (Larsson, Ingmarsson, & Sun, 2007): here, user interfaces are distributed across different hardware devices. An ontology of devices and their capabilities is combined with a set of rules to make sure that each user interface component is displayed by a hardware component that has the required capabilities.

In the examples above, the rules for adapting user interfaces have been actively defined by the developer or the user, either at design or at run-time. Another approach is observing the user and learning those rules from the user's behavior during run-time, or off-line from log files. Such an approach is described by Schmidt, Dörflinger, Rahmani, Sahbi, and Thomas (2008). Here, learned rules, based on ontologies characterizing both the IT system and the real world domain, are used to optimize the information presentation in a portal. Information items that are more likely to be relevant for the user are given more prominent positions on the screen than others.

Another adaptation mechanism is the selection of visualization modules (software widgets, algorithms, or even hardware devices) that are suitable for a given information. This requires an ontology of those modules (i.e., the system domain software and/or hardware) in a degree of formality which allows reasoning to answer the queries for appropriate visualization modules. Such an approach is shown by (Potter & Wright, 2006), where input and output devices are selected at run time given the current information and visualization needs.

Ontologies for adapting user interfaces can be used both at design and at run time, depending on whether the user interfaces is supposed to adapt dynamically, or if pre-adapted user interfaces are to be shipped (Table 3). It may take place in the background, with the ontologies completely hidden from the user, or visibly. The user may also be granted the possibility to express their own rules for adaptation. Since the reasoning employed for

Table 3. Characterization of examined approaches to adapation of UI appearance

Ontology domain:	Real world, IT system and user
Ontology complexity:	High
Ontology visualization:	None, lists, or graphs
Interaction with the ontology:	View or extend
Ontology usage time:	Design and run time

adaptation is fairly complex, the ontologies also have to be highly expressive. Information about the real world, the IT system to adapt, and the user may be included for adaptation.

Using Ontologies for Improving the Interaction Possibilities

Besides visualizing data, the second important purpose of a user interface is to provide an access point to a system's functionalities. To this end, the user has to interact with the system by entering data, selecting items, issuing commands, etc. There are several approaches for employing ontologies to improve the interaction with IT systems.

Ontology-based Browsing: While we concentrated on information visualization as a run-once task so far (i.e., a given set of information items is visualized in an optimal form), the user usually interacts with these visualizations by browsing from one information item to another. Ontologies can be used to improve this browsing process. Hyvönen, Styrman, and Saarela (2002) use the term "semantic browsing"; however, we prefer the term "ontology-based browsing" since any kind of browsing information always requires a semantic understanding of that information (which, on the other hand, does not need to be formalized in an ontology).

One example of a semantic browser is *Ozone* (Burel, Cano, & Lanfranchi, 2009). Ozone uses RDF embedded in web pages to provide so-called "semantic overlays", i.e., textual and/or graphical information provided on demand when selecting an information item. For example, city names in texts annotated with concepts from an ontology defining their geographical position can be displayed on a map when selected.

Embedded RDF, however, is currently rather rare on the web. The browser *Magpie* (Dzbor, 2008) uses overlays like Ozone, but does not rely on embedded RDF. Instead, HTML pages are pre-processed, and the annotations are generated automatically. This is an approach also followed by *PiggyBank* (Huynh, Mazzocchi, & Karger, 2005): here, so-called "screen scrapers" automatically transform web page contents into RDF. This RDF can then be used to provide additional information on the web page's contents. Piggy Bank also allows the user to store and share the RDF information gathered from scraping the web.

Another popular approach for ontology-based browsing is *faceted browsing*. Here, data (such as product information, or websites) is annotated with ontologies. The user can then select from different lists of ontological categories and orthogonal property values to view filtered lists of relevant information (Heim, Ziegler, & Lohmann, 2008). While the basic faceted browsing approaches only use list-based views, there are some interesting extensions. The *SearchPoint* web search interface presents a graph of topics (which can be filled from an ontology) and their relations, and the user can click on any point in the graph to view the search results which belong to the topics which are displayed closest to the selected point (Pajntar & Grobelnik, 2008). The faceted browsing approach introduced by Hussein and Münter (2010) allows for defining arbitrary as well as domain-specific interaction elements (called "facet decorators") for different facet types, e.g., sliders for numeric values, maps for geographic values, etc.

Ontology-based browsing cannot be performed on the web alone. The *Semantic Desktop* (Sauermann, Bernardi, & Dengel, 2005; Cheyer, Park, & Giuli, 2005) allows for browsing data contained in different applications on a single desktop computer. For example, there may be papers from authors (stored as text files), some of the authors may also be email contacts (stored in an email client program), and their web pages are bookmarked in a standard web browser. Semantic Desktop software links this data and explicitly presents these links to the user, so that the user

Table 4. Characterization of examined ontology-based browsing approaches

Ontology domain:	Real world
Ontology complexity:	Informal, higher complexity possible
Ontology visualization:	None, lists, or graphs
Interaction with the ontology:	View only
Ontology usage time:	Run time

can navigate from one resource to another, even if they are stored in different programs.

When resources are annotated with ontologies, an ontology-based browser can point to relevant other resources (Table 4). Unlike finding related documents by measuring text similarities or access correlations, the user can also be informed about *how* the documents are related. Ontologies of low complexity (in the simplest case topic lists) about the documents' real world domain are sufficient for providing ontology-based browsing, but more sophisticated browsing functionality requires at least medium complexity. Visualization can range from invisible ontologies (in case related documents are proposed with help of the ontology, but without showing the ontology itself) to lists of concepts and more sophisticated graphical visualization.

User Input Assistance: In most kinds of interfaces, the user has to enter data into the system at a certain point, either in the form of textual input or by selecting values from predefined lists. In a form-based user interface, not every combination of input options is feasible. An ontology formalizing knowledge about the domain of the objects whose data is entered in a user interface may be employed to provide plausibility checking on the user's input.

It may be argued that plausibility checking is a functionality of the business logic, not of the user interface. Nevertheless, when being applied *during* the input process and not *afterwards*, plausibility

checking can help *reducing the complexity of input forms*. Thus, plausibility checking can improve the usability of a user interface.

An example is introduced by Liu, Chen, and He (2005). In a flower shop application, the customer has to step through an input wizard consisting of different forms. If a male person is selected as the recipient of a bouquet, then options such as "mother's day greeting card" are not included in subsequent selection lists. Here, an ontology reasoner can decide that a male person cannot be a mother and will therefore not receive a mother's day greeting card. Another example for a real world setting is e-government, where ontologies can be used to ease input in a large amount of forms, as shown in the *SeGoF* project (Stadlhofer & Salhofer, 2008). Another setting where filtering selection lists is useful are user interfaces for configuring complex products, as demonstrated in the *CAWICOMS* project (Ardissono et al., 2002).

Feasible input options can also be extracted from context information at run-time. In the semantic e-mail client *Semanta* (Scerri, Davis, Handschuh, & Hauswirth, 2009), for example, the content of an e-mail is extracted at run-time (e.g., it contains a meeting request), and possible answers (e.g., accept or decline the request) are determined by a reasoner and shown to the user in a selection list for automatically generating an answer mail. Here, the complex input task of writing an e-mail is simplified and reduced to selecting a template and filling the gaps.

In addition to supporting the user in selecting from pre-defined values, ontologies may also be employed *improving textual input*. In the case of searching for information, as shown, for example, in *OntoSeek*, the number of search results can be increased by not only searching for documents containing one term, but also for those containing a term related to the one the user entered, where those related terms are defined in an ontology (Guarino, Masolo, & Vetere, 1999).

Another way of improving textual input is the provision of *autocomplete functionality*, where the user types the beginning of a word, and the system proposes completion based on terms defined in an ontology (Hildebrand & Ossenbruggen, 2009). This ensures that the user only enters terms that the system understands and follows the idea of using ontologies as a shared vocabulary (Gruber, 1995). In this scenario, the ontology again contains domain knowledge, but it requires only little formalization, since no reasoning is applied, and it is invisible for the user.

In many ontology-based systems, large knowledge bases are created, e.g., in the field of life sciences (Mendes, McKnight, Sheth, & Kissinger, 2008). While querying those knowledge bases is very useful, it is a difficult task for the end user who is not familiar with querying languages such as SPARQL. Therefore, assistance in *query construction* is a desirable feature in those applications. This approach requires an ontology which models the real world domain the knowledge base is about, and its complexity can range from informal (when only single query terms are selected) to high (when complex queries are issued). In most cases, lists of concepts are shown to the user, although more sophisticated visual interfaces are possible (Spahn, Kleb, Grimm, & Scheidl, 2008).

In the simplest case, query construction can be done by selecting terms from a list. More sophisticated query construction interfaces let the user specify additional properties and relations of the selected concept. For example, the user selects the concept "employee" and then restricts the query by adding the relation "worksFor" and providing a value for the relation, thus querying for all users working for a given company, as shown in the projects *QuizRDF* (Davies, Weeks, & Krohn, 2004) and *TAMBIS* (Paton et al., 1999). A similar mechanism is used in the online news portal *PlanetOnto* (Domingue & Motta, 1999): here, the user may also store their queries and get notifications when there are new results. Other systems such as *SEWASIE* try to construct the first cut of the query from natural language input and allow further graphical refinement of that query (Catarci et al., 2004).

The ontologies are usually not visually presented to the user. As it is typically information from the real world domain (e.g., customer data) which is entered into a form, the ontology used for plausibility checking at run-time has to model that domain in a highly formal way to enable reasoners to decide whether an input combination is plausible (Table 5). While plausibility checking may also take place in the background without any visualization, ontologies are often presented in the form of lists (e.g., selection lists in forms) or graphs, as in the case of query construction support.

Table 5: Characterization of examined user input assistance approaches

Ontology domain:	Real world
Ontology complexity:	Informal, higher complexity possible
Ontology visualization:	None, lists, or graphs
Interaction with the ontology:	View only
Ontology usage time:	Run time

Providing Help: More general approaches of user assistance provide help for the user, especially in form of help texts, which can range from tool tips of a few words to large, interlinked help documents. Examples are projects such as *SACHS* and *CPoint* (Kohlhase & Kohlhase, 2009), where ontologies are used to generate user assistance. That process is called "Semantic Transparency" by the authors. User assistance *making the system transparent* can be created in the form automatically generated help documents, small tooltips displayed on demand (Paulheim, 2010), and graphical visualizations of how the system works.

Gribova (2007) presents an approach which accounts for the user's context. Besides the system and its real world domain, the ontologies have to model the user's possible tasks as well. By observing the user's activities and the system's state, the system determines the user's current task. Based on this information, context-sensitive help can be provided on demand, thus freeing the user from searching the relevant help text sections themselves (Table 6).

Approaches for providing help for the user employ ontologies characterizing both the system itself as well as parts of its real world domain and present them to the user in verbalized form. As discussed above for text generation, the provision of useful help texts requires at least a medium level of formality and can be done at design-time or at run-time.

User Interface Integration: When performing a complex task, the user often does not only use one application, but several ones in parallel. This generates additional workload for the user for coordinating work with the different applications, such as finding related information stored in different applications, or copying and pasting data from one application to another.

To provide *unified views on data* stored in different applications, portals or mash-ups displaying different applications as *portlets* or *mashlets* at the same time can be used. A few projects exist in which ontologies are used in building web portals. The approach described by Dettborn, König-Ries, and Welsch (2008) uses semantic web services to retrieve related data in different applications unified in one portal. Thus, applications can display data which is relevant according to the data displayed in other portlets. A similar approach for mashup development is shown by Ankolekar, Krötzsch, Tran, and Vrandecic (2007).

Integrated user interfaces can ease those tasks by *facilitating cross-application interactions*, i.e., interactions that span more than one application, such as highlighting related data in different applications or dragging objects from on application to the other. Thus, the integrated applications are extended with new interaction possibilities. Existing solutions for integration on the user interface layer, however, suffer from significant shortcomings when trying to implement such interactions (Daniel et al., 2007).

Table 6: Characterization of examined approaches to providing help

Ontology domain:	Real world, IT system, and user
Ontology complexity:	Medium or higher
Ontology visualization:	Verbalized or graphical
Interaction with the ontology:	View only
Ontology usage time:	Design or run time

While ontologies have been used to integrate applications on the database and business logic layer (Doan & Halevy, 2005; Martin et al., 2004; Lausen et al., 2005), using ontologies for user interface integration is a new and widely unexplored field. Daz, Iturrioz, and Irastorza (2005) discuss an approach which allows pre-filling form fields in different applications based on data from other applications. The input and output data are annotated by using ontologies defining the real world domain, and based on those annotations, data pipes between the different forms are defined. A more flexible approach facilitating integration at run time is shown by Paulheim (2009). Here, not only the real world data, but also the systems to be integrated are defined in ontologies. A reasoner can be used at run-time to determine the possible cross-application interactions and facilitating event exchange between the applications. In this approach, the ontology itself is not visible for the user, but used as an underlying mechanism to enhance the user interface's functionality.

In all of those approaches, the ontologies are evaluated at run-time for coordinating the behavior of integrated user interfaces. The ontology is not visible to the user, in fact, the user may not even know that the integration is based on ontologies (Table 7). Both the technical components as well as the real world information they process have to be formally characterized in an ontology to automate the coordination of user interface components.

Using Ontologies for Improving the Development of User Interfaces

Ontologies can be used at different stages in the software development process; starting from requirements engineering and ending up with maintenance (Hesse, 2005; Calero, Ruiz, & Piattini, 2006). This also holds for user interface development. Whereas in most of the approaches shown above, the ontologies are used at the system's run time for supporting the user, the following approaches most often employ ontologies at a system's design time, and the end user of the system does not see the ontologies, nor interact with them.

Identifying and Tracking Requirements: The task of *identifying the requirements* of a software system includes modelling the real world domain to a certain level. In the case of a form-based user interface, for example, it is necessary to define the real-world concepts for which data is entered, the ranges of their relations, etc. The approach described by Furtado et al. (2002) how such ontological models can be used in user interface development. Such an approach helps decoupling domain knowledge and user interface code and allows reuse of the domain ontology when developing different user interfaces for related applications in the same domain.

After a user interface has been developed from the requirements originally identified, those requirements may change, e.g., due to adaptation of business processes. In that case, parts of the

Table 7. Characterization of examined user interface integration approaches

Ontology complexity:	Informal, higher complexity possible
Ontology visualization:	None
Interaction with the ontology:	None
Ontology usage time:	Run time

system, including the user interface, have to be rewritten, and it is not always trivial to *track the requirements* and identify those parts. The approach presented by Sousa (2009) uses ontologies for modelling both business processes and the user interfaces. Based on these ontologies, rules describing the dependencies between elements in the user interfaces and in the business processes can be defined. In case of business process changes, those rules are used to find the spots where the user interfaces need to be adapted.

Adaptations of a user interface may not only be triggered by changes in business processes, but also by changes in technical requirements, e.g., support of additional platforms. Such *system migrations* require decisions on which components and widgets of a platform to use for a given component. Modelling the system as well as the target platforms in formal ontologies can help assisting developers with those decisions (Moore, Rugaber, & Seaver, 1994) and thus improve the migration process.

In all the cases discussed, reasoning is employed to assist the developer, therefore, formal ontologies are required. To model requirements, both the real world and the IT system have to be taken into account (Table 8).

Generating User Interfaces: An area which has been increasingly gaining attention is the automatic generation of user interfaces from ontologies. This can be seen as a special case of model driven architectures (MDA), where software is generated from models (not necessarily ontological models).

Similar to the problem of system migration described above, platform independent models in MDAs can also be used in conjunction with rules defining the mappings of UI components to specific widgets and components on different target platforms (Calvary et al., 2003). Similarly, combining the system ontology with ontologies of users and user preferences, personalized versions of user interfaces can be created, like shown in the *OntoWeaver* project (Lei, Motta, & Domingue, 2003).

For being able to automatically derive a software system from an ontology, this ontology has to model the system as well as parts of its the real-world domain (Table 9). Although reasoning is not necessary, the ontology has to be complex enough to model the system on a reasonable level of detail (Liu et al., 2005; Sergevich & Viktorovna, 2003).

Reusing User Interface Components: The development of a system's user interfaces consumes about 50% of the overall development efforts (Myers & Rosson, 1992). Thus, reusing existing user interface components is especially desirable.

Reusing software components requires *finding suitable components* as a first step. Similar to defining and retrieving web services in the field of semantic web services, those components are annotated with ontologies describing their

Table 8. Characterization of examined approaches to identifying and tracking requirements

Ontology domain:	Real world and IT system
Ontology complexity:	High
Ontology visualization:	None
Interaction with the ontology:	None
Ontology usage time:	Design time

Table 9. Characterization of examined UI generation approaches

Ontology domain:	Real world and IT system
Ontology complexity:	Medium or higher
Ontology visualization:	None
Interaction with the ontology:	None
Ontology usage time:	Design time

functional and non-functional properties. Base on these annotations, developers can find components suitable for their specific problems based on more precise queries then text-based search. One example for a component repository (not specifically UI components) implementing these ideas is *KOntoR* (Happel, Korthaus, Seedorf, & Tomczyk, 2006).

Once user interface components have been retrieved, they have to be integrated into one coherent user interface. This requires communication between those components and a language for composing those components (Daniel et al., 2007). Ontologies can serve these purposes by modelling the components as well as the operations that can be performed with them and the data objects they use. Based on these ontologies, integration rules can be defined, which, when interpreted at run-time by a reasoner, implement an integrated user interface. Such rules may either be triggered by events (Paulheim, 2009), or evaluated when assembling a user interface at run-time, e.g., a complex web page built from different components (Pohjalainen, 2010).

User interface components are not restricted to software components. Besides standard input and output components (keyboard, mouse, screen), more specialized and advanced devices have recently been developed. From a more general point of view, selecting suitable components for developing a user interface therefore also includes choosing the right hardware devices. There are ontologies which can be used to define hardware devices, such as the *GLOSS ontology* (Coutaz, Lachenal, & Dupuy-Chessa, 2003) and

the *FIPA device ontology* (Intelligent Phyiscal Agents, 2002). With the help of those ontologies, the process of *selecting suitable hardware devices* can be supported efficiently as a larger number of highly specialized devices becomes available.

Similarly to components, design practices and patterns can also be stored in annotated databases and retrieved by developers. Ontology-based pattern languages have been proposed to formalize those patterns (Gaffar, Javahery, Seffah, & Sinnig, 2003). With the help of such ontologies, developers can query a knowledge base of patterns in order to find patterns suitable for their problems and find additional information such as related patterns, patterns that can be combined, etc. (Henninger, Keshk, & Kinworthy, 2003).

To provide a model of a user interface component, both the component itself as well as the real world information it processes has to be modeled in the ontology. For finding components in a repository, a hierarchy of concepts is sufficient, although more complex ontologies can be employed to specify more concise queries and retrieve more accurate results (Table 10).

Summary of Survey Results

Table 11 summarizes the approaches discussed and their characterization in our classification scheme. In the following section, we will discuss some of the findings from this survey in more detail.

Table 10. Characterization of examined approaches to reusing UI components

Ontology domain:	Real world and IT system
Ontology complexity:	Low or higher
Ontology visualization:	None
Interaction with the ontology:	None
Ontology usage time:	Design time

Table 11. Summary of approaches. Legend: Ontology Domain (W=Real World, S=IT System, U=Users & Roles), Ontology Formality (I=Informal, L=Low, M=Medium, H=High, + indicates a minimum level of formality required), Ontology Visualization (N=None, L=Lists, G=Graphical, V=Verbalized), Interaction with the ontology (N=None, V=View only, E=Edit), Usage Time (D=Design Time, R=Run Time

Purpose	Approach	Domain	Complexity	Visualization	Interaction	Usage Time
33cmImproving Visualization Capabilities	Information Clustering	W	L+	L,G	V	R
	Text Generation	W	M+	V	V,E	D,R
	Adaptation of UI Appearance	W,S,U	H	N,L,G	V,E	D,R
43cmImproving Interaction Possibilities	Ontology-based Browsing	W	I+	N,L,G	V	R
	Input Assistance	W	I+	N,L,G	N,V	R
	Providing Help	W,S,U	M+	V,G	V	R
	UI Integration	W,S	L+	N	N	D,R
33cmImproving Development	Identifying & Tracking Requirements	W,S	H	N	N	D
	Generating UIs	W,S	M+	N	N	D
	Reusing UI Components	W,S	L+	N	N	D

DISCUSSION AND CONCLUSION

With this article, we have given a definition for ontology-enhanced user interfaces and presented a characterization schema for such interfaces and the requirements for their implementation. Those criteria encompass the ontology's domain and formality, the type of visualization of the ontology, the possibility of interaction with the ontology, and the time at which the ontology is employed.

We have given a survey of approaches how ontologies can be used to improve the usability, appearance and development of user interfaces. The variety of approaches shows that ontology-enhanced user interfaces are a vivid, promising research area. Regarding the placement of the approaches in our classification, some interesting gaps can be identified:

Alterable Ontologies

Most approaches use static ontologies; approaches where ontologies can be altered or at least extended by the user are rather rare. This finding is also supported by the analysis in Heitmann et al. (2009), which states that authoring interfaces are the least common feature in semantic web applications. The reasons may be two-fold – the developers either see no useful scenario for modifiable ontologies; or they consider the users not to have the necessary experience to edit ontologies. The latter may also be a hint at the need for more intuitive user interfaces for editing and manipulating ontologies, as pointed out by Garcì a-Barriocanal, Sicilia, and Sánchez-Alonso (2005).

Advanced Visualization

Among those approaches that visualize ontologies, lists are by far the most often used form of visualization. Visualization as source code is only rarely used for providing expert users' interfaces; this is probably due to the fact that in most cases, non-expert (w.r.t. knowledge about ontologies) users are addressed. Although advanced forms of visualization could be applied in many of the approaches discussed in this article, they are used in a relatively small number of actual projects, despite the large variety of techniques available in that field (Katifori et al., 2007). This finding, which is supported by the analysis done by Heitmann et al. (2009), is surprising, because graphical visualizations are considered helpful for the user, and in many of the approaches analysed in this article, the complexity of the ontologies was large enough (more than taxonomies), so that a graphical visualization would have indeed been beneficial. One reason for the small number of approaches using such visualizations could be the developing efforts (compared to, e.g., implementing a list visualization). However, with a growing number of graphical visualization solutions which can be used off-the-shelf, this aspect should gain more attention in the future.

Highly Formal Ontologies

Regarding ontology formality, many approaches discussed do not use more than a class hierarchy; some also work with a collection of categories without any relations. This means that in these cases, the full power of using ontologies – providing an expressive description of a domain and

being able to use reasoning – is often not utilized in user interfaces. It is possible that a larger number of approaches using highly formal ontologies will emerge in the near future, allowing for more sophisticated applications of ontologies in user interfaces. On the other hand, recent development in the linked open data community shows many applications based on ontologies which are not too rigid and formal (Hausenblas, 2009). Therefore, it is still an open question whether more applications based on rather formal ontologies will emerge, or whether "a little semantics will go a long way" (Hendler, 2003).

Further Findings

There are two more remarkable findings. First, many approaches deal with ontologies encompassing more than one domain. Especially the IT system domain and the real world domain are often modeled in ontologies within the same approach. For creating long-living, reusable ontologies, it is important to separate those concerns and model each ontology in a domain of its own (Klien & Probst, 2005). Thus, modular ontologies (Stuckenschmidt, Parent, & Spaccapietra, 2009) are essentially important in ontology-enabled user interfaces.

Second, many of the approaches discussed use ontologies at run-time, often involving reasoning. Since for user interfaces, reaction times are essential to assure good usability, performance marks of reasoners and ontology programming frameworks are important in the area of ontology-enabled user interfaces. Thus, carefully designing software architectures is essential to create software which is accepted by the end user (Paulheim, 2010).

Summary

The characterization schema presented in this article serves two main purposes: first, it helps in designing new solutions by pointing out the relevant requirements to be met by the designer. Second, it allows a clear analysis of the approaches that exist and identifies interesting research directions and promising application areas. There are clear research gaps in using alterable ontologies, advanced visualizations, and exploiting the possibilities of highly formal ontologies in user interfaces. Due to those potentials and the growing impact of ontologies in software development, we are confident that the employment of ontologies in user interfaces will add interesting features and possibilities to future software.

ACKNOWLEDGMENT

The work presented in this article has been partly funded by the German Federal Ministry of Education and Research under grant no. 01ISO7009.

REFERENCES

W3C. (2009). *WAI-ARIA Overview.* Retrieved from http://www.w3.org/WAI/intro/aria

Ankolekar, A., Krötzsch, M., Tran, T., & Vrandecic, D. (2007). The Two Cultures: Mashing Up Web 2.0 and the Semantic Web. In C. L. Williamson, M. E. Zurko, P. F. Patel-Schneider, & P. J. Shenoy (Eds.), *Proceedings of WWW* (pp. 825-834). New York: ACM.

Antoniou, G., Franconia, E., & van Harmelen, F. (2005). Introduction to Semantic Web Ontology Languages. In Eisinger, N., & Maluszynski, J. (Eds.), *Reasoning Web* (*Vol. 3564*, pp. 1–21). New York: Springer.

Ardissono, L., Felfernig, A., Friedrich, G., Jannach, D., Zanker, M., & Schäfer, R. (2002). A Framework for Rapid Development of Advanced Web-based Configurator Applications. In F. van Harmelen (Ed.), *Proceedings of the 15th Eureopean Conference on Artificial Intelligence (ECAI'2002)*, Lyon, France (pp. 618-622). Amsterdam: IOS Press.

Bontcheva, K., & Wilks, Y. (2004). Automatic Report Generation from Ontologies: The MIAKT Approach. In *Proceedings of the 9th International Conference on Applications of Natural Language to Information Systems* (pp. 324-335).

Burel, G., Cano, A. E., & Lanfranchi, V. (2009). Ozone Browser: Augmenting the Web with Semantic Overlays. In C. Bizer, S. Auer, & G. A. Grimnes (Eds.), *Proceedings of the 5th Workshop on Scripting and Development for the Semantic Web.*

Calero, C., Ruiz, F., & Piattini, M. (Eds.). (2006). *Ontologies for Software Engineering and Software Technology.* New York: Springer. doi:10.1007/3-540-34518-3

Calvary, G., Coutaz, J., Thevenin, D., Limbourg, Q., Bouillon, L., & Vanderdonckt, J. (2003). A Unifying Reference Framework for multi-target user interfaces. *Interacting with Computers, 15*(3), 289–308. doi:10.1016/S0953-5438(03)00010-9

Carr, L., Hall, W., Bechhofer, S., & Goble, C. (2001). Conceptual linking: ontology-based open hypermedia. In *Proceedings of the 10th international conference on World Wide Web* (pp. 334-342). New York: ACM.

Catarci, T., Dongilli, P., Mascio, T. D., Franconi, E., Santucci, G., & Tessaris, S. (2004). An Ontology Based Visual Tool for Query Formulation Support. In R. L. de Mántaras & L. Saitta (Eds.), *Proceedings of ECAI* (pp. 308-312). Amsterdam: IOS Press.

Cheyer, A., Park, J., & Giuli, R. (2005). IRIS: Integrate. Relate. Infer. Share. In *Proceedings of the Workshop on the Semantic Desktop: Next Generation Personal Information Management and Collaboration Infrastructure.*

Coutaz, J., Lachenal, C., & Dupuy-Chessa, S. (2003). Ontology for Multi-surface Interaction. In *Proceedings of IFIP INTERACT03: Human-Computer Interaction* (pp. 447-454).

Daniel, F., Yu, J., Benatallah, B., Casati, F., Matera, M., & Saint-Paul, R. (2007). Understanding UI Integration: A Survey of Problems, Technologies, and Opportunities. *IEEE Internet Computing, 11*(3), 59–66. doi:10.1109/MIC.2007.74

Davies, J., Weeks, R., & Krohn, U. (2004). QuizRDF: Search Technology for the Semantic Web. In *Proceedings of the Hawaii International Conference on System Sciences, 4,* 40112.

Dettborn, T., König-Ries, B., & Welsch, M. (2008). Using Semantics in Portal Development. In *Proceedings of the 4th International Workshop on Semantic Web Enabled Software Engineering.*

Dìaz, O., Iturrioz, J., & Irastorza, A. (2005). Improving portlet interoperability through deep annotation. In *Proceedings of the 14th international conference on World Wide Web (WWW '05)* (pp. 372-381). New York: ACM.

Dix, A., Hussein, T., Lukosch, S., & Ziegler, J. (Eds.). (2010). In *Proceedings of the First Workshop on Semantic Models for Adaptive Interactive Systems (SEMAIS).*

Doan, A., & Halevy, A. Y. (2005). Semantic Integration Research in the Database Community: A Brief Survey. *AI Magazine, 26*(1), 83–94.

Domingue, J., & Motta, E. (1999). A Knowledge-Based News Server Supporting Ontology-Driven Story Enrichment and Knowledge Retrieval. In *Proceedings of the 11th European Workshop on Knowledge Acquisition, Modeling and Management (EKAW '99)* (pp. 103-120). London: Springer-Verlag.

Dzbor, M. (2008). Best of Both: Using Semantic Web Technologies to Enrich User Interaction with the Web and Vice Versa. In V. Geffert, J. Karhumäki, A. Bertoni, B. Preneel, P. Návrat, & M. Bieliková (Eds.), *Proceedings of Theory and Practice of Computer Science, 34th Conference on Current Trends in Theory and Practice of Computer Science (SOFSEM 2008),* Nový Smokovec, Slovakia (Vol. 4910, pp. 34-49). New York: Springer.

Fluit, C., Sabou, M., & Harmelen, F. V. (2003). Supporting User Tasks through Visualisation of Light-weight Ontologies. In *Handbook on Ontologies in Information Systems* (pp. 415–434). New York: Springer.

Furtado, E., Furtado, J. J. V., Silva, W. B., Rodrigues, D. W. T., da Silva Taddeo, L., & Limbourg, Q. (2002). An Ontology-Based Method for Universal Design of User Interfaces. In *Proceedings of Task Models and Diagrams For User Interface Design.* TAMODIA.

Gaffar, A., Javahery, H., Seffah, A., & Sinnig, D. (2003). A Pattern Framework for Eliciting and Delivering UCD Knowledge and Practices. In *Proceedings of the Tenth International Conference on Human-Computer Interaction* (pp. 108-112). Mahwah, NJ: Lawrence Erlbaum Associates.

García-Barriocanal, E., Sicilia, M. A., & Sánchez-Alonso, S. (2005). Usability evaluation of ontology editors. *Knowledge Organization, 32*(1), 1–9.

Gómez-Pérez, A., Fernández-López, M., & Corcho, O. (2004). *Ontological Engineering.* New York: Springer.

Gribova, V. (2007). Automatic Generation of Context-Sensitive Help Using a User Interface Project. In V. P. Gladun, K. K. Markov, A. F. Voloshin, & K. M. Ivanova (Eds.), *Proceedings of the 8th International Conference "Knowledge-Dialogue-Solution"* (Vol. 2).

Gruber, T. R. (1995). *Toward Principles for the Design of Ontologies Used for Knowledge Sharing* (*Vol. 43,* pp. 907–928). New York: Academic Press.

Gruninger, M., & Lee, J. (2002). Ontology Applications and Design. *Communications of the ACM, 45*(2), 39–41.

Guarino, N. (1998). *Formal Ontology and Information Systems.* Amsterdam: IOS Press.

Guarino, N., Masolo, C., & Vetere, G. (1999). OntoSeek: Content-Based Access to the Web. *IEEE Intelligent Systems, 14*(3), 70–80. doi:10.1109/5254.769887

Happel, H. J., Korthaus, A., Seedorf, S., & Tomczyk, P. (2006). KOntoR: An Ontology-enabled Approach to Software Reuse. In K. Zhang, G. Spanoudakis, & G. Visaggio (Eds.), *Proceedings of the Eighteenth International Conference on Software Engineering & Knowledge Engineering (SEKE)* (pp. 349-354).

Happel, H. J., & Seedorf, S. (2006, November 5-9). Applications of Ontologies in Software Engineering. In *Proceedings of the Workshop on Semantic Web Enabled Software Engineering (SWESE) on the 5th International Semantic Web Conference (ISWC 2006),* Athens, Georgia.

Hausenblas, M. (2009). Exploiting Linked Data to Build Web Applications. *IEEE Internet Computing, 13*, 68–73. doi:10.1109/MIC.2009.79

Heim, P., Ziegler, J., & Lohmann, S. (2008). gFacet: A Browser for the Web of Data. In S. Auer, S. Dietzold, S. Lohmann, & J. Ziegler (Eds.), *Proceedings of the International Workshop on Interacting with Multimedia Content in the Social Semantic Web (IMC-SSW'08)* (Vol. 417, pp. 49-58).

Heitmann, B., Kinsella, S., Hayes, C., & Decker, S. (2009). *Implementing Semantic Web Applications: Reference Architecture and Challenges* (Kendall, E. F., Pan, J. Z., Sabbouh, M., Stojanovic, L., & Zhao, Y., Eds.). *Vol. 524*).

Hendler, J. (2003). *On Beyond Ontology.* Retrieved from http://iswc2003.semanticweb.org/hendler_files/v3_document.htm

Henninger, S., Keshk, M., & Kinworthy, R. (2003). Capturing and Disseminating Usability Patterns with Semantic Web Technology. In *Proceedings of the CHI 2003 Workshop: Concepts and Perspectives on HCI Patterns.*

Herman, I., Melançon, G., & Marshall, M. S. (2000). Graph Visualization and Navigation in Information Visualization: A Survey. *IEEE Transactions on Visualization and Computer Graphics, 6*(1), 24–43. doi:10.1109/2945.841119

Hesse, W. (2005). Ontologies in the Software Engineering Process. In R. Lenz, U. Hasenkamp, W. Hasselbring, & M. Reichert (Eds.), *Proceedings of the 2nd GI-Workshop on Enterprise Application Integration (EAI)* (Vol. 141). CEUR-WS.org.

Hildebrand, M., & van Ossenbruggen, J. (2009, February). Configuring Semantic Web Interfaces by Data Mapping. In *Proceedings of the Workshop on Visual Interfaces to the Social and the Semantic Web (VISSW2009).*

Hussein, T., & Münter, D. (2010). Automated Generation of Faceted Navigation Interfaces Using Semantic Models. In A. Dix, T. Hussein, S. Lukosch, & J. Ziegler (Eds.), *Proceedings of the First Workshop on Semantic Models for Adaptive Interactive Systems (SEMAIS).*

Huynh, D., Mazzocchi, S., & Karger, D. R. (2005). Piggy Bank: Experience the Semantic Web Inside Your Web Browser. In Y. Gil, E. Motta, V. R. Benjamins, & M. A. Musen (Eds.), *International Semantic Web Conference* (Vol. 3729, pp. 413-430). New York: Springer.

Hyvönen, E., Styrman, A., & Saarela, S. (2002). Ontology-Based Image Retrieval. In E. Hyvönen & M. Klemettinen (Eds.), *Towards the semantic Web and Web services, Proceedings of the XML Finland 2002 Conference.* Helsinki, Finland: HIIT Publications.

Intelligent Phyiscal Agents, F. (2002). *FIPA Device Ontology Specification.* Retrieved from http://www.fipa.org/specs/ fipa00091/index.html

Kagal, L., Finin, T., & Joshi, A. (2003). A policy language for a pervasive computing environment. In *Proceedings of the IEEE 4th International Workshop on Policies for Distributed Systems and Networks (POLICY 2003).*

Kaljurand, K., & Fuchs, N. E. (2007). Verbalizing OWL in Attempto Controlled English. In C. Golbreich, A. Kalyanpur, & B. Parsia (Eds.), *Proceedings of the OWLED 2007 Workshop on OWL: Experiences and Directions,* Innsbruck, Austria (Vol. 258). CEUR-WS.org.

Karim, S., & Tjoa, A. M. (2006). Towards the Use of Ontologies for Improving User Interaction for People with Special Needs. In Miesenberger, K., Klaus, J., Zagler, W. L., & Karshmer, A. I. (Eds.), *ICCHP* (*Vol. 4061*, pp. 77–84). New York: Springer.

Katifori, A., Halatsis, C., Lepouras, G., Vassilakis, C., & Giannopoulou, E. G. (2007). Ontology visualization methods - a survey. *ACM Computing Surveys, 39*(4). doi:10.1145/1287620.1287621

Klien, E., & Probst, F. (2005). Requirements for Geospatial Ontology Engineering. In F. Toppen & M. Painho (Eds.), *Proceedings of the 8th Conference on Geographic Information Science (AGILE 2005)*, Estoril, Portugal.

Kohlhase, A., & Kohlhase, M. (2009). Semantic Transparency in User Assistance Systems. In *Proceedings of the 27th annual ACM international conference on Design of Communication. Special Interest Group on Design of Communication (SIGDOC-09)*, Bloomingtion, IN. New York: ACM Press.

Korpipää, P., Häkkilä, J., Kela, J., Ronkainen, S., & Känsälä, I. (2004). Utilising context ontology in mobile device application personalisation. In *Proceedings of the 3rd international conference on Mobile and ubiquitous multimedia (MUM '04)* (pp. 133-140). New York: ACM.

Larsson, A., Ingmarsson, M., & Sun, B. (2007). A Development Platform for Distributed User Interfaces. In *Proceedings of the Nineteenth International Conference on Software Engineering & Knowledge Engineering (SEKE '2007)*, Boston (pp. 704-709).

Lausen, H., Polleres, A., Roman, D., de Bruijn, J., Bussler, C., & Domingue, J. (2005). In *Proceedings of the Web Service Modeling Ontology (WSMO)*. Retrieved from http://www.w3.org/Submission/WSMO/

Lee, A. (2010). Exploiting Context for Mobile User Experience. In A. Dix, T. Hussein, S. Lukosch, & J. Ziegler (Eds.), *Proceedings of the First Workshop on Semantic Models for Adaptive Interactive Systems (SEMAIS)*.

Lei, Y., Motta, E., & Domingue, J. (2003). Design of customized web applications with OntoWeaver. In *Proceedings of the 2nd international conference on Knowledge capture (K-CAP '03)* (pp. 54-61). New York: ACM.

Liu, B., Chen, H., & He, W. (2005). Deriving User Interface from Ontologies: A Model-Based Approach. In *Proceedings of the 17th IEEE International Conference on Tools with Artificial Intelligence (ICTAI '05)* (pp. 254-259). Washington, DC: IEEE Computer Society.

Martin, D., Burstein, M., Hobbs, J., Lassila, O., McDermott, D., & McIlraith, S. (2004, November). *OWL-S: Semantic Markup for Web Services*. Retrieved from http://www.w3.org/Submission/OWL-S/

Masolo, C., Borgo, S., Gangemi, A., Guarino, N., & Oltramari, A. (2003). *WonderWeb Deliverable D18 – Ontology Library (final)* (Tech. Rep.). Laboratory For Applied Ontology, Trento, Italien. http://wonderweb.semanticweb.org/deliverables/documents/D18.pdf

Mendes, P. N., McKnight, B., Sheth, A. P., & Kissinger, J. C. (2008). TcruziKB: Enabling Complex Queries for Genomic Data Exploration. In *Proceedings of the 2008 IEEE International Conference on Semantic Computing (ICSC '08)* (pp. 432-439). Washington, DC: IEEE Computer Society.

Moore, M. M., Rugaber, S., & Seaver, P. (1994). Knowledge-Based User Interface Migration. In *Proceedings of the International Conference on Software Maintenance* (pp. 72-79). Washington, DC: IEEE Computer Society.

Myers, B. A., & Rosson, M. B. (1992). Survey on user interface programming. In *Proceedings of the SIGCHI conference on Human factors in computing systems (CHI '92)* (pp. 195-202). New York: ACM.

Pajntar, B., & Grobelnik, M. (2008). SearchPoint - a New Paradigm of Web Search. In *Proceedings of the WWW 2008 Developers Track.*

Paton, N. W., Stevens, R., Baker, P., Goble, C. A., Bechhofer, S., & Brass, A. (1999). Query processing in the TAMBIS bioinformatics source integration system. In *Proceedings of the Eleventh International Conference on Scientific and Statistical Database Management* (pp. 138-147).

Paulheim, H. (2009). Ontologies for User Interface Integration. In Bernstein, A., (Eds.), *The Semantic Web - ISWC 2009* (*Vol. 5823*, pp. 973–981). New York: Springer. doi:10.1007/978-3-642-04930-9_63

Paulheim, H. (2010). In Aroyo, L., (Eds.), *Efficient Semantic Event Processing: Lessons Learned in User Interface Integration* (*Vol. 6089*, pp. 60–74). New York: Springer.

Pohjalainen, P. (2010). Self-configuring User Interface Components. In A. Dix, T. Hussein, S. Lukosch, & J. Ziegler (Eds.), *Proceedings of the First Workshop on Semantic Models for Adaptive Interactive Systems (SEMAIS).*

Potter, R., & Wright, H. (2006). An Ontological Approach to Visualization Resource Management. In Doherty, G. J., & Blandford, A. (Eds.), *Interactive Systems. Design, Specification, and Verification, 13th International Workshop, DSVIS 2006, Dublin, Ireland* (*Vol. 4323*, pp. 151–156). New York: Springer.

Rebstock, M., Fengel, J., & Paulheim, H. (2008). *Ontologies-based Business Integration*. New York: Springer.

Ruiz, F., & Hilera, J. R. (2006). In Calero, C., Ruiz, F., & Piattini, M. (Eds.), *Using Ontologies in Software Engineering and Technology* (pp. 49–102). New York: Springer. doi:10.1007/3-540-34518-3_2

Sauermann, L., Bernardi, A., & Dengel, A. (2005). Overview and Outlook on the Semantic Desktop. In S. Decker, J. Park, D. Quan, & L. Sauermann (Eds.), *Proceedings of the 1st Workshop on The Semantic Desktop at the ISWC 2005 Conference.*

Scerri, S., Davis, B., Handschuh, S., & Hauswirth, M. (2009). In Aroyo, L., (Eds.), *Semanta - Semantic Email Made Easy* (*Vol. 5554*, pp. 36–50). New York: Springer.

Schmidt, K. U., Dörflinger, J., Rahmani, T., Sahbi, M., & Thomas, L. S. S. M. (2008). An User Interface Adaptation Architecture for Rich Internet Applications. In S. Bechhofer, M. Hauswirth, J. Hoffmann, & M. Koubarakis (Eds.), In *Proceedings of the Semantic Web: Research and Applications, the 5th European Semantic Web Conference (ESWC 2008)* (pp. 736-750).

Seeling, C., & Becks, A. (2003, July). Exploiting metadata for ontology-based visual exploration of weakly structured text documents. In *Proceedings of the Seventh International Conference on Information Visualization* (pp. 652-657).

Sergevich, K. A., & Viktorovna, G. V. (2003). From an Ontology-Oriented Approach Conception to User Interface Development. *International Journal of Information Theories and Applications, 10*(1), 89–98.

Smith, B., & Welty, C. (2001). FOIS introduction: Ontology—towards a new synthesis. In *Proceedings of the international conference on Formal Ontology in Information Systems (FOIS '01)* (pp. 3-9). New York: ACM.

Sousa, K. (2009). Model-Driven Approach for User Interface - Business Alignment. In *Proceedings of the 1st ACM SIGCHI Symposium on Engineering Interactive Computing Systems (EICS'2009)* (pp. 325-328). New York: ACM Press.

Spahn, M., Kleb, J., Grimm, S., & Scheidl, S. (2008). Supporting business intelligence by providing ontology-based end-user information self-service. In *Proceedings of the first international workshop on Ontology-supported business intelligence (OBI '08)* (pp. 1-12). New York: ACM.

Stadlhofer, B., & Salhofer, P. (2008). SeGoF: semantic e-government forms. In *Proceedings of the 2008 international conference on Digital government research* (pp. 427-428). Digital Government Society of North America.

Stuckenschmidt, H., Parent, C., & Spaccapietra, S. (Eds.). (2009). *Modular Ontologies - Concepts, Theories and Techniques for Knowledge Modularization*. New York: Springer.

Tane, J., Schmitz, C., & Stumme, G. (2004). Semantic resource management for the web: an e-learning application. In *Proceedings of the 13th international World Wide Web conference on Alternate track papers & posters (WWW Alt. '04)* (pp. 1-10). New York: ACM.

Uschold, M., & Gruninger, M. (2004). Ontologies and semantics for seamless connectivity. *SIGMOD Record, 33*(4), 58–64. doi:10.1145/1041410.1041420

Uschold, M., & Jasper, R. (1999). A framework for understanding and classifying ontology applications. In *Proceedings of the IJCAI99 Workshop on Ontologies* (pp. 16-21).

van Heijst, G., Schreiber, A. T. G., & Wielinga, B. J. (1997). Using explicit ontologies in KBS development. *International Journal of Human-Computer Studies, 46*(2-3), 183–292. doi:10.1006/ijhc.1996.0090

Visser, U., & Schuster, G. (2002). Finding and Integration of Information - A Practical Solution for the SemanticWeb. In J. Euzénat, A. Gómez-Pérez, N. Guarino, & H. Stuckenschmidt (Eds.), *Proceedings of the ECAI-02 Workshop on Ontologies and Semantic Interoperability.*

Völkel, M., Krötzsch, M., Vrandecic, D., Haller, H., & Studer, R. (2006). Semantic Wikipedia. In *Proceedings of the 15th international conference on World Wide Web(WWW '06)* (pp. 585-594). New York: ACM.

This work was previously published in International Journal of Semantic Web and Information Systems, Volume 6, Issue 2, edited by Amit P. Sheth, pp. 36-59, copyright 2010 by IGI Publishing (an imprint of IGI Global).

Chapter 11
Integrating Interactive TV Services and the Web through Semantics

Vassileios Tsetsos
University of Athens, Greece

Antonis Papadimitriou
University of Athens, Greece

Christos Anagnostopoulos
University of Athens, Greece

Stathes Hadjiefthymiades
University of Athens, Greece

ABSTRACT

Interactive TV has started to penetrate broadcasting markets, providing a new user experience through novel services to subscribers and new revenue opportunities for companies. Personalization and intelligent behavior, such as proactive content delivery are considered key features for the services of the future TV. However, most of the work in this area is limited to personalization of electronic program guides and advanced program recommendation. In this article, the authors adopt a more horizontal approach and describe the application of concepts, practices and modern Web trends to the TV domain in the context of the POLYSEMA platform. A key characteristic of this approach is the formal modeling of multimedia and user semantics that enables novel TV services. Specifically, Semantic Web methodologies are employed (e.g., ontologies and rules) while compatibility with the MPEG-7 standard is also pursued. The paper describes the overall architecture of the platform, provides implementation details and investigates business issues.

DOI: 10.4018/978-1-4666-0185-7.ch011

INTRODUCTION

During the last two decades, we witnessed many radical changes in the computing paradigms and environments. The recent advances in many areas of Information Technology (IT) seem to converge to a new global computing infrastructure that will be based on an enhanced World Wide Web (WWW). This enhanced WWW will be the cornerstone for human communication, interoperable computing systems, intelligent ultra-wide scale applications and, eventually, improved used experience. Among the aforementioned advances and trends we can distinguish: a) the technologies and social networking principles of Web 2.0, b) the huge online collections of multimedia content, c) the Service Oriented Architectures (SOA), d) the networked multimedia applications (e.g., IPTV, interactive TV) and, finally, e) the explicit representation of content and application semantics through structured metadata. This semantically enhanced application framework is, generally, referred to as Web 3.0. These new technologies can alter the current human-computer interaction practices and facilitate the consolidation of diverse IT solutions into really innovative products and services.

To better illustrate the type of services we refer to, let us consider a sample service that continuously displays information relevant to a currently playing documentary in a small window in a corner of the TV screen. We assume that each scene of the film is annotated with special metadata describing the entities presented (e.g., place, objects, time, persons, activities). These are correlated with the profile of the user as set prior to using the service so that the system decides what information to display. The actual information may be retrieved by different sources in the Web, such as Wikipedia, Flickr, IMDb, etc. Hence, we eventually have a kind of a "Web mashup" in the residential environment created through representation and reasoning of semantics. Another example service can be an advanced parental control service, where the rules for characterizing the content are based on its metadata. Such service would enable the characterization of specific scenes instead of the entire film. We will describe in more detail such service in a following section.

However, despite the maturity of most of the aforementioned technologies, their integration into platforms able to deliver services like those just described has not made much progress. One reason for this is that most researchers focused on specific technology integration tasks. For example, some researchers addressed the integration of TV and Web content while others focused on personalizing specific TV services, usually the EPG (Electronic Program Guide). On the other hand, most of the works ignore the semantics of the content or users. The only metadata they exploit are simple tags or keywords. One reason for this is that rich and formal semantic metadata are hardly available. There are no easy-to-use tools and the publicly available metadata collections do not usually refer to audiovisual content. Unfortunately, this lack of semantics data results in greater effort for developing sophisticated algorithms. Our thesis is that by exploiting the semantics metadata of TV content, we can rely on declarative ways of personalizing services that simplify a lot the development of such systems.

In this article, we describe the application of the Web 3.0 paradigm to a residential infotainment environment that is developed over interactive digital TV (iTV). The discussed approach, implemented in the context of the POLYSEMA project (POLYSEMA, 2009), employs Web technologies and services, multimedia semantics and an extensible residential infrastructure that can support a flexible service lifecycle. Specifically, the main contributions of our solution are:

1. Semantic annotation of audiovisual content through Semantic Web ontologies (e.g., MPEG-7). This results in formal metadata descriptions and advanced support for multimedia content indexing and retrieval.

Based on an existing ontology we adapted it and we built a tool for annotating video files (Valkanas et al., 2007).

2. Declarative representation of user profiles and preferences with (Semantic Web-compliant) rules.

3. A testbed for standardized industry technologies (e.g., DVB-T, DVB-MHP, OSGi) and research techniques and tools (context-aware Web content retrieval, rule-based personalization).

4. An open platform that exploits the Web 3.0 framework in the home infotainment domain. The design principles of this platform facilitate the introduction of residential SOA architectures and the introduction of more flexible business models.

In this article, the main architectural orientations of this platform are discussed, as well as core implementation technologies. The requirements that drove the design and development of the platform were collected by a Digital TV provider, member of the POLYSEMA consortium. The findings of the requirements analysis indicated a strong demand for a flexible iTV solution that would:

- Be capable of delivering well known iTV services (e.g., advanced Electronic Program Guide - EPG, video on demand, TV of yesterday)

- Be based on standardized broadcasting technologies such as DVB and be compatible with existing broadcasting platforms and residential gateways (thus reducing the time-to-market)

- Be able to integrate with other data communication channels such as the Web

- Support flexible business models through its support for novel infotainment services.

In the rest of this article we describe how the identified requirements were materialized in the developed system. The flexibility and openness of

the solution is demonstrated through the description of a sample parental control service and new business models that can be supported.

RELATED WORK ON SEMANTICS-ENABLED INTERACTIVE TV AND TV-WEB INTEGRATION

Since the appearance of digital TV, both academia and industrial stakeholders have focused on the integration of the Web with the world of television broadcasting. A strong indication of this is the fact that the DVB-MHP (Digital Video Broadcast – Multimedia Home Platform) specification includes a profile which supports Web browsing and e-mail client functionality. Web browsing is realized via the introduction of the DVB-HTML markup language. Unfortunately, DVB-HTML has not been widely adopted yet by STB manufacturers, because it is a quite complex specification, thus leading to higher device costs and interoperability/transcoding issues. An alternative to DVB-HTML was recently proposed in (Ferretti et al., 2007). The authors developed a method for transcoding Web pages to MHP-compliant visual components that can be displayed in TV screens by DVB-enabled set-top-boxes. In this way, they try to integrate the Web with a TV environment. Moreover, the authors proposed an integrated solution for intelligent Web content browsing/retrieval through mobile agents that search the Web for user-relevant content. Towards the same direction, the author of (Tanaka, 2007) has proposed an approach for augmenting TV content with Web content, by exploiting intelligent information retrieval techniques applied to closed captions.

However, in our view, convergence of WWW with iTV does not only refer to browsing the Web from a television screen using a remote control, which was the main topic of the aforementioned works. It also signifies that a broad scope of diverse applications can migrate from the Web to the TV broadcasting world. Two major research efforts towards this direction are the AVATAR (Blanco Fernandez et al., 2006) and the MediaNet (MediaNET, 2009) projects. AVATAR is a project which shares many techniques and technologies with POLYSEMA, such as annotation of DVB video streams, ontology-based modeling, multimedia metadata, user profiling and personalization through semantic reasoning. However, the project's main objective is to create a personalized digital TV program recommender and not transferring Web content in the residential infotainment domain in a personalized way. The system accomplishes the task by taking into account the user's profile and TV-Anytime meta-information of each TV programme. The MediaNET project is divided in five sub-projects, each of which covers a significant area of the multimedia content lifecycle: creation, service providers, network operators, etc. As far as interactive services are concerned, it delivers the AmigoTV platform and a PVR. Moreover, MediaNET offers integrated iTV/Web services such as e-voting and e-shopping. AmigoTV is a social TV platform that delivers services over triple-play networks. Although the service makes significant progress towards importing popular social networking applications into the iTV domain (e.g., messaging, voice communications, games), it does not investigate the benefits from using metadata during the various phases of the multimedia content and service lifecycles. Hence, all actions are user-initiated and the system does not provide means for intelligent automation of service executions or (Web) content retrieval.

Another project that exploits semantic metadata in order to provide personalized access to TV content is the SenSee framework (Aroyo et al., 2007). This framework harvests TV metadata from various sources (e.g., BBC, IMDb) and provides a personalized TV guide. Several ontologies are used for integrating the harvested metadata and to model the current user context. All this information is used for inferring content of interest to the user.

The use of multimedia semantics in different phases of the multimedia content lifecycle is of course not a new approach. Several researchers have performed significant contributions through designing and demonstrating the use of multimedia ontologies (Arndt et al., 2007; Tsinaraki et al., 2004; W3C Multimedia Semantics Incubator Group, 2009). However, in most of the related works, semantics are used mainly for content classification and for (meta-)data integration purposes and not for actual reasoning. Moreover, most efforts deal with still images and less dynamic types of media. In this work we also exploit an MPEG-7 ontology to describe video files. Moreover, we model all other information involved in the service provisioning though ontologies and eventually apply rules on the resulting knowledge base.

Finally, in terms of middleware infrastructure a very similar approach that integrates the MHP and OSGi platforms is presented in (Vilas et al., 2006). The architecture presented in (Vilas et al., 2006) relies on a hybrid MHP/OSGi component called XBundLET. This component serves as a proxy between the two platforms, enabling bidirectional service discovery and invocation. In our case, since we did not require so tight integration between the two platforms, we adopted a more lightweight approach relying on communication over HTTP, as described in section "The POLYSEMA Platform". Apart from this technological similarity the two approaches do not have much in common, since our middleware is enhanced by the Semantic Component and constitutes an integrated iTV service platform.

From the survey just presented, it becomes apparent that all these related works do not try to develop a general-purpose framework that can provide intelligent and personalized services to the users, but rather focus on specific parts of such system (e.g., Web-TV content integration, personalized EPGs). In the following sections we present the POLYSEMA platform that adopts a more horizontal approach.

THE POLYSEMA PLATFORM

The POLYSEMA platform is one of the first prototypes to deliver next generation services to TV viewers. It constitutes a proof-of-concept system for developing and assessing personalized iTV services. It covers the whole service lifecycle by providing a residential gateway and some basic server-side functionality. Specifically, the platform provides: content preparation (segmentation), metadata creation and delivery, Web content retrieval and presentation, personalization based on rule-based inference. One challenge addressed by such platform was the introduction of rich metadata (based on Semantic Web practices) in the entire workflow of service provisioning. All metadata are aligned to domain models that represent shared vocabularies for the development of services. This way many interoperability problems are handled. The main difficulty in this task was to build the models (i.e., ontologies) in a suitable form and populate them with the actual

data. For example, the MPEG-7 ontology should enable standard reasoning tasks (such as concept classification) but not be too strict and demanding. Towards this end several ontology elements were devised accordingly or totally removed.

Architecture Overview

Components

Figure 1 presents a bird's eye view of the end-to-end architecture. The architectural components can be divided to those residing on the server side, responsible for delivering content and applications to the iTV subscribers and those deployed on the client side. The main server-side component is the Video Playout Server, which performs streaming of the audiovisual content. Moreover, several other (Web) servers may be available for providing other types of content. The client is implemented as a residential gateway, which handles service execution, user interaction, service personalization, and

Figure 1. Overall POLYSEMA architecture

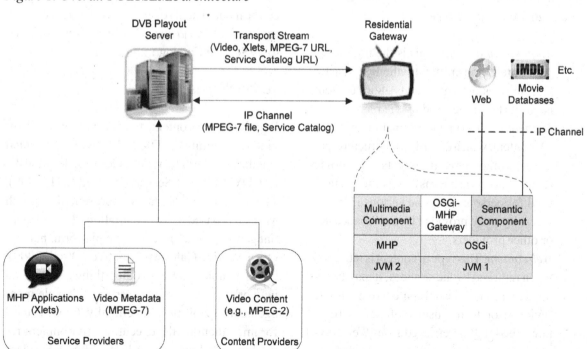

content presentation. The core components inside this gateway are the Multimedia Component and the Semantic Component. The first is responsible for decoding/displaying the broadcast video stream, executing iTV applications, receiving content-relevant notifications from the broadcaster and handling the user interaction issues of the platform. The Semantic Component is responsible for deciding and executing additional personalized actions that should be taken during the play-out period of the audiovisual content. Such actions are decided (in real-time) based on the service, user and content semantics. Typical actions are service invocations (e.g., video recording, parental control) and retrieval of metadata and related content from the Web. Evidently, coordination of the Multimedia and Semantic Components is necessary for delivering the POLYSEMA Services. Such coordination is achieved through a gateway between the two components/platforms.

Content

Until now we referred to content in a rather abstract way. In the context of POLYSEMA, content can be categorized to three types:

A. *Audiovisual content.* This is the traditional TV content transmitted by the broadcaster (e.g., movies, advertisements). Such content is not further processed by the platform.

B. *Metadata.* This is meta-information about the TV content, which describes its structure and captures other semantic aspects (e.g., movie cast, scene descriptions). This metadata is used for personalizing the various iTV services. It can be provided by the broadcaster or other providers.

C. *Web content.* This type of content is retrieved when required by the services. It may be related to the audiovisual content (e.g., movie reviews) or to the user preferences (e.g., news feeds). It is retrieved from Web servers, typically not owned by the broadcaster.

Services

Before delving into the details of the platform we should clarify that a POLYSEMA Service is a value added service (VAS) exploiting TV content semantics in order to provide additional relevant content (typically retrieved from the Web in a context-aware manner) and intelligent behavior. A POLYSEMA Service consists of three parts: a) the Multimedia part, b) the Semantic part (it may be the business logic of a service or a wrapper for an external system, such as Personal Video Recorder - PVR) and c) a Service Description with details about service functionality and operational semantics. The "Multimedia part" is used by the Multimedia Component for presentation and human-computer interaction purposes (e.g., for displaying text messages and multimedia content, switching channels, or adjusting sound volume). The "Semantic part" contains the implementation of the core service logic. Finally, the "Service Description", is used for service discovery and configuration purposes. In addition, it is used by the Semantic Component so that the correct method calls to the Semantic or Multimedia service parts can be made. The set of all service descriptions that are available *for a specific subscriber* is referred to as Service Catalog in Figure 1.

Technologies

Regarding the content, the technology used for video streaming is DVB-T, a widely adopted standard for digital TV. For video broadcasting the IRT DVB Playout Server was used (IRT, 2009). The content metadata is represented through MPEG-7–based video annotation. The residential gateway is an open service platform, namely Open Service Gateway Initiative (OSGi, 2009). OSGi enables, among other things, advanced networking and provides service lifecycle management capabilities. Specifically, OSGi is used for implementing the execution environment for the business logic of the POLYSEMA Services (i.e., Semantic Component). Moreover, we achieve seamless service upgrade, through the OSGi framework. We exploit the OSGi mechanisms in order to install new services and allow for future integration of the system with home networking and automation applications.

The Multimedia Component of the residential gateway, on the other hand, relies on the Multimedia Home Platform (MHP) middleware and Execution Environment (MHP, 2009). MHP is a Java-based execution platform (i.e., it runs on top of a Java Virtual Machine - JVM) for MHP applications, called Xlets. Xlets are to the digital TV what applets are to the Web. Such execution environment fully controls the Xlet lifecycle, including initialization, activation, and destruction. MHP contains several code libraries for the development of Xlets. Many of these libraries rely on other specifications such as Home Video Audio Interoperability (HAVi, 2009) and Java TV (JavaTV, 2009).

OSGi and MHP environments have different properties as they adopt different design principles (Vilas et al., 2006). In order to retain full compatibility with industry standards such as MHP and DVB, and still exploit the service openness and flexibility of OSGi, we decided to build a proxy bundle in the OSGi platform that conceals the nature of MHP applications from the rest of the system (MHP-OSGi Gateway). The MHP-based Multimedia Component communicates with this proxy bundle via the IP return channel of the receiver. Similarly, the OSGi-based components of the Semantic Component interact with the Multimedia Component by accessing the respective MHP-delegate OSGi service.

Finally, the POLYSEMA services are implemented as a mixture of technologies. The Multimedia part is implemented as an MHP application (i.e., Xlet). The Semantic part is implemented as an OSGi bundle (i.e., a packaged Java application). The Service Description is represented through XML.

Multimedia Component

The Multimedia Component consists of MHP applications that can be downloaded and executed by any DVB-MHP receiver. The only requirement is that the MHP middleware running at the Set-Top-Box (STB) supports Return Channel (RC) communication, which is based on TCP/IP. This is necessary for the interaction between the Multimedia Component and the Semantic Component (see OSGi-MHP Gateway in Figure 1).

The operation of the Multimedia Component relies on a basic MHP application running at the receiver's end. This Xlet (called "POLYSEMA Xlet") includes the Multimedia parts of all the services supported by the broadcaster. Another task assigned to this Xlet is to read the broadcast file system (Digital Storage Media Command and Control or DSM-CC or 'Carousel', in MHP terminology) and retrieve the URL that will provide the MPEG-7 metadata. Such metadata describe the audiovisual content and the Service Catalog for the subscribed POLYSEMA Services. Both these URLs are, subsequently, fed to the Semantic Component which is responsible for fetching, locally storing and processing the respective files.

Finally, the POLYSEMA Xlet subscribes and listens to incoming stream events, inserted into the DVB Transport Stream (TS) by the broadcaster. Typically, these events indicate the beginning of a new video scene (a.k.a., segment) and are automatically generated at the playout server from the corresponding MPEG-7 temporal decomposition of the video, as provided by the service provider. Upon the reception of a stream event, the POLYSEMA Xlet inquires the Semantic Component for services that should be invoked for the specific video scene. These services are specified in a plan, as described in the following section. Hence, through these events the streaming video can be synchronized with the VAS.

Semantic Component

At the heart of the platform lies the Semantic Component. It is responsible for the coordination of the VAS offered by the platform as well as the inference processes that drive the personalized service provisioning. In a few words, one could describe this component as the knowledge- and rule-based infrastructure that provides personal-

ized 'mashups' of content inside a TV receiver. A diagram with the basic elements of its architecture and their main interactions is shown in Figure 2.

Upon retrieval of the Service Catalog file, a graphical user interface (GUI) for managing the service and user profiles is automatically generated using Java Server Pages. These profiles, once defined by the user, are automatically translated into ontological instances. These profiles are

Figure 2. POLYSEMA semantic component

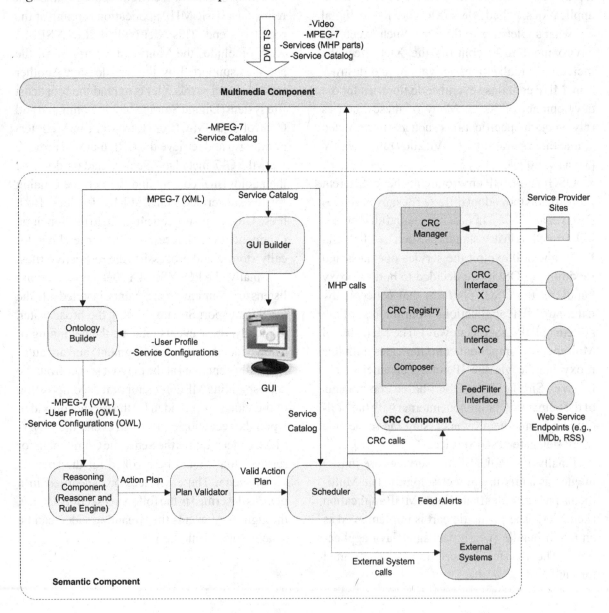

static, in the sense that they are not dynamically adjusted by the system. Once a user defines her profile, it remains unchanged until the next update. The MPEG-7 data are also translated to instances of a MPEG-7 ontology (see also section "Semantics-based Personalization of iTV Services"). We should remind that ontology is an "explicit specification of a conceptualization" according to (Gruber, 1993). In our case it provides a hierarchical representation of concepts along with their relationships that describes the specific multimedia domain. Hence, according to the classifications in (Mizoguchi, 2004), the MPEG-7 ontology is a type of light-weight ontology: it is mainly used for data integration reasons and not for the formal definition of the domain concepts.

The instantiation of this ontology is performed by the Ontology Builder component and is necessary so that all data are represented in a common format, compatible with the inference engine (Jang & Sohn, 2004) of the Reasoning Component. The Ontology Builder consists of a specially designed parser for valid MPEG-7 XML files. It exploits naming conventions between the XML elements of the MPEG-7 standard and the class names in the MPEG-7 ontology in order to populate the latter.

The rules that are applied to these ontological data are specified by the individual third party service providers in the Service Catalog. Once the rules are executed, a first execution plan is in place, which describes the actions that should be scheduled for the current user and the current TV program. Before submitting this action plan to the Scheduler, who is responsible for the plan execution, the Plan Validator is invoked in order to produce a more refined version of the plan and resolve possible conflicts among actions. Such conflicts may be forced by device specifications, the semantics of individual services or the temporal relationships between the scheduled actions. For instance, the Plan Validator does not allow the execution of two Personal Video Recorder (PVR) services with temporal overlap, as the Set-Top-Box (STB) may not support concurrent

recording of two different TV programs. Moreover, a Web information retrieval service should not be executed when a parental control service is already running, since the additional information may also be inappropriate for underage viewers. Another validation rule example is the following: if two services should present Web content in the same region of the screen concurrently, one of them is removed from the plan. In general, the rules for performing plan validation are based on heuristics and common sense, and their aim is to ensure "smooth" invocation of the services and presentation of their results. These rules are applied once the actions for each video segment have been decided by the Reasoning Component. Hence, conflict resolution is not performed in the typical way that rule engines do, but on the inferred action set. Currently, we have implemented validation rules like the aforementioned, but many more should be probably needed in an actual deployment. Moreover, more sophisticated and formal ways of handling conflicting actions should be investigated in the future.

Finally, the Scheduler component invokes the methods that correspond to the inferred actions. For these mappings between actions and service methods, it consults with the Service Catalog. Such methods may be MHP calls, calls to external Web servers or calls to external systems (PVR, networked home devices, etc.).

Interfaces with Web and Other External Content/Service Providers

One of the objectives of the POLYSEMA platform is to constitute a residential implementation of the Web 2.0 that will introduce rich internet applications to the home environment. Through its infrastructure, open and proprietary APIs can be accessed in order to bridge the gap between Web resources and home infotainment. The data fetched from the WWW can be either in textual (movie information, encyclopedic knowledge, sport statistics, translation services etc.), visual (e.g., images) or any other format that can be "consumed" by the STB middleware.

The integration of a home infotainment TV environment with the modern Web technologies and trends is mainly implemented through the Content Retrieval & Composition Component (CRC). Once the Reasoning Component has pre-processed the semantic video description and has "inferred" that certain Web information should be fetched and displayed to the viewer, the Scheduler instructs the CRC component to start downloading the relevant data.

CRC consists of several interfaces (implemented as OSGi bundles) that provide access to external Web resources. For instance, in the prototype system we have developed bundles which access content from the Internet Movie Database (IMDb) and Wikipedia. The respective classes follow a common abstract design, which involves management of created objects, caching of retrieved data till the end of the corresponding TV program and basic formatting of the requested Web information. Through this modular design data heterogeneity is handled too, since content retrieval is performed by these specialized bundles. Each bundle handles content retrieval from specific sources and, thus, "knows" how to parse it and what to present to the user.

Surely, the various CRC interfaces may differ with regard to the actual information they can retrieve. Hence, each installed bundle updates a registry, called CRC Registry, which is used by the Scheduler to map user requested information to CRC interface method calls. Typical information stored in this registry includes the specific methods and parameters that correspond to types of available information as well as the format of this information (image, text, etc.). For example, if we can retrieve the director of a given movie from IMDb, there is a corresponding option in the relevant Service Description, which can be selected by the user through the GUI and further mapped to a CRC method call. This mapping is performed in the CRC Registry. We should note that a CRC interface is actually the Semantic part of a POLYSEMA Service (for this example, the IMDb Web content retrieval service). Hence, a service creator/provider is the sole responsible for deciding what info each service can retrieve. Of course, most CRC methods take some input parameters. For example, a method retrieving an actor's biography takes its name as input. The values for these parameters are extracted from the MPEG-7 metadata. Such metadata is expressed through ontologies, as it will be described in section "Semantics-based Personalization of iTV Services". Hence, a MPEG-7 document that supports the IMDb service should annotate the actors based on a special purpose IMDb ontology containing all valid actor names (a sample ontology can be found in (POLYSEMA, 2009)).

The additional content retrieved by the CRC interfaces is returned to the Scheduler, which then stores it in text or image files at a local lightweight HTTP Server. This server is running within the Semantic Component and is the core component of the OSGi-MHP Gateway. Subsequently, the Multimedia Component (after a Scheduler's call) accesses the HTTP Server in order to retrieve the Web content and display it to the user (this workflow is shown in Figure 3). A special component in the CRC design is the FeedFilter interface. A user can register feeds of interest and define the way she wants to receive notifications about feed updates (currently only RSS feeds are supported).

Finally, the CRC component has its own updating mechanism, which is responsible for communicating with the service provider sites and installing new CRC interfaces or upgrading existing ones. Such updating is totally handled by the OSGi framework.

POLYSEMA SERVICES

Several services have been implemented in our prototype:

Figure 3. UML sequence diagram describing the content retrieval process

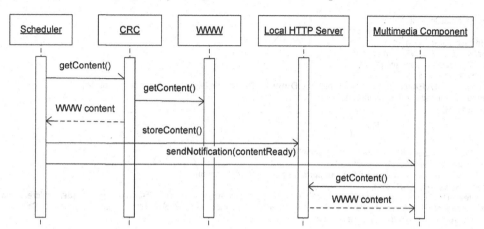

- A parental control service
- A service that retrieves and displays Web content from IMDb. Such content can be actor-specific, and is, thus, displayed in every segment that contains some new actor, or movie-specific (e.g., rating, reviews, director details) and is displayed during the beginning/end of a movie
- A service that retrieves and displays Web content from Wikipedia for segments that contain specific objects
- A PVR service that records segments that contain specific activities, objects, places or actors (these are specified by the user and adhere to the terminology of the LSCOM ontology (Naphade, 2006)
- A notification service bound to user-specified RSS feeds.

As an example, the parental control service performs some action (e.g., mutes sound, changes channel, toggles off video, displays alert) for video segments that are not appropriate for the current user, judging from her age. This service differs from typical parental control services, in that it performs a more fine-grained control over content display, i.e., on a per video segment basis and not on the video as a whole. Figure 4a shows the code that is executed in the MHP environment upon

service invocation (Multimedia part); while Figure 4b shows the service description that defines the service invocation rule templates and other service metadata[1]. Rule templates are expressed in the rule language described in (Jang & Sohn, 2004). Each rule template defines when a service should be invoked and with which input parameters. The actual values of these parameters can be obtained from the MPEG-7 file and the current status of the system. In our example, the only parameter is *currentUser* the value of which is set upon user logon.

Knowledge Engineering Details

The exploitation of user, service and content semantics is the cornerstone of our system. Specifically, all the video content is assumed to be annotated according to the MPEG-7 Multimedia Description Scheme (MDS). However, we limited the MDS expressiveness only to Description Schemes (DS) and Descriptors relevant to "high-level semantics" of video files (e.g., those describing persons, activities, places, time, objects). A significant differentiation with respect to the MPEG-7 standard is that we did not adopt its term definition and term reference mechanisms (e.g., TermUseType and ControlledTermUseType elements, classification schemes) and used only

Figure 4. An example parental control service a) Multimedia part, b) Service description

```
public class ParentalControl{
   //we overide the paint method of the HContainer..
   public void paint(Graphics g) {
      DVBGraphics dvbG = (DVBGraphics) g;
      DVBAlphaComposite compositingRule;
      // When alpha = 1, the display gets black
      compositingRule = DVBAlphaComposite.getInstance(DVBAlphaComposite.DST_OVER, (float) this.alpha);
      dvbG.setDVBComposite(compositingRule);
      super.paint(dvbG);
   }
}
```

(a)

```
<service id="2" name="parentalControlService" version="1">
  <GUIName>Parental Control</GUIName>
  <description>Takes actions upon detection of inappropriate content</description>
  <API_method>NULL</API_method>
  <ruleTemplate>if TVUO:Under7(?u) and [?u = TVUO:*currentUser*] and mds:Why(?sat, MPAA:directed_to_older_children) and
    mds:TextAnnotation(?vst, ?tat) and mds:VideoSegmentType(?vst) and mds:StructuredAnnotation(?tat, ?sat) then iTVServices:action(?vst,
    iTVServices:parentalControlService)</ruleTemplate>
  <params>
    <param id="1">
      <name>action</name>
      <GUIName>Action</GUIName>
      <description>Determines the action for parental control</description>
      <type primitive="false">exclusive-list</type>
      <exclusive-list>
        <item>
          <value>toggle.video</value>
          <GUIName>Toggle video</GUIName>
        </item>
        <item>
          <value>alert</value>
          <GUIName>Alert Viewer</GUIName>
        </item>
      </exclusive-list>
    </param>
  </params>
</service>
```

(b)

domain ontologies for describing video semantics, instead. Hence, the MPEG-7 ontology we used, although retains most of the vocabulary of the MPEG-7, it allows extension of the annotation terms through third-party ontology resources.

Moreover, we did not adopt the MPEG-7 Semantic DS elements (e.g., Semantic, SemanticBase, SemanticType, Time, Event), which allows for very expressive high level semantic descriptions, for the following reasons:

- The effort required by the annotator for such descriptions is too high. An indication of this is the fact that none of the available (commercial or not) video annotation tools does support such descriptions. One excep-

tion to this is the COMM (Core Ontology on Multimedia) API (Arndt et al., 2007).

- There is no sound and accepted methodology that defines how such annotation should be performed or how the applications should exploit such information. The lack of such methodology causes ambiguity during metadata interpretation. This problem is also reported in (Rahman et al., 2006), where an ontology for the semantics of MPEG-7 Semantic DS is proposed as a potential solution.

Since the intelligence of the system is provided by a rule-based system, it was necessary that all data related to the user, TV program, and services are represented in a common knowledge representation formalism. This formalism was decided to be the Web Ontology Language (OWL) due to its popularity and its adoption by the World Wide Web Consortium (W3C). For the ontology-based representation of the metadata we elaborated the model of Tsinaraki et al. (2004), implemented in OWL, too. In (W3C Multimedia Semantics Incubator Group, 2009), some other candidate models are also listed but they are either too abstract or too detailed for our needs. We performed several changes to the original MPEG-7 ontology in order to render it more flexible (e.g., omitted certain concepts and properties). Flexibility mainly refers to the ability to: a) automatically populate such ontology from original MPEG-7 XML files, b) perform typical reasoning tasks such as classification, and c) allow for linking to external domain ontologies for describing video segments. In general, we kept only MPEG-7 elements relevant to the provision of iTV services. The ontology resulted in consisting of 53 classes, 53 datatype properties and 63 object properties. The corresponding OWL file can be found in the POLYSEMA site (POLYSEMA, 2009). Indicative modifications are:

1. The classes TermUseType and ControlledTermUseType were removed, as already mentioned at the beginning of the section, since the role of such vocabularies is substituted by domain ontologies. Moreover, the Term class (or some subclass) was removed from the range of all properties.
2. The elements for relative time reference were removed (e.g., MediaRelTimePointType, RelIncrTimePointType) as well as the elements for "incremental" timing (e.g., MediaIncrDuration, IncrDuration).
3. The elememts relevant to Classification Schemes were removed (e.g., ClassificationSchemeBaseType, ClassificationSchemeDescriptionType).
4. All elements relevant to the Semantic DS were removed, as already explained.
5. All elements describing graphs were removed (e.g., GraphType, Node).
6. Several object properties that in practice will assume primitive data types were converted to datatype properties (e.g., FreeTextAnnotation, Language, GivenName).

We should note that the performed modifications can surely affect the interoperability between our ontology and the original one. However, interoperability was not one of our requirements. The original ontology was used just as a starting point for the design of a more "pragmatic" ontology that could be directly used in annotation tools and in reasoning tasks.

All actual data (instances) in this MPEG-7 ontology were expressed through domain ontologies. Some of these ontologies derive from the MPEG-7 and TV-Anytime classification schemes (e.g., those related to parental rating and video categorization). Others are custom ontologies that restrict the vocabulary that can be used by certain services. For example, as already mentioned, we have designed an IMDb ontology that contains valid actor names. These ontologies are used both during video annotation (Valkanas et al., 2007) and service execution. Since these ontologies are used for rule execution, some singleton instances were also created besides the class hierarchies. As a convention, each singleton instance has the name of the class it belongs (and a prefix). For instance, in MPEG7RoleCS ontology that described movie roles we have the following instance assertion: <Art_Director rdf:ID="art_Director"/>.

Similarly to the translation of MPEG-7 XML data to OWL data, each service configuration is transformed to a proprietary service ontology (iTVServices) and each user profile to a TV user ontology (TVUO). The TVUO class hierarchy is shown in Figure 5. As one can see, this model can be instantiated with some demographic information about the user, and her preferences regarding the content delivered and the services provided

Figure 5. TVUO class hierarchy

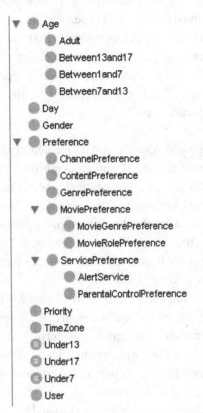

(i.e., which services should be executed and with what parameters). All the ontologies mentioned in this section are available in (POLYSEMA, 2009).

The adoption and engineering of formal ontologies for structuring the metadata (i.e., MPEG-7, TVUO) and their instantiation through domain ontologies (and not just literal values), makes the platform a pure knowledge-based system, capable of inferencing and reasoning over explicit and implicit knowledge.

In Figure 6, some sample data are presented so that the reader can understand how the system performs reasoning and computation of the action plan. In Figure 6a, a rule (of a parental control service) is depicted. In natural language, it states that "if the current user is under 7 years old and the current video segment is directed to older children, according to the MPAA (Motion Picture Association of America) classification scheme, then the service should be triggered for that segment" (we assume that parental ratings are expressed in the "Why" element of MPEG-7). This is a generic rule applied to the actual metadata of the video

Figure 6. Example data for rule-based service personalization

```
rule parentalControl is if
TVUO:CurrentUser(?u) and TVUO:Under7(?u) and mds:Why(?sat, MPAA:directed_to_older_children) and
mds:TextAnnotation(?vst, ?tat) and mds:VideoSegmentType(?vst) and mds:StructuredAnnotation(?tat, ?sat)
then
iTVServices:action(?vst, iTVServices:parentalControlService)
```
a) service rule

```
<TVUO:User rdf:ID="bill">
  <TVUO:hasUsername rdf:datatype="http://www.w3.org/2001/XMLSchema#string">Bill</TVUO:hasUsername>
  <TVUO:hasGender rdf:resource="http://polysema.di.uoa.gr/ont/TVUO.owl#male"/>
  <TVUO:hasAge>
    <TVUO:Between1and7 rdf:ID="ageOfBill"/>
  </TVUO:hasAge>
</TVUO:User>
```
b) user profile

```
Under7 ≡ User ⊓ ∃hasAge.Between1and7
```
c) a user profile definition

```
<mds:VideoType rdf:ID="MultimediaContent3">
  <mds:Video>
  ......
    <mds:VideoSegmentType rdf:ID="segment7">
      <mds:MediaTime>
      ......
      </mds:MediaTime>
      <mds:TextAnnotation>
        <mds:TextAnnotationType rdf:ID="TextAnnotation20">
          <mds:StructuredAnnotation>
            <mds:StructuredAnnotationType rdf:ID="StructuredAnnotation21">
              <mds:Why rdf:resource="&MPAA;#directed_to_older_children"/>
            </mds:StructuredAnnotationType>
          </mds:StructuredAnnotation>
        </mds:TextAnnotationType>
      </mds:TextAnnotation>
    </mds:VideoSegmentType>
  ......
```
d) extract of the MPEG-7 instances

and the user (i.e., the variables, starting with "?", will be evaluated with some instances of the video MPEG-7 ontology and the ontological instances of the other ontologies). In case the user is described in a user ontology as presented in Figure 6b and 6c (represented in Description Logics notation), and the video metadata are that of Figure 6d, then the service will be added to the plan for all video segments that satisfy the rule conditions. The specific action taken will depend on the value of the "action" service parameter (see Figure 4). The "mds" namespace refers to the MPEG-7 ontology, the "TVUO" and the "iTVServices" to the respective profiles (i.e., the description of Figure 4b is transformed to iTVServices instances) and MPAA to a domain ontology that defines parental rating classes.

New Business Models for Interactive TV

The openness and extensibility of the POLYSEMA implementation technologies along with the innovative exploitation of semantics allows for new business models in the iTV domain. An indicative business model that is supported by the platform is illustrated in Figure 7. In this figure, one can see the revenue (Ri, i=1,2,...) and information (Ij, j=1,2,...) flows between the core players and roles of this model. The innovation of this model is the introduction of the Metadata Provider role and the Service Aggregator role (the last will be typically assumed by the Broadcaster). Another new role is that of a Service & Metadata Provider. Although, separate Service Providers and Metadata Providers may exist, a new role that combines both of their responsibilities is also supported by this model. This new role may even be necessary so that the service logic (rules) can be paired with meaningful metadata. For example, if one Service Provider provides localized Web information retrieval to augment documentaries, then it should make sure that such geospatial information is also available in the documentary metadata, or else, the rules of its service may never "fire".

The need for the Service Aggregator is attributed to the fact that each user will be typically registered for several POLYSEMA services. Hence, the Service Catalog has to be dynamically composed. If, for a certain video file, there are numerous metadata from different providers, these should be aggregated too. Such metadata aggregation is a very challenging issue, unless the same annotation tools and conventions are

Figure 7. Business model roles and information/revenue flows between them

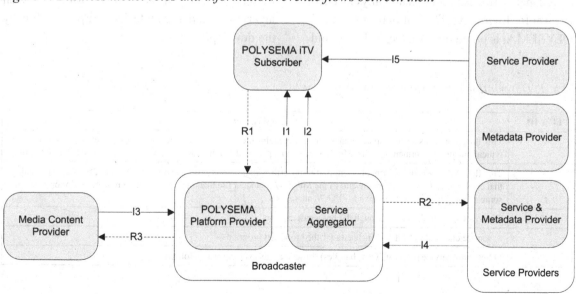

used by all Metadata Providers. Similar issues are also met in other areas, such as metadata harvesting in digital libraries. The aggregation process may encounter difficulties at the syntax level (e.g., different syntax describing the same semantics) or at the semantics level (e.g., inconsistency of descriptions). However, this topic is out of the scope of this work and will not be further discussed.

A more detailed description of the information flows between the various players of the business model is summarized in Table 1. Finally, regarding the revenue flows we should note that various payment models and subscription types can be supported. For example, a user may subscribe for a fixed set of services or for unlimited use of services (flow R1). Alternatively, she can pay for some basic set of services and be additionally charged depending on her service usage. The flow R2 can be also implemented through several compensation methods. The 'pay-per-install' method gives income to the Service Providers depending on the installations of their services by the users. Another, Internet-oriented, method is 'pay-per-impression'. According to this model, each provider receives commission for several hundreds or thousands of views (it is similar to the 'pay-per-view' model).

CHALLENGES AND FUTURE WORK

In this paper, we presented a semantically enriched platform for Interactive TV. Our platform, called POLYSEMA, is based on open technologies and emerging standards (e.g., MPEG-7, OSGi, OWL). We provided an extensive overview of the POLYSEMA architecture emphasizing on the issues of knowledge engineering, Web-iTV integration and the business models supported through the particular features of the platform.

Our future plans for extensions/improvements include a thorough study of the adopted metadata formalisms. Specifically, in our approach we have used the MPEG-7 standard for capturing multimedia content semantics. However, there is growing skepticism among the multimedia metadata community on the value of MPEG-7. Its high complexity has played critical role for its low adoption and tool support. In fact, many researchers try to develop formalisms that substitute (parts of) the standard. From our experience, both in metadata production (Valkanas et al., 2007) and metadata consumption, MPEG-7 is indeed an inefficient standard. Our conclusions are that sophisticated and user-friendly semi-automatic video annotation tools are necessary for the standard to survive the "metadata war" as well as a further modularization and layering of the specification. Modularization is merely supported by the MPEG-7 structure (Description Schemes), but should be extended and better documented. Layering refers to the definition of various species of the standard in a way analogous to the Web Ontology Language (Lite, DL and Full). Moreover, such layering would facilitate its comprehension by the developers and users.

Table 1. Description of information flows

Flow ID	Description
I1	This flow represents the Transport Stream that also contains the DVB Carousel. It consists of a) the video content, b) typical broadcast information, c) the Multimedia service part and d) a link to the Service Aggregator service endpoint
I2	This flow represents the information sent to the subscriber upon login to the platform. It consists of the Service Catalog that corresponds to its subscription, and b) the MPEG-7 metadata file that may also depend on its subscription (in case some services come with their own MPEG-7 annotations)
I3	The video content delivered through the broadcast channel
I4	a) service data and b) MPEG-7 metadata for the broadcast program
I5	a) Semantic service part (e.g., CRC bundles), b) service-specific domain ontologies

From our experience we noticed that the MHP is a heavyweight middleware platform for Web-enabled interactive TV. On the other hand, more open and lightweight solutions (possibly implemented through IPTV and Web-based technologies), such as (Opera, 2009), are not widely adopted and tested, yet. Hence, choosing an iTV platform for building value added service platforms like POLYSEMA is an issue that deserves further study.

Finally, what is not addressed to a satisfactory degree in our platform yet, is the support for social networking and advanced recommendation services. These are key elements of the Web 2.0 ecosystem. Therefore, we are currently working on the proof-of-concept implementation of similar services in POLYSEMA.

REFERENCES

W3C Multimedia Semantics Incubator Group. (2009). *Multimedia Vocabularies on the Semantic Web*. Retrieved July 25, 2009 from http://www.w3.org/2005/Incubator/ mmsem/XGR-vocabularies/

Anisur Rahman, M., Hossain, A., Kiringa, I., & El Saddik, A. (2006, November). *Towards an Ontology for MPEG-7 Semantic Descriptions*. Paper presented at the Intelligent Interactive Learning Object Repositories (I2LOR) Conference, Montreal, QC, Canada.

Arndt, R., Troncy, R., Staab, S., Hardman, L., & Vacura, M. (2007). COMM: Designing a Well-Founded Multimedia Ontology for the Web. In *Proceedings of the 6th International Semantic Web Conference: The Semantic Web,* Busan, Korea (LNCS 4825, pp. 30-43). Berlin: Springer.

Aroyo, L., Bellekens, P., Bjorkman, M., Houben, G. J., Akkermans, P., & Kaptein, A. (2007). SenSee Framework for Personalized Access to TV Content. In *Proceedings of the Interactive TV: a Shared Experience,* Amsterdam, The Netherlands (LNCS 4471, pp. 156-165). Berlin: Springer.

Blanco Fernandez, Y., Pazos Arias, J. J., Lopez Nores, M., Gil Solla, A., & Ramos Cabrer, M. (2006). AVATAR: An Improved Solution for Personalized TV based on Semantic Inference. *IEEE Transactions on Consumer Electronics, 52*(1), 223–231. doi:10.1109/TCE.2006.1605051

Ferretti, S., Roccetti, M., & Palazzi, C. (2007). Web Content Search and Adaptation for IDTV: One Step Forward in the Mediamorphosis Process toward Personal-TV. *Advances in Multimedia, 2007,* 1–13. doi:10.1155/2007/16296

Gruber, T. R. (1993). A Translation Approach to Portable Ontology Specifications. *Knowledge Acquisition, 5*(2), 199–220. doi:10.1006/knac.1993.1008

HAVi. (2009). *Home Audio / Video Interoperability*. Retrieved July 25, 2009 from http://www.havi.org

IRT. (2009). *DVB Playout Server*. Retrieved July 25, 2009 from http://www.irt.de/en/products/digital-television/dvb-playout-server.html

Jang, M., & Sohn, J. (2004). Bossam: An Extended Rule Engine for OWL Inferencing. In *Proceedings of the Rules and Rule Markup Languages for the Semantic Web: RuleML,* Hiroshima, Japan (LNCS 3323, pp. 128-138). Berlin: Springer.

Java, T. V. (2009). *JavaTV Specification*. Retrieved July 25, 2009 from http://java.sun.com/products/javatv/

Media, N. E. T. (2009). *The MediaNET Project*. Retrieved July 25, 2009 from http://www.ip-medianet.org

MHP. (2009). *DVB – Multimedia Home Platform Specification 1.1.1, ETSI TS 102 812 V1.2.2*. Retrieved July 25, 2009 from http://www.mhp.org/fullspeclist.htm

Mizoguchi, R. (2004). Tutorial on ontological engineering, Part 3: Advanced course of ontological engineering. *New Generation Computing, 22*(2), 198–220. doi:10.1007/BF03040960

Naphade, M., Smith, J. R., Tesic, J., Chang, S. F., Hsu, W., & Kennedy, L. (2006). Large-Scale Concept Ontology for Multimedia. *IEEE MultiMedia, 13*(3), 86–91. doi:10.1109/MMUL.2006.63

Opera. (2009). *Opera for Devices iTV SDK*. Retrieved July 25, 2009 from http://www.opera.com/products/devices/

OSGi. (2009). *Open Service Gateway Initiative Alliance*. Retrieved July 25, 2009 from http://www.osgi.org

POLYSEMA. (2009). *The POLYSEMA Project*. Retrieved July 25, 2009 from http://polysema.di.uoa.gr

Tanaka, K. (2007). Towards New Content Services by Fusion of Web and Broadcasting Contents. In *Proceedings of the 20th International Conference on Industrial, Engineering and Other Applications of Applied Intelligent Systems: New Trends in Applied Artificial Intelligence*, Kyoto, Japan (LNCS 4570, pp. 1-11). Berlin: Springer.

Tsinaraki, C., Polydoros, P., & Christodoulakis, S. (2004). Interoperability support for Ontology-based Video Retrieval Applications. In *Proceedings of the 3rd International Conference on Image and Video Retrieval (CIVR 2004)*, Dublin, Ireland (LNCS 3115, pp. 582-591). Berlin: Springer.

Valkanas, G., Tsetsos, V., & Hadjiefthymiades, S. (2007). The POLYSEMA MPEG-7 Video Annotator. In *Proceedings of the Poster and Demo Conference on Semantic and Digital Media Technologies*, Genova, Italy.

Vilas, A. F., Díaz Redondo, R., Ramos Cabrer, M., Pazos Arias, J., Gil Solla, A., & García Duque, J. (2006). MHP-OSGi convergence: a new model for open residential gateways. *Software, Practice & Experience, 36*(13), 1421–1442. doi:10.1002/spe.727

ENDNOTE

[1] Note that the specific service does not have a Semantic part

This work was previously published in International Journal of Semantic Web and Information Systems, Volume 6, Issue 1, edited by Amit P. Sheth, pp. 1-18, copyright 2010 by IGI Publishing (an imprint of IGI Global).

Chapter 12
Music Retrieval and Recommendation Scheme Based on Varying Mood Sequences

Sanghoon Jun
Korea University, South Korea

Seungmin Rho
Korea University, South Korea

Eenjun Hwang
Korea University, South Korea

ABSTRACT

A typical music clip consists of one or more segments with different moods and such mood information could be a crucial clue for determining the similarity between music clips. One representative mood has been selected for music clip for retrieval, recommendation or classification purposes, which often gives unsatisfactory result. In this paper, the authors propose a new music retrieval and recommendation scheme based on the mood sequence of music clips. The authors first divide each music clip into segments through beat structure analysis, then, apply the k-medoids clustering algorithm for grouping all the segments into clusters with similar features. By assigning a unique mood symbol for each cluster, one can transform each music clip into a musical mood sequence. For music retrieval, the authors use the Smith-Waterman (SW) algorithm to measure the similarity between mood sequences. However, for music recommendation, user preferences are retrieved from a recent music playlist or user interaction through the interface, which generates a music recommendation list based on the mood sequence similarity. The authors demonstrate that the proposed scheme achieves excellent performance in terms of retrieval accuracy and user satisfaction in music recommendation.

DOI: 10.4018/978-1-4666-0185-7.ch012

1. INTRODUCTION

With the explosive growth of digital media population, content-based retrieval has come to play an important role in the multimedia domain, due to its rich and intuitive expressiveness in query formulation. The details of content-based multimedia retrieval are deeply dependent on the media type. For instance, in the case of audio data, low-level acoustic features such as MFCCs and ZCR are extracted from audio clips and indexed for retrieval purposes (Ghias, Logan, Chanberlin, & Smith, 1995; Birmingham, Dannenberg, & Pardo, 2006; Rho, Han, Hwang, & Kim, 2008). However, these low-level features fail to provide semantic information of music contents such as mood or emotion. This is a serious limitation in retrieving and recommending appropriate music in many applications. To handle this limitation, many researchers have tried to utilize high-level musical features such as harmonics and beat.

On the other hand, many researchers (Feng, Zhuang, & Pan, 2003; Juslin & Sloboda, 2001; Lu, Liu, & Zhang, 2006) have investigated the influence of music features such as loudness and tonality on the perceived emotional expression. They analyzed such data using diverse techniques, some of which are involved in measuring psychological and physiological correlations between the state of a particular musical factor and emotion evocation. Feng et al. (2003) approached the problem from the viewpoint of Computational Media Aesthetics (CMA) and mapped two dimensions of tempo and articulation into four categories of moods: happiness, anger, sadness and fear. This categorization is based on Juslin's theory (Juslin & Sloboda, 2001) in which the authors investigated the utilization of acoustic cues in the communication of music emotions between performers and listeners, and measured the correlations between emotional expressions (i.e., anger, sadness and happiness) and acoustic cues (i.e., tempo, spectrum and articulation). Lu et al. (2006) classified various features into three categories: intensity, timber and rhythm and mapped all the moods

into Thayer's two-dimensional space (Juslin & Sloboda, 2001). They used the Gaussian mixture model (GMM) as a classifier. To track music moods, they considered musical mood variation and proposed a mood boundary detection scheme based on threshold adaptation. To the best of our knowledge, no effort has been made to measure the similarities of music clips based on the musical mood change pattern.

Some music genres such as classical usually invoke more than one musical mood. For instance, Beethoven's Symphony No. 5 is famous for mood changes ranging from magnificence to nimbleness. Distinct musical features invoke different musical moods. In Jun et al. (2009), we considered a single global feature for mood classification and used it for music retrieval. However, in many cases, a single global feature could not summarize various moods in a music clip effectively and hence provide incorrect result. To solve this problem, in this paper, we first divide music clips into segments, extract various low-level features from each segment and then classify them into clusters with similar features. By assigning an appropriate mood symbol for each cluster, we can get musical mood sequences for music clips and use them for music retrieval and recommendation.

The rest of this paper is organized as follows: In Section 2, we present a brief overview on the recent music retrieval and mood classification techniques. Section 3 presents the overall system architecture and some details on the similar music retrieval and recommendation. Section 4 describes the experiments we performed and some of the results. In the last section, we conclude the paper with directions for future work.

2. RELATED WORK

In this section, we introduce some of the recent efforts in the area of music mood recognition, retrieval and recommendation. We first investigate the state of the art musical mood/emotion recognition techniques.

2.1. Musical Mood/ Emotion Recognition

Music is a language of emotions, and hence music emotion could play an important role in the various music-related applications such as music understanding, retrieval, and recommendation. Many issues for music emotion recognition have been addressed by different disciplines such as physiology, psychology, cognitive science and musicology. A regression approach for MER (Music Emotion Recognition) was proposed by Yang et al. (2008), where MER was formulated as a regression problem to predict the arousal and valence values (AV values) of each music sample which correspond to a point in the AV plane. As a result, users can efficiently retrieve desired music samples by specifying a point in the emotion plane. For performance improvement, they reduced the correlations between arousal and valence values using the Principal Component Analysis (PCA). They evaluated the accuracy in terms of the R^2 statistics, which were 58.3% for arousal and 28.1% for valence with the support vector machine (SVM) as the regressor.

While Yang et al. trained support vector regressors (SVR) on the Cartesian coordinate system, we brought the regression problem to the Polar coordinate system and improved the classification accuracy in Han et al. (2009a).

To tackle the challenging issues for recognizing music emotions, in Jun et al. (2008) we focused on the relationship between subjective human emotions and acoustic music signal features. We explored various musical features such as loudness, harmony, tempo, key, etc., and concluded that musical moods can be inferred from low-level musical features and used for music retrieval and recommendation effectively.

2.2. Sequence-Based Similar Music Retrieval

In Jun et al. (2009), we proposed a music retrieval scheme based on the musical mood change sequence. For this, we first divided music clips into segments based on six low-level musical features. Then, we applied the k-means clustering algorithm for grouping those segments into clusters with similar features. By assigning a musical mood symbol for each cluster, we transform each music clip into a mood symbol sequence. Also, we used the longest common subsequence (LCS) algorithm to estimate the similarity between mood sequences.

2.3. Music Recommendation

Most of the existing music recommendation systems are based on the user's musical preferences, which can be inferred from his or her listening history. For instance, popular music recommendation sites such as Last.fm (http://www.Last.fm), GarageBand (http://www.garageband.com), and MyStrands (http://www.mystrands.com) extrapolate correlations between like-minded listeners in order to create recommendations. In general, there are two major approaches for music recommendation: content-based and collaborative filtering-based. The former analyzes the content of music that the user preferred in the past and recommends similar music. The latter considers users' musical preferences and recommends music preferred by a user group of similar preferences.

Cano et al. (2005) presented the MusicSurfer, a meta-data free system, to provide content-based music recommendation. The system automatically extracts descriptions related to instrumentation, rhythm and harmony from music audio signals and provides music browsing and recommendation based on a high-level music similarity metric.

Pauws et al. (2002) developed Personalized Automatic Track Selection (PATS) to provide personalized playlist using a collaborative filtering method. For the creation of such playlist, a dynamic clustering was performed to group songs based on their attribute similarity and an inductive learning algorithm based on decision trees was then employed to reveal the attribute values that might explain the removal of songs.

In Han et al. (2009b), we made three distinctive contributions to the idea of context awareness in the music recommendation. Firstly, we proposed an emotion state transition model (ESTM) to model the effect of music on the human emotion state transitions. ESTM acts like a bridge between the user's situation information along with his/her emotions and the low-level music features. Using ESTM, the most appropriate music that could transit current emotion state to the desired emotion can be recommended to the user. Secondly, we presented the context-based music recommendation (CO-MUS) ontology to model the user's musical preferences and context and support reasoning about the user's desired emotions and preferences. The COMUS is a music-dedicated ontology in OWL and constructed by incorporating domain-specific classes for music recommendation into the music ontology including situation, mood and musical features. Thirdly, for mapping low-level features to ESTM, we collected various high-dimensional music features and applied nonnegative matrix factorization (NMF) for dimension reduction. We also used the support vector machine (SVM) as the emotional state transition classifier. We constructed a prototype music recommendation system based on these features.

3. SYSTEM ARCHITECTURE

In this section, we describe the overall architecture of our prototype music retrieval and recommendation system. In particular, we focus on how to generate music mood sequences and how to retrieve similar music or recommend a music list to users based on these sequences. The overall system architecture is depicted in Figure 1.

3.1. Database Construction

For music retrieval and recommendation, we generate musical mood sequence and component

Figure 1. Overall system architecture

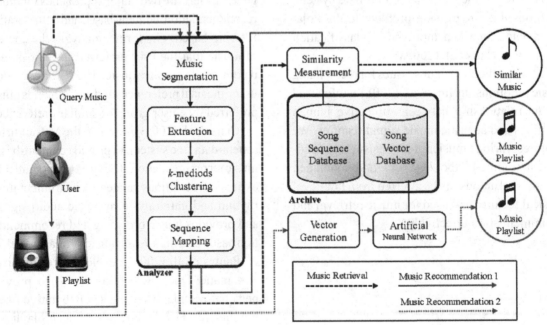

Figure 2. Overall flow for database construction

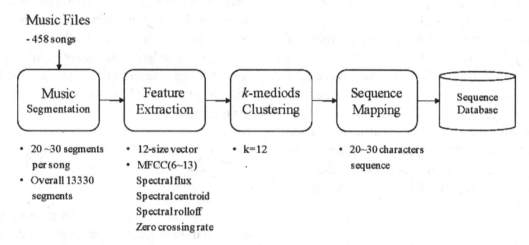

ratio vector for each music file in database and store them in the database. Music mood sequences are generated by the following steps: segmentation, feature-extraction, clustering and sequence mapping. The details are shown in Figure 2. Processing query music involves similar steps and its mood sequence is compared with sequences in the database to find out similar ones.

3.1.1. Music Segmentation Using Beat Tracking Algorithm

To divide a music clip into segments, we used the beat tracking algorithm proposed by Ellis (2007). The beat tracking algorithm derives a sequence of beat instants from a music clip by providing its approximate beat structure and bar position. Here, each beat instant corresponds to when a human listener would tap his foot.

Since 1-beat segments are too small for analysis, we use 16-beat segments, assuming 4-quadruple time music. Hence, the boundary B of segment i for total N tracked beat music is calculated using the following equations:

$$B(i) = b(16*i - 15)$$

$$(1 \leq i \leq \frac{N}{16}) \tag{1}$$

Here, b is the tracked beat position.

3.1.2. Feature Extraction

The next step is clustering similar music segments. For this purpose, we extracted 5 timbre features including Mel-frequency cepstral coefficients (MFCC), spectral centroid (SC), spectral flux (SF), spectral roll-off (SR) and zero crossing rate (ZCR). These features are represented by an 11-dimensional vector.

- *Mel-frequency cepstral coefficient*: MFCC is one of the most popular features for speech recognition. A typical example is recognizing numbers spoken into a telephone. Also, this can be used for speaker recognition, where the task is to identify who is speaking from his or her voice (Ganchev, Fakotakis, & Kokkinakis, 2005). Recently, it has been used in the music information retrieval for genre classification and audio similarity measurement (Müller, 2007) etc. The detailed procedure for computing MFCC is well described in (Zheng, Zhang, & Song, 2001).

Spectral centroid: The spectral centroid is a measure for characterizing a spectrum. It indicates the "center of mass" of the spectrum. Perceptually, it has a robust connection with the impression of the "brightness" of a sound (Shuber, Wolfe, & Tarnopolsky, 2004). It is calculated as the weighted mean of the frequencies present in the signal, using the magnitudes as the weights. The equation for computing the spectral centroid C at frame t is as follows:

$$C_t = \frac{\sum\limits_{n=1}^{N} M_t[n] * n}{\sum\limits_{n=1}^{N} M_t[n]} \qquad (2)$$

where $M_t[n]$ is the magnitude of the Fourier transform at frame t and frequency bin n.

Spectral roll-off: The spectral roll-off is another measure of spectral shape and can be defined as the frequency R_t below which 85% of the magnitude distribution is concentrated. The following equation shows the estimation of spectral roll-off.

$$\sum_{n=1}^{R_t} M_t[n] = 0.85 * \sum_{n=1}^{N} M_t[n] \qquad (3)$$

Spectral flux: The spectral flux is a measure of how quickly the power spectrum of a signal changes and can be calculated by comparing the power spectrum of one frame with that of the previous one. More precisely, it is calculated by the 2-norm Euclidean distance between two normalised spectra. The spectral flux can be used to determine the timbre of an audio signal. The following equation shows the estimation of spectral flux F at frame t:

$$F_t = \sum_{n=1}^{N} (N_t[n] - N_{t-1}[n])^2 \qquad (4)$$

Here, $N_t[n]$ and $N_{t-1}[n]$ are the normalized magnitude of the Fourier transform at the current frame, and the previous one, respectively.

Time domain zero-crossing rate: Time domain zero crossing rate indicates a measure of how noisy a signal is, and can be defined by the following equation.

$$Z_t = \frac{1}{2} \sum_{n=1}^{N} \left| sign(x[n]) - sign(x[n-1]) \right| \qquad (5)$$

Here, the *sign* function is 1 for positive arguments and 0 for negative arguments, and $x[n]$ is the time domain signal at frame t

3.1.3. K-Mediod Clustering and Sequence Generation

Both the *k*-means algorithm (MacQueen, 1967) and *k*-medoids algorithm (Kaufman & Rousseeuw, 1990) are classical clustering techniques that cluster a data set of n objects into k clusters known a priori and attempt to minimize the distance between points labeled as being in a cluster, and a point designated as the center of that cluster. They are both known to be fast, light and effective. However, compared to the *k*-means algorithm, the *k*-medoids algorithm is more robust to noise and outliers. Because of this robustness, in this paper, we use the *k*-medoids algorithm for clustering purpose.

For clustering, we first collected aforementioned features from the dataset of about 13,000 music segments. Also, we set the number of clusters k to 12 which was chosen empirically since it showed good performance in terms of accuracy and complexity.

In order to define a dominant music mood for each cluster, we recruited volunteers without any restriction on the musical background and asked them to listen to music clips in the cluster and annotate appropriate moods according to our hierarchically defined mood list. The ground truth mood of each group is determined by a majority vote of the labeled data. Even though we performed mood annotation manually, this step can be easily automated either by collecting mood tags, if available, using a collaborated filter or by some well-defined feature-mood mapping function.

By assigning a mood symbol for each cluster, we can transform each music clip into a sequence of mood symbols. For example, assume that there are 6 clusters, C_1 through C_6 for the music dataset with M_1 through M_6 as their mood symbols. If a music clip m has four segments, s_1 through s_4 where $s_1 \in C_1$, $s_2 \in C_5$, $s_3 \in C_3$, and $s_4 \in C_6$, then the music clip m is represented by the sequence M_1 $M_5 M_3 M_6$.

3.1.4. Vector Generation

Since music clips are segmented by small frame size, their mood sequences may contain various

size of repeating groups depending on the mood symbol. We believe that moods with larger repeating group have more influence on the overall music mood than those with smaller one. The quantitative weight of component moods over the whole music clip can be easily represented by the component ratio vector. For instance, suppose that music mood sequence for music clip m is (M_1 M_1 $M_1 M_5 M_5 M_5 M_5 M_5 M_5 M_5 M_5 M_3 M_6 M_6$). Since the sequence length is 14, its component ratio vector V for 12 mood symbols is [0.21, 0, 0.07, 0, 0.57, 0.14, 0, 0, 0, 0, 0, 0]. For comparison, we show the component ratio vector of different genre songs in Figure 3.

Figure 3. Component ratio vector of different genre music

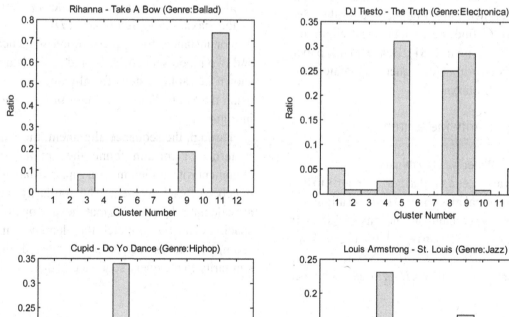
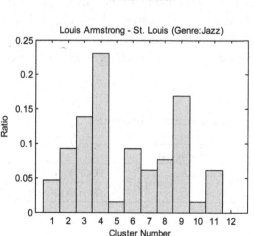

3.2. Similarity-based Music Retrieval

3.2.1. Smith-Waterman Algorithm

Sequence alignment is one of the most popular methods for arranging sequences present in the various domains such as natural language, financial data and bioinformatics. For instance, for the sequences in the bioinformatics, it is known to be effective in identifying regions of similarity that may be a consequence of functional, structural, or evolutionary relationships. Sequence alignment techniques generally fall into two categories: global alignments and local alignments. Global alignments perform global optimization that forces the alignment to span the entire length of all query sequences. By contrast, local alignments identify regions of similarity within long sequences. Considering partial query sequence and full database sequences, local alignments are more appropriate. The Smith-Waterman algorithm is a well-known local alignment algorithm that guarantees to find the optimal local alignment (Smith & Waterman, 1981). Hence, in this paper, we use this algorithm for sequence alignment and similarity measurement.

3.2.2. Similarity Measurement

The Smith-Waterman is a dynamic programming algorithm and uses a similarity score matrix to find the optimal local alignment. The local alignment is obtained by searching for the maximal score in the similarity score matrix, and tracing back the optimal path until a score of zero is encountered. The similarity score matrix H for a query sequence S_q of size m and database sequence S_d of size n is built as follows:

$$H(i,0) = 0$$

$$(0 \leq i \leq m)$$

$$H(0,j) = 0$$

$$(0 \leq j \leq n)$$

$$H(i,j) = \max \begin{cases} 0 \\ H(i-1,j-1) + w(Sq_i, Sd_j) & Match \, / \, Mismatch \\ H(i-1,j) + w(Sq_i, -) & Deletion \\ H(i,j-1) + w(-, Sd_j) & Insertion \end{cases}$$

(3)

Here, w is the substitution matrix that contains the match/mismatch score and gap penalties. The similarity score of a pair of sequences is derived by the maximum score in matrix H.

For instance, for a query mood sequence Q and two mood sequences D_1 and D_2 in database shown in Table 1, steps for aligning sequences using the Smith-Waterman algorithm are shown in Figure 4.

Through the sequence alignment, the Smith-Waterman algorithm found the optimal local alignment with minimum open gaps and maximum matches of each element. The similarity scores are calculated by counting matches and open gaps spacing elements to match the elements. In the example, database sequence D_1 showed higher similarity to the query sequence Q than D_2 since

Table 1. Sample music sequences

Query sequence	GGFFIGIGGGGGFFF
Database sequence D_1	FGGFFGGGGFFGFGGFFGGIIF
Database sequence D_2	CHGCGGGGGGGGGCCGGGGGGGGGGCCGGBBCC

Figure 4. Local sequence alignment using Smith-Waterman Algorithm

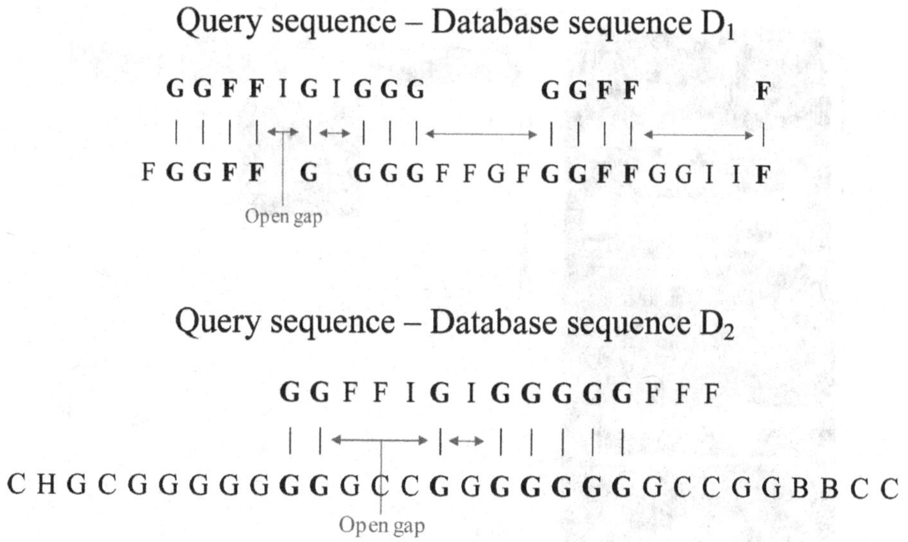

Query sequence – Database sequence D_1

G G F F I G I **G G G**   **G G F F**   **F**

| | | | ↔ | ↔ | | | ← → | | | | ← → |

F **G G F F** G **G G G** F F G F **G G F F** G G I I F

Open gap

Query sequence – Database sequence D_2

G G F F I **G** I **G G G G G** F F F

| | ← → | ↔ | | | | | |

C H G C **G G G G G G G G G** C C **G** G G G G G G G C C G G B B C C

Open gap

the former has more matches even though it has more open gaps.

3.3. Music Recommendation

Music recommendation attempts to recommend a set of songs that are likely to be of interest to the user and can be done using diverse techniques. In this paper, we perform music recommendation based on our retrieval scheme and user preference. For comparison, we also developed artificial neural network (ANN)-based recommendation scheme.

3.3.1. User Preferences

User preferences for music are very crucial for the effective music recommendation. In this paper, we collected user preferences using two methods: One involves analyzing music playlist data, and the other involves playing with user interface such that the user can rate his/her preferences for music easily. In this section, we describe the former method and the latter method will be described in the section 4.3.

Figure 5 shows the music playlist of the Apple iPod with rating interface where the user can rate

music clips while listening. We used the Apple iPod for music rating since it provides easy rating interface of just clicking or turning dial. Rated metadata are synchronized in the PC when the iPod is connected. This feature is also easily found in the Microsoft Windows Media Player. Rated metadata are stored as an ID3 tag in a music clip.

3.3.2. Music Recommendation

After collecting user preferences for music, we need to decide the list of music for recommendation. If we know user preferred music, we can retrieve similar music based on the mood sequence. This approach guarantees that recommended music have similar mood sequences. For the comparison, we also developed artificial neural network -based music recommendation scheme where artificial neural network is used to obtain user preferences from preferred music clips and generate music recommendation.

The artificial neural network is one of the most popular machine learning algorithms that has been used in various research areas such as face identification, medical diagnosis and financial applications (Rumelhart & McClelland, 1986).

Figure 5. Music rating interfaces

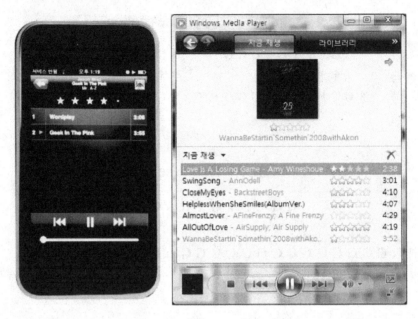

The artificial neural network takes the component ratio vectors as input and the user rating data as the target function (0~5).

4. EXPERIMENTAL RESULTS

To evaluate the effectiveness of our proposed scheme, we implemented a prototype system and carried out various experiments on it. The system was implemented on the PC with Intel Core2Duo 2.80GHz with 4GB ram. MATLAB programming was used to implement most of the system. Web user interface was implemented on Apache web server with PHP language and Mysql database.

For the experiment, we first collected music data from a Korean online music store (http://www.mnet.com) which provides music clips by genre and popularity. We collected 458 songs (MP3 files) from six different genres including electronic, hip-hop, jazz, ballad, new age and rock. They were stored as 41,000 Hz, 16-bit and 2 channel stereo PCM.

4.1. Feature Analysis on Music Segments

As we mentioned before, we use timbre features such as spectral roll-off, spectral flux and zero crossing rate for music feature analysis. Even in the same music clip, each timbre feature may show diverse variation on time. For example, we depicted three different timbre features together in the same space in Figure 6. In the figure, the global timbre feature of the music clip is marked 'X' and its segment features are denoted by '●'. The figure shows that even though there are different timbres in the music clip, the global feature dilutes them by averaging.

Figure 7 shows timbre feature variations of three different music clips on the SR-SF-ZCR space. Each music clip is denoted by 3 different symbols ('●', square, and diamond). In the figure, we can observe that music clips provide similar global feature even though their segments have totally different timbre patterns.

Figure 6. SR-SF-ZCR variation and non-segmented feature

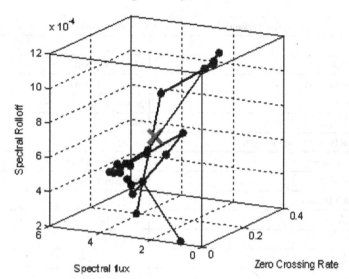

Figure 7. SR-SF-ZCR variation of 3 songs

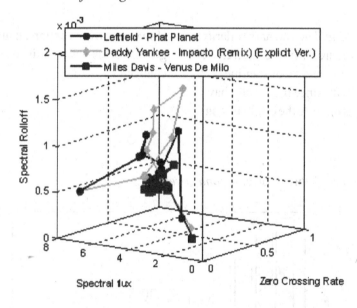

4.2. Similarity Measurement of Similar Music

In this experiment, we show the effectiveness of our mood sequence-based music retrieval scheme. We first show the evaluation on the original songs and their cover versions. We will show its general performance in terms of user satisfaction in the next section. Even though original and cover songs have delicate or distinct local differences in the musical timbre, in many cases they still keep similar musical timbres and mood variations on the whole. For instance, '*Bohemian Rhapsody*' is a well-known song with diverse cover versions. Table 2 shows the list of songs that we considered and brief annotation on the genre or degree of perceptual similarity. The last column shows their ranking by the similarity score of the

Table 2. Original and cover songs of 'Bohemian Rhapsody'

Original	Cover version	Manual annotation	Rank
Queen			
	Ten Tenors	Similar to original	1
	Constantine M	Similar to original	2
	Helmut Lotti	Similar to original	3
	The Cast Of We Will Rock You	Similar to original	4
	Royal Philharmonic Orchestra	Orchestra version	5
	Dream Queen	Similar to original	6
	Maksim	Orchestra version	7
	Russell Watson	Electronic version	8
	Braids	Hiphop version	9
	Thierry Lang	Piano version	10
	The Flaming Lips	Acoustic version	11
	The Euphorics	A cappella version	12
	Todacosta	Latin version	13

Smith-Waterman algorithm. Their actual similarity scores are shown in Figure 8. In the figure, we can see that "Ten Tenors" and "Constantine M" have the highest similarity since they really have similar overall mood variation to the original song.

However, cover versions that belong to different genres get lower ranks since musical timbres were changed a lot.

Figure 8. Similarity scores between original and cover song

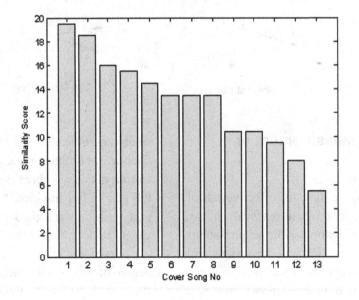

Table 3. User satisfaction evaluation

Subject	1	2	3	4	5	6	7	8	9	10
Sequence-based	79	83	62	100	94	93	83	83	86	99
Segment+ANN	45	76	50	94	61	76	79	59	48	83
Global+ANN	48	75	49	68	80	68	75	59	44	25
Random	34	67	32	44	50	33	22	40	12	48
Subject	11	12	13	14	15	16	17	18	19	20
Sequence-based	60	80	84	76	96	85	84	99	70	91
Segment+ANN	40	82	74	57	96	97	78	70	45	89
Global+ANN	36	57	43	39	85	95	76	72	26	80
Random	11	55	41	28	59	9	50	52	9	15

	Average	Standard deviation
Sequence-based	84.35	11.35
Segment+ANN	69.95	18.20
Global+ANN	60.00	20.32

4.3. Music Recommendation

In this section, we measure the effectiveness of our music recommendation system in terms of user satisfaction. We have 20 volunteers recruited inside the campus. They were asked to listen to 20 music clips and rate them. Subjects evaluated the recommended songs using a scale from 0 to 100. Figure 10 shows the graphical user interface we developed for the evaluation. Based on these ratings, the system can infer user preference. User preference can be obtained directly from users or indirectly. For the indirect inference, we used the artificial neural network model. If we have user preferences, then we can generate recommendable music list based on our mood sequence-based similarity measurement. For the comparison, we used four different recommendation schemes: (i) random, (ii) global feature-based ANN, (iii) segment feature-based ANN, and (iv) mood

Figure 9. Comparison of user satisfaction between recommendation and random selection

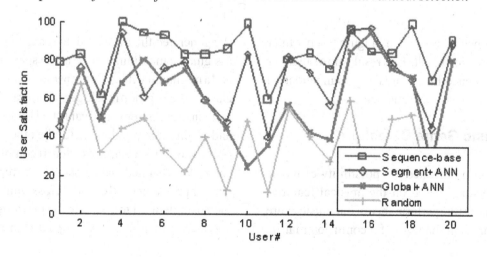

Figure 10. Web GUI for training and recommendation

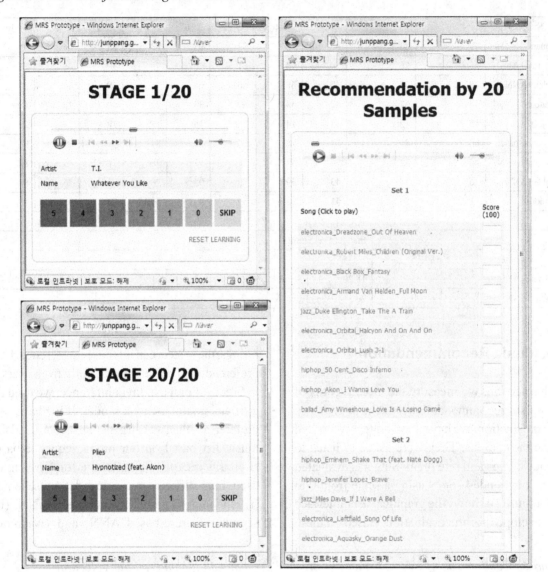

sequence-based. Table 3 and Figure 9 show their user satisfaction result. This result shows that our mood sequence-based music recommendation achieved highest user satisfaction.

4.4. Music Genre Detection

Lastly, we investigated the possibility of music genre detection based on the musical features. Table 4 shows the performance of our music genre classification in the form of a confusion matrix.

We generated the training data for each genre by assigning a maximum value to the specific genre and a minimum value to the others. For instance, to classify the Hip-hop music genre, the training data contains a maximum rated value for Hip-hop music and a minimum rated value for the others. Based on these training data, our system recommends 20 songs. We assumed that the same genre represents similar preferences. Recently, cross-validation is increasingly used to evaluate the performance of classifiers; therefore, we adopted it in order to

Table 4. Confusion matrix for music genre classification

.	EL	HH	JA	BA	NE	RO
Electronic (EL)	17	0	0	5	0	0
Hiphop (HH)	2	20	2	5	0	1
Jazz (JA)	0	0	15	0	6	1
Ballad (BA)	0	0	0	10	0	0
Newage (NE)	1	0	1	0	11	1
Rock (RO)	0	0	2	5	3	17
Accuracy	85%	100%	75%	50%	55%	85%
(a) Sequence-based model						
.	EL	HH	JA	BA	NE	RO
Electronic (EL)	14	4	0	5	0	0
Hiphop (HH)	4	15	1	3	0	1
Jazz (JA)	0	1	12	0	5	4
Ballad (BA)	0	0	1	12	0	0
Newage (NE)	0	0	2	0	15	1
Rock (RO)	2	0	4	0	0	14
Accuracy	70%	75%	60%	60%	75%	70%
(a) Segment feature-based ANN model						
.	EL	HH	JA	BA	NE	RO
Electronic (EL)	9	3	1	3	1	2
Hiphop (HH)	4	14	3	6	0	1
Jazz (JA)	2	2	7	1	6	2
Ballad (BA)	2	0	1	7	1	0
Newage (NE)	1	0	7	2	11	1
Rock (RO)	2	1	1	1	1	14
Accuracy	45%	70%	35%	35%	55%	70%
(b) Global feature-based ANN model						

divide the dataset into two sets: training samples (231) and testing samples (227).

In a confusion matrix, the columns and rows correspond to the actual and predicted genre, respectively. For example, in Table 4 (a), the value of a cell in the 5th row and 5th column is 11, which means that New Age music was correctly classified with 55% accuracy. As we can observe from the table, the classification performance could be very varied depending on the genre. Still, our sequence-based approach achieved best performance on the average.

5. CONCLUSION

In this paper, we proposed a new music retrieval and recommendation scheme based on varying musical mood sequences. For this, we first divided music clips into segments and grouped them into clusters using the *k*-medoids clustering algorithm. For each cluster, we defined a unique mood symbol, which enabled each music clip to be transformed into a sequence of musical mood symbols. For similarity-based music retrieval, we used the Smith-Waterman algorithm to estimate the similarity between music sequences. For music recommendation, we first collected user preferences directly or indirectly and then generated recommendation list of music clips with similar musical mood sequence. For performance evaluation, we compared our scheme with three other methods. We also investigated the accuracy of music genre classification. On the average, our scheme showed excellent performance compared to the other methods.

REFERENCES

Birmingham, W. P., Dannenberg, R. B., & Pardo, B. (2006). An Introduction to Query by Humming with the Vocal Search System. *Communications of the ACM, 49*(8), 49–52. doi:10.1145/1145287.1145313

Cano, P., Koppenberger, M., & Wack, N. (2005). Content-based music audio recommendation. In *Proceeding of ACM Multimedia.*

Ellis, D. (2007). Beat Tracking by Dynamic Programming. *Journal of New Music Research. Special Issue on Beat and Tempo Extraction, 36*(1), 51–60.

Feng, Y., Zhuang, Y., & Pan, Y. (2003, October). Music information retrieval by detecting mood via computational media aesthetics. In *Proceedings of IEEE/WIC International Conference on* (pp. 235-241).

Ganchev, T., Fakotakis, N., & Kokkinakis, G. (2005). Comparative evaluation of various MFCC implementations on the speaker verification task. In *Proceedings of the 10th International Conference on Speech and Computer.*

Garageband. (n.d.). Retrieved November 30, 2009, from http://www.garageband.com/

Ghias, A., Logan, J., Chanberlin, D., & Smith, B. C. (1995). Query by humming - musical information retrieval in an audio database. In *Proceedings of ACM Multimedia.*

Han, B., Rho, S., Dannenberg, R. B., & Hwang, E. (2009a, October 26). SMERS: Music Emotion Recognition using Support Vector Regression. In *Proceedings of the International Society for Music Information Retrieval 09*, Kobe, Japan.

Han, B., Rho, S., Jun, S., & Hwang, E. (2009b). Music Emotion Classification and Context-based Music Recommendation. In *Proceedings of the Multimedia Tools and Applications.*

Jun, S., Han, B., & Hwang, E. (2009, April). A Similar Music Retrieval Scheme based on Musical Mood Variation. In *Proceedings of the Asian Conference on Intelligent Information and Database Systems.*

Jun, S., Rho, S., Han, B., & Hwang, E. (2008, August). A Fuzzy Inference-based Music Emotion Recognition System. In *Proceedings of the Visual Information Engineering.*

Juslin, P. N., & Sloboda, J. A. (2001). *Music and Emotion: Theory and research.* New York: Oxford University Press.

Kaufman, L., & Rousseeuw, P. (1990). *Finding groups in data: an introduction to cluster analysis.* New York: John Wiley and Sons.

Last.fm. (n.d.). Retrieved November 30, 2009, from http://www.last.fm/

Lu, L., Liu, D., & Zhang, H. (2006). Automatic Mood Detection and Tracking of Music Audio Signals. *IEEE Transactions on Audio. Speech and Audio Processing*, *14*(1), 5–18. doi:10.1109/TSA.2005.860344

MacQueen, J. (1967). Some methods for classification and analysis of multivariate observations. In *Proceedings of Knowledge Discovery and Data Mining*.

Müller, M. (2007). *Information Retrieval for Music and Motion* (p. 65). New York: Springer. ISBN 9783540740476.

Mystrands. (n.d.). Retrieved November 30, 2009, from http://www.mystrands.com/

Pauws, S., & Eggen, B. (2002). Realization and user evaluation of an automatic playlist generator. In *Proceedings of International Society for Music Information Retrieval*. PATS.

Rho, S., Han, B., Hwang, E., & Kim, M. (2008). MUSEMBLE: A Novel Music Retrieval System with Automatic Voice Query Transcription and Reformulation. *Journal of Systems and Software*, *81*(7), 1065–1080. doi:10.1016/j.jss.2007.05.038

Rumelhart, D. E., & McClelland, J. L. (1986). *Parallel distributed processing* (*Vol. 1*). Cambridge, MA: MIT Press.

Schubert, E., Wolfe, J., & Tarnopolsky, A. (2004). Spectral centroid and timbre in complex, multiple instrumental textures. In *Proceedings of the International Conference on Music Perception and Cognition*, Evanston, IL.

Smith, T. F., & Waterman, M. S. (1981). Identification of Common Molecular Subsequences. *Journal of Molecular Biology*, *147*, 195–197. doi:10.1016/0022-2836(81)90087-5

Yang, Y., Lin, Y., Su, Y., & Chen, H. (2008). A Regression Approach to Music Emotion Recognition. *IEEE Transactions on Audio. Speech and Audio Processing*, *16*(2), 448–457. doi:10.1109/TASL.2007.911513

Zheng, F., Zhang, G., & Song, Z. (2001). Comparison of Different Implementations of MFCC. *Journal of Computer Science & Technology*, *16*(6), 582–589. doi:10.1007/BF02943243

This work was previously published in International Journal of Semantic Web and Information Systems, Volume 6, Issue 2, edited by Amit P. Sheth, pp. 1-16, copyright 2010 by IGI Publishing (an imprint of IGI Global).

Compilation of References

Abbasi, R., Staab, S., & Cimiano, P. (2007). Organizing Resources on Tagging Systems using t-org. In *Proceedings of the 4th European Semantic Web Conference* (pp. 97-110). Heidelberg, Germany: Springer.

Adriaens, G., & Schreurs, D. (1992). From COGRAM to ALCOGRAM: Toward a controlled English grammar checker. In *Proceedings of the Conference on Computational Linguistics (COLING'92),* Nantes, France (pp. 595-601).

Akkiraju, R., Srivastava, B., Ivan, A.-A., Goodwin, R., & Syeda-Mahmood, T. (2006). SEMAPLAN: Combining Planning with Semantic Matching to Achieve Web Service Composition. In *Proceedings of the 6th International Conference on Web Services (ICWS).* Washington, DC: IEEE Computer Society.

Alexander, C. (1979). *The Timeless Way of Building.* New York: Oxford University Press.

Altschul, S. F., Madden, T. L., Schaffer, A. A., Zhang, J., Zhang, Z., & Miller, W. (1997). Gapped BLAST and PSI-BLAST: a new generation of protein database search programs. *Nucleic Acids Research, 25*(17), 3389–3402. doi:10.1093/nar/25.17.3389

Ames, S., Bobb, N., Greenan, K. M., Hofmann, O. S., Storer, M. W., Maltzahn, C., et al. (2006). LiFS: An Attribute-Rich File System for Storage Class Memories. In *Proceedings of the 23rd IEEE / 14th NASA Goddard Conference on Mass Storage Systems and Technologies.*

An, Y., & Mylopoulos, J. (2005). Translating XML Web Data into Ontologies. In *Proceedings of the OTM Workshops* (pp. 967-976).

An, Y., Borgida, A., & Mylopoulos, J. (2005). Constructing Complex Semantic Mappings between XML Data and Ontologies. In *Proceedings of the International Semantic Web Conference* (pp. 6-20).

Angeletou, S., Sabou, M., & Motta, E. (2008). Semantically Enriching Folksonomies with FLOR. In *Proceedings of the 1st International Workshop on Collective Semantics; Collective Intelligences & the Semantic Web at the 5th European Semantic Web Conference,* Tenerife, Spain (pp.65-79).

Angeletou, S., Sabou, M., Spacia, L., & Motta, E. (2007). Bridging the Gap Between Folksonomies and the Semantic Web: An Experience Report. In *Proceedings of the Workshop: Bridging the Gap between Semantic Web and Web 2.0, European Semantic Web Conference,* Vienna, Austria.

Angelov, K., & Ranta, A. (2009). Implementing controlled languages in gf. In *Proceedings of CNL* (pp. 82-101).

Anisur Rahman, M., Hossain, A., Kiringa, I., & El Saddik, A. (2006, November). *Towards an Ontology for MPEG-7 Semantic Descriptions.* Paper presented at the Intelligent Interactive Learning Object Repositories (I2LOR) Conference, Montreal, QC, Canada.

Ankolekar, A., Krötzsch, M., Tran, T., & Vrandecic, D. (2007). The Two Cultures: Mashing Up Web 2.0 and the Semantic Web. In C. L. Williamson, M. E. Zurko, P. F. Patel-Schneider, & P. J. Shenoy (Eds.), *Proceedings of WWW* (pp. 825-834). New York: ACM.

Antoniou, G., Franconia, E., & van Harmelen, F. (2005). Introduction to Semantic Web Ontology Languages. In Eisinger, N., & Maluszynski, J. (Eds.), *Reasoning Web* (*Vol. 3564*, pp. 1–21). New York: Springer.

Ardissono, L., Felfernig, A., Friedrich, G., Jannach, D., Zanker, M., & Schäfer, R. (2002). A Framework for Rapid Development of Advanced Web-based Configurator Applications. In F. van Harmelen (Ed.), *Proceedings of the 15th Eureopean Conference on Artificial Intelligence (ECAI'2002)*, Lyon, France (pp. 618-622). Amsterdam: IOS Press.

Arndt, R., Troncy, R., Staab, S., Hardman, L., & Vacura, M. (2007). COMM: Designing a Well-Founded Multimedia Ontology for the Web. In *Proceedings of the 6th International Semantic Web Conference: The Semantic Web*, Busan, Korea (LNCS 4825, pp. 30-43). Berlin: Springer.

Aroyo, L., Bellekens, P., Bjorkman, M., Houben, G. J., Akkermans, P., & Kaptein, A. (2007). SenSee Framework for Personalized Access to TV Content. In *Proceedings of the Interactive TV: a Shared Experience*, Amsterdam, The Netherlands (LNCS 4471, pp. 156-165). Berlin: Springer.

Auer, S. (n.d.). *Powl – a web based platform for collaborative semantic web development.* Retrieved from http://powl.sourceforge.net/overview.php

Auer, S., & Lehmann, J. (2007). What have Innsbruck and Leipzig in common? extracting semantics from wiki content. In *Proceedings of Eswc* (pp. 503-517).

Baader, F., Calvanese, D., McGuinness, D. L., Nardi, D., & Patel-Schneider, P. F. (2003). *The Description Logic Handbook: Theory, Implementation, and Applications.* Cambridge, UK: Cambridge University Press.

Bailey, B. (2006). *Getting the complete picture with usability testing.* Washington, DC: U.S. Department of Health and Human Services. Retrieved December 16, 2010, from http://usability.gov/articles/newsletter/pubs/030106news.html

Baldauf, M., Dustar, S., & Rosenberg, F. (2007). A Survey on Context-Aware Systems. *Intl. Journal of Ad Hoc and Ubiquitous Computing, 2*(4), 263–277. doi:10.1504/IJAHUC.2007.014070

Bansiya, J., & Davis, C. (2002). A hierarchical model for object-oriented design quality assessment. *IEEE Transactions on Software Engineering*, 4–17. doi:10.1109/32.979986

Bao, J., Smart, P., Braines, D., & Shadbolt, N. (2009, March). *A controlled natural language interface for semantic media wiki using the rabbit language.* Paper presented at the Workshop on Controlled Natural Language (CNL'09).

Bardram, J. E. (2005). The Java Context Awareness Framework (JCAF). In *Proceedings of the 3rd intl. conf. on pervasive computing.*

Barrasa, J., Corcho, O., & Gómez-Pérez, A. (2004). R_2O, an Extensible and Semantically Based Database-to-Ontology Mapping Language. In *Proceedings of the Second Workshop on Semantic Web and Databases (SWDB2004).*

Barrasa, J. (2007). *Modelo para la Definición Automática de Correspondencias Semánticas entre Ontologías y Modelos Relacionales.* Madrid, Spain: Facultad de Informática, Universidad Politécnica de Madrid.

Basili, V., Caldiera, G., & Rombach, H. D. (1994). The Goal Question Metric Paradigm, Encyclopedia of Software Engineering. In Marciniak, J. J. (Ed.), *Encyclopedia of Software Engineering* (pp. 528–532). New York: John Wiley & Sons.

Batchelor, C. (2008). Formal ontology in information systems. In *Frontiers in Artificial Intelligence and Applications* (Vol. 183, pp. 195-207).

Begelman, G., Keller, P., & Smadja, F. (2006). Automated Tag Clustering: Improving Search and Exploration in the Tag Space. In *Proceedings of the Collaborative Web Tagging Workshop at the 15th WWW Conference*, Edinburgh, Scotland.

Berman, H. M., Bhat, T. N., Bourne, P. E., Feng, Z., Gilliland, G., & Weissig, H. (2000). The PDB and the Challenge of Structural Genomics. *Nature Structural Biology, 11*, 957–959. doi:10.1038/80734

Berman, H. M., Westbrook, J., Feng, Z., Gilliland, G., Bhat, T. N., & Weissig, H. (2000). The Protein Data Bank. *Nucleic Acids Research, 28*, 235–242. doi:10.1093/nar/28.1.235

Berners-Lee, T., Chen, Y., Chilton, L., Connolly, D., Dhanaraj, R., Hollenbach, J., et al. (2006, November). Tabulator: Exploring and analyzing linked data on the semantic web. In *Proceedings of the 3rd International Semantic Web User Interaction Workshop (SWUI)*, Athens, GA. Retrieved from http://swui.semanticweb.org/swui06/papers/Berners-Lee/Berners-Lee.pdf

Berners-Lee, T., Handler, J., & Lassila, O. (2001, May). The Semantic Web. *Scientific American*, 28–37.

Bhat, T. N. (2009a). Chemical Taxonomies and Ontologies for Semantic Web. *Semantic Universe*. Retrieved from http://www.semanticuniverse.com/articles-chemical-taxonomies-and-ontologies-semantic-web.html

Bhat, T. N. (2009b). *On the creation of structural FaceBook using rule-based methods to build and exchange ontology for drug design*. Retrieved from http://sunsite.informatik.rwth-aachen.de/Publications/CEUR-WS/Vol-549

Bhat, T. N., & Barkley, J. (2007). Semantic Web for the Life Sciences - Hype, Why, How and Use Case for AIDS Inhibitors. In *Proceedings of the IEEE Congress on Services* (pp. 87-91).

Bhat, T. N., & Barkley, J. (2008). Development of a Use case for Chemical Resource Description Framework for Acquired Immune Deficiency Syndrome Drug Discovery. *The Open Bioinformatics Journal*, 2, 20–27. doi:10.2174/1875036200802010020

Birbeck, M., & McCarron, S. (2009). *CURIE Syntax 1.0 — A Syntax for Expressing Compact URIs*. World Wide Web Consortium.

Birmingham, W. P., Dannenberg, R. B., & Pardo, B. (2006). An Introduction to Query by Humming with the Vocal Search System. *Communications of the ACM*, 49(8), 49–52. doi:10.1145/1145287.1145313

Bizer, C., & Gauß, T. (2007). *Disco - hyperdata browser*. Retrieved from http://sites.wiwiss.fu-berlin.de/suhl/bizer/ng4j/disco/

Bizer, C., Lee, R., & Pietriga, E. (2006). Fresnel: A Browser Independent Presentation Vocabulary for RDF. In *Proceedings of the Second International Workshop on Interaction Design and the Semantic Web* (pp. 158-171).

Bizer, C. (2009). The Emerging Web of Linked Data. *IEEE Intelligent Systems*, 24(5), 87–92. doi:10.1109/MIS.2009.102

Bizer, C., Cyganiak, R., & Heath, T. (2007). *How to Publish Linked Data on the Web*. Berlin: Freie Universität Berlin.

Bizer, C., Heath, T., & Berners-Lee, T. (2009). Linked Data — The Story So Far. *International Journal on Semantic Web and Information Systems*, 5(3), 1–22.

Blanco Fernandez, Y., Pazos Arias, J. J., Lopez Nores, M., Gil Solla, A., & Ramos Cabrer, M. (2006). AVATAR: An Improved Solution for Personalized TV based on Semantic Inference. *IEEE Transactions on Consumer Electronics*, 52(1), 223–231. doi:10.1109/TCE.2006.1605051

Bloehdorn, S., Görlitz, O., Schenk, S., & Völkel, M. (2006). *TagFS – Tag Semantics for Hierarchical File Systems*. Paper presented at the 6th International Conference on Knowledge Management (I-KNOW'06).

Blundell, T. L., Sibanda, B. L., Montalvao, R. W., Brewerton, S., Chelliah, V., & Worth, C. L. (2006). Structural biology and bioinformatics in drug design: opportunities and challenges for target identification and lead discovery. *Philosophical Transactions of the Royal Society B. Biological Sciences*, 361(1467), 413–423. doi:10.1098/rstb.2005.1800

Blunschi, L., Dittrich, J.-P., Girard, O. R., Karakashian, S. K., & Salles, M. A. V. (2007). A Dataspace Odyssey: The iMeMex Personal Dataspace Management System. In *Proceedings of the Third Biennial Conference on Innovative Data Systems Research* (pp. 114-119).

Boardman, R. (2001). Multiple Hierarchies in User Workspace. In *Proceedings of CHI '01 Extended Abstracts on Human Factors in Computing Systems* (pp. 403-404). New York: ACM Press.

Bonino da Silva Santos, L. O., Wijnen, R. P.-v., & Vink, P. (2007, November). A Service-Oriented Middleware for Context-Aware Applications. In *Proceedings of the 5th international workshop on middleware for pervasive and ad-hoc computing (mpac 2007)*, Newport Beach, CA (pp. 37-42). New York: ACM. Retrieved from http://eprints.eemcs.utwente.nl/11446/.

Bontcheva, K., & Wilks, Y. (2004). Automatic Report Generation from Ontologies: The MIAKT Approach. In *Proceedings of the 9th International Conference on Applications of Natural Language to Information Systems* (pp. 324-335).

Brandon, D. (2005). Recursive Database Structures. *Journal of Computing Sciences in Colleges.*

Brickley, D., & Guha, R. V. (2000). *Resource Description Frame Work (RDF) Schema Specification 1.0, W3C Candidate Recommendation.* Retrieved from http://www.w3.org/TR/rdf-schema

Brin, S., & Page, L. (1998). The anatomy of a large-scale hypertextual Web search engine. In *Proceedings of the 7th International World Wide Web Conference* (pp. 107-117). Amsterdam: Elsevier.

Brooke, J. (1996). SUS: a "quick and dirty" usability scale. In P. Jordan, B. Thomas, B. Weerdmeester, & A. McClelland (Eds.), *Usability evaluation in industry.* London: Taylor and Francis. Retrieved December 16, 2010, from http://www.usabilitynet.org/trump/documents/Suschapt.doc

Burel, G., Cano, A. E., & Lanfranchi, V. (2009). Ozone Browser: Augmenting the Web with Semantic Overlays. In C. Bizer, S. Auer, & G. A. Grimnes (Eds.), *Proceedings of the 5th Workshop on Scripting and Development for the Semantic Web.*

Byrne, E. J. (1992). A Conceptual Foundation for Software Re-engineering. In *Proceedings of the International Conference on Software Maintenance and Reengineering* (pp. 226-235). Washington, DC: IEEE Computer Society.

Cai, Y., Dong, X. L., Halevy, A., Liu, J. M., & Madhavan, J. (2005). Personal Information Management with SEMEX. In *Proceedings of the 2005 ACM SIGMOD Conference on Management of Data* (pp. 921-923). New York: ACM Press.

Calero, C., Ruiz, F., & Piattini, M. (Eds.). (2006). *Ontologies for Software Engineering and Software Technology.* New York: Springer. doi:10.1007/3-540-34518-3

Calvary, G., Coutaz, J., Thevenin, D., Limbourg, Q., Bouillon, L., & Vanderdonckt, J. (2003). A Unifying Reference Framework for multi-target user interfaces. *Interacting with Computers, 15*(3), 289–308. doi:10.1016/S0953-5438(03)00010-9

Cano, P., Koppenberger, M., & Wack, N. (2005). Content-based music audio recommendation. In *Proceeding of ACM Multimedia.*

Caracciolo, C., Heguiabehere, J., Presutti, V., & Gangemi, A. (2009). *Initial Network of Fisheries Ontologies.* NeOn project.

Carey, M. J., DeWitt, D. J., Richardson, J. E., & Shekita, E. J. (1986). Object and File Management in the EXODUS Extensible Database System. In *Proceedings of the 12th International Conference on Very Large Data Bases* (pp. 91-100). San Francisco: Morgan Kaufmann Publishers Inc.

Carkenord, B. (2002). *Why Build a Logical Data Model.* Retrieved from http://etnaweb04.embarcadero.com/resources/tech_papers/datamodel.pdf

Carr, L., Hall, W., Bechhofer, S., & Goble, C. (2001). Conceptual linking: ontology-based open hypermedia. In *Proceedings of the 10th international conference on World Wide Web* (pp. 334-342). New York: ACM.

Catarci, T., Dongilli, P., Mascio, T. D., Franconi, E., Santucci, G., & Tessaris, S. (2004). An Ontology Based Visual Tool for Query Formulation Support. In R. L. de Mántaras & L. Saitta (Eds.), *Proceedings of ECAI* (pp. 308-312). Amsterdam: IOS Press.

Chang, C.-C., & Lin, C.-J. (2001). *Libsvm: a library for support vector machines.* Retrieved from http://www.csie.ntu.edu.tw/ cjlin/libsvm

Chen, G., & Kotz, D. (2000, November). *A Survey of Context-Aware Mobile Computing Research* (Tech. Rep. No. TR2000-381). Hanover, NH: Dartmouth College, Dept. of Computer Science.

Chen, H., Finin, T., & Joshi, A. (2003). An Ontology for Context-Aware Pervasive Computing Environments. In *Proceedigns of the Workshop on ontologies and distributed systems (ijcai-2003).*

Chen, H., Perich, F., Finin, T., & Joshi, A. (2004). SOUPA: Standard Ontology for Ubiquitous and Pervasive Applications. In *Proceedings of the Intl. conf. on mobile and ubiquitous systems: Networking and services.*

Cheyer, A., Park, J., & Giuli, R. (2005). IRIS: Integrate. Relate. Infer. Share. In *Proceedings of the Workshop on the Semantic Desktop: Next Generation Personal Information Management and Collaboration Infrastructure.*

Chin, J. P., Diehl, V. A., & Norman, K. L. (1988, June 15-19). Development of an instrument measuring user satisfaction of the human-computer interface. In E. Soloway, D. Frye, & S. B. Sheppard (Eds.), *Interface Evaluations: Proceedings of ACM CHI'88 Conference on Human Factors in Computing Systems,* Washington, DC (pp. 213-218).

Chomsky, N. (1965). *Aspects of the theory of syntax.* Cambridge, MA: MIT Press.

Clark, P., Thompson, J., & Porter, B. W. (2000). Knowledge Patterns. In *Proceedings of KR2000* (pp. 591–600). Principles of Knowledge Representation and Reasoning.

Corcho, O., López-Cima, A., & Gómez-Pérez, A. (2006). A platform for the development of semantic web portals. In *Proceedings of the 6th International Conference on Web Engineering (ICWE2006)* (pp. 145-152). New York: ACM Press.

Cortes, C., & Vapnik, V. (1995). Support-Vector Networks. *Machine Learning, 20,* 273–297. doi:10.1007/BF00994018

Coutaz, J., Lachenal, C., & Dupuy-Chessa, S. (2003). Ontology for Multi-surface Interaction. In *Proceedings of IFIP INTERACT03: Human-Computer Interaction* (pp. 447-454).

Cruz, I. F., Xiao, H., & Hsu, F. (2004). An Ontology-Based Framework for XML Semantic Integration. In *IDEAS '04: Proceedings of the International Database Engineering and Applications Symposium* (pp. 217-226). Washington, DC: IEEE Computer Society.

d'Aquin, M., Baldassarre, C., Gridinoc, L., Angeletou, S., Sabou, M., & Motta, E. (2007). Characterizing Knowledge on the Semantic Web with Watson. In *Proceedings of the 5th International Workshop on Evaluation of Ontologies and Ontology-Based Tools (EON2007), ISWC/ASWC* (Vol. 329, pp. 1-10). CEUR Workshop Proceedings. Retrieved from http://sunsite.informatik.rwth-aachen.de/Publications/CEUR-WS/Vol-329

d'Aquin, M., Motta, E., Sabou, M., Angeletou, S., Gridinoc, L., & Lopez, V. (2008). Toward a New Generation of Semantic Web Applications. *IEEE Intelligent Systems, 23*(3), 20–28. doi:10.1109/MIS.2008.54

da Rocha, R. C. A., Endler, M., & de Siqueira, T. S. (2008). Middleware for ubiquitous context-awareness. In *Proceedings of the 6th international workshop on middleware for pervasive and ad-hoc computing (Mpac '08)* (pp. 43-48). New York: ACM.

Daniel, F., Yu, J., Benatallah, B., Casati, F., Matera, M., & Saint-Paul, R. (2007). Understanding UI Integration: A Survey of Problems, Technologies, and Opportunities. *IEEE Internet Computing, 11*(3), 59–66. doi:10.1109/MIC.2007.74

d'Aquin, M., Sabou, M., Dzbor, M., Baldassarre, C., Gridinoc, L., Angeletou, S., et al. (2007). Watson: A Gateway for the Semantic Web. In *Proceedings of the Poster Session of the 4th European Semantic Web Conference,* Vienna, Austria.

d'Aquin, M., Motta, E., Sabou, M., Angeletou, S., Gridinoc, L., & Lopez, V. (2008). Toward a New Generation of Semantic Web Applications. *IEEE Intelligent Systems, 23*(3), 20–28. doi:10.1109/MIS.2008.54

Davies, J., Weeks, R., & Krohn, U. (2004). QuizRDF: Search Technology for the Semantic Web. In. *Proceedings of the Hawaii International Conference on System Sciences, 4,* 40112.

Davis, I. (2005). *Talis, web 2.0 and all that.* Retrieved from http://iandavis.com/blog/2005/07/talis-web-20-and-all-that?year=2005&monthnum=07&name=talis-web-20-and-all-that

Decker, S. (2002). *Semantic web methods for knowledge management.* Unpublished doctoral dissertation, University of Karlsruhe, Germany.

Decker, S., & Frank, M. R. (2004). *The Networked Semantic Desktop.* Paper presented at the WWW Workshop on Application Design, Development and Implementation Issues in the Semantic Web.

Dettborn, T., König-Ries, B., & Welsch, M. (2008). Using Semantics in Portal Development. In *Proceedings of the 4th International Workshop on Semantic Web Enabled Software Engineering.*

Dìaz, O., Iturrioz, J., & Irastorza, A. (2005). Improving portlet interoperability through deep annotation. In *Proceedings of the 14th international conference on World Wide Web (WWW '05)* (pp. 372-381). New York: ACM.

Dimitrova, V., Denaux, R., Hart, G., Dolbear, C., Holt, I., & Cohn, A. (2008). Involving Domain Experts in Authoring OWL Ontologies. In *Proceedings of the 7th International Semantic Web Conference (ISWC 2008)*, Karlsruhe, Germany.

Ding, L., Finin, T., Joshi, A., Pan, R., Cost, R. S., Peng, Y., et al. (2004). Swoogle: A Search and Metadata Engine for the Semantic Web. In *Proceedings of the 13th ACM International Conference on Information and Knowledge Management* (pp. 652-659). New York: ACM Press.

Dix, A., Hussein, T., Lukosch, S., & Ziegler, J. (Eds.). (2010). In *Proceedings of the First Workshop on Semantic Models for Adaptive Interactive Systems (SEMAIS).*

DMOZ. (1998). *ODP - The Open Directory Project.* Retrieved February 2008 from http://dmoz.org

Doan, A., & Halevy, A. Y. (2005). Semantic Integration Research in the Database Community: A Brief Survey. *AI Magazine, 26*(1), 83–94.

Domingue, J., & Motta, E. (1999). A Knowledge-Based News Server Supporting Ontology-Driven Story Enrichment and Knowledge Retrieval. In *Proceedings of the 11th European Workshop on Knowledge Acquisition, Modeling and Management (EKAW '99)* (pp. 103-120). London: Springer-Verlag.

Dong, X., Madhavan, J., & Halevy, A. (2004). Mining Structures for Semantics. *ACM Special Interest Group on Knowledge Discovery and Data Mining Explorations Newsletter, 6*(2).

Dourish, P., Edwards, W. K., LaMarca, A., & Salisbury, M. (1999). PRESTO: An Experimental Architecture for Fluid Interactive Document Spaces. *ACM Transactions on Computer-Human Interaction, 6*(2), 133–161. doi:10.1145/319091.319099

Draft, W. W. (2009). *Owl 2 web ontology language* (Tech. Rep.). Retrieved from http://www.w3.org/TR/owl2-overview

Drews, J. (2000). Drug discovery: a historical perspective. *Science, 287*, 1960–1964. doi:10.1126/science.287.5460.1960

Dymetman, M., Lux, V., & Ranta, A. (2000). Xml and Multilingual Document Authoring: convergent trends. In *Proceedings of the 18th Conference on Computational Linguistics* (Vol. 1, pp. 243-249). Morristown, NJ: Association for Computational Linguistics.

Dzbor, M. (2008). Best of Both: Using Semantic Web Technologies to Enrich User Interaction with the Web and Vice Versa. In V. Geffert, J. Karhumäki, A. Bertoni, B. Preneel, P. Návrat, & M. Bieliková (Eds.), *Proceedings of Theory and Practice of Computer Science, 34th Conference on Current Trends in Theory and Practice of Computer Science (SOFSEM 2008)*, Nový Smokovec, Slovakia (Vol. 4910, pp. 34-49). New York: Springer.

Edwards, H., Puckettm, R., & Jolly, A. (2006). Analyzing Communication Patterns in Software Engineering Projects. In *Software Engineering Research and Practice* (pp. 310-315).

Efron, B., & Tibshirani, R. (1986). Bootstrap methods for standard errors, confidence intervals, and other measures of statistical accuracy. *Statistical Science, 1*(1), 54–75. doi:10.1214/ss/1177013815

Ejigu, D., Scuturici, M., & Brunie, L. (2008). Hybrid Approach to Collaborative Context-Aware Service Platform for Pervasive Computing. *JCP, 3*(1), 40–50. doi:10.4304/jcp.3.1.40-50

Ellis, D. (2007). Beat Tracking by Dynamic Programming. *Journal of New Music Research. Special Issue on Beat and Tempo Extraction, 36*(1), 51–60.

Engelbrecht, P. C., Hart, G., & Dolbear, C. (2009). Talking rabbit: A user evaluation of sentence production. In *Proceedings of CNL* (pp. 56-64).

Euzenat, J., Pierson, J., & Ramparany, F. (2008). Dynamic context management for pervasive applications. *The Knowledge Engineering Review*, *23*(1), 21–49. doi:10.1017/S0269888907001269

Fagin, R., Kumar, R., McCurley, K. S., Novak, J., Sivakumar, D., Tomlin, J. A., et al. (2003). Searching the workplace web. In *Proceedings of the International World Wide Web Conference* (pp. 366-375). New York: ACM.

Feldman, S., & Sherman, C. (2004). The High Cost of Not Finding Information. *KM World, 13*.

Feng, Y., Zhuang, Y., & Pan, Y. (2003, October). Music information retrieval by detecting mood via computational media aesthetics. In *Proceedings of IEEE/WIC International Conference on* (pp. 235-241).

Fernández-López, M., Gómez-Pérez, A., & Juristo, N. (1997, March). Methontology: from ontological art towards ontological engineering. In *Proceedings of the AAAi97 Spring Symposium* (pp. 33-40).

Ferretti, S., Roccetti, M., & Palazzi, C. (2007). Web Content Search and Adaptation for IDTV: One Step Forward in the Mediamorphosis Process toward Personal-TV. *Advances in Multimedia, 2007*, 1–13. doi:10.1155/2007/16296

Fischer, G., & Giaccardi, E. (2006). Meta-design: A framework for the future of end-user development. In Lieberman, H., Paternò, F., & Wulf, V. (Eds.), *End User Development: Empowering people to flexibly employ advanced information and communication technology* (pp. 427–457). Berlin: Springer.

Fischer, G., Giaccardi, E., Ye, Y., Sutcliffe, A., & Mehandjiev, N. (2004). Meta-design: a manifesto for end-user development. *Communications of the ACM*, *47*(9), 33–37. doi:10.1145/1015864.1015884

Floréen, P., Przybilski, M., Nurmi, P., Koolwaaij, J., Tarlano, A., & Wagner, M. (2005). Towards a Context Management Framework for MobiLife. In *Proceedings of the ist summit*.

Fluit, C., Sabou, M., & Harmelen, F. V. (2003). Supporting User Tasks through Visualisation of Light-weight Ontologies. In *Handbook on Ontologies in Information Systems* (pp. 415–434). New York: Springer.

Fluit, C., van Harmelen, F., & Sabou, M. (2002). Ontology-based information visualisation. In Geroimenko, V. (Ed.), *Visualising the Semantic Web* (pp. 36–48). Berlin: Springer Verlag.

Foxvog, D., & Bussler, C. (2006). Ontologizing EDI Semantics. In *Proceedings of the ER Workshops* (pp. 301-311).

Franz, T., Scherp, A., & Staab, S. (2009). *Are Semantic Desktops Better? — Summative Evaluation Comparing a Semantic against a Conventional Desktop.* Paper presented at the Fifth International Conference on Knowledge Capture (K-CAP 2009).

Franz, T., Staab, S., & Arndt, R. (2007). The X-COSIM Integration Framework for a Seamless Semantic Desktop. In *Proceedings of the 4th International Conference on Knowledge Capture* (pp. 143-150). New York: ACM.

Fuchs, N. E., Kaljurand, K., Kuhn, T., Schneider, G., Royer, L., & Schröder, M. (2006). *Attempto Controlled English and the semantic web* (Deliverable No. I2D7). Retrieved December 16, 2010, from http://rewerse.net/deliverables/m24/i2-d7.pdf

Fuchs, N., & Schwitter, R. (1996). Attempto Controlled English (ACE). In *CLAW96: Proceedings of the First International Workshop on Controlled Language Applications*, Leuven, Belgium.

Funk, A., Tablan, V., Bontcheva, K., Cunningham, H., Davis, B., & Handschuh, S. (2007). Clone: Controlled language for ontology editing. In *Proceedings of ISWC/ASWC* (pp. 142-155).

Furnas, G. W., Deerwester, S., Dumais, S. T., Landauer, T. K., Harshman, R. A., Streeter, L. A., et al. (1988). Information retrieval using a singular value decomposition model of latent semantic structure. In *Proceedings of the Annual ACM Conference on Research and Development in Information Retrieval* (pp. 465-480). New York: ACM.

Furtado, E., Furtado, J. J. V., Silva, W. B., Rodrigues, D. W. T., da Silva Taddeo, L., & Limbourg, Q. (2002). An Ontology-Based Method for Universal Design of User Interfaces. In *Proceedings of Task Models and Diagrams For User Interface Design*. TAMODIA.

Gaffar, A., Javahery, H., Seffah, A., & Sinnig, D. (2003). A Pattern Framework for Eliciting and Delivering UCD Knowledge and Practices. In *Proceedings of the Tenth International Conference on Human-Computer Interaction* (pp. 108-112). Mahwah, NJ: Lawrence Erlbaum Associates.

Ganchev, T., Fakotakis, N., & Kokkinakis, G. (2005). Comparative evaluation of various MFCC implementations on the speaker verification task. In *Proceedings of the 10th International Conference on Speech and Computer*.

Gangemi, A., Navigli, R., & Velardi, P. (2003). The OntoWordNet Project: Extension and Axiomatization of Conceptual Relations in WordNet. In *Proceedings of the CoopIS/DOA/ODBASE Conference*.

Gangemi, A., Guarino, N., Masolo, C., & Oltramari, A. (2003). Sweetening WordNet with DOLCE. *AI Magazine*, *24*(3), 13–24.

Gangemi, A., Pisanelli, D., & Steve, G. (1998). Experiences with Medical Terminologies. In *Ontology in Information Systems* (pp. 163–178). Ontology Integration.

Garageband. (n.d.). Retrieved November 30, 2009, from http://www.garageband.com/

García, R., & Celma, O. (2005). Semantic Integration and Retrieval of Multimedia Metadata. In *Proceedings of the ISWC 2005 Workshop on Knowledge Markup and Semantic Annotation (Semannot'2005)*.

García-Barriocanal, E., Sicilia, M. A., & Sánchez-Alonso, S. (2005). Usability evaluation of ontology editors. *Knowledge Organization*, *32*(1), 1–9.

García-Silva, A., Gómez-Pérez, A., Suárez-Figueroa, M. C., & Villazón-Terrazas, B. (2008). A Pattern Based Approach for Re-engineering Non-Ontological Resources into Ontologies. In *ASWC '08: Proceedings of the 3rd Asian Semantic Web Conference* (pp. 167-181). Berlin: Springer-Verlag.

Gediga, G., & Hamborg, K. C. (1999). IsoMetrics: An usability inventory supporting summative and formative evaluation of software systems. In *Proceedings of the 8th International Conference on Human-Computer Interaction* (pp. 1018-1022). Hillsdale, NJ: Lawrence Erlbaum Associates Inc.

Ghias, A., Logan, J., Chanberlin, D., & Smith, B. C. (1995). Query by humming - musical information retrieval in an audio database. In *Proceedings of ACM Multimedia*.

Gifford, D. K., Jouvelot, P., Sheldon, M. A., & O'Toole, J. W. (1991). Semantic File Systems. In *Proceedings of the 13th ACM Symposium on Operating Systems Principles* (pp. 16-25). New York: ACM Press.

Gómez-Pérez, A., & Suárez-Figueroa, M. C. (2009). Scenarios for Building Ontology Networks within the NeOn Methodology. In *Proceedings of the Fifth International Conference on Knowledge Capture (K-CAP 2009)*.

Gómez-Pérez, A., Fernández-López, M., & Corcho, O. (2003). *Ontological Engineering*. Berlin: Springer-Verlag.

Gómez-Pérez, A., & Manzano-Macho, D. (2004). An overview of methods and tools for ontology learning from text. *The Knowledge Engineering Review*, *19*(3), 187–212. doi:10.1017/S0269888905000251

Gracia, J. (2009). *Integration and Disambiguation Techniques for Semantic Heterogeneity Reduction on the Web*. Zaragoza, Spain: University of Zaragoza.

Greenberg, S., & Roseman, M. (1996). GroupWeb: A WWW Browser as Real Time Groupware. In *Proceedings of the Conference companion on human factors in computing systems (Chi96)* (pp. 271-272). New York: ACM.

Gribova, V. (2007). Automatic Generation of Context-Sensitive Help Using a User Interface Project. In V. P. Gladun, K. K. Markov, A. F. Voloshin, & K. M. Ivanova (Eds.), *Proceedings of the 8th International Conference "Knowledge-Dialogue-Solution"* (Vol. 2).

Gridinoc, L., & Guidi, D. (2007). *PowerMagpie- a Semantic Web Browser*. Retrieved February 2008 from http://powermagpie.open.ac.uk

Grimes, R. (2004). Code Name WinFS: Revolutionary File Storage System Lets Users Search and Manage Files Based on Content. *MSDN Magazine, 19*(1).

Groza, T., Handschuh, S., Moeller, K., Grimnes, G., Sauermann, L., & Minack, E. (2007). The NEPOMUK Project — On the Way to the Social Semantic Desktop. In *Proceedings of I-Semantics, 07*, 201–211.

Gruber, T. (2007). Ontology of Folksonomy: A Mash-up of Apples and Oranges. *International Journal on Semantic Web and Information Systems, 3*(2), 1–11.

Gruber, T. R. (1993). A Translation Approach to Portable Ontology Specification. *Knowledge Acquisition, 5,* 199–220. doi:10.1006/knac.1993.1008

Gruber, T. R. (1995). *Toward Principles for the Design of Ontologies Used for Knowledge Sharing* (*Vol. 43,* pp. 907–928). New York: Academic Press.

Gruninger, M., & Lee, J. (2002). Ontology Applications and Design. *Communications of the ACM, 45*(2), 39–41.

Guarino, N. (1998). *Formal Ontology and Information Systems.* Amsterdam: IOS Press.

Guarino, N., Masolo, C., & Vetere, G. (1999). OntoSeek: Content-Based Access to the Web. *IEEE Intelligent Systems, 14*(3), 70–80. doi:10.1109/5254.769887

Gu, T., Pung, H. K., & Zhang, D. Q. (2005). A Service-Oriented Middleware for Building Context-Aware Services. *Journal of Network and Computer Applications, 28*(1), 1–18. doi:10.1016/j.jnca.2004.06.002

Haase, P., Rudolph, S., Wang, Y., & Brockmans, S. (2006). *Networked Ontology Model Networked Ontology Model.* NeOn project.

Hahn, U., & Schulz, S. (2003). Towards a broad-coverage biomedical ontology based on description logics. *Pacific Symposium on Biocomputing, 8,* 577-588).

Hahn, V. (2003). Turning informal thesauri into formal ontologies: a feasibility study on biomedical knowledge re-use. *Comparative and Functional Genomics, 4*(1), 94–97. doi:10.1002/cfg.247

Hakkarainen, S., Hella, L., Strasunskas, D., & Tuxen, S. (2006). A Semantic Transformation Approach for ISO 15926. In *Proceedings of the OIS 2006 First International Workshop on Ontologizing Industrial Standards.*

Han, B., Rho, S., Dannenberg, R. B., & Hwang, E. (2009a, October 26). SMERS: Music Emotion Recognition using Support Vector Regression. In *Proceedings of the International Society for Music Information Retrieval 09,* Kobe, Japan.

Han, B., Rho, S., Jun, S., & Hwang, E. (2009b). Music Emotion Classification and Context-based Music Recommendation. In *Proceedings of the Multimedia Tools and Applications.*

Handschuh, S. (2005). *Creating ontology-based metadata by annotation for the semantic web.* Unpublished doctoral dissertation, University of Karlsruhe, Germany

Handschuh, S., & Staab, S. (2002). Authoring and annotation of web pages in cream. In *Proceedings of WWW* (pp. 462-473).

Happel, H. J., & Seedorf, S. (2006, November 5-9). Applications of Ontologies in Software Engineering. In *Proceedings of the Workshop on Semantic Web Enabled Software Engineering (SWESE) on the 5th International Semantic Web Conference (ISWC 2006),* Athens, Georgia.

Happel, H. J., Korthaus, A., Seedorf, S., & Tomczyk, P. (2006). KOntoR: An Ontology-enabled Approach to Software Reuse. In K. Zhang, G. Spanoudakis, & G. Visaggio (Eds.), *Proceedings of the Eighteenth International Conference on Software Engineering & Knowledge Engineering (SEKE)* (pp. 349-354).

Hart, G., Johnson, M., & Dolbear, C. (2008, June). Rabbit: Developing a control natural language for authoring ontologies. In *Proceedings of the 5th European Semantic Web Conference (ESWC2008)* (pp. 348-360).

Hausenblas, M. (2009). Exploiting Linked Data to Build Web Applications. *IEEE Internet Computing, 13,* 68–73. doi:10.1109/MIC.2009.79

HAVi. (2009). *Home Audio / Video Interoperability.* Retrieved July 25, 2009 from http://www.havi.org

Hawking, D. (2004). Challenges in enterprise search. In *Proceedings of the ACM International Conference Proceeding Series* (Vol. 52, pp. 15-24). Darlinghurst, Australia: Australian Computer Society, Inc.

Hayes, P. (2004). *RDF Semantics (W3C Recommendation 10 February 2004).* World Wide Web Consortium.

Heery, R., & Patel, M. (2000). Application Profiles: Mixing and Matching Metadata Schemas. *Ariadne, September*(25).

Heim, P., Ziegler, J., & Lohmann, S. (2008). gFacet: A Browser for the Web of Data. In S. Auer, S. Dietzold, S. Lohmann, & J. Ziegler (Eds.), *Proceedings of the International Workshop on Interacting with Multimedia Content in the Social Semantic Web (IMC-SSW'08)* (Vol. 417, pp. 49-58).

Heitmann, B., Kinsella, S., Hayes, C., & Decker, S. (2009). *Implementing Semantic Web Applications: Reference Architecture and Challenges* (Kendall, E. F., Pan, J. Z., Sabbouh, M., Stojanovic, L., & Zhao, Y., Eds.). *Vol. 524*).

Hendler, J. (2003). *On Beyond Ontology.* Retrieved from http://iswc2003.semanticweb.org/ hendler_files/ v3_document.htm

Henninger, S., Keshk, M., & Kinworthy, R. (2003). Capturing and Disseminating Usability Patterns with Semantic Web Technology. In *Proceedings of the CHI 2003 Workshop: Concepts and Perspectives on HCI Patterns.*

Hepp, M., & de Brujin, J. (2007). GenTax: A generic Methodology for Deriving OWL and RDF-S Ontologies from Hierarchical Classifications, Thesauri, and Inconsistent Taxonomies. In *Proceedings of the 4th European Semantic Web Conference (ESWC2007)*. Berlin: Springer-Verlag.

Hepp, M. (2006). Products and Services Ontologies: A Methodology for Deriving OWL Ontologies from Industrial Categorization Standards. *International Journal on Semantic Web and Information Systems, 2*(1), 72–99.

Hepp, M. (2007). Possible Ontologies: How Reality Constrains the Development of Relevant Ontologies. *IEEE Internet Computing, 11*(1), 90–96. doi:10.1109/MIC.2007.20

Herman, I., Melançon, G., & Marshall, M. S. (2000). Graph Visualization and Navigation in Information Visualization: A Survey. *IEEE Transactions on Visualization and Computer Graphics, 6*(1), 24–43. doi:10.1109/2945.841119

Hesse, W. (2005). Ontologies in the Software Engineering Process. In R. Lenz, U. Hasenkamp, W. Hasselbring, & M. Reichert (Eds.), *Proceedings of the 2nd GI-Workshop on Enterprise Application Integration (EAI)* (Vol. 141). CEUR-WS.org.

Hildebrand, M., & van Ossenbruggen, J. (2009, February). Configuring Semantic Web Interfaces by Data Mapping. In *Proceedings of the Workshop on Visual Interfaces to the Social and the Semantic Web (VISSW2009).*

Hinz, M., Pietschmann, S., & Fiala, Z. (2007). A Framework for Context Modeling in Adaptive Web Applications. *IADIS Intl. Journal of WWW/Internet, 5.*

Hirst, G. (2004). Ontology and the Lexicon. In *Handbook on Ontologies in Information Systems* (pp. 209–230). Berlin: Springer.

Hodge, G. (2000). Systems of Knowledge Organization for Digital Libraries: Beyond Traditional Authority Files.

Hoefler, S. (2004). *The syntax of Attempto Controlled English: An abstract grammar for ACE 4.0* (Tech. Rep. No. Ifi-2004.03). Zurich, Switzerland: Department of Informatics, University of Zurich. Retrieved December 16, 2010, from http://www.ifi.unizh.ch/attempto/publications/papers/hoefler2004theSyntax.pdf

Holzinger, A. (2005). Usability engineering methods for software developers. *Communications of the ACM, 48,* 71–74. doi:10.1145/1039539.1039541

Hsu, C.-W., Chang, C.-C., & Lin, C.-J. (2007). *A Practical Guide to Support Vector Classification.*

Huiskes, M. J., & Lew, M. S. (2008). The MIR flickr retrieval evaluation. In *Proceedings of the 1st ACM Int'l Conference on Multimedia Information Retrieval*, Vancouver, Canada (pp. 39-43).

Hull, D. (1993). Using statistical testing in the evaluation of retrieval experiments. In *Proceedings of the 16th ACM SIGIR Conference on Research and Development in Information Retrieval.*

Hussein, T., & Münter, D. (2010). Automated Generation of Faceted Navigation Interfaces Using Semantic Models. In A. Dix, T. Hussein, S. Lukosch, & J. Ziegler (Eds.), *Proceedings of the First Workshop on Semantic Models for Adaptive Interactive Systems (SEMAIS).*

Huynh, D., Mazzocchi, S., & Karger, D. (2005). Piggy bank: Experience the semantic web inside your web browser. In *Proceedings of the International Semantic Web Conference (ISWC)*(LNCS 3729, pp. 413-430).

Huynh, D., Miller, R., & Karger, D. (2008). Potluck: Data mash-up tool for casual users. *Web Semantics: Science. Services and Agents on the World Wide Web, 6*(4), 274–282. doi:10.1016/j.websem.2008.09.005

Hyvönen, E., Styrman, A., & Saarela, S. (2002). Ontology-Based Image Retrieval. In E. Hyvönen & M. Klemettinen (Eds.), *Towards the semantic Web and Web services, Proceedings of the XML Finland 2002 Conference.* Helsinki, Finland: HIIT Publications.

Hyvönen, E., Viljanen, K., Tuominen, J., & Seppälä, K. (2008). Building a National Semantic Web Ontology and Ontology Service Infrastructure - The FinnONTO Approach. In *Proceedings of the European Semantic Web Conference, ESWC* (pp. 95-109).

Iman, R. L., & Davenport, J. M. (1980). Approximations of the critical region of the Friedman statistic. *Communications in Statistics, A9*(6), 571–595. doi:10.1080/03610928008827904

Intelligent Phyiscal Agents, F. (2002). *FIPA Device Ontology Specification.* Retrieved from http://www.fipa.org/specs/ fipa00091/index.html

IRT. (2009). *DVB Playout Server.* Retrieved July 25, 2009 from http://www.irt.de/en/products/ digital-television/dvb-playout-server.html

ISO. (1986). *Documentation - Guidelines for the establishment and development of monolingual thesaurus (Rep. ISO 2788).* Geneva, Switzerland: ISO.

ISO/IEC. (2004). *Information technology - Metadata registries - Part 1: Framework (Rep. ISO/IEC FDIS 11179-1).* Geneva, Switzerland: ISO.

Jang, M., & Sohn, J. (2004). Bossam: An Extended Rule Engine for OWL Inferencing. In *Proceedings of the Rules and Rule Markup Languages for the Semantic Web: RuleML,* Hiroshima, Japan (LNCS 3323, pp. 128-138). Berlin: Springer.

Java, T. V. (2009). *JavaTV Specification.* Retrieved July 25, 2009 from http://java.sun.com/products/javatv/

Joachims, T., Nedellec, C., & Rouveirol, C. (1998). Text categorization with Support Vector Machines: Learning with many relevant features. In *Proceedings of the 10th European Conference on Machine Learning.* Berlin: Springer.

Joachims, T. (2003). Evaluating retrieval performance using clickthrough data. In Franke, J., Nakhaeizadeh, G., & Renz, I. (Eds.), *Text Mining* (pp. 79–96). New York: Springer.

Joachims, T., & Radlinski, F. (2007). Search Engines that Learn from Implicit Feedback. *IEEE Computer, 40*(8), 34–40.

Jun, S., Han, B., & Hwang, E. (2009, April). A Similar Music Retrieval Scheme based on Musical Mood Variation. In *Proceedings of the Asian Conference on Intelligent Information and Database Systems*.

Jun, S., Rho, S., Han, B., & Hwang, E. (2008, August). A Fuzzy Inference-based Music Emotion Recognition System. In *Proceedings of the Visual Information Engineering*.

Juslin, P. N., & Sloboda, J. A. (2001). *Music and Emotion: Theory and research.* New York: Oxford University Press.

Kagal, L., Finin, T., & Joshi, A. (2003). A policy language for a pervasive computing environment. In *Proceedings of the IEEE 4th International Workshop on Policies for Distributed Systems and Networks (POLICY 2003)*.

Kaljurand, K. (2008, October 26-27). ACE View — an ontology and rule editor based on Attempto Controlled English. In *Proceedings of the 5th OWL Experiences and Directions Workshop (OWLED 2008)*, Karlsruhe, Germany.

Kaljurand, K., & Fuchs, N. E. (2006, June). Bidirectional mapping between OWL DL and Attempto Controlled English. In *Proceedings of the 4th Workshop on Principles and Practice of Semantic Web Reasoning.*, Budva, Montenegro.

Kaljurand, K., & Fuchs, N. E. (2007). Verbalizing OWL in Attempto Controlled English. In C. Golbreich, A. Kalyanpur, & B. Parsia (Eds.), *Proceedings of the OWLED 2007 Workshop on OWL: Experiences and Directions,* Innsbruck, Austria (Vol. 258). CEUR-WS.org.

Karger, D. R. (2007). Haystack: Per-User Information Environments Based on Semistructured Data. In Kaptelinin, V., & Czerwinski, M. (Eds.), *Beyond the Desktop Metaphor* (pp. 49–100). Cambridge, MA: Massachusetts Institute of Technology.

Karim, S., & Tjoa, A. M. (2006). Towards the Use of Ontologies for Improving User Interaction for People with Special Needs. In Miesenberger, K., Klaus, J., Zagler, W. L., & Karshmer, A. I. (Eds.), *ICCHP* (*Vol. 4061*, pp. 77–84). New York: Springer.

Katifori, A., Halatsis, C., Lepouras, G., Vassilakis, C., & Giannopoulou, E. G. (2007). Ontology visualization methods - a survey. *ACM Computing Surveys, 39*(4). doi:10.1145/1287620.1287621

Kaufer, F., & Klusch, M. (2006). WSMO-MX: A Logic Programming Based Hybrid Service Matchmaker. In *Proceedings of the 4th IEEE European Conference on Web Services (ECOWS 2006)*, Zurich, Switzerland. Washington, DC: IEEE Computer Society.

Kaufman, L., & Rousseeuw, P. (1990). *Finding groups in data: an introduction to cluster analysis*. New York: John Wiley and Sons.

Kaufmann, E. (2007). *Talking to the semantic web: natural language query interfaces for casual end-users*. Unpublished doctoral dissertation, University of Zurich.

Kernchen, R., Bonnefoy, D., Battestini, A., Mrohs, B., Wagner, M., & Klemettinen, M. (2006, June). Context-Awareness in MobiLife. In *Proceedings of the 15th ist mobile summit*, Mykonos, Greece.

Kiefer, C., & Bernstein, A. (2008). The Creation and Evaluation of iSPARQL Strategies for Matchmaking. In *Proceedings of the 5th European Semantic Web Conference (ESWC)* (LNCS 5021).

Kifer, M., Lausen, G., & Wu, J. (1995). Logical foundations of object-oriented and frame-based languages. *Journal of the ACM, 42*, 741–843. doi:10.1145/210332.210335

Kimball, R., & Caserta, J. (2004). The Data Warehouse ETL Toolkit: Practical Techniques for Extracting, Cleaning. In *The Data Warehouse ETL Toolkit*. New York: John Wiley & Sons.

Klien, E., & Probst, F. (2005). Requirements for Geospatial Ontology Engineering. In F. Toppen & M. Painho (Eds.), *Proceedings of the 8th Conference on Geographic Information Science (AGILE 2005)*, Estoril, Portugal.

Klusch, M., & Kapahnke, P. (2008). Semantic Web Service Selection with SAWSDL-MX. In *Proceedings of the 2nd Workshop on Service Matchmaking and Resource Retrieval in the Semantic Web (SMR2)*, Karlsruhe, Germany. CEUR.

Klusch, M., & Kapahnke, P. (2009). OWLS-MX3: An Adaptive Hybrid Semantic Service Matchmaker for OWL-S. In *Proceedings of the 3rd International Workshop on Semantic Matchmaking and Resource Retrieval (SMR2) at ISWC*. CEUR.

Klusch, M., Fries, B., & Sycara, K. (2006). Automated Semantic Web Service Discovery with OWLS-MX. In *Proceedings of the 5th International Conference on Autonomous Agents and Multi-Agent Systems (AAMAS)*, Hakodate, Japan. New York: ACM Press.

Klusch, M., Kapahnke, P., & Zinnikus, I. (2009). SAWSDL-MX2: A Machine-Learning Approach for Integrating Semantic Web Service Matchmaking Variants. In *Proceedings of the IEEE 7th International Conference on Web Services (ICWS)*, Los Angeles. Washington, DC: IEEE Computer Society.

Klusch, M., Fries, B., & Sycara, K. (2009). OWLS-MX: A Hybrid Semantic Web Service Matchmaker for OWL-S Services. *Web Semantics, 7*(2), 121–133.

Kohlhase, A., & Kohlhase, M. (2009). Semantic Transparency in User Assistance Systems. In *Proceedings of the 27th annual ACM international conference on Design of Communication. Special Interest Group on Design of Communication (SIGDOC-09)*, Bloomingtion, IN. New York: ACM Press.

Korpipää, P., Häkkilä, J., Kela, J., Ronkainen, S., & Känsälä, I. (2004). Utilising context ontology in mobile device application personalisation. In *Proceedings of the 3rd international conference on Mobile and ubiquitous multimedia (MUM '04)* (pp. 133-140). New York: ACM.

Kourtesis, D., & Paraskakis, I. (2008). Combining SAWSDL, OWL-DL and UDDI for Semantically Enhanced Web Service Discovery. In *Proceedings of the 5th European Semantic Web Conference (ESWC)* (LNCS 5021).

Krötzsch, M., Vrandečić, D., & Völkel, M. (2006). Semantic MediaWiki. In *The semantic web - Iswc 2006* (LNCS 4273, pp. 935-942).

Krötzsch, M., Vrandečić, D., Völkel, M., Haller, H., & Studer, R. (2007). Semantic Wikipedia. *Journal of Web Semantics*, *5*(4), 251–261. doi:10.1016/j.websem.2007.09.001

Kuhn, T. (2006, March). Attempto Controlled English as ontology language. In F. Bry & U. Schwertel (Eds.), *Proceedings of the REWERSE Annual Meeting 2006*.

Kuhn, T. (2008). AceWiki: Collaborative Ontology Management in Controlled Natural Language. In *Proceedings of the 3rd Semantic Wiki Workshop*. CEUR Workshop Proceedings.

Kuhn, T. (2010a). *Controlled English for knowledge representation*. Unpublished doctoral dissertation, University of Zurich. Retrieved December 10, 2010, from http://attempto.ifi.uzh.ch/site/pubs/

Kuhn, T. (2010b). An evaluation framework for controlled natural languages. In N. E. Fuchs (Ed.), *Proceedings of the Workshop on Controlled Natural Language (CNL 2009)* (LNCS 5972, pp. 1-20).

Larsson, A., Ingmarsson, M., & Sun, B. (2007). A Development Platform for Distributed User Interfaces. In *Proceedings of the Nineteenth International Conference on Software Engineering & Knowledge Engineering (SEKE'2007)*, Boston (pp. 704-709).

Lassila, O., & Swick, R. (1999). *Resource Description Framework (RDF) Model and Syntax Specification, W3C Recommendation*. Retrieved from http://www.w3.org/TR/REC-rdf-syntax

Last.fm. (n.d.). Retrieved November 30, 2009, from http://www.last.fm/

Lausen, H., Polleres, A., Roman, D., de Bruijn, J., Bussler, C., & Domingue, J. (2005). In *Proceedings of the Web Service Modeling Ontology (WSMO)*. Retrieved from http://www.w3.org/Submission/WSMO/

Lausen, H., Ding, Y., Stollberg, M., Fensel, D., Lara, R., & Han, S.-K. (2005). Semantic web portals: state-of-the-art survey. *Journal of Knowledge Management*, *9*(5), 40–49. doi:10.1108/13673270510622447

Lauser, B., & Sini, M. (2006). From AGROVOC to the agricultural ontology service/concept server: an OWL model for creating ontologies in the agricultural domain in the agricultural domain. In *DCMI '06: Proceedings of the 2006 International Conference on Dublin Core and Metadata Applications* (pp. 76-88). Dublin, Ireland: Dublin Core Metadata Initiative.

Lee, A. (2010). Exploiting Context for Mobile User Experience. In A. Dix, T. Hussein, S. Lukosch, & J. Ziegler (Eds.), *Proceedings of the First Workshop on Semantic Models for Adaptive Interactive Systems (SEMAIS)*.

Lee, S., & Yong, H. (2007). Tagplus: A Retrieval System using Synonym tag in Folksonomy. In *Proceedings of the International Conference on Multimedia and Ubiquitous Engineering*, Seoul, Korea (pp. 294-298).

Lei, Y., Motta, E., & Domingue, J. (2003). Design of customized web applications with OntoWeaver. In *Proceedings of the 2nd international conference on Knowledge capture (K-CAP '03)* (pp. 54-61). New York: ACM.

Le-Phuoc, D., Polleres, A., Hauswirth, M., Tummarello, G., & Morbidoni, C. (2009). Rapid prototyping of semantic mash-ups through semantic web pipes. In *WWW '09: Proceedings of the 18th International Conference on World Wide Web* (pp. 581-590). New York: ACM.

Lerman, K., Plangpoasopchok, A., & Wong, C. (2007). Personalizing Image Search Results on Flickr. In *Proceedings of the AAAI 5th Workshop on Intelligent Techniques for Web Personalization*, Vancouver, Canada.

Levesque, H. J., & Lakemeyer, G. (2001). *The Logic of Knowledge Bases*. Cambridge, MA: MIT Press.

Li, X., Snoek, C. G. M., & Worring, M. (2008). Learning Tag Relevance by Neighbor Voting for Social Image Retrieval. In *Proceedings of the 1st ACM Int'l Conference on Multimedia Information Retrieval*, Vancouver, Canada (pp. 39-43).

Li, K., Verma, K., Mulye, R., Rabbani, R., Miller, J. A., & Sheth, A. P. (2006). Designing Semantic Web Processes: The WSDL-S Approach. In Cardoso, J., & Sheth, A. (Eds.), *Semantic Web Services, Processes and Applications*. New York: Springer. doi:10.1007/978-0-387-34685-4_7

Liu, B., Chen, H., & He, W. (2005). Deriving User Interface from Ontologies: A Model-Based Approach. In *Proceedings of the 17th IEEE International Conference on Tools with Artificial Intelligence (ICTAI '05)* (pp. 254-259). Washington, DC: IEEE Computer Society.

Liu, D., Hua, X., Yang, L., Wang, M., & Zhang, H. (2009). Tag Ranking. In *Proceedings of the 18th International World Wide Web Conference,* Madrid, Spain (pp. 351-360).

Lu, L., Liu, D., & Zhang, H. (2006). Automatic Mood Detection and Tracking of Music Audio Signals. *IEEE Transactions on Audio. Speech and Audio Processing, 14*(1), 5–18. doi:10.1109/TSA.2005.860344

Maala, M., Deiteil, A., & Azough, A. (2007). A Conversion Process from Flickr tags to RDF descriptions. In *Proceedings of the 10th International Conference on Business Information Systems,* Poznan, Poland.

Macías, J., & Castells, P. (2007). Providing end-user facilities to simplify ontology-driven web application authoring. *Interacting with Computers, 19*(4), 563–585. doi:10.1016/j.intcom.2007.01.006

MacQueen, J. (1967). Some methods for classification and analysis of multivariate observations. In *Proceedings of Knowledge Discovery and Data Mining.*

Maedche, A., & Staab, S. (2001). Ontology Learning for the Semantic Web. *IEEE Intelligent Systems.*

Malinowski, E., & Zimányi, E. (2006). Hierarchies in a multidimensional model: From conceptual modeling to logical representation. *Data & Knowledge Engineering, 59*(2). doi:10.1016/j.datak.2005.08.003

Martin, B. (2006). The World is a libferris Filesystem. *Linux Journal, 2006*(146).

Martin, D., Burstein, M., Hobbs, J., Lassila, O., McDermott, D., & McIlraith, S. (2004, November). *OWL-S: Semantic Markup for Web Services.* Retrieved from http://www.w3.org/Submission/OWL-S/

Masolo, C., Borgo, S., Gangemi, A., Guarino, N., & Oltramari, A. (2003). *WonderWeb Deliverable D18 – Ontology Library (final)* (Tech. Rep.). Laboratory For Applied Ontology, Trento, Italien. http://wonderweb.semanticweb.org/ deliverables/documents/D18.pdf

Maßun, M. (2008). *Collaborative Information Management in Enterprises.* Regensburg, Germany: University of Regensburg.

Mayrhofer, R. (2004). *An Architecture for Context Prediction.* Unpublished doctoral dissertation, Johannes Kepler University of Linz, Austria.

McNaught, A. (2003). *What's in a Name.* The Alchemist.

McNemar, Q. (1947). Note on the sampling error of the difference between correlated proportions or percentages. *Psychometrika, 12,* 153–157. doi:10.1007/BF02295996

Media, N. E. T. (2009). *The MediaNET Project.* Retrieved July 25, 2009 from http://www.ip-medianet.org

Mendes, P. N., McKnight, B., Sheth, A. P., & Kissinger, J. C. (2008). TcruziKB: Enabling Complex Queries for Genomic Data Exploration. In *Proceedings of the 2008 IEEE International Conference on Semantic Computing (ICSC '08)* (pp. 432-439). Washington, DC: IEEE Computer Society.

MHP. (2009). *DVB – Multimedia Home Platform Specification 1.1.1, ETSI TS 102 812 V1.2.2.* Retrieved July 25, 2009 from http://www.mhp.org/fullspeclist.htm

Micarelli, A., Gasparetti, F., Sciarrone, F., & Gauch, S. (2007). Personalized search on the World Wide Web. In Brusilovsky, P., Kobsa, A., & Nejdl, W. (Eds.), *The Adaptive Web: Methods and Strategies for Web Personalization* (pp. 195–230). Berlin: Springer.

Mika, P. (2005). Ontologies are us: a Unified Model of Social Networks and Semantics. In *Proceedings of the 4th International Semantic Web Conference* (pp. 522-536). Heidelberg, Germany: Springer.

Miller, A. (1995). WordNet: A Lexical Database for English. *Communications of the ACM, 38*(11), 39–41. doi:10.1145/219717.219748

Mitchell, T. (1997). *Machine Learning.* New York: McGraw-Hill.

Mitschick, A., Nagel, R., & Meißner, K. (2008). Semantic Metadata Instantiation and Consolidation within an Ontology-based Multimedia Document Management System. In *Proceedings of the Int. Workshop on Semantic Metadata Management and Applications (ESWC 2008),* Tenerife, Spain.

Mizoguchi, R. (2004). Tutorial on ontological engineering, Part 3: Advanced course of ontological engineering. *New Generation Computing*, *22*(2), 198–220. doi:10.1007/BF03040960

Moore, M. M., Rugaber, S., & Seaver, P. (1994). Knowledge-Based User Interface Migration. In *Proceedings of the International Conference on Software Maintenance* (pp. 72-79). Washington, DC: IEEE Computer Society.

Motta, E., & Sabou, M. (2006). Next Generation Semantic Web Applications. *The 1st Asian Semantic Web Conference* (pp. 24-29). Heidelberg, Germany:Springer.

Mühlbacher, S. (2008). *Scientific Information Literacy in Enterprises*. Regensburg, Germany: University of Regensburg.

Müller, M. (2007). *Information Retrieval for Music and Motion* (p. 65). New York: Springer. ISBN 9783540740476.

Muñoz, S., Pérez, J., & Gutiérrez, C. (2007, June 3-7). Minimal Deductive Systems for RDF. In *Proceedings of the 4th European Semantic Web Conference*, Innsbruck, Austria (pp. 53-67).

Murray-Rust, P., Rzepa, H. S., Tyrrell, S. M., & Zhang, Y. (2004). Representation and use of chemistry in the global electronic age. *Organic & Biomolecular Chemistry*, *2*(22), 3192–3203. doi:10.1039/b410732b

Myers, B. A., & Rosson, M. B. (1992). Survey on user interface programming. In *Proceedings of the SIGCHI conference on Human factors in computing systems (CHI '92)* (pp. 195-202). New York: ACM.

Mystrands. (n.d.). Retrieved November 30, 2009, from http://www.mystrands.com/

Nadeau, D., & Sekine, S. (2007). A survey of named entity recognition and classification. *Linguisticae Investigationes*, *30*, 3–26. doi:10.1075/li.30.1.03nad

Naphade, M., Smith, J. R., Tesic, J., Chang, S. F., Hsu, W., & Kennedy, L. (2006). Large-Scale Concept Ontology for Multimedia. *IEEE MultiMedia*, *13*(3), 86–91. doi:10.1109/MMUL.2006.63

Niederhausen, M., Pietschmann, S., Ruch, T., & Meißner, K. (2009). *Web-Based Support By Thin-Client Co-Browsing*. Berlin: Springer.

Niederhausen, M., Pietschmann, S., Ruch, T., & Meißner, K. (2010, April). Emergent Web Intelligence: Advanced Semantic Technologies. In Badr, Y., Chbeir, R., Abraham, A., & Hassanien, A. E. (Eds.), *Web-Based Support By Thin-Client Co-Browsing* (*Vol. XVI*). Berlin: Springer.

Nordstrom, B., Petersson, K., & Smith, J. M. (1990). *Programming in Martin-Löf's Type Theory: An Introduction*. New York: Oxford University Press.

Noy, N. F., & McGuinness, D. L. (2001, March). *Ontology development 101: A guide to creating your first ontology* (Tech. Rep. No. KSL-01-05). Stanford, CA: Stanford Knowledge Systems Laboratory. Retrieved December 5, 2009, from http://protege.stanford.edu/publications/ontologydevelopment/ontology101-noy-mcguinness.html

O'Reilly, T. (2005). *What is web 2.0. Design patterns and business models for the next generation of software.* Retrieved from at http://oreilly.com/web2/archive/what-is-web-20.html

Okoli, A., & Schandl, B. (2009). *Extraction of Contextual Metadata from File System Interactions.* Paper presented at the Workshop on Exploitation of Usage and Attention Metadata (EUAM 09).

Opera. (2009). *Opera for Devices iTV SDK.* Retrieved July 25, 2009 from http://www.opera.com/products/devices/

Oren, E., Delbru, R., Moller, K., Volkel, M., & Handschuh, S. (2006). Annotation and navigation in semantic wikis. In *Proceedings of the ESWC Workshop on Semantic Wikis.* Retrieved from http://ftp.informatik.rwth-aachen.de/Publications/CEUR-WS/Vol-206

Oren, E., Delbru, R., Catasta, M., Cyganiak, R., Stenzhorn, H., & Tummarello, G. (2008). Sindice.com — A Document-oriented Lookup Index for Open Linked Data. *International Journal on Metadata, Semantics, and Ontologies*, *3*(1), 37–52. doi:10.1504/IJMSO.2008.021204

Oren, E., Heitmann, B., & Decker, S. (2008). Activerdf: Embedding semantic web data into object-oriented languages. *Web Semantics*, *6*(3), 191–202.

OSGi. (2009). *Open Service Gateway Initiative Alliance*. Retrieved July 25, 2009 from http://www.osgi.org

Padioleau, Y., Sigonneau, B., & Ridoux, O. (2006). Lisfs: A logical information system as a file system. In *Proceedings of the 28th International Conference on Software Engineering* (pp. 803-806). New York: ACM Press.

Pajntar, B., & Grobelnik, M. (2008). SearchPoint - a New Paradigm of Web Search. In *Proceedings of the WWW 2008 Developers Track.*

Patel, C., Supekar, K., Lee, Y., & Park, E. (2003). OntoKhoj: A Semantic Web Portal for Ontology Searching, Ranking, and Classification. In *Proceedings of the 5th ACM International Workshop on Web Information and Data Management*, USA (pp. 58-61).

Paton, N. W., Stevens, R., Baker, P., Goble, C. A., Bechhofer, S., & Brass, A. (1999). Query processing in the TAMBIS bioinformatics source integration system. In *Proceedings of the Eleventh International Conference on Scientific and Statistical Database Management* (pp. 138-147).

Paulheim, H. (2009). Ontologies for User Interface Integration. In Bernstein, A., (Eds.), *The Semantic Web - ISWC 2009* (*Vol. 5823*, pp. 973–981). New York: Springer. doi:10.1007/978-3-642-04930-9_63

Paulheim, H. (2010). In Aroyo, L., (Eds.), *Efficient Semantic Event Processing: Lessons Learned in User Interface Integration* (*Vol. 6089*, pp. 60–74). New York: Springer.

Pauws, S., & Eggen, B. (2002). Realization and user evaluation of an automatic playlist generator. In *Proceedings of International Society for Music Information Retrieval*. PATS.

Perlman, G. (1997, April 18-23). Practical usability evaluation. In *CHI '97: Extended Abstracts on Human Factors in Computing Systems,* Los Angeles (pp. 168-169). New York: ACM.

Peterson, E. (2006). Beneath the Metadata: Some Philosophical Problems with Folksonomy. *D-Lib Magazine, 12*(11). doi:10.1045/november2006-peterson

Pfisterer, F., Nitsche, M., Jameson, A., & Barbu, C. (2008). User-Centered Design and Evaluation of Interface Enhancements to the Semantic MediaWik. In *Proceedings of the Semantic Web User Interaction Workshop at CHI 2008: Exploring HCI Challenges*. CEUR Workshop Proceedings.

Phillips, J. L. (1996). *How to think about statistics*. New York: W. H. Freeman and Company.

Pietriga, E. (2001). *Isaviz: A visual authoring tool for rdf.* Retrieved from http://www.w3.org/2001/11/IsaViz

Pietschmann, S., Niederhausen, M., Ruch, T., Wilkowski, R., & Richter, J. (2007). Instant Collaborative Web-Browsing with VCS. In *Proceedings of the "virtuelle organisationen und neue medien" (geneme 2007).*

Pietschmann, S., Voigt, M., Rümpel, A., & Meißner, K. (2009, June). CRUISe: Composition of Rich User Interface Services. In M. Gaedke, M. Grossniklaus, & O. Díaz (Eds.), *Proceedings of the 9th intl. conf. on web engineering (icwe 2009),* San Sebastian, Spain (pp. 473-476). Berlin: Springer Verlag.

Pinto, H. S., Tempich, C., & Staab, S. (2004). DILIGENT: Towards a fine-grained methodology for DIstributed, Loosely-controlled and evolvInG Engineering of oNTologies. In *Proceedings of the 16th European Conference on Artificial Intelligence (ECAI 2004)* (pp. 393-397).

Plebani, P., & Pernici, B. (2009). URBE: Web Service Retrieval Based on Similarity Evaluation. *IEEE Transactions on Knowledge and Data Engineering, 21*(11), 1629–1642. doi:10.1109/TKDE.2009.35

Pohjalainen, P. (2010). Self-configuring User Interface Components. In A. Dix, T. Hussein, S. Lukosch, & J. Ziegler (Eds.), *Proceedings of the First Workshop on Semantic Models for Adaptive Interactive Systems (SEMAIS).*

POLYSEMA. (2009). *The POLYSEMA Project*. Retrieved July 25, 2009 from http://polysema.di.uoa.gr

Pooley, R., & Stevens, P. (1998). *Software Reengineering Patterns*. Retrieved from http://www.reengineering.ed.ac.uk/csgrep.pdf

Porter, M. (1980). An Algorithm for Suffix Stripping Program. *Program, 14*, 130–137.

Potter, R., & Wright, H. (2006). An Ontological Approach to Visualization Resource Management. In Doherty, G. J., & Blandford, A. (Eds.), *Interactive Systems. Design, Specification, and Verification, 13th International Workshop, DSVIS 2006, Dublin, Ireland* (*Vol. 4323*, pp. 151–156). New York: Springer.

Power, R., O'Sullivan, D., Conlan, O., Lewis, D., & Wade, V. (2004). Utilizing Context in Adaptive Information Services for Pervasive Computing Environments. In *Proceedings of the pervasive web services and contex aware computing workshop (ah'2004).*

Prasanna, M. D., Vondrasek, J., Wlodawer, A., Rodriguez, H., & Bhat, T. N. (2006). Chemical compound navigator: a web-based chem-BLAST, chemical taxonomy-based search engine for browsing compounds. *Proteins, 63*(4), 907–917. doi:10.1002/prot.20914

Prasanna, M., Vondrasek, J., Wlodawer, A., & Bhat, T. N. (2005). Application of InChI to curate, index and query 3-D structures. *Proteins, Structure, Function, and Bioinformatics, 60,* 1–4. doi:10.1002/prot.20469

Presutti, V., Gangemi, A., David, S., de Cea, G. A., Suárez-Figueroa, M. C., & Montiel-Ponsoda, E. (2008). *NeOn Deliverable D2.5.1: A Library of Ontology Design Patterns: reusable solutions for collaborative design of networked ontologies.* Retrieved from http://www.neon-project.org

Prud'hommeaux, E., & Seaborne, A. (2008). *SPARQL Query Language for RDF* (W3C Recommendation). Retrieved from http://www.w3.org/TR/rdf-sparql-query/

Quan, D., & Karger, D. (2004). How to Make a Semantic Web Browser. In *Proceedings of the 13th International Conference on the World Wide Web. Session: Semantic Interfaces and OWL Tools.* ISBN:1-58113-844-X

Ranta, A. (2004). Grammatical Framework: A Type-Theoretical Grammar Formalism. *Journal of Functional Programming, 14*(2), 145–189. doi:10.1017/S0956796803004738

Rebstock, M., Fengel, J., & Paulheim, H. (2008). *Ontologies-based Business Integration.* New York: Springer.

Reeve, L., & Han, H. (2005). Survey of semantic annotation platforms. In *Proceedings of the Symposium on Applied Computing* (pp. 1634-1638). New York: ACM.

Rho, S., Han, B., Hwang, E., & Kim, M. (2008). MUSEMBLE: A Novel Music Retrieval System with Automatic Voice Query Transcription and Reformulation. *Journal of Systems and Software, 81*(7), 1065–1080. doi:10.1016/j.jss.2007.05.038

Richter, J., & Poelchau, J. (2008). DeepaMehta — Another Computer is Possible. In Rech, J., Decker, B., & Ras, E. (Eds.), *Emerging Technologies for Semantic Work Environments: Techniques, Methods, and Applications.* Hershey, PA: Idea Group.

Rico, M., Camacho, D., & Corcho, Ó. (2008). VPOET: Using a Distributed Collaborative Platform for Semantic Web Applications. In C. Badica, G. Mangioni, V. Carchiolo, & D. Burdescu (Eds.), *Intelligent Distributed Computing, Systems and Applications: Proceedings of the 2nd International Symposium on Intelligent Distributed Computing (IDC'2008)* (pp. 167-176). Berlin: Springer. ISBN: 978-3-540-85256-8

Rico, M., Camacho, D., & Corcho, Ó. (2009a). Macros vs. scripting in VPOET. In *Proceedings of the 5th Workshop on Scripting and Development for the Semantic Web (SFSW2009), 6th Annual European Semantic Web Conference (ESWC).* (Vol. 449). CEUR Online Proceedings.

Rico, M., Camacho, D., & Corcho, Ó. (2009b). VPOET Templates to Handle the Presentation of Semantic Data Sources in Wikis. In *Proceedings of the 4th Workshop on Semantic Wikis: The Semantic Wiki Web (SemWiki2009), 6th Annual European Semantic Web Conference (ESWC)* (Vol. 464, pp. 186-190). CEUR Online Proceedings.

Rico, M., Camacho, D., & Corcho, Ó. (2010). A Contribution-based Framework for the Creation of Semantically-enabled Web Applications. *Journal of Information Science, 180*(10), 1850–1864. doi:10.1016/j.ins.2009.07.004

Rocchio, J. J. (1971). Relevance feedback in information retrieval. In Salton, G. (Ed.), *The SMART Retrieval System - Experiments in Automatic Document Processing* (pp. 313–323). Englewood Cliffs, NJ: Prentice-Hall.

Rochen, R., Rosson, M., & Pérez, M. (2006). End user Development of Web Applications. In Lieberman, H., Paternò, F., & Wulf, V. (Eds.), *End-User Development* (pp. 161–182). Berlin: Springer.

Roussaki, I., Strimpakou, M., Pils, C., Kalatzis, N., & Anagnostou, M. (2006). Hybrid Context Modeling: A Location-Based Scheme Using Ontologies. In *Proceedings of the 4th annual iee intl. conf. on pervasive computing and communications workshop.*

Ruiz, F., & Hilera, J. R. (2006). In Calero, C., Ruiz, F., & Piattini, M. (Eds.), *Using Ontologies in Software Engineering and Technology* (pp. 49–102). New York: Springer. doi:10.1007/3-540-34518-3_2

Rumelhart, D. E., & McClelland, J. L. (1986). *Parallel distributed processing (Vol. 1)*. Cambridge, MA: MIT Press.

Salton, G., Wong, A., & Yang, C. S. (1975). A vector space model for automatic indexing. *Communications of the ACM, 18*, 613–620. doi:10.1145/361219.361220

Sauermann, L., & Heim, D. (2008). Evaluating Long-Term Use of the Gnowsis Semantic Desktop for PIM. In *Proceedings of the 7ᵗʰ International Semantic Web Conference* (pp. 467-482). Berlin: Springer.

Sauermann, L., Bernardi, A., & Dengel, A. (2005). Overview and Outlook on the Semantic Desktop. In S. Decker, J. Park, D. Quan, & L. Sauermann (Eds.), *Proceedings of the 1st Semantic Desktop Workshop*, Galway, Ireland. CEUR Workshop Proceedings.

Scerri, S., Davis, B., Handschuh, S., & Hauswirth, M. (2009). In Aroyo, L., (Eds.), *Semanta - Semantic Email Made Easy (Vol. 5554*, pp. 36–50). New York: Springer.

Schaert, S. (2006). *Ikewiki: A semantic wiki for collaborative knowledge management*. Paper presented at the 1st International Workshop on Semantic Technologies in Collaborative Applications (STICA06).

Schandl, B. (2009a). *An Infrastructure for the Development of Semantic Desktop Applications*. Unpublished PhD thesis, University of Vienna, Department of Distributed and Multimedia Systems.

Schandl, B. (2009b). Representing Linked Data as Virtual File Systems. In *Proceedings of the 2nd International Workshop on Linked Data on the Web*, Madrid, Spain.

Schandl, B., & Haslhofer, B. (2009). The Sile Model – A Semantic File System Infrastructure for the Desktop. In *Proceedings of the 6th European Semantic Web Conference*, Heraklion, Greece.

Schandl, B., & King, R. (2006). The SemDAV Project: Metadata Management for Unstructured Content. In *Proceedings of the 1ˢᵗ International Workshop on Contextualized Attention Metadata: Collecting, Managing and Exploiting of Rich Usage Information* (pp. 27-32). New York: ACM Press.

Schandl, B., & Popitsch, N. (2010). *Lifting File Systems into the Linked Data Cloud with TripFS*. Paper presented at the 3rd International Workshop on Linked Data on the Web, Raleigh, NC.

Schmedding, F., Hanke, C., & Hornung, T. (2008). RDF Authoring in Wikis. In C. Lange, S. Schaffert, H. Skaf-Molli, & M. Völkel (Eds.), *Proceedings of the 3rd Semantic Wiki Workshop (SemWiki 2008)*. CEUR Workshop Proceedings.

Schmidt, K. U., Dörflinger, J., Rahmani, T., Sahbi, M., & Thomas, L. S. S. M. (2008). An User Interface Adaptation Architecture for Rich Internet Applications. In S. Bechhofer, M. Hauswirth, J. Hoffmann, & M. Koubarakis (Eds.), In *Proceedings of the Semantic Web: Research and Applications, the 5th European Semantic Web Conference (ESWC 2008)* (pp. 736-750).

Schmidt, A. (2006). The Challenges of Imperfection and Time-Dependence. In *Proceedings of odbase 2006, on the move federated conferences (otm)*. Ontology-Based User Context Management.

Schmitz, P. (2006). Inducing Ontology from Folksonomy tags. In *Proceedings of the Collaborative Tagging Workshop at the 15th International WWW Conference*, Edinburgh, Scotland.

Schubert, E., Wolfe, J., & Tarnopolsky, A. (2004). Spectral centroid and timbre in complex, multiple instrumental textures. In *Proceedings of the International Conference on Music Perception and Cognition*, Evanston, IL.

Schumacher, M., Helin, H., & Schuldt, H. (Eds.). (2008). *CASCOM – Intelligent Service Coordination in the Semantic Web*. Berlin: Birkhäuser Verlag. doi:10.1007/978-3-7643-8575-0

Schwitter, R. (2007). *Controlled natural languages*. Retrieved, July 15, 2008, from http://www.ics.mq.edu.au/rolfs/controlled-natural-languages

Sebastiani, F. (2002). Machine learning in automated text categorization. *ACM Computing Surveys, 34*, 1–47. doi:10.1145/505282.505283

Sechrest, S., & McClennen, M. (1992). Blending Hierarchical and Attribute-Based File Naming. In *Proceedings of the 12th International Conference on Distributed Computing Systems* (pp. 572-580). Washington, DC: IEEE Computer Society.

Seeling, C., & Becks, A. (2003, July). Exploiting metadata for ontology-based visual exploration of weakly structured text documents. In *Proceedings of the Seventh International Conference on Information Visualization* (pp. 652-657).

Sergevich, K. A., & Viktorovna, G. V. (2003). From an Ontology-Oriented Approach Conception to User Interface Development. *International Journal of Information Theories and Applications*, *10*(1), 89–98.

Shadbolt, N., Gibbins, N., Glaser, H., Harri, S., & Schraefe, M. (2004). CS AKTive Space, or How We Learned to Stop Worrying and Love the Semantic Web. *IEEE Intelligent Systems*, *19*(3), 41–47. doi:10.1109/MIS.2004.8

Shiman, R. N., Michel, G., Krauthammer, M., Fuchs, N. E., Kaljurand, K., & Kuhn, T. (2010). Writing clinical practice guidelines in controlled natural language. In N. E. Fuchs (Ed.), *Proceedings of the Workshop on Controlled Natural Language (CNL 2009)* (LNCS 5972, pp. 265-280).

Sintek, M., van Elst, L., Scerri, S., & Handschuh, S. (2007a). Distributed Knowledge Representation on the Social Semantic Desktop: Named Graphs, Views and Roles in NRL. In E. Franconi, M. Kifer, & W. May (Eds.), *Proceedings of the 4th European Semantic Web Conference (ESWC 2007)*, Innsbruck, Austria (pp. 594-608). Berlin: Springer.

Sintek, M., van Elst, L., Scerri, S., & Handschuh, S. (2007b). *NEPOMUK Representational Language Specification (Technical Rep.)*. NEPOMUK Project Consortium.

Smart, P. R. (2008). *Controlled natural languages and the semantic web*. Southampton, UK: School of Electronics and Computer Science, University of Southampton.

Smith, B., & Welty, C. (2001). FOIS introduction: Ontology—towards a new synthesis. In *Proceedings of the international conference on Formal Ontology in Information Systems (FOIS '01)* (pp. 3-9). New York: ACM.

Smith, T. F., & Waterman, M. S. (1981). Identification of Common Molecular Subsequences. *Journal of Molecular Biology*, *147*, 195–197. doi:10.1016/0022-2836(81)90087-5

Soergel, D. (1995). *Data models for an integrated thesaurus database*. Retrieved from http://www.dsoergel.com/cv/B54.pdf

Soergel, D., Lauser, B., Liang, A., Fisseha, F., Keizer, J., & Katz, S. (2004). *Reengineering Thesauri for New Applications: The AGROVOC Example*. Rome, Italy: FAO.

Sousa, K. (2009). Model-Driven Approach for User Interface - Business Alignment. In *Proceedings of the 1st ACM SIGCHI Symposium on Engineering Interactive Computing Systems (EICS'2009)* (pp. 325-328). New York: ACM Press.

Souzis, A. (2006, June 12). Bringing the wiki-way to the semantic web with rhizome. In M. Völkel & S. Schaffert (Eds.), *SEMWIKI 2006: Proceedings of the First Workshop on Semantic Wikis,* Budva, Montenegro. Retrieved from http://www.ceur-ws.org/Vol-206/paper19.pdf

Spahn, M., Kleb, J., Grimm, S., & Scheidl, S. (2008). Supporting business intelligence by providing ontology-based end-user information self-service. In *Proceedings of the first international workshop on Ontology-supported business intelligence (OBI '08)* (pp. 1-12). New York: ACM.

Specia, L., & Motta, E. (2007). Integrating Folksonomies with the Semantic Web. In *Proceedings of the 4th European Semantic Web Conference* (pp. 624-639). Heidelberg, Germany: Springer.

Staab, S., Schnurr, H., Studer, R., & Sure, Y. (2001). Knowledge Processes and Ontologies. *IEEE Intelligent Systems*, *16*(1), 26–34. doi:10.1109/5254.912382

Stadlhofer, B., & Salhofer, P. (2008). SeGoF: semantic e-government forms. In *Proceedings of the 2008 international conference on Digital government research* (pp. 427-428). Digital Government Society of North America.

Stojanovic, L., Stojanovic, N., & Volz, R. (2002). A Reverse Engineering Approach for Migrating Data-intensive Web Sites to the Semantic Web. In *Proceedings of the Conference on Intelligent Information Processing*.

Strang, T., & Linnhoff-Popien, C. (2004). A Context Modeling Survey. In *Proceedings of the Workshop on advanced context modeling, reasoning and management - 6th intl. conf. on ubiquitous computing.*

Stroulia, E., & Wang, Y. (2004). Structural and Semantic Matching for Assessing Web-Service Similarity. *Cooperative Information Systems, 14*(4).

Stuckenschmidt, H., Parent, C., & Spaccapietra, S. (Eds.). (2009). *Modular Ontologies - Concepts, Theories and Techniques for Knowledge Modularization.* New York: Springer.

Suárez-Figueroa, M. C., & Gómez-Pérez, A. (2008). First Attempt towards a Standard Glossary of Ontology Engineering Terminology. In *Proceedings of the 8th International Conference on Terminology and Knowledge Engineering (TKE2008),* Copenhagen, Denmark.

Suárez-Figueroa, M. C. (2010). *NeOn Methodology for Building Ontology Networks: Specification, Scheduling and Reuse.* Madrid, Spain: Facultad de Informática, Universidad Politécnica de Madrid.

Sure, Y. (2003). *Methodology, tools and case studies for ontology based knowledge management.* Unpublished doctoral dissertation, University of Karlsruhe, Germany.

Tanaka, K. (2007). Towards New Content Services by Fusion of Web and Broadcasting Contents. In *Proceedings of the 20th International Conference on Industrial, Engineering and Other Applications of Applied Intelligent Systems: New Trends in Applied Artificial Intelligence,* Kyoto, Japan (LNCS 4570, pp. 1-11). Berlin: Springer.

Tane, J., Schmitz, C., & Stumme, G. (2004). Semantic resource management for the web: an e-learning application. In *Proceedings of the 13th international World Wide Web conference on Alternate track papers & posters (WWW Alt. '04)* (pp. 1-10). New York: ACM.

Toch, E., Gal, A., Reinhartz-Berger, I., & Dori, D. (2007). A semantic approach to approximate service retrieval. *ACM Transactions on Internet Technology, 8*(2).

Tsinaraki, C., Polydoros, P., & Christodoulakis, S. (2004). Interoperability support for Ontology-based Video Retrieval Applications. In *Proceedings of the 3rd International Conference on Image and Video Retrieval (CIVR 2004),* Dublin, Ireland (LNCS 3115, pp. 582-591). Berlin: Springer.

Tullis, T. S., & Stetson, J. N. (2004, June). *A comparison of questionnaires for assessing Website Usability.* Paper presented at the Usability Professionals' Association Conference, Minneapolis, MN.

Ungrangsi, R., & Simperl, E. (2008). OMEGA: An Automatic Ontology Metadata Generation Algorithm. In *Proceedings of the 16th International Conference on Knowledge Engineering and Knowledge Management* (pp. 239-254). Heidelberg, Germany: Springer.

Ungrangsi, R., Anutariya, C., & Wuwongse, V. (n.d.). *SQORE Web Services.* Retrieved June 2009 from http://research.shinawatra.ac.th:8080/sqore

Ungrangsi, R., Anutariya, C., & Wuwongse, V. (2008). combiSQORE: A Combinative-ontology Retrieval System for Next Generation Semantic Web Applications. *IEICE Transactions on Information and Systems. E (Norwalk, Conn.), 91-D*(11), 2616–2625.

Ungrangsi, R., Anutariya, C., & Wuwongse, V. (2009). SQORE: An Ontology Retrieval Framework for the Next Generation Web. *Concurrency and Computation, 21*(5), 651–671. doi:10.1002/cpe.1385

Uren, V. S., Cimiano, P., Iria, J., Handschuh, S., Vargas-Vera, M., & Motta, E. (2006). Semantic annotation for knowledge management: Requirements and a survey of the state of the art. *Journal of Web Semantics, 4*(1), 14–28. doi:10.1016/j.websem.2005.10.002

Uschold, M., & Jasper, R. (1999). A framework for understanding and classifying ontology applications. In *Proceedings of the IJCAI99 Workshop on Ontologies* (pp. 16-21).

Uschold, M., & Gruninger, M. (2004). Ontologies and semantics for seamless connectivity. *SIGMOD Record, 33*(4), 58–64. doi:10.1145/1041410.1041420

Valkanas, G., Tsetsos, V., & Hadjiefthymiades, S. (2007). The POLYSEMA MPEG-7 Video Annotator. In *Proceedings of the Poster and Demo Conference on Semantic and Digital Media Technologies*, Genova, Italy.

Van Assem, M., Gangemi, A., & Schreiber, G. (2006). Conversion of WordNet to a standard RDF/OWL representation. In *Proceedings of the Fifth International Conference on Language Resources and Evaluation (LREC '06)*, Genova, Italy.

Van Assem, M., Menken, M., Schreiber, G., & Wielemaker, J. (2004). A Method for Converting Thesauri to RDF/OWL. In *Proceedings of the Third International Semantic Web Conference (ISWC)*. Berlin: Springer.

Van Assem, M., Malaisé, V., Miles, A., & Schreiber, G. (2006). A Method to Convert Thesauri to SKOS. In *The Semantic Web* (pp. 95–109). Research and Applications.

van Heijst, G., Schreiber, A. T. G., & Wielinga, B. J. (1997). Using explicit ontologies in KBS development. *International Journal of Human-Computer Studies, 46*(2-3), 183–292. doi:10.1006/ijhc.1996.0090

Vilas, A. F., Díaz Redondo, R., Ramos Cabrer, M., Pazos Arias, J., Gil Solla, A., & García Duque, J. (2006). MHP-OSGi convergence: a new model for open residential gateways. *Software, Practice & Experience, 36*(13), 1421–1442. doi:10.1002/spe.727

Villazón-Terrazas, B., Gómez-Pérez, A., & Calbimonte, J. P. (2010). NOR$_2$O: a Library for Transforming Non-Ontological Resources to Ontologies. In *Proceedings of the Seventh Extended Semantic Web Conference (ESWC 2010)*.

Visser, U., & Schuster, G. (2002). Finding and Integration of Information - A Practical Solution for the Semantic Web. In J. Euzénat, A. Gómez-Pérez, N. Guarino, & H. Stuckenschmidt (Eds.), *Proceedings of the ECAI-02 Workshop on Ontologies and Semantic Interoperability.*

Völkel, M., Krötzsch, M., Vrandecic, D., Haller, H., & Studer, R. (2006). Semantic Wikipedia. In *Proceedings of the 15th international conference on World Wide Web(WWW '06)* (pp. 585-594). New York: ACM.

Von Ahn, L., & Dabbish, L. (2004). Labeling images with a computer game. In *Proceedings of the Conference on Human Factors in Computing Systems* (pp. 319-326). New York: ACM.

W3C Multimedia Semantics Incubator Group. (2009). *Multimedia Vocabularies on the Semantic Web*. Retrieved July 25, 2009 from http://www.w3.org/2005/Incubator/mmsem/XGR-vocabularies/

W3C. (2009). *WAI-ARIA Overview*. Retrieved from http://www.w3.org/WAI/intro/aria

Wang, X., Gorlitsky, R., & Almeida, J. S. (2005). From XML to RDF: how semantic web technologies will change the design of 'omic' standards. *Nature Biotechnology, 23*(9), 1099–1103. doi:10.1038/nbt1139

Watt, W. C. (1968). Habitability. *American Documentation, 19*, 338–351. doi:10.1002/asi.5090190324

Wielinga, B., Schreiber, A. T., Wielemaker, J., & Sandberg, J. (2001). From thesaurus to ontology. In *K-CAP '01: Proceedings of the 1st international conference on Knowledge capture* (pp. 194-201). New York: ACM Press.

Wilcoxon, F. (1945). Individual comparisons by ranking methods. *Biometrics Bulletin*, 80–83. doi:10.2307/3001968

Wills, C., Giampaolo, D., & Mackovitch, M. (1995). Experience with an Interactive Attribute-based User Information Environment. In *Proceedings of the 1995 IEEE Fourteenth Annual International Phoenix Conference on Computers and Communications* (pp. 359-365).

Wlodawer, A., & Erickson, J. W. (1993). Structure-based inhibitors of HIV-1 protease. *Annual Review of Biochemistry, 62*, 543–585. doi:10.1146/annurev.bi.62.070193.002551

Wright, S., & Budin, G. (1997). *Handbook of terminology management, Basic aspects of terminology management*. Amsterdam, The Netherlands: John Benjamins Publishing Company.

Xue, G. R., Zeng, H. J., Chen, Z., Ma, W. Y., Zhang, H. J., & Lu, C. J. (2003). Implicit link analysis for small web search. In *Proceedings of the Annual ACM Conference on Research and Development in Information Retrieval* (pp. 56-63). New York: ACM.

Yahoo. Inc. (n.d.). *Flickr APIs*. Retrieved June 2009 from http://www.flickr.com/services/api/

Yahoo. Inc. (n.d.). *Flickr- Photo Sharing.* Retrieved June 2009 from http://www.flickr.com

Yang, Y., Lin, Y., Su, Y., & Chen, H. (2008). A Regression Approach to Music Emotion Recognition. *IEEE Transactions on Audio. Speech and Audio Processing, 16*(2), 448–457. doi:10.1109/TASL.2007.911513

Zhang, Y., Vasconcelos, W., & Sleeman, D. (2005). OntoSearch: An Ontology Search Engine. In *Proceedings of the 24th SGAI International Conference on Innovative Techniques and Applications of AI*, UK (pp. 58-69).

Zheng, F., Zhang, G., & Song, Z. (2001). Comparison of Different Implementations of MFCC. *Journal of Computer Science & Technology, 16*(6), 582–589. doi:10.1007/BF02943243

Zhou, Y., Pan, J., Ma, X., Luo, B., Tao, X., & Lu, J. (2007). Applying ontology in architecture-based self-management applications. In Cho, Y., Wainwright, R. L., Haddad, H., Shin, S. Y., & Koo, Y. W. (Eds.), *Sac* (pp. 97–103). New York: ACM.

Zinnikus, I., Rupp, H.-J., & Fischer, K. (2006). Detecting Similarities between Web Service Interfaces: The WSDL Analyzer. In *Proceedings of the 2nd International Workshop on Web Services and Interoperability (WSI 2006)*.

About the Contributors

Amit Sheth is an educator, researcher, and entrepreneur. He is a LexisNexis Eminent Scholar (an endowed faculty position, funded by LexisNexis and the Ohio Board of Regents) at Wright State University. He directs the Ohio Center of Excellent in Knowledge-enabled Computing (http://knoesis.org), which conducts research in Web 3.0 (Semantic Web, semantics enhanced social/sensor/service/mobile/cloud/WoT computing) and applications to healthcare and life sciences, cognitive science, and defense/intelligence. He was a Professor at the University of Georgia where he founded and directed the LSDIS Lab. Prior to that, he served in R&D groups at Bellcore, Unisys, and Honeywell. His research has led to several commercial products and two companies which he founded and managed in various executive roles: Infocosm, which had products in enterprise workflow management and Taalee/Voquette/Semagix, which was one of the earliest companies with Semantic Web applications and application development platforms. Professor Sheth is an IEEE Fellow and has received recognitions such as the IBM Faculty award. He is a highly cited author in Computer Science (h-index of 71 based on Google scholar citations) and among the top cited authors in WWW, given over 200 invited talks and colloquia including over 40 keynotes, and (co)-organized/chaired 65+ conferences/workshops. He is on several journal editorial boards, is the Editor-in-Chief of the *International Journal on Semantic Web and Information Systems (IJSWIS)* and the joint-EIC of *Distributed & Parallel Databases Journal*.

* * *

Christos B. Anagnostopoulos has received his BSc in Computer Science from the Department of Informatics and Telecommunications at the National & Kapodistrian University of Athens (NKUA), Greece, in 2001 and his MSc in Computer Science, Advanced Information Systems from the same department in 2003. He holds a PhD in Modeling Mobile Computing Systems (2008) from NKUA. His research interest is focused on Mobile Computing, Distributed Systems, Context- aware Computing, Approximate Reasoning (Fuzzy Logic), Semantic Web and Ontological Engineering. He had also participated in projects realized in the context of European Union Programs.

Talapady N. Bhat, a Project leader in the Biochemical Science Division at the National Institute of Standards and Technology. He is the author of over 80 refereed scientific articles and he has given over hundred presentations at national and international professional meetings. His publications have been widely cited (over 13,000 scientific citations) and this is the highest among all NIST staff. Dr. Bhat has won several scientific awards including: two Best Publication Awards from the Science Applications International Corporation; the Science Spectrum Traiblazer Award in 2006; and the prestigious Judson C. French award of the National Institute of Standards and Technology in 2005. In 2007 Dr. Bhat received the prestigious Emerald Honors.

Hamish Cunningham has been a researcher in language and knowledge technologies for around fifteen years, and currently runs a research team of 15 as part of the Natural Language Processing group in Computer Science at the University of Sheffield. He is principal investigator on a number of significant (in their own lunchtime) research initiatives, and a member of the scientific board of the Information Retrieval Facility. He has published widely, sits on a number of editorial boards and reviews project proposals for the EC, EPSRC, BBSRC, ESRC and NWO. Prof. Cunningham's team produces the GATE open source platform for language and knowledge research, which is used by organisations as diverse as WHO cancer research, OntoText, Matrixware, Generic, Garlik, Spock, Solcara, Fizzback, Innovantage, Astra Zeneca, Merck, Eli Lilly, Ontos, OntoPrise, Thompson, Greenstone, ANC, Perseus, NCSA, AT&T, IBM, British Telecom, Hewlett Packard and thousands of others.

Pradeep Dantuluri is a Research Masters Student and a Research Assistant, working at DERI, National University of Ireland, Galway. His research topic is Controlled Natural Languages and their application to Semantic web interfaces. He obtained a bachelors degree(BTech) in Information Technology from IIIT Allahabad, India. His main interests include Controlled Natural Languages, Linked Open Data and Mobile Application Development.

Brian Davis graduated in 2001 with an Honours B.Sc in Computational Linguistics and German from Dublin City University. After receiving an M.Sc. in Computer Science by Research from Trinity College Dublin in 2003, he worked as a Software Engineer at Sun Microsystems Ireland for 2 years. He joined DERI, National Univeristy of Ireland, Galway in 2006 as a Language Engineer attached to the Lion/Nepomuk projects from 2006-2009. He is currently a PhD researcherin the Unit for Semantic Collaborative Systems (USCS) under the supervision of Dr. Siegfried Handschuh and Prof. Hamish Cunnigham (Sheffield NLP group). His PhD work focuses on Controlled Natural Languages for ontology authoring and semantic annotation. He is a specialist in the GATE framework and Ontology based Information Extraction. He is also an IBM CAS Faculty Fellow.

Mari Carmen Suárez Figueroa belongs to the Ontology Engineering Group (OEG) of the Artificial Intelligence Department of the Computer Science School (http://www.fi.upm.es) at Universidad Politécnica de Madrid (UPM). She graduated in Computer Science from UPM in 2001. She got the PhD in Artificial Intelligence in UPM in June 2010. She was Associate Professor (January-March 2002) and now she is Teaching Assistant from 1st September 2008 at the Computer Science School at UPM. Her research activities are focused on Ontology Engineering and the Semantic Web. Particularly, her research lines include methodologies for ontology network development, ontology network development, ontology development tools, ontology evaluation, and the Semantic Web. She has participated in different European and national projects: OntoWeb, Esperonto, PIKON, Knowledge Web, OntoGrid, REIMDOC, SEEMP, NeOn, mIO!, and BuscaMedia. She has been research visitor at Department of Computer Science (University of Liverpool) in 2004 and at KMi at the Open University in 2007. She has published more than 20 papers in journals, conferences and workshops. She co-organized the EON 2006 Workshop at WWW'06, the KRRSW 2008 Workshop at ESWC 2008, the tutorial called "NeOn Methodology: how to build ontology networks?" at EKAW 2008, and the tutorial called "Ontology Engineering: the NeOn Methodology through the NeOn Toolkit" at ISWC 2009.

Asunción Gómez-Pérez is Full Professor at the Universidad Politécnica de Madrid (UPM). She is the Director of the Artificial Intelligence Department (2008) and Director of the Ontology Engineering Group (OEG) at UPM (1995). She is a member of the AENOR CTN_148 Geographical Information Committee, the corresponding Spanish Committee that participates in the Working Group of ISO 1950. She has a B.A. in Computer Science (1990), M.S.C. on Knowledge Engineering (1991), Ph.D. in Computer Sciences (1993) and MS.C. on Business Administration (1994). She was visiting (1994-1995) the Knowledge Systems Laboratory at Stanford University. Her main research areas are: Ontological Engineering, Semantic Web and Knowledge Management. She led at UPM the following EU projects: MKBEEM, Ontoweb, Esperonto, Knowledge Web, NeOn, SEEMP, OntoGrid, Admire, Dynalearn, SemSorGrid4Env, SEALS and Monnet. She coordinated OntoGrid and now she is coordinating Sem-SorGrid4Env and SEALS. She is also leading at UPM projects funded by Spanish agencies. The most relevants are: España Virtual, Webn+1, Geobuddies and the Spanish network on Semantic Web. She has published more than 150 papers and she is author of one book on Ontological Engineering and co-author of a book on Knowledge Engineering. She has been co-director of the summer school on Ontological Engineering and the Semantic Web since 2003 up to now. She was program chair of ASWC'09, ESWC'05 and EKAW'02 and co-organiser of many workshops on ontologies. She reviews papers in many conferences and journals.

Stathes Hadjiefthymiades received the BSc, MSc and PhD in Informatics & Telecommuncations from the University of Athens, Athens, Greece. He also holds an Joint MSc in engineering-economics awarded by the National Technical University of Athens. In 1992, he joined the Greek consulting firm Advanced Services Group, Ltd., as an analyst/developer of telematic systems. In 1995, he joined the Communication Networks Laboratory, University of Athens. From September 2001 to July 2002, he was a visiting assistant professor at the Department of Information and Communication Systems Engineering, University of Aegean. In July 2002, he joined the faculty of the Hellenic Open University, Patras, Greece, as an assistant professor. Since December 2003, he has been with the faculty of the Department of Informatics and Telecommunications, University of Athens, where he is currently an assistant professor. He has participated in numerous projects realized in the context of EU program and national initiatives. His research interests include the areas of mobile, pervasive computing, web systems engineering, and networked multimedia applications. He is the author of more than 150 publications in these areas.

Siegfried Handschuh is a Senior Lecturer at the National University of Ireland, Galway (NUIG). He is the research leader of the Social Semantic Collaboration research stream at the Digital Enterprise Research Institute (DERI) and heads the research group for Semantic Information Systems and Language Engineering (SmILE). Siegfried holds an Honours Degrees in both Computer Science and Information Science and a PhD from the University of Karlsruhe. He has published over 100 papers as books and journal, book chapters, conference, and workshop contributions, mainly in the areas of Semantic Annotation, Knowledge Acquisition, Information Extraction, Controlled Natural Language, Information Visualization and Social Semantics. Since 2000 he has initiated, participated and/or coordinated several R&D projects at an international level, such as DAML (DARPA), aceMedia (IP), HALO 2 (Vulcan Inc.), Knowledge Web (NOE), NEPOMUK (IP), FAST(STREP) and Digital.me (STREP).

Eenjun Hwang received his BS and MS Degree in Computer Engineering from Seoul National University, Seoul, Korea, in 1988 and 1990, respectively; and his PhD Degree in Computer Science from the University of Maryland, College Park, in 1998. From September 1999 to August 2004, he was with the Graduate School of Information and Communication, Ajou University, Suwon, Korea. Currently he is a member of the faculty in the School of Electrical Engineering, Korea University, Seoul, Korea. His current research interests include database, multimedia systems, audio/visual feature extraction and indexing, semantic multimedia, information retrieval and Web applications.

Sanghoon Jun received his BS Degree in Electrical engineering from Korea University, Korea, in 2008, respectively. Currently, he is in a master's course at the Multimedia information lab of the School of electrical engineering in Korea University. His current research interests include music retrieval and recommendation, multimedia systems, machine learning, emotional computing and Web applications.

Patrick Kapahnke received his master of science degree in computer science from Saarland University, Germany in 2005. Since then, he is working for DFKI and has been involved in research projects SCALLOPS, MODEST, VITAL and ISReal. Topics of interest include semantic Web service coordination and multiagent systems.

Matthias Klusch is head of the Research Group on Multi-Agent Systems and distinguished Research Fellow of the German Research Center for Artificial Intelligence (DFKI) as well as Adjunct Professor of Computer Science at the Swinburne University of Technology in Melbourne, Australia, and Private Lecturer (PD) for Computer Science at the Saarland University, Germany. He received his MSc (1992) and PhD (1997) from the University of Kiel, Germany, and his habilitation (2009) in computer science from the Saarland University, Germany. Among other, he is on the scientific advisory board of the international CETINIA center for intelligent information technologies in Madrid, the founder and steering committee member of the German conference series on multi-agent system technologies, chair of the international semantic service selection contest series. He is editor of several major international journals in the areas of the Web, semantic Web, and information systems, and served on numerous conference organization boards and science funding agencies worldwide including NSERC, FWF, FNSNF, RGC and NWO. Besides, he was nominee for the ACM SIGART 2008 Award for Excellence in Autonomous Agent Research, and co-/authored 27 books and published about 130 papers. His research group has been involved in many research projects funded by industry, regional and national government as well as the European Commission including SEMAS, SCALLOPS, MODEST, ISReal, CASCOM, VITAL, ATHENA, i2home, SHAPE, SAID, COIN.

Klaus Meißner is Professor of the Chair of Multimedia Technology at the Department of Computer Science of the Dresden University of Technology. He has over 15 years industry background in different management functions at Philips and Digital Equipment. His research interest includes tools and methods for adaptive multimedia Web applications, for social and collaborative application scenarios and life cycle management of multimedia content especially for mobile and home environments.

Annett Mitschick is a Research Associate and Teaching Assistant at the Chair of Multimedia Technology of the Department of Computer Science at Dresden University of Technology, Germany. She obtained her Diploma in Media Computer Science from the Dresden University of Technology and started her research as part of the K-IMM (Knowledge through Intelligent Media Management) project. Her research focuses on the generation and modeling of semantic descriptions for multimedia documents and their context to enable individual media and knowledge management.

Antonis Papadimitriou holds a MSc degree from the National & Kapodistrian University of Athens and belongs to the Pervasive Computing Research Group of the same institution. He is also a former member of the ASAP Research Group of the French National Institute for Research in Computer Science and Control (INRIA). His research interests focus on engineering secure and scalable applications in distributed computing environments (P2P Systems, WSNs, Ad-hoc Networks).

Heiko Paulheim works as a research associate at SAP Research CEC Darmstadt, Germany, with his research focus on semantic web and ontologies. He has worked in both academic and applied research as well as in commercial software development. His research interests encompass a large variety of applications of semantic web technologies, including ontology engineering, ontology matching, semantic annotation, ontology-based systems integration, and ontology-driven software development, as well as engineering-oriented problems such as developing frameworks and infrastructures for ontology-based software, in particular in the area of user interfaces. Heiko holds an MSc in Computer Science from Technische Universität Darmstadt (Darmstadt University of Technology).

Stefan Pietschmann is a Research Associate and PhD candidate at the Department of Computer Science of the Dresden University of Technology. After graduation with a diploma thesis on adaptation of context-aware Web architectures, as part of the AMACONT project, he concentrated on browser-based, synchronous collaboration on web pages with different end devices within the VCS project. His current research is carried out within the scope of the research project CRUISE, with a special accent on the modeling, deployment and runtime of web-based user interfaces based on service-oriented paradigms.

Florian Probst works as researcher at SAP Research, CEC Darmstadt, Germany. His research interests are in the field of formal ontology, geospatial ontology engineering and semantic web technologies. Florian is an information scientist developing methods for improved web-based communication. He received his PhD in Geoinformatics from University of Münster, Germany. He worked in the group of Prof. Werner Kuhn, the Institute for Geoinformatics (ifgi) and the Muenster Semantic Interoperability Lab (MUSIL).

Seungmin Rho received his MS and PhD Degrees in Computer Science from Ajou University, Korea, in Computer Science from Ajou University, Korea, in 2003 and 2008, respectively. In 2008-2009, he was a Postdoctoral Research Fellow at the Computer Music Lab of the School of Computer Science in Carnegie Mellon University. He is currently working as a Research Professor at School of Electrical Engineering in Korea University. His research interests include database, music retrieval, multimedia systems, machine learning, knowledge management and intelligent agent technologies. He has been a reviewer in Multimedia Tools and Applications (MTAP), Journal of Systems and Software, Information Science (Elsevier), and Program Committee member in over 15 international conferences. He has published 17 papers in journals and book chapters and 25 in international conferences and workshops. He is listed in Who's Who in the World.

Vassileios Tsetsos received his BSc in Informatics from the Department of Informatics & Telecommunications at the University of Athens, Greece in 2003 and his M.Sc. in "Communication Systems and Data Networks" from the same Department in 2005. Nowadays, he is a Ph.D. candidate in the department. He is a member of the Communication Networks Laboratory (CNL) of the University of Athens and the Pervasive Computing Research Group (p-comp). He has participated in the PoLoS (Integrated Platform for Location Based Services) project, funded by the EU IST programme, and in several national research projects. His research interests are in the areas of pervasive and mobile computing, Semantic Web technologies and middleware for context-aware and sensor-based services.

Boris Villazón-Terrazas is a researcher and a PhD student in Artificial Intelligence at the Universidad Politécnica de Madrid. His University granted him a 4 year fellowship to carry out his PhD studies in the Ontology Engineering Group (OEG). Previously, the Ontology Engineering Group granted him a fellowship to carry out his master studies. He has previously worked as a researcher and software developer at the Research Institute of Informatics at the Universidad Católica Boliviana San Pablo. He obtained a BSc in computer Science (2002) from the Universidad Católica Boliviana San Pablo in Bolivia. He obtained the "Diploma de Estudios Avanzados (DEA)", equivalent to the current Master from the Universidad Politécnica de Madrid (2007). His research interests are focus on Semantic Web and Ontology Engineering, among others. He has participated in several European research projects such as Knowledge Web, SEEMP and NeOn as well as in national projects such as Reimdoc, Servicios Semánticos, Plata, Gis4Gov, and WebN+1. He has published more than 20 papers in journals, conferences and workshops.

Ingo Zinnikus graduated from Saarland University, Germany in 1998 and is since then working for DFKI. He has been working on the application of multiagent systems for a number of topics such as logistics, recommendation systems and business process execution. Besides numerous publications he has contributed to a number of successful national and European proposals. He served as program committee member for a number of international workshops. Fields of Interest: Multiagent systems, service-oriented architectures and Semantic Web services. Experience with projects: the German government funded project TeleTruck, the EU funded projects SAID (FP5), VITAL (FP6, Technical Coordination), ATHENA (FP 6), and COIN (FP7), as well as domestic industry projects in German.

Index